Stuart Robinson

Discourses of Redemption

Stuart Robinson

Discourses of Redemption

ISBN/EAN: 9783744753937

Printed in Europe, USA, Canada, Australia, Japan

Cover: Foto ©ninafisch / pixelio.de

More available books at **www.hansebooks.com**

DISCOURSES

OF

REDEMPTION:

AS REVEALED AT

"SUNDRY TIMES AND IN DIVERS MANNERS,"

DESIGNED BOTH AS

BIBLICAL EXPOSITIONS FOR THE PEOPLE AND HINTS
TO THEOLOGICAL STUDENTS

OF A POPULAR METHOD OF EXHIBITING THE

"DIVERS" REVELATIONS THROUGH PATRIARCHS, PROPHETS,
JESUS, AND HIS APOSTLES.

BY REV. STUART ROBINSON,

PASTOR OF THE SECOND CHURCH, LOUISVILLE, AND LATE PROFESSOR OF
CHURCH GOVERNMENT AND PASTORAL THEOLOGY AT
DANVILLE, KENTUCKY.

THIRD AMERICAN EDITION.

RICHMOND:
PRESBYTERIAN COMMITTEE OF PUBLICATION.

PREFACE.

THAT the noble conception of British and American Christians, half a century since, of the Bible, "the religion of Protestants," in every household has produced its fruits, is evinced in the general Bible *Renaissance* of our age—as seen in the elaborate Biblical disquisitions of infidelity itself; in the multiplication of learned critical helps for the expositions of scripture; and, more than all, in the almost innumerable issues of expositions and illustrations of scripture to meet the general demand for such knowledge among the people.

However we may account for the fact, this *Renaissance* has not yet manifested itself in an equal degree in the pulpit —that divinely appointed agency for the special and authoritative teaching of the Word of God to the people. With the exception of perhaps a slight increase of the expository lecture, the prevailing method of preaching is still that of theological disquisition, ethical essay, rhetorical, persuasive or emotional appeal—founded upon a shred of the Sacred Text chosen as a motto, or, at best, as suggesting simply the theological topic of the occasion. Whereas the true theory of preaching as gathered from the scriptures, manifestly assumes its purpose to be the showing of the people how to read the Word of God; and leading them to feel that " this day is the scripture fulfilled in their ears," and that these are the words of a Jesus who not only *spake* by holy men of old, but who *is now speaking* with living utterance to the men of this generation.

Having, through a ministry of twenty years, to congregations variously composed, in four different cities, been accustomed, in pursuance of the latter theory of preaching, to appropriate one of the public services of the Sabbath to showing the people how to read the scriptures, and to follow the development of the one great central thought of the Book through the successive eras of revelation—the author can testify from practical experience that the people need no other attraction to draw them to the house of God than a simple, rational and practical exposition and illustration of the Bible.   And he who may once attract them by such teaching will find no occasion for devising sermons on special subjects, or any other theatrical devices to draw men to the sanctuary. The author's first experiment was in a congregation composed largely of the professional and public men that gather in the capital of a state ; his last experiment in a city of colleges and in a congregation composed in large measure of professional men and students in every stage of professional education ; in two intervening experiments in commercial cities among business men.   And his experience is, that with all classes alike the preaching which aims most directly at making the scriptures a living message from God to men, translating them into the current forms of thought and speech, is more permanently attractive than any other.   Perhaps the most encouraging assurance he ever received that his labours were profitable to hearers, was in a recent testimony from the

Students of Arts, Law, Medicine and Theology in the various institutions of learning in Toronto, which specially and very intelligently pointed out the benefits which they considered themselves to have received from the exposition of the gospel in the order of the successive revelations, under the several covenants in the history of redemption.

The present volume is the result of an attempt to give permanent form, so far as oral instruction can be transferred to the printed page, to such outline specimens of the author's Biblical Expositions in the several sections of the inspired Word as might be most suggestive to younger preachers in their attempts to develop the various parts of Scripture to the comprehension of the people, and at the same time be instructive to Christians, and inquirers, and other earnest persons troubled with doubts touching the inspiration or the doctrines of the Bible. From the titles of the several sections, it will be seen that this is not a collection of miscellaneous discourses, but a logical development of the gospel in the order of its communication. And from the titles of the several discourses under each section it will be seen that the general aim is to discuss some of the more germinal points of each revelation. Want of space for the full execution of his plan has compelled the author to omit several subjects embraced in the programme originally, and has suggested the purpose, if the present effort is acceptable to the public, to prepare a second series of " Discourses of Redemption," filling up more completely this outline, while yet constituting a volume complete in itself, devoted more especially to the great cardinal truths developed in the symbols of the Protestant Reformation.

Of course students and others accustomed to more exact forms of presenting religious truth will not expect to find in this volume the precise and scientific style of discussion of the systems of divinity; nor must literary critics look for the carefulness and finish of the religious essay where the author is aiming to transfer spoken language, in its popular forms, to the printed page. It is hoped, however, that students will find many valuable suggestive hints; and that earnest-minded persons—whether Christian believers, or inquirers after the way of salvation, or those harassed and tempted by sceptical doubts—may find these discourses of some advantage to them.

In the Appendix, the author has discussed two or three points having a direct relation to the subjects of the discourses —especially the place of the Church in the scheme of Redemption, its ordinances of public worship, and its relation to the Civil Government—in a more elaborate manner than suited the style and limits of a sermon. The conviction grows upon him daily, that the questions there discussed have a far higher importance in the Gospel system than that hitherto attached to them by the Protestant ministry; and that these are destined to be the great questions of the next ten years both in the British and American Churches.

NEW YORK, March 26th, 1866.

CONTENTS.

INTRODUCTORY DISCOURSES

DISCOURSE I.

THE DIVERSITY IN UNITY OF THE REVELATION OF REDEMPTION.

Hebrews i. 1, 2, and ii. 1-4.

DISCOURSE II.

THE SCRIPTURES OF THE "SUNDRY TIMES" INSPIRED OF GOD: THE ONLY SOURCE OF SAVING KNOWLEDGE: THE ANTIDOTE TO PERILOUS ERROR.

II. Timothy iii. 1, 16.

SECTION I.

DISCOURSE III.

REDEMPTION AS REVEALED TO THE PATRIARCHS IN THE THEO-PHANIES. THE GOSPEL COVENANT AND WORSHIP OF THE LOST EDEN.

Genesis ii. 8-17; iii. 15, 24, and iv. 4.

Principles of the interpretation of these ancient records. The estate of man anterior to Eden. The Eden covenant of works. The

CONTENTS.

DISCOURSE VI.

THE GOSPEL OF THE SINAI COVENANT: ITS RULE OF LIFE TO
CONVICT OF SIN: ITS RITUAL TO TEACH THE TAKING AWAY
OF SIN: AND ITS MOULDING OF THE SOCIAL ORDER AS A
TYPE OF CHRIST'S SPIRITUAL COMMONWEALTH.

Exodus xix. 3-6, xx. 1-17, xxiv. 7-9.—Deuteronomy v. 2, 3, 22, vi. 1-5, x. 1-5.

SECTION III

REDEMPTION AS REVEALED THROUGH THE SPIRIT OF CHRIST IN
THE PROPHETS.

DISCOURSE VII.

THE GOSPEL CHURCH BY COVENANT TYPICALLY SET FORTH
AS THE ETERNAL KINGDOM OF DAVID'S SON.

II. Samuel vii. 1-24.—Psalm lxxii. 1, 8, 17.—xxxix 3, 4.—Luke i. 32.—Acts ii. 30.

DISCOURSE XI.

DISCOURSE XII.

DISCOURSE XIII.

DISCOURSE XIV.

REDEMPTION AS PREACHED AT THE FINAL APOSTASY OF THE TYPICAL KINGDOM, IN THE "LIFTING UP" AND THE "PIERCING" OF JESUS ON THE CROSS.

John xix. 15 37; iii. 14, and xii. 32, 33.

SECTION V.

REDEMPTION AS PREACHED BY APOSTLES UNDER THE DISPENSATION OF THE SPIRIT.

DISCOURSE XV.

THE APOSTOLIC STATEMENT OF THE TERMS OF SALVATION.

Acts. xvi. 29 31.

DISCOURSE XVI.

THE APOSTOLIC SUMMARY OF THE CHRISTIAN CREED.

1 Timothy i. 15.

DISCOURSE XVII.

THE APOSTOLIC GROUND OF CHRISTIAN COMFORT AMD COURAGE.

Romans viii. 28-31.

DISCOURSE XVIII.

THE GOSPEL DOCTRINE OF IMMORTALITY CONTRASTED WITH THAT OF THE SCHOOLS.

II Timothy i. 10—I Cor. xv. 22, 53, 54.

DISCOURSE XIX.

THE GOSPEL ALARUM.—ITS IMPORT.

Ephesians v. 11.

SECTION VI.

REDEMPTION AS PROCLAIMED BY JESUS ASCENDED; CONFIRMING ALL THAT HAD BEEN REVEALED AT THE "SUNDRY TIMES AND IN DIVERS MANNERS."

DISCOURSE XX.

THE GOSPEL ADAPTED TO THE CONSCIOUS WANTS OF THE HUMAN SOUL; ITS ARGUMENTS, TERMS AND AGENCIES.

Revelations xxii. 16-18.

APPENDIX.

NOTE A. TO DISCOURSE III.

THE RECENT OBJECTION IN THE CHURCH OF SCOTLAND CONCERN-
ING THE PERPETUAL OBLIGATION OF THE SINAI COVENANT,
AND ITS SABBATH.

NOTE B. TO DISCOURSE IV.

THE PLACE OF THE CHURCH IN THE SCHEME OF REDEMPTION.

NOTE C. TO DISCOURSE X

THE ORDINANCES OF PUBLIC WORSHIP AS SET FORTH IN SCRIP-
TURE; THEIR RELATION TO THE IDEA OF THE CHURCH.

NOTE D. TO DISCOURSE X.

THE RELATION OF THE TEMPORAL AND THE SPIRITUAL POWERS
HISTORICALLY CONSIDERED.   THE SCOTO-AMERICAN THEORY.

INTRODUCTORY DISCOURSE.

I.

THE DIVERSITY IN UNITY OF THE REVELATION OF REDEMPTION.

HEBREWS i. 1, 2.—God, who at sundry times and in divers manners spake in time past unto the fathers by the prophets, hath in these last days spoken unto us by his Son.

HEBREWS ii. 1, 3.—Therefore we ought to give the more earnest heed to the things which we have heard, lest at any time we should let them slip. For if the word spoken by angels was steadfast, and every transgression and disobedience received a just recompense of reward; how shall we escape if we neglect so great salvation?

IT will be perceived that these two passages, though the opening sentences of different chapters, stand in the close logical relation to each other of premise and conclusion; the intervening portion of the first chapter being of the nature of a parenthesis. The first, by way of premise, declares the fact that, instead of speaking once for all in making his revelation, God spake at " sundry times " through his prophets, and at last through his Son, " God manifest in the flesh." Nor that either in any uniform mode of utterance, but " in divers manners " through the successive ages: He spake now through the Theophanies of the Patriarchal era, now through the oracles of the Theocratic era, now through the inspiration of the Spirit of Christ in the prophets of later ages, and lastly through Jesus the Incarnate Word.

B

From these facts as a premise, Rationalism argues to the conclusion of the uncertainties and contradictions of Scripture ; and Romanism to the conclusion of the need of excluding the people from the free perusal thereof, and the need of an infallible interpreter, through whose harmonizing voice only the speech of God shall be spoken to the people. But, you will observe, the Apostle, from the same premise, reasons to a precisely opposite conclusion from both, viz., the increased responsibility of those who have the benefit of all these varieties of the revelations of God, and the inevitable doom of those who now neglect such advantage.

The purpose of the present discourse will be to fix your attention upon :

First.—The significance of the facts of the Apostle's premise—the " sundry times and divers manners " of revelation.

Second.—The significance of the Apostle's reasoning and conclusion from this premise.

I. The fact here set forth, of God's revelation to men through successive and diversified developments of his scheme of Redemption, furnishes a most important key to the interpretation of the Scriptures. For their peculiar form and structure arises chiefly from this, that, instead of a single utterance, in systematic and scientific form, God chose to speak " at sundry times and in divers manners," gradually developing more and more clearly a scheme of salvation, *which was perfect from the first.*

It is the fundamental blunder, alike of the sceptics and of the philosophic theologians, to assume that, if God speak to man, his perfections require the utterance to be exclusively in the terms of a scientific theology. Had he gathered the more intelligent of the race around some Horeb summit, and thence communicated his attributes and purposes, in the style of a " Code Napoleon," or of scientific papers before the Paris Academy, or the Royal Society of London, then would the communication, they think, have had an exactness and a certitude more worthy a Divine Author; and then would no room have been left for disputes and diversities of opinion in religion.

Now it might be a sufficient answer to all such suggestions —What if God hath chosen to reveal himself in his Word as in his Works?   What if in Revelation, as in Nature, he hath chosen to scatter his truths broadcast, leaving men to gather them with laborious care, and arrange them in their scientific systems?   But a little reflection must make it plain that it was for reasons in the essential nature of the case, that he spake thus at " sundry times," connecting his revelation with the progressive history of humanity through all its varying developments.

What man needed was not merely a revelation concerning the mysteries of God, but concerning the mysteries of his own nature as well; and the paradoxes of which his soul is full.   Man needed a revelation which should become the articulate voice of these mysterious instincts of his spiritual nature.   How could such a revelation be made in any other conceivable method so well as by this of connecting it with, and developing it through, the ever varying history of humanity, under the leadings of his Providence, through all its phases and civilizations?

Accordingly, you find this revelation a record, not merely of the utterances of God speaking from heaven to men, but of the utterances, also, of the human soul answering back from earth to the voice of God.   That answer is now in cries of mysterious terror, now in shouts of defiant impenitency, now in penitential wailings, now in the joyous cries of child-like faith and trust.   The Bible is not a Divine *monologue;* it is an amazing *dialogue* of the ages, between earth and heaven.   The gospel which it reveals is not a mere melody

of " Peace on earth " sung by angel voices ; it is the strain
of a mighty orchestra rather. Notes from the stricken chords
of the heart of God lead the strain, and notes from all the
stricken chords of the human soul answer back in responsive
chorus.

As already suggested, the Bible method consists in the
development more and more fully, through the successive
" sundry times " of humanity, of a scheme of salvation which
was perfect from the first, though revealed only in germ.
Men build their systems of knowledge as they build their
houses ; beam is laid upon beam ; nor does the structure
really exist, as a structure, until the last fragment has been
adjusted to its place. Hence their proneness to regard a
theology as imperfect, which is not thus artificially *systemized.*
But when God constructs a theology, he builds, just as he
builds the oak of the forest, or the cedar of Lebanon, by the
continual development of a germ, perfect from the first,
through the successive " sundry times" of the humanity
with whose origin the development began.

As the oak, perfect and entire, is in the acorn that buries
itself in the soil, and expands and extends an ever perfect
life till it becomes the gigantic monarch of the forest; so the
entire gospel of redemption was in that germinal promise
concerning " the seed of the woman" which, buried in the
clods of a wasted Eden, shot forth its life parallel with the
growth of humanity. Now it appears as the tender twig of
promise to Enoch and Noah ; now the vigorous sapling to the
faith of Abraham ; now the refreshing shade tree leafing
out in the gorgeous ritual of Moses ; now the well-known
pilot's signal tree that guides the course of David and Isaiah ;
now putting forth its blossom of plenteous promise in the
Gospel of John the Baptist ; and now bearing the rich harvest of ripe fruit in the preaching of the Apostles under " the
ministration of the Spirit." Thus through all the ages, and

in all the divers manners of its communication, it is one and the same Gospel, embodying the same great truths in its various stages of development.

To the cant of Rationalism concerning the narrower, less enlightened and legendary system of religion which *preceded* the Christian gospel, our response is, therefore, Christianity *had no* predecessor. In a sense that the English deist Tindal never conceived of, " *Christianity is old as Creation.*" The Bible is the history and development of Christianity, and nothing else. It is " the Gospel according to " Moses and David, Isaiah and Daniel, just as truly as it is the Gospel according to Matthew and Mark and Luke and John. And this is manifest from the unity of idea that underlies all " the divers manners" of the revelation. For of all the books in the world, the Bible is emphatically the " book of one idea." That idea is the grand enterprise of " the seed of the woman" in conflict with the Serpent and his seed, gathering his elect body, the Bride of the Lamb, out of all the successive ages. It is this Redeemer, Jehovah Jesus, who, assuming transiently the shadowy form of humanity, speaks with Adam and Abraham, and Jacob and Joshua. It is Jehovah Jesus who sits between the Cherubim as the Theocratic king of Israel. It is " the spirit of Christ in them " that utters through the prophets " the sufferings of Christ and the glory which should follow." In these cases, just as truly is it the record of Jesus Christ, as when it is the story of his walking on earth as " the Son of man" or of his communicating his will through the Holy Spirit to his Apostles after his ascension.

Not only is this Great Personage the subject of all the revelation alike, but the fundamental articles of its theology, even to the detailed forms of their expression, are one and the same from first to last. The wrath of God appeased, and sin pardoned by vicarious blood, is the theology of Adam, Abel, and Noah. Vicarious blood shed for sin, is the central thought of the theology of Abraham and Moses, of David and Isaiah, just as truly as in that of Peter and John and Paul, who declare " In him we have redemption through his blood ; " and " His blood cleanseth from all sin." So the central idea of the worship which embodies this theology in ritual form. In the worship of Abel the sacrificial *lamb* was the peculiar feature. In the worship of Abraham, two thousand years later, it is still the lamb substituted for the lamb of his own bosom. In the worship of Moses four hundred years later, it is still the lamb whose blood is sprinkled, and which figures in the gorgeous ritual of the tabernacle. Seven hundred years later, in the visions of Isaiah, it is still the " Lamb led to the slaughter." Again, seven hundred years, and John the Baptist, pointing to Jesus the ante-type of all the preceding types, cries " Behold the Lamb of God that taketh away the sins of the world," and, at the close of the revelation, as John the Evangelist is permitted through " the door opened in heaven" to catch a glimpse of the glorious Church of the future, the worship has still the same central attraction—" the Lamb in the midst of the throne ;" around whom are gathered the shouting myriads who have " washed their robes and made white in the blood of the Lamb."

And, as the objective theology of the " sundry times," even to its forms of expression, is still the same, so also is the expression of the subjective faith which apprehends it. The only reliance of the saints is upon the vicarious blood ; and upon the promise " When I see the blood I will pass over." And with this reliance for the soul's refreshment, and for " peace and joy in believing," the very forms of the experimental utterances of the soul are the same in all ages. With David the cry is " my soul *thirsteth* for God, as the hart panteth after the water brooks." And Isaiah proclaims to such—" Ho every one that *thirsteth* come ye to the waters." Just so the Son of God incarnate, standing in the temple on the great day of the feast, proclaims, " If any man *thirst* let him come unto me and drink." And so again, as the Son of God ascended, Jesus sends back from his throne his last message to the sinners, for whom he had " endured the cross, despising the shame," " Let him that is *athirst* come, and whosoever will let him take the water of life freely."

But what leaves the charge of contradiction between the Old and the New Testament scriptures without apology, even on the part of those who cannot enter into the spirit of the objective theology of the Bible, or into the subjective experience of the saints, is the fact of the substantial identity, amid all the diversity, of even the externals of this scheme of redemption revealed at the " sundry times."

It cannot fail to attract the attention of the reader of this book, that the mode of its revelation is through a series of *covenants*, each one a larger development of that which precedes it. These covenants imply the idea of a distinct body of people with whom the *covenant* or contract is made. The entire revelation may be analyzed, as consisting of three classes of truths :—First, the record of historic events which prepared the way for certain *covenants:* next, the covenant and revelation connected with it ; and next the history and revelations connected with the development of that covenant. The story of creation and of Eden prepares the way for the covenant of grace with Adam ; the history developing this, prepares again the way for the covenant of protection to the race made with Noah. Then, under this covenant, begins the history preparatory to the Church covenant with Abraham, the history of whose development prepares the way for the Passover covenant to redeem the Church, and that again for the Sinai covenant ; then the history of the development of this Church, as Jehovah's spiritual commonwealth, prepares the way for the covenant with David, establishing the typical throne and kingdom of Messiah in the Church. From this time forward all the history and revelations through the prophets are to the end of preparing the way of the Lord's coming, as the king of a universal kingdom; and for the new covenant in his blood, under which his commissioned agents shall "go into all the world and preach the gospel to every creature."

And what is specially noteworthy, as indicating the unity existing under the "divers manners" of this covenant body, is the sameness of its administrations under all the changes. The patriarchs, or natural elders of the church, while it was still embosomed in the family constitution, are succeeded by the official "elders" when the shortening of human life makes it necessary to choose among many patriarchs. And such continued to be the form of administration of the visible church in all succeeding ages. Before the national organization under Moses, the elders were in charge of the covenant people, to receive and decide upon the genuineness of Moses' call from God (Ex. iii. 15, and iv. 29); through the elders was received the covenant seal of the passover (Ex. xii. 3, 21); and through them was preparation made for receiving the law; and through them again was negotiated the Sinai Covenant (Ex. xix. 7, 8, and xxiv. 7, 8). Before the elders was the typical rock smitten (Ex. xvii. 5, 6); and the elders partook of the sacrificial feast preparatory to receiving the ecclesiastical constitution and ritual (Ex. xxiv. 9, 11). The elders with the priests constituted the supreme ecclesiastical court to decide appeals under the instruction of the oracle (Deut. xvii. 9, 12). The elders are found, even during the apostasy, sitting in council with Elisha (II Kings, vi. 32); in the exile with Ezekiel (Ezek. viii. 1); and, in apostate Jerusalem, sat with the priests upon the case of Jeremiah (Jer. xxvi. 8, 17). So when Messiah "came unto his own, and his own received him not," his rejection was by the priests and elders

in council, of an apostate church (Math. xxiv. 1). Under
the dispensation of the Spirit, the elders still sit in council
with Apostles (Acts xv. 23). And in that glorious vision
of the church of the future, through the door opened in
heaven, John saw the great congregation, represented by the .
" four and twenty elders," twelve for the Old, and twelve for
the New Testament Church, acting together, casting their
crowns—the symbols of their official authority—at the feet
of the great king (Rev. iv. 4).

This, then, is our short method with the treacherous Rationalism which would persuade us to cast aside what " God at
sundry times and in divers manners spake to the fathers,"
anterior to the teaching of Jesus, the Son of man, as no
gospel for us. We answer, it is all gospel ; one gospel ; and
the same gospel ; not only in its creed, but in the details and
results of that creed when accepted. It must therefore stand
in its complete integrity or not stand at all. If one part is
not divine, no part is divine. If Moses and the prophets are
not divine utterances, then neither can Jesus and the apostles
be, who claim to be simply the full development of Moses
and the prophets, and fully endorse them. And, therefore,
this pretence of receiving Jesus as history, while rejecting
Moses as legend, is founded either upon an ignorance that
has never grasped the idea of him whom it so dogmatically
pronounces upon, or upon a hypocritical infidelity,—that by
gradual and insidious approaches, would undermine the foundations of our faith.

On the other hand, the view here taken furnishes an equally
short method with the Romanism that harps upon the diversities of revelation as creating a necessity for an infallible
interpreter, and the exclusion of the people from the free use
of the scriptures. What the people need is not an infallible
interpreter of scripture, but simply to be shown how to read
the scriptures, thus given at the " sundry times," and the

divers manners of several successive forms of civilization and thought and speech. Properly instructed as to these incidental questions, and having the scriptures translated into their fashion of thought, the people can far more readily interpret the scriptures for themselves than interpret the infallible interpreter.

It is indeed true, that the rule of faith being of " divers manners" of expression will lead to corresponding diverse opinions in incidentals and non-essentials, according as more or less stress is laid upon this or that manner of utterance of the same truth. In this sense it may produce sectarianism. But, in this sense, sectarianism is obviously pre-supposed by the gospel, and implied in the very nature of Christianity. Yet this diversity by no means mars the essential unity of the Church of God. It is rather a necessity to the completeness of the Holy Catholic Church, as the visible embodiment of such a gospel. Just as we have four biographies of Jesus in the Evangelists, and yet all of them one life so thoroughly, that neither of the four is the life of Jesus without the other three. Just as we find the harmonists of the gospels labouring to make the four one, and yet each successive harmonist begins his work by shewing that all his predecessors have failed in some important particular. So with the Church of God, founded upon these Evangelists; it is manifold, yet one. And so with these perpetual endeavours to fashion the Church into one invariable form in all the details of its liturgy and expression of faith.

Hence, long before the controversy with Protestantism concerning sects, and the need of an infallible interpreter, the children of the Church of Rome herself loved to find the symbols of a church manifold, yet one, in the four rivers, flowing from one fount in Paradise; and, in the four-fold, yet one, living creature seen in the visions of Ezekiel and Daniel and John in the Apocalypse. Long before the apostasy of

Rome, Jerome had said : " As the one river of Paradise divided into four streams, so the gospel doctrine of Christ Jesus distributes itself through the channel of four different ministers, to water and fructify the garden of God." Even in the " dark ages," as long ago as A.D. 1172, Adam, of St. Victor, the great hymnologist, taught the Latin Church to sing:

> " Circa thronum majestatis,
> Cum spiritibus beatis,
> Quatuor diversitatis
> Adstant animalia.
>
> .   .   .
>
> Formae formant figurarum
> Formas evangelistarum,
> Quorum imber doctrinarum
> Stillat in ecclesia."

Of which—though rudely and feebly rendered—the sense and spirit is,—

> " Before the throne of majesty,
> With spirits blessed beyond the sky,
> The four-fold creature stood.
>
> .   .   .
>
> Strange mystic figure ! four in one !
> Of Matthew, Mark, and Luke, and John,
> Who jointly shed their dews upon
> The blessed Church of God."

If the unity of the rule of faith is not marred by reason of the " divers manners " of its utterances, why may not the Church, founded upon such a rule of faith, be one in reality, notwithstanding it may exhibit diversity in the manner of uttering its faith and worship ?

I may add, moreover, that even though there were no such diversity in the rule of faith, yet from the " divers manners" of the humanity upon which its truths operate, to be reflected back in a subjective theology, the reflection must naturally exhibit these diversities of religious views. It is one of the fine analogies of Edmund Burke, that "the metaphysical rights of man, coming into contact with the actual life of society, are, as the rays of light passing from a rarer into a denser medium, refracted out of a straight line." Slightly modifying the great orator's figure, I may say that the beams of light from the divine oracles, falling as they do upon humanity, as upon a prism, are not only refracted in the subjective theology of Christian experience, but their *colours* separated to the view of the beholder, as in the spectrum; shewing here the Presbyterian *blue*—here the Episcopal *orange*—here the Methodist *red*—and so through all the seven colours of which the pure white light is composed. And so, reversing the process, when the separating causes are counteracted by some common devotional movement that brings them to pray and praise together, all the colours are combined again, as they commune with God, and they reflect the one pure white light, as it fell upon the prism.

This unity of spirit, in devotion and communion with God, is that unity to which the Apostles exhort; this is the unity which fulfils the Master's intercessory prayer "that they all may be one." And this spiritual unity is far more real and true than the boasted unity of Rome, depending not on spiritual attraction, but a mere external power of government under one head, making the several fragments artificially cohere together. So, on the other hand, this unity of spirit is the true unity as against the latitudinarian sentimentalism which, in our day, affects to long for the abolition of sects and creeds, and would merge all into one, by utterly ignoring the doctrine of a church as one of the essential elements of the gospel; and by making light of Christ's appointed order and ordinances for his spiritual commonwealth. The marvellous unity of doctrine evinced by the various confessions of the Protestant Reformation is the true secret of the unity of spirit in devotion among Christians of these various churches ; it is not merely sentimental. Discerning the image of Christ in each other, they learn to recognize each other as brethren ; and the very zeal for maintaining Christ's order and ordinances as each understands them, is only a guarantee, each to the other, of a common zeal for the faith once delivered to the saints.

II. Having considered the Apostle's premise, it now remains that we consider, very briefly, the significancy of the Apostle's reasoning and conclusion from the premise of a revelation " at sundry times and in divers manners." He argues, " Therefore we ought to give the more earnest heed, etc., for if the word spoken by angels was steadfast, how shall we escape if we neglect so great salvation ?"

You will observe that this argument is a compound syllogism, which may be resolved into these two :

1st. Impenitency under the fuller light of a completed revelation involves greater guilt than under a revelation incomplete.

But, since Christ's advent under the ministration of the Spirit, we have the revelation, begun in earlier ages, fully and completely developed.

Therefore, the guilt of impenitency is greater now than ever before.

2nd. The certainty of judgment without mercy is greater, in proportion to the greater guilt of neglecting clearer light.

But, as a matter of fact, even under the inferior light of a partially developed gospel, " Every transgression and disobedience received a just recompense of reward."

Therefore, more certain and inevitable must be the doom of such as now reject the great and fully developed salvation.

Thus the power of the two arguments is made to converge upon the one tremendous conclusion of the inevitable doom of transgressors, under the last dispensation of the gospel.

To comprehend fully the force of the argument, we need only inquire,—with whom precisely is the Apostle here reasoning? and what does he assume concerning them?

Observe then, that he is not reasoning with sceptics who either deny any inspiration, or who conceive of faith as merely a submission to the overwhelming power of proofs addressed to the understanding, or under the crushing power of difficulties which the mind cannot master. So, indeed, many conceive of the gospel salvation; they regard it as something bestowed in the way of reward to the logical and the learned minds, in consideration of their toil in working out demonstrations of the gospel; or, in the case of the unlearned, something bestowed as a reward for the credulity which can accept without question impossible truths. They imagine that the only reason why they are not Christians is simply from want of ability to force their minds into the belief of the gospel, or want of time to examine its evidences. They have the misfortune to be gifted with such an astuteness of logical perception, or such a capacity of intellect, that the loose reasoning which satisfied a Bacon, or a Newton, or a Locke, cannot satisfy them. But they intend, at a leisure time, to gather up all the books on the evidences, and demonstrate themseves into the kingdom of heaven. Meanwhile, they appear to themselves to be sincerely longing after that simple, uninquiring faith, which they think is the peculiar privilege of the unlearned masses.

Not with such is the Apostle reasoning; for then the argument would be, " God at sundry times hath piled argument upon argument, and in divers manners hath presented the argument, until nothing more could be added to its force; therefore, how shall we be converted if not by this ?" That would, indeed, be a true statement, and sound reasoning, but it is not the argument here. It is directed not to those who *reject*, but to those who " *neglect* " salvation.

Nor, again, is the reasoning with that class who, though not unbelievers, as they think, yet find their chief reason for not being Christians in the difficulties of the gospel doctrines, which they cannot reconcile with their reason. There are many of our educated youth and professional men to whom the gospel presents the aspect of the Sphinx of the old tragedy, sitting by the wayside to propound the riddle, and demanding of each passer-by " Solve it or die !" Whereas, it is the peculiar feature of the gospel of Christ that it demands neither the solution of paradoxes, nor even the acceptance of opinions, as a condition precedent to salvation. Its call is not " solve or die," but " believe with thine heart or die." Not believe a creed, either, but " believe on the Lord Jesus Christ," a personal Saviour. Not with such is the reasoning here. For then the argument would be, God hath at " sundry times and in divers manners" added explanation to explanation, and solved difficulty after difficulty, till no longer is it conceivable how any sincere mind can cavil ; therefore, if still in the dark,—how shall we ever have the mystery solved ? That would be valid reasoning, but it is not the argument here. He reasons not with those who *mystify*, but those who " *neglect* " salvation.

Nor, again, is the reasoning here with the careless and profane scoffers, who say, " let us eat and drink, for to-morrow we die ;" nor with the frivolous devotees of fashion and the world, who never care to listen to the higher calls of the soul; nor with the servile worshippers of Mammon, who recklessly take the dollar in exchange for the soul. For then the reasoning would be—God hath so highly regarded this work of saving sinners, that, amid all the cares of the Universe, he hath "at sundry times and in divers manners" manifested special concern, and sent down the chariot of heaven to bear communication to earth respecting it.   If then ye are careless, frivolous and reckless in a matter that has interested all heaven during ages past, what hope is there for you? How can such as ye escape ?   That would be valid reasoning, but it is not the argument here.   He reasons not with those that *insult* and *contemn*, but those that "*neglect*" salvation.

But the parties addressed in the argument of the text are those of whom it is assumed,

First,—That "they have heard these things" and recognize them as things spoken by God's angels (messengers).   In so far, they are those found in all our Sabbath congregations, who treat the gospel with great outward respect, and even thank God that they are not as other men—even as these sceptics, scoffers, frivolous and thoughtless.

Second,—That they have not only the objective knowledge of the gospel, but also a subjective consciousness of a danger to be "escaped," and a ruin from which the rescue must be a "great salvation." It is indeed a striking feature of the gospel that it assumes, as truths known to human conscious-ness, most of those things which men speculate about as religious opinions.   It makes no argument to prove immor-tality to him who is ambitious to prove himself an ox or an ass, or as any of "the brutes that perish."   It assumes not only the conviction of immortality in every soul, but, as con-nected with that, the conviction of a condition of present moral ruin, and of a wrath to come.   These are instincts with which the spiritual nature of man is assumed in the gospel to have been originally endowed.

As in the realms of animated nature, the creatures seem, by some mysterious law, to be endowed with instincts, whose blind impulses prove more watchful guardians of their safety than the proud intelligence of man ; so that the wild scream of the sea-bird is often the first warning of the coming tempest, even when the most experienced mariner can discover no "cloud big as a man's hand": so the soul of man seems to be endowed with certain spiritual instincts,—blind impulses, it may be,—but efficient to warn him of wrath to come. And even when the voyage of life is happiest, its sea calmest, and its sun brightest—amid your shouts of joy and songs of gladness, there would be heard, if you listened for it, the low soul-wail of a coming storm of retribution, through which none but the Great Captain of our salvation can pilot us in safety.

Third,—It is assumed that those here addressed have had, in addition to this objective knowledge and subjective conviction, some practical development and confirmation of both, in the great facts of God's providential history, showing that every transgression and disobedience has actually received a just recompense. It is, in fact, to this end that the record has been made by holy men of old.

Fourth,—It is assumed, however, that, with all this, the men who enjoy such light may yet *neglect* it, and through neglect *perish;* " seeing they may see and not perceive that God shall save them." Saddest of all truths concerning man the creature ever boasting of his powers of reason !

Now may we see the force of the Apostle's argument to the conclusion of the inevitable doom of all that neglect salvation. For the greatness of this salvation is of that very sort, that the neglect of it logically necessitates damnation. If God hath, as it were, exhausted all his infinite resources, and infinitely surpassed all your own conceptions ; if he hath carried on an argument through four thousand years, gradually cumulating to its full completion, and now, in His Providence, hath placed you upon the very apex of the infinite demonstration ; if, in the way of argument, he hath given every conceivable exposition; if, in the way of persuasion, he hath used every conceivable appeal of tenderness and love ;

if, in the way of warning and alarm, he hath arrayed before
you every conceivable terror among the recompenses of
reward to transgressors—then what more is there to wait for?
what more to hope for? how can he possibly escape who
neglects so great salvation? The very method of his revelation, "at sundry times and in divers manners," leaves you
without one plea for neglecting it, or from putting off from
you its calls, a moment longer. Do you plead that you have
yet doubts as to the certainty and reality of these things?
That plea might have had some plausibility in the case of those
to whom Noah preached righteousness; for then the salvation was but dimly revealed. But even their transgressions
received a just recompense of reward! How then can you
escape? Do you plead that you desire to believe, but this
gospel is full of doctrines hard to be understood? That plea
had some plausibility as urged by those to whom Ezekiel and
Jeremiah preached, when these cavillers urged that their
sufferings, intended to bring them to repentance, were not
for their own sins, but because "the fathers had eaten sour
grapes, and the children's teeth are set on edge." For still
the revelation of redemption was comparatively dim and
mysterious. But even they, for their transgressions received
a just recompense of reward, under the law "the soul that
sinneth it shall die." How then can you escape on such a
plea? Do you still urge that, though you can accept all the
doctrines of the gospel as a theology, still somehow it seems
not to apply practically to your case? That plea would have
had great plausibility, if God had spoken, as the sceptical
men of science would have him speak, by but one utterance
of the abstract truths of his gospel in scientific form. For it is
easily conceivable that, in such a case, many a poor sinner
would have had trouble in applying the abstract truths to the
multitudinous forms of the soul trouble. But God "spake at
sundry times and in divers manners," connecting the revela-

tion of His plan of mercy with all the practical diversities of human character and condition, for four thousand years: and among all the multitudes of sinners saved, and of cases put on record, some one must surely be parallel with yours: at least so nearly parallel as to furnish you with a precedent. Do you plead, "but I am so great a sinner, and have neglected the great salvation so long?" That plea might have had some plausibility when sinners under the law heard Isaiah preach "your hands are full of blood." But even Isaiah said to them —" though your sins be as scarlet, never mind ; come on,— and they shall be made as snow ; though you are spiritually bankrupt—never mind ; Ho every one that thirsteth, come ye to the waters ; and he that hath no money, come ye, buy and eat—without money and without price." And surely you have no excuse for hesitating, who on the back of all this, know that " God in these last times hath spoken unto us by his Son," saying " Whosoever will let him take of the water of life FREELY."

II.

THE SCRIPTURES OF THE "SUNDRY TIMES" INSPIRED OF GOD; THE ONLY SOURCE OF SAVING KNOWLEDGE AND ANTIDOTE TO PERILOUS ERROR.

I. TIMOTHY, iii. 1 16.—This know also, that in the last days perilous times shall come. • • • All Scripture is given by inspiration of God, and is profitable for doctrine, for reproof, for correction, for instruction in righteousness.

VIEWED simply in its aspect as Divine, nothing incidental can add solemnity and importance to any utterance of "holy men of old who spake as they were moved by the Holy Ghost." Viewed on its human side, however, this passage in the Epistle to Timothy, "his son in the gospel," has special solemnity and power, as the farewell counsel and warning of an aged martyr for Jesus, now in prison awaiting execution, and saying of himself, in this immediate connection, "I am now ready to be offered, and the time of my departure is at hand. I have fought a good fight, I have finished my course, I have kept the faith; henceforth there is laid up for me a crown of righteousness, which the Lord, the righteous judge, shall give me."

Though from a prison, therefore, and though a picture of the world drawn by one whom it had maligned, scorned, scourged, imprisoned, and condemned to death, it is not in the snarling spirit of a cynic, but in the joyous spirit of a martyr, shaded, indeed, for a moment, as he recurs from the glorious prospect before him to the sad prospects of the way-ward and erring church of his love that he leaves behind him. Nor is it in the spirit of an empirical enthusiast that he pre-scribes the scriptures as the only antidote for the anticipated perils of error, but in the profoundest convictions of his own heart's experience, and his large observation and experience in dealing with the errors and passions of men.

We should note carefully, at least the general outlines of the Apostle's picture of perilous times in the last days, as preparatory to any proper appreciation of the antidote for all those perils which he finds in the scriptures inspired of God.

You will observe, in the first place, that unbounded as is the confidence of the Apostle in the power of the gospel to regenerate society, and large as are his anticipations of its success, neither he in this place, nor the inspired writers any where else, give any countenance to the dreams so popular in these last times, of a progress of society under the gospel with its Christian reforms and philanthropies, to a golden age of universal perfection. Nor do they give any ground for the infidel scoff and cavil, so popular also in these last times, that Christianity is a failure ; because, in spite of all the efforts of the Church, the society, even of christendom, is still so largely corrupt, insincere, selfish, God-despising, sham-worshipping, sensual, devilish. Nay, they give no ground, either for the disappointments and despondencies of that Arcadian piety which, assuming the saintly perfection of the Church, anticipated nothing but peace, purity, and love, within its sacred enclosures, and having failed to realize its ideal, falls back into censoriousness, uncharitableness, distrust and unbelief. For it is evidently within the limits of Chris-tianized communities, and even of the Church itself, that the Apostle prophetically sees these. " men that shall be *lovers of their own selves, covetous, boasters, proud, blasphemers, disobedient to parents, unthankful, unholy, without natural affections, trucebreakers, false accusers, incontinent, fierce, despisers of those that are good, traitors, heady, high minded, lovers of pleasure more than lovers of God.''* That he anticipates the realization of this appalling list of sins within the limits of Christianized communities, and among those making pretence to religion, is very manifest from the last item in the catalogue—*" Having a form of godliness, but denying the power thereof.''* The predictions of the scriptures uniformly represent that humanity shall go on from generation to generation, until the era of millennial glory, exhibiting the same depravity and the same passions, even under all the light of the gospel; and that the gospel, parallel with the progress of humanity, shall gather out of the corrupt generations Christ's elect, by the same exercise of Divine power and grace that converts the most fierce and savage of the species. Nay, that even the visible Church shall constantly be liable to corruption from the world without, and from unsanctified nature within its enclosures. And, therefore, not only shall the tares continue to grow with the wheat till the reapers come for the harvest, but not unfrequently the tares shall utterly choke out the wheat in large portions of the field.

Having drawn this general outline of the picture, the Apostle proceeds to point out the influences at work in the Church to produce such corruption of faith and morals. And here he presents certain portraits of character which may well lead us to study, with special interest, both the perils and the antidote in the infallible Word of God which he sets before us.

The first of these special portraitures, in filling up the picture, is the religious pretence of the errorism of the last days. For observe, the special peril here described is not from the " scoffers," whose coming in the last days the Apostle Peter predicted, but rather from the hypocrites whom

both the Apostles Peter and Jude predict and describe as
" false teachers, who shall privily bring in damnable heresies,
even denying the Lord that bought them," (II. Peter,
ii. 1); and as " certain men crept in unawares, ungodly
men, turning the grace of our God into lasciviousness, and
denying the only Lord God, even our Lord Jesus Christ"
(Jude i. 4). Yet all this is done under the guise of " a
form of godliness." Nay, generally, as we see from the
fulfilment, under the guise of a form of *extra* godliness.
The Church of Jesus Christ, as he hath organized it, is represented by them to be a laggard and a sluggard in the great
movement of philanthropy for the regeneration of humanity.
So far advanced is this new and improved form of godliness,
that even Jesus and His Apostles, though patronizingly smiled
upon as well-meaning men, are regarded as far in the rear
of the modern philanthropy. But especially are the Apostles
far in the rear of the improved form of godliness whose
flexibility so readily adapts itself to the tastes of men, and
thereby beguiles them into the kingdom of God. It devises,
now, a poetic religionism for the sentimental ; now a gorgeous
ceremonial for the lovers of the æsthetic ; now penances for
the self-righteous ; now indulgences for the lovers of pleasure ;
now fires the zeal of bigots with " genealogies and old wives'
fables ;" and now assures the careless and sluggish Gallios
that it is "no matter about belief if one is sincere." In
short, while it quiets the craving of the human soul for
a religion of some sort, it skilfully adapts itself to every phase
of human self-love and human weakness. It preserves, for
policy's sake, the semblance of gospel religion ; but under
well-feigned zeal for its outward form, it assiduously subverts
its power.

A second feature in the picture is the very peculiar *propagandism* of this sham religion—" which creeps into houses
and leads captive silly women "—γυναικάρια—in the neuter,

and hence the word may well be taken as descriptive of the brainless of either sex. This is the remarkable characteristic of *most* mere formal religionism, that its propagandism expends itself, not in going forth to "the highways and hedges," nor to the people that sit in darkness and the shadow of death," but in creeping within the enclosures of the covenant, either to seduce off its victims or to infuse into the weak minds self-conceit, self-righteousness, dissatisfaction with the law and ordinances of Christ's house, and suspicion and distrust of those who administer them.

A third feature in the picture of this sham-religion of the last days is its *purely negative* character—" *Ever learning and never able to come to the knowledge of the truth.*" How apt the description of that religionism which, while professing to accept the gospel as Christians, assures us at the same time that nothing is settled as the positive truth of God, but all things are open to dispute as mere opinions. It has no faith, but only an opinion. Its gospel is not " *credo* "—" I believe," but ever " *nego* "—" I deny." Its prayer and confession is not, " Lord, I believe, help thou mine unbelief," but " Lord, I deny, reject, eschew all creeds, *reward* Thou mine unbelief." The creed, or rather the *no-creed*, on which it founds its hopes of salvation—no, not of salvation, for it neither needs, nor would accept salvation—but on which it founds its hope of heaven, is, " I believe not God as maker of heaven and earth, since I know not whether heaven and earth were *made*, or only developed ; I believe *not* Jesus Christ *the* Son of God, for all of us are in like manner sons of God. I believe *not* the Holy Ghost, in any sense of a personal spirit and sanctifier, but only as a figure of speech. I believe *not* that we are justified by faith, but every one of us will for our works be rewarded with God's favour. And as to other points, I have not been able to come to the knowledge of the truth ; and even if I had, could not say I believe, since that would trammel free thought with a creed.

Another feature of the picture is the *plausibility and inge-nuity* of the teachers of this sham religion ; they shall be able so to counterfeit the truth as to deceive even the very elect. " As Jannes and Jambres withstood Moses,"—counterfeiting the very miracles intended to demonstrate the presence and power of Jehovah with him, and thereby destroying the effect of the miracle on Pharaoh's mind—" *so do these also resist the truth.*" They counterfeit the very seal of heaven, and so counterfeit the current coin of Christ's kingdom, that the real people of the kingdom are imposed upon by their high sound-ing phrases of faith and piety !

Brethren, those of you who are at all familiar with the current style of the insidious infidelity of these times—its pretended zeal for the honour of Christianity—its affected sighings after a more spiritual faith than either Moses and the Prophets, or Jesus and his Apostles teach—its noisy philanthropism—and its pretentious claims to have met the demands of science and the progress of modern thought—will readily perceive that the aged martyr here paints no ideal picture, nor a picture, either, of men and things only of the ages gone by !

Now, for such perils as these to the Church of God, the Apostle points out the remedy which, if faithfully applied, shall prove infallible. " Thou hast known, from a child, the holy scriptures which are able to make thee wise unto salva-tion." And they are thus able to teach the infallible way of salvation :—

First, because of their intrinsic dignity and infallible authority, as the inspiration of God :

Secondly, because their inspiration gives their contents a Divine adaptation to every positive want of the mind and heart in reference to the question of religion, and to the exposure of every form of religious error. For they give Divine, and therefore infallible direction, *for doctrine—teac-*

καὶ ει—the didactic teaching of the truth concerning God; "for reproof"—ελεγχον—the refutation, by proof, of error concerning God; "*for correction*"—επανόρθωσιν—the setting right or rectifying the wrong principles of practical ethics; "*for instruction in righteousness*"—παιδείαν τὴν ἐν δικαιοσύνῃ—the positive nurture of the soul in experimental knowledge of the way in which a sinner may be accounted righteous before God.

And this, it will be perceived on a little reflection, is no mere random citation of certain uses to which the word of God may be applied, as specimens of that use simply. It is a marvellously logical classification of their uses ; and it is *exhaustive*, as covering all the possible wants that man can desire to have met by a revelation. As a being endowed with reason, and capable of believing only what he conceives to be truth, his religion must embrace a *doctrine* of God and his relation to God. As a creature liable to be deceived, by error and unbelief, concerning God and his relations to God, his religion must have a guide to warn him against and expose the treacherous wiles of error, that are ever tampering with his " evil heart of unbelief." As a being whose passions are ever blinding his conscience in reference to duty toward God and man, his religion must supply him with an ethical rule of right, by which to correct his crooked judgments and amend his crooked ways. As a being capable of a birth to a new and everlasting life, his religion must supply him with a *nurture* under the new law of righteousness which the faith that is unto salvation teaches him. So that it may be affirmed, with truth, that no want of the human soul can be conceived which is not provided for under one or other of these four heads.

We proceed now to consider briefly the twofold aspect in which the scriptures are here presented :

First, of the intrinsic dignity and authority of the scriptures as inspired by God.

In what sense and to what extent are we to accept this proposition, "All Scripture is given by inspiration of God?" This inquiry is the more needful in an age like this when, on the one hand, science and philosophy are demanding, though in very courteous and reverential terms, that religion shall make some concessions to its advance of thought, and, on the other, many who stand as representatives of religion are disposed, in various degrees, to make concessions, explanations, apologies, and limitations of the high claims of the scriptures, at which the men of science stagger and doubt.

We answer, then:

1. The "inspiration of God" in the fullest and plainest sense which the words convey; for such is evidently the meaning and drift of all the language which these scriptures use, in other places, concerning their own origin and authorship. They are declared to be "the Word," "the Law," "the Testimonies," "the Oracles of God." They claim to report, in many cases, the very words of Jehovah, appearing to them in shadowy form, or in the visions of the night; in other cases to utter the words which the "Spirit of Christ in the prophets" spake; which they describe as the words "of the holy men of old, who spake as they were moved by the Holy Ghost." They purport to be, in part, the recorded words of the Son of God himself, who spake on earth as never man spake. They expressly declare, further, that not only did God speak "in time past, to the fathers by the prophets, and in these last times by his Son;" but, also, that the same general truths were repeated, enlarged upon, and enforced by Apostles whom God attested, as speaking for him, "by signs and wonders and divers miracles and gifts of the Holy Ghost." It is simply impossible to give such declarations their natural and proper sense, and at the same time, accept the limitations and interpretations suggested by the current liberal criticism, which, in truth, is liberal only in

the sense of granting what is not its own, but Christ's, the Prophet of the Church, by way of removing the difficulties that "the progress of modern thought" and "the advance of philosophy" has found in the Bible

For however this criticism may urge that its purpose is merely to translate into more scientific forms of expression the thought of an ancient record, belonging to a more poetic and less scientific age ; very manifestly, the sacred writers themselves mean to convey the idea that the book is designed to be the utterance of the mind of God, not in scientific form, but in the forms of thought and speech current among the masses of humanity in the successive ages of its progress during the period of inspiration. Just as, in the person of Jesus Christ, the infinite nature of God assumed a finite human body and soul, conforming to our finite conceptions, that we might commune with him,—so, in the scripture, the infinite mind of God, the Saviour, assuming a finite human form of thought and expression, reveals himself to our finite comprehension, that he may communicate to us his way of salvation.

To all those treacherous forms of unbelief, therefore, which affect to receive the scriptures as the inspiration of God, and yet reject their teachings of Christ as God in human form because incomprehensible, there is this very simple answer : It is utterly incompetent to those who, in any real sense, accept the scriptures, as inspired of God, to reject any teaching, or even any interpretation of their teaching, be- cause it is thus incomprehensible ; since in the very act of receiving the Scriptures, as truly inspired of God, you have already accepted a truth equally incomprehensible. For not more so is the proposition that the infinite nature should have assumed the finite form of the human body animated by a human soul, than the proposition that the infinite mind should have assumed the finite form of the human mind to utter its. thought to man.

The scriptures then are, in the fullest sense, the inspiration of God. It is God, the Saviour, using the machinery of human nature—its intellect, emotions, will, fashions of thought and organs of utterance—through which to express to man his infinite concern for him, and his method of saving him. As these utterances of God extended through different ages and civilizations, therefore the speech varies in its forms, according to the varieties of thought and speech which the humanity assumed to itself in its progress through the ages. For so thoroughly human in its form was God's speech designed to be, that it moulded itself in the successive forms into which humanity moulded its thought and speech in the different eras. Hence the scriptures became so thoroughly divine thoughts, moulded so thoroughly in human forms of expression. And the Bible, while a divine book, is, at the same time, the most thoroughly human book in the world. Flexible thus to mould itself, during the process of its utterance to the varying phases of human thought in successive ages, the divine thought, as soon as its utterance was completed, and the revelation closed, became in its turn a power that moulded the thought and speech of all the successive ages and civilizations since, to its own form of thought and fashion of utterance. So that now the Bible stands forth, before the modern ages, neither a curious petrifaction—a fossil of a divine human organism that once lived and breathed, ages ago, nor a statue—cold, rigid and lifeless, however beautiful—carved by science out of the primeval rock, but a living and breathing human expression of the thoughts of "Jesus Christ, the same yesterday, to-day, and for ever."

2. And as we take the expression "inspiration of God" in its fullest sense; so also we take in its fullest sense the expression "All Scripture." For the description of inspiration just given excludes the idea of one portion of scripture as inspired, another not inspired, and still another *demi-*

inspired. The too current popular notion that the New Testament is, somehow, inspired in a sense higher than the Old Testament ; or, that of the New Testament itself, some portions, as the words of Jesus in the Evangelists, are inspired in some higher sense than the teachings of John and Paul and Peter, is utterly incompatible with the conception of the Bible as a God-inspired book. With regard to the inspiration of the New Testament and the non-inspiration of the Old, it is sufficient to remind you, that Jesus and his Apostles, not only endorsed the Old Testament writers as inspired, but founded their own teachings wholly upon it. It is manifest, therefore, that the stream can rise no higher than its source. " If they believe not Moses and the prophets," saith Jesus, " neither will they believe though one rose from the dead." " Had ye believed Moses, ye would have believed me for he wrote of me," said Jesus on another occasion. And so we say now, to those who affect to accept the inspiration of the gospels while they reject the Old Testament—" Had ye really believed Jesus, ye would believe Moses," for Jesus spake of Moses and endorsed him,—saying " I came not to destroy the law but to fulfil ;" and to his disciples, after his resurrection, " beginning at Moses and all the prophets he expounded unto them in all the Scriptures the things concerning himself," saying, " All things must be fulfilled which were written in the law of Moses, and in the prophets, and in the Psalms concerning me."

If then the sayings of Moses and the prophets are not the inspiration of God, how can ye pretend to receive as inspiration the sayings of Jesus ? How could inspired teachers in the New Testament mistake so widely as to account for inspired that which is not inspired ? The truth is that this popular conception of the superior inspiration of what Jesus said above that which Moses, or David, or Paul, or John said, is the merest fallacy. For the book claims that it is all really what Jesus, the Saviour, said; only this part he said through Moses, this part through David and the prophets, by his spirit in them, and this part through Evangelists and Apostles, by his spirit upon them. What boots it to us, if it only be Christ speaking, whether he gives utterance to his divine thoughts through the mind of the legal man Moses, or the poetic men David and Isaiah, or the logical man Paul, or the transcendental man John? The scripture therefore is the inspiration of God in the sense of being in all portions alike inspired.

3. Still further, as we take the expression " inspiration of God," and " all scripture " in their fullest sense, so we understand them as signifying that the *forms of speech*, in each portion, are selected under inspired guidance. We are not disposed, with too many of the critics, to make abatement on the score of the want of scientific accuracy of the scripture rhetoric, or of supposed accommodation to the unscientific spirit of the eras of the writers. We decline the proffered aid of such apologists, not merely because we judge that the difficulties which they labor to remove arise from " an evil heart of unbelief" that " would not believe though one rose from the dead;" but because, also, the apologies themselves are founded, for the most part, upon assumptions that are not true.

As to the apology for the unscientific structure and style of the scripture, that it grew out of the want of scientific knowledge on the part of the agents employed by the spirit of God, or want of scientific capacity to comprehend the " higher modern thought," it is simply untrue in fact. For the written history of the ages of Apostles, Evangelists and Prophets, and the recently disentombed records of the early civilization on the Euphrates and the Nile, all go to show, that if there had been any desire to give scientific form to this revelation, there was philosophy enough in the world to have enabled men to comprehend then, just as well as now, a revelation made according to the fashion of the "higher form of thought." In the mystic schools of Egypt, in the Pantheistic schools of Chaldea and the East, all the jargon of the modern philosophic schools of Germany, France, Great Britain and America, was in full blast; and, in fact, higher flights of transcendentalism and profounder thoughts were in the process of utterance, than the schools of modern Germany, France, Britain and America, may yet have had the capacity to comprehend. However that may be, there was surely philosophy enough in the world in the age of Jesus, John and Paul, had they chosen scientific forms of utterance, to have made them as comprehensible to their age as Socrates, Plato and Cicero. Beyond all doubt a larger number of their generation could have comprehended them, than the number of our generation which comprehends the transcendental "higher thought" of Germany, France, Old England or New England! But so far from desiring to satisfy the "higher thought" of his age, as he certainly had the capacity to do, Paul declared that of a set purpose, he preached a gospel which "was to the Greek foolishness."

It is not consistent with the limits of a single discourse to go into the merits of the question concerning the difficulties of the theory of plenary inspiration. There are doubtless difficulties here, as there are in all our endeavours to comprehend the things of God. It is easy to suggest difficulties; easier than to solve them. It is easy to descend to the lowest depths of unbelief; not so easy to retrace one's steps and rise out of the depths. But does scepticism on this subject relieve us of difficulties? Are they all on the side of belief? Come then, ye that find difficulties in our belief—take ye the laboring oar, and let us propound in turn our difficulties with your theory of unbelief.

Come, expound to us the curious riddle—how it is that

D

this Bible alone of all the books in the world, attempts the bold endeavour of a calm, historic statement of the first origin of the race. How is it, that as we attempt to trace up, through other channels, the present order of things in the world to its source, we can get no farther back than some three thousand years, either by aid of history or plausible legend ; and there find ourselves upon a vast historic desert ? But, when all other history stops, this book becomes, like its own pillar of fire that blazed across the Arabian desert, a beacon light to guide us onward and upward to the birth spot of the present generations ? Nay, having brought us there to Ararat slowly emerging from a vast desert of waters, then, like its own ark, floats us over the waste of waters and up to the very birthplace of time itself ?

Or solve for us the still profounder difficulty, on your sceptical theory, how these mysterious writings have so deeply rooted themselves in the world's thought, in spite of the perpetual conflict they have had with the general thought of every successive generation. And how they still have not only survived but triumphed in this perpetual war with the opinions of mankind ?

Or solve for us the curious fact that this book alone, of all books in the world, instead of uttering the opinions of the successive ages that produced it, has been the antagonist of those opinions ;—maintaining the unity of God amid all the darkness of the Western Polytheism; the vivid personality of God against the Eastern Pantheism ; the ineffable purity and holiness of God against the obscenities of Egyptian and Canaanitish idolatry ; the omnipresence of God against the theory of gods many and lords many ; teaching salvation by grace without works, just when and where the great schools of the world were glorying in the perfection of their ethical schemes for human regeneration ; teaching the resurrection of the body and how the " mortal must put on immortality," just when and where Socrates and Plato had theorized for man an immortality that excluded the mortal body, on the one hand, and Epicurus and his swinish herd were grunting their practical atheism of the degradation of both soul and body, on the other !

Or expound for us this mystery, how, in the modern ages, this book at war with human ideas, has stood its ground, not only, but made constant aggressions on the domain both of ignorance and learned unbelief. How now it bursts forth into new splendor to chase away the darkness, just as Papal tyranny has exiled it from Europe. How now it spreads its ideas over the enlightened world of the nineteenth century in face of the combined powers of scoffing and maligning atheism; of cavilling and witty deism ; of sneering and contemptuous pantheism ; of plausible and insinuating spiritualism ; of a treacherous and sanctimonious rationalism !

Or expound to us the mystery that this book, while all other books evince an adaptedness to the mind of some one country and age—as Persian Zoroaster, Greek Socrates, or Roman Cicero—is the book alike of all countries and ages ? Nay more, is the book that adapts itself alike to every phase of mind in every state and period of individual life, from the young dreams of the nursery, and the heart throbbings of the rudest peasant, up to the profoundest conviction of the philosopher and the sublimest inspiration of the poet ?

Let those who stagger under the difficulties of belief in scripture as the inspiration of God, make the experiment of solving some of the difficulties of unbelief. Then may they find that difficulties do not always imply error.

Second.—Of the Divine adaptation of these inspired scriptures to the need of man as a religious creature. We have space for brief hints, merely, under the several heads of the Apostle's exhaustive fourfold classification.

1. The Scripture, God-inspired—in the sense just ex-

plained, of God the Saviour revealing to man, the sinner, a way of salvation—is "*profitable for doctrine*," and the only reliable source of doctrine on the subject of salvation. As God the Creator, he speaks in "the heavens that tell the glory of God;" and the "invisible things of God are made manifest from the things that are made." From these man may learn something of his relation to God his Creator; and this revelation in nature is that which forms his guide in establishing law and justice and government for himself and for society. Yet even when, in the highest exercise of his capacity, man thus haply feels after and finds God, that knowledge, in connection with his own moral instincts, discovers to his conscience not only a *law*, but a *law violated*. And therefore the highest stretch of his knowledge of God, through nature, is only to demonstrate the probability of an existence of disorder and misery in store for him hereafter, as well as here.

If then, standing in the relation of a Saviour to man the sinner, God makes a revelation of a method whereby he may be saved, this must be not merely a source, but the *only* source, of all such knowledge of God the Saviour. And just here lies the fallacy of all those deceptive forms of religionism, on either extreme, which suppose the scriptures to be *a* source, but not the *only* source of all doctrine concerning salvation. It is such a mockery to the powers of reason with which God has endowed man to conceive him capable of *believing truth*, as a mere act of obedience to authority, on the one hand, and such a mockery of the scriptures as God-inspired, on the other, to suggest a concurrent jurisdiction of mere human reason with God's word in the authoritative statement of the doctrine of salvation to man, that none who are capable of intelligently conceiving of the nature of religion, or who are not given over to blindness, can well be led far astray by such a theory. The chasm between a

God inspired doctrine of religion, and a doctrine of mere authority, on the one hand, or of mere human reason, on the other, is infinite and bridgeless.

2. These God-inspired scriptures are also " *profitable for reproof*,"—or as the original signifies, " for controverting and exposing errors,"—contrary to the "doctrine" of salvation. So far as concerns errors of theology, to which this expression has, no doubt, reference, if we cease to stand upon the ground of the scriptures, we have no standard by which to test and expose the subtile wiles of error.   If we consent to follow the errorist into the region of speculative truth, it must be an endless chase, or a combat where there are no laws of battle to determine the victory.   And beside, the reason of man, to which in such case we really appeal, is a partial and corrupt judge, with a bias against the moral laws of God. Hence the unprofitableness of so much that passes for theological controversy.   It appeals, on both sides to the authority of reason merely, and leaves all as uncertain as before. Hence the uncertainty of all creeds in theology that interpolate reason as a co-ordinate source of doctrine with revelation.   Their source being variable and uncertain, these creeds seldom remain stationary long enough to be examined. Their theology floats loose, as some poetic isle of Delos that floated on the sea, so that no navigator could ever fix its place.   Or sadly uncertain as our great American river, the Mississippi, whose channel so changes, year by year, that no pilot can fix it upon his chart.   He who, this year, would run his craft by his knowledge of last year, finds himself high and dry upon a sand-bar, or a "sawyer," and is coolly informed " that *was* the channel last year," but " the progress " of the last " June rise," not satisfied therewith, has forced a new channel.

The Divine method with the gainsayers is chiefly through the ordinances of the sanctuary,—not with endless " strifes of words"—to put before the mind and heart the clear

statement of " doctrine," to meet the soul-wants ; that the
Holy Ghost, using the doctrine,—may give effectual proof
of sin, of righteousness and of judgment.

3. The God-inspired scriptures are not only thus the
source of doctrine, and the armory whence are drawn divine
weapons against errors in theology, but also the test whereby
to rectify all ethical errors. They are profitable also, for
" correction " of the practical life. It would not be difficult
to show, if space permitted, that, independent of the scriptures, there can be no ethical system of force enough to
make its power practically felt in the conscience of man.
For, with nothing more than the vague conceptions of God
derived through reason, there can be no moral law, save in
a loose metaphysical sense. Hence the tendency of a loose
theology must ever be to generate a loose moral life ; however much it may aim to exalt " works " and belittle
" grace." Hence too the folly of the cant, that pretends to
accept the beautiful morality of the gospel, but rejects the
theology of the gospel. It is " the play of Hamlet with the
part of Hamlet omitted." Only as it is founded upon the
theology of the gospel, has the morality of the gospel any
more force than the morality of Socrates. But upon this
wide field we cannot here enter, otherwise it would be easy
to show that the difference between the ethics of the scriptures and all other systems, is a difference not merely of
degree, but also an infinite difference of *kind*.

4. As to the fourth and last point in the Apostle's classification, that the God-inspired scriptures are the great means
of *Christian nurture—of " instruction in righteousness,"*
there is less need of argument, since here no rival instruction
pretends even to set up a claim. Whatever wisdom other
schemes may claim to teach, they do not claim " to make
thee wise unto salvation." It is not only a " doctrine," a
" reproof " of error in theology, and a " correction " of

wrong ethics, but is also a " power."—the " power of God unto salvation." It hath a *nurture* which shall train even the most depraved for the purity of heaven. It comes not therefore to seek out exceptional cases of high moral virtue, but " to seek and to save that which is lost,"—" not to call the righteous but sinners to repentance." And, so thoroughly does it confide in the power of this nurture, that it proclaims without any limits or exception, " able to save to the uttermost all that come to God by him."

SECTION I.

DISCOURSE III

THE GOSPEL COVENANT AND WORSHIP OF THE LOST EDEN.

GENESIS ii. 8, 9, 15, 17; iii. 15, 24; and iv. 4.—And the Lord God planted a garden eastward in Eden; and there he put the man whom he had formed * * *. The tree of life also in the midst of the garden, and the tree of knowledge of good and evil.

And the Lord God TOOK the man, and PUT HIM INTO the garden of Eden to dress it and to keep it.

And the Lord God commanded the man, saying, of every tree of the garden thou mayest freely eat; but of the tree of knowledge of good and evil, thou shalt not eat of it: for in the day that thou eatest thereof thou shalt surely die.

And I will put enmity between thee and the woman, and between thy seed and her seed; it shall bruise thy head, and thou shalt bruise his heel.

So he drove out the man; and he placed at the east of the garden of Eden Cherubims, and a flaming sword which turned every way, to keep the way of the tree of life.

And Abel, he also brought of the firstlings of his flock and of the fat thereof. And the Lord had respect unto Abel and his offering.

FROM overlooking a few very obvious facts and principles which must govern the interpretation of this record of the primeval estates of man: the origin of sin: and the gospel for sinners, many true believers are greatly puzzled in the reading thereof; and many unbelievers take occasion to scoff. Chief among these facts and principles are these:

1. That the *design* of this inspired record is not to present a history of the universe and of God's relation to the universe; but a history of man, and the relation of God in Christ to man. It is not, therefore, to solve problems in the philosophy of human nature, as a science, nor even in the philosophy of God, as a science, but simply to enunciate the problem of the relation of man to God, as Father, Son, and Holy Ghost, and to answer the question, "What shall I do to be saved?"

2. That the *method* of the book is to record the successive developments of a scheme of mercy which God interposed, after the ruin of the race, for the purpose of gathering out of the wreck the materials for the reconstruction of humanity through a Divine Mediator connecting himself with the race.

3. That the *style* of the book accommodates itself to the modes of thought and speech common among men in their successive generations, rather than to the technicalities of science or the modes of thought and speech current among learned men. While a divine book, therefore, it is the most human of books. The infinite mind that suggests its truths presents their finite side towards finite men that they may apprehend and commune with them.

4. That the *structure* of the book is singularly brief and fragmentary, comprising the history of twenty centuries in half as many pages. But, at the same time, it is not the brevity of a compend, as one of our school histories; nor is it disconnected, fragmentary memoirs. For each of the fragments has a marvellous logical relation to the others, and to the whole, and aids in the development of the grand subject. Just as the joints of the animal frame have such a relation to each other and to the whole structure, that a Cuvier may from a single fossil bone construct the complete form of the *Saurian* or *Mastodon* of pre-historic ages, so the skilful student of God's word finds each fragment bearing such relation to the others and to the whole, that he may logically

construct from it the outlines of the whole scheme of redemption.

5. That the *measure* of the thought of this book is not according to the standard of other books. The mind that suggests them being an infinite mind before which the past and future lie ever open as the present, its utterances may not seem to us always to make that marked distinction which our habits of thinking make between the past, the future and the present; between history and prophecy; and between the immediate finite bearing of the truths and their remote infinite bearing. Nay more, its finite facts and truths merging continually into the infinite, it must needs be that while we see them, yet we " see through a glass darkly."

Under the limits and the guidance of these and their correlative facts and truths, I propose, by an interpretation of this record in the second and third chapter of Genesis, to bring out in brief outline, historically, the ORIGIN OF THE GOSPEL OF REDEMPTION, AND THE GERMINAL FORM OF ITS DEVELOPMENT.

It is necessary to any proper understanding of the record,—and it demolishes at once most of the fictions of the scoffers at the doctrine of the fall,—to note, very particularly, the distinction between man's *primal* estate at his creation and his *subsequent* estate in Eden. This distinction is very plainly brought out in the record. For having given an account of man's creation and the peculiar endowments of his nature, it proceeds to declare that *after* that—we know not how long, it may have been a century—Jehovah having planted a garden, with its tree of life and tree of knowledge, TOOK the man and PUT HIM into the garden. And subsequently, after the fall, it is particularly said,—he drove out the man to till the *ground whence he was taken.* That this is no overstraining of the language is made evident also, by the fact that the sacred writer, in beginning the history of the

Eden transaction, begins with it to apply a new title to God. Before, the title is simply "*Elohim*," God ; now it is the title which is ever afterwards used to express his covenant relation to man, "*Jehovah Elohim*," the Jehovah God.

To comprehend fully, therefore, the Eden condition of man, we must needs conceive clearly and distinctly, first, of the relation in which he stood to God during that estate which was, both in time and in idea, anterior to the Eden estate.

First,—as to his nature. He stood forth at his creation an entirely new order of being, so far as we know, in the universe. There were, before this, angels, purely spiritual creatures : there were animals on earth, mere physical creatures ; but this is a compound nature, spiritual as the angel, physical as the animal. Into an organism fashioned out of dust, God hath breathed a living soul. The account of it seems to imply that the vital principle in man was not, as in the other animals, the result of the organism, but produced by a separate and distinct creative act. The process suggests that the vital principle in man is not necessarily dependent upon the physical organism, and, therefore, may exist apart from it. It is connected rather with the spiritual principle ; so that, while the separation of the soul from the body is the death of the body, yet the soul may continue to exist in connection with the vital principle after the dissolution of the body.

But not only is man a new order of existence in the universe, personally ; but, by virtue of his compound nature, he stands forth as representative head of a race of beings ; in this respect unlike the angels who, Jesus tells us, " neither marry nor are given in marriage ;" and therefore there are no *races* of angels, but each one must be dealt with as a separate order of being.

Thus, then, man stands a subject toward his Creator, and a sovereign toward the creatures of his system. He is in the image of God. His vital principle is inseparably united with his soul. He is free from every sort of evil, physical, mental, moral, or spiritual. He is capable of communing with God and with the angelic orders of being. He is capable of an endless life, just as he is: and more than that, of transmitting the power of a like endless existence to an innumerable race of beings in his own image :—Now, out of such a state of facts arises, necessarily, certain relations to God his Creator and to other creatures ;—thus,—

To God, as the author of his being, he owes perfect obedience and service ;

To God, as the bestower of so much loving-kindness, he owes, in return, a grateful love and self-consecration.

To the creatures of his dominion he owes a just and benevolent administration of his authority and rule.

To the beings who may spring from him he owes a loving care and parental guardianship, that they may keep steadfastly " their first estate " of bliss, and not fall irrecoverably by sinning against God.

Thus upon man, considered simply as a creature, a law was laid in this his first estate. Whether a law was formally revealed to him, or he left with such a nature to be " a law unto himself," matters not to the argument.

We infer, however, that a law was formally given to him, since, in accordance with such an idea, would be the obligation to observe one-seventh part of his time, as specially consecrated to be a perpetual reminder of his Creator's goodness.

So, had there been no Eden with its covenant, and no fall, there would have been a creed of three articles of theology, and, with it, a law imbedded in the very nature of man :—The blessedness of the Adam-race as specially constituted of God a compound creature, and his consecration to God: man's dominion over the creatures : and man's obligation to consecrate one-seventh of his time specially to God.

Out of such a state of the case grows, necessarily, the idea of obligation to a dependent creature : and out of this the idea of good and evil, according to some rule in the will of the Creator ; and from obligation and duty springs also the idea of penalty for disobedience.

But, in the very nature of the case, there can be no room for anything like pardon in such a system ; but, precisely as now when we violate physical laws, the penalty must inexorably work itself out.

Any transgression must, as far as it reaches, defeat the whole scheme.

Conceive then of the new being, Adam, left without any further law, and, unlike the angel creatures, becoming the head of a whole race of beings in his own likeness ; and still under no special covenant. Then, to every individual of the race, the only condition of his continuance in blessedness, must have been that he continued to love and serve God perfectly. And failure, in the least, must be irretrievable ruin, as it had been to " the angels who kept not their first estate." With the same inevitable certainty with which the penalty now follows violation of physical laws, such transgressor must become at once a devil, with an unchangeable doom.

Obviously, therefore, but two conceivable forms of moral constitution are possible to such a creature, under which to perpetuate such a relation between God and man. Either, *first*,—that each individual of the race, through endless generations, shall take the risk for himself, as fallible, and thus each individual of the race continue perpetually on trial, receiving his proper doom, in case of transgression : or, *second*,—the race as such may be put upon trial by concentrating universal obedience in some special proof of it, and through one representative head of the whole ; and, in case the trial is sustained, the reward shall be the establishment of the whole by divine favour, in steadfastness and blessedness forever. So, from divers intimations in scripture, we may infer that the angels in heaven have been established in their steadfastness by some constitution dating far back in eternity.

Now, the record proceeds to inform us that, by special act of God's grace, this second order of constitution was appointed for man. Instead of leaving the Adam race under the original and natural law of his existence to stand or fall, irrecoverably, on the myriads of trials of each one of all the generations ; God entered into a covenant of life with him conditioned upon one special act of obedience. He placed him under a special dispensation ; that is, he changed the original moral constitution under which he, simply as a creature, stood towards his Creator. He surrounded him with every element of blessedness : taking away all temptation to disobedience : and, laying upon him the obligation of abstinence from a single tree of all the thousands that surrounded him, he put him to the test whether he was indeed willing to perform all duty.

Of all the trees he may eat, to nourish the physical life : of the tree of life, even, whose fruit might impart the power of endless endurance to his physical life ; but of the tree of knowledge of good and evil, appointed as the sacramental seal of the covenant now made, he shall not eat, as a pledge of his readiness to serve and obey.

The whole transaction is thus, manifestly, in the nature of a covenant entered into between Jehovah and man, embodying the general principles of man's relation to God in specified form. It is just as when men in their transactions with each other, not simply leaving the general principles of justice to operate their proper results, enter into contract specially, by solemn instrument with seals affixed. Hence, Hosea, alluding to this Eden covenant, says (Hos. vi. 7) : "They, like Adam, have transgressed the covenant ;" and elsewhere in scripture this is treated as a covenant with Adam. It is a covenant, not simply personal with Adam, but with him as representative of his race. We know that, in it, he represented Eve also, who though probably yet uncreated, was a party to its obligation and penalty. It was therefore not personally with Adam ; and on the same principle that he represented one he represented the whole race. That the race is involved in the consequences is manifest enough ; which would not have been the case under the original constitution. And, moreover, the scriptures everywhere represent this arrangement as analogous to the covenant of redemption with Christ, who stood, not personally, but as the representative of all the redeemed.

And the condition of this covenant—namely, obedience in one specified act, to a positive command of the Creator, and that merely a command of abstinence where there was no overpowering, or even strong temptation—was certainly as favourable as could be asked by any fallible being. It would sorely puzzle those who scoff at this, to conceive of a better test or a fairer trial.

The result of all was a failure, by an act of disobedience. This brings man now into a *third* estate ; the estate of spiritual death under a broken covenant, with as yet no hope of recovery set before him. And the record proceeds to detail the workings of the human soul under this new phase.

The first feature in the picture is that " their eyes were opened ;" that is, to the experimental knowledge of evil. The second is, that " they knew that they were naked"—that is, in the spiritual and typical sense, as when Moses saw that Aaron had made the people naked by the golden calf at Sina (Ex. xxxii. 25) ; or, as Ahaz's sin made Judah naked (II Chron. xxviii. 19). The third is, that hearing that sound once so gladdening to them, " The voice of the Lord God walking in the garden," they were afraid and hid themselves. The fourth is, that being by compulsion brought face to face with Jehovah, they seek to evade and palliate the sin.

Thus, then, this creature made in the image of God—so glorious, in his estate of creation at first, as the new compound order of existence, angel and animal ; so blessed in his second estate of covenant with God, lies fallen, and without hope, in this his *third* estate.

But so ordering and arranging the judgment upon the transgressors that the tempter should not for a moment enjoy complete triumph, the sentence is pronounced first upon him : and in that sentence upon the tempter is embodied the whole gospel in germ, as subsequently revealed. For, as I now proceed to show you, just as the oak, in germ, is in the acorn, so all the gospel system is in this sentence, " I will put enmity between thee and the woman, and between thy seed and her seed : it shall bruise thy head, and thou shalt bruise his heel."

Thus it will be seen, on careful analysis of these words, and deducing the truths embodied by implication in them, that they set forth these eight points of the gospel creed.

1. That the Redeemer and Restorer of the race is to be *man*, since he is to be the seed of the woman.

2. That he is, at the same time, to be a being *greater than man*, and greater even than Satan ; since he is to be the conqueror of man's conqueror, and, against all his efforts, to recover a sinful world which man had lost ; being yet sinless, he must therefore be divine.

3. That this redemption shall involve a *new nature*, at " enmity " with the Satan nature, to which man has now become subject.

4. That this new nature is a *regeneration by Divine power ;* since the enmity to Satan is not a natural emotion, but, saith Jehovah, " I WILL PUT ENMITY," &c.

5. This redemption shall be accomplished by *vicarious suffering ;* since the Redeemer shall suffer the bruising of his heel in the work of recovery.

E

6. That this work of redemption shall involve the gathering out of an *elect seed* a " peculiar people " at enmity with the natural offspring of a race subject to Satan.

7. That this redemption shall involve a *perpetual conflict* of the peculiar people, under its representative head, in the effort to bruise the head of Satan, that is, " to destroy the works of the Devil."

8. This redemption shall involve the ultimate triumph, after suffering, of the woman's seed ; and therefore involves a triumph over *death* and a restoration of the humanity to its original estate, as a spiritual in conjunction with a physical nature, in perfect blessedness as before its fall.

Such, then, is the gospel theology here revealed, in germ, through the very terms of the curse pronounced upon the destroyer of the race. It will be seen that here are all the peculiar doctrines of salvation, by grace, which every Christian accepts, who exercises the faith which is unto salvation. And in the broader and higher sense of the terms, Moses, as truly as Mark at the opening of his evangel, might have prefixed to this third chapter of Genesis the title, " The *beginning* of the gospel of Jesus Christ the Son of God."

Observe, then, that we have traced man through *three* estates up to this point. *First*, as simply a perfect creature, peculiarly constituted, under the natural law of obligation to his Creator. *Second*, as, under a special covenant, placed under a special positive law, for the trial, once for all, of his obedience. *Third*, as, under this special covenant and law, a sinner without any gospel of hope, and therefore wholly subject to the curse. Now we have next presented to us, in the record, man the creature, the covenanting subject, the sinner under the curse, in a *Fourth* estate. Henceforth he is man the sinner, under a gospel of hope and salvation held forth to his faith. Have we evidence that these first sinners comprehended this gospel of the lost Eden and accepted it by faith ?

Bearing in mind what has already been suggested of the brief and fragmentary, yet logical, structure of this record, we shall find evidence that they not only comprehended it, but that, also, their " sorrow of the world that worketh death " was changed to a " Godly sorrow that worketh repentance ;" and that, in the exercise of a living faith, they cast their souls upon this promised Redeemer for salvation.

The first evidence of this faith is in the fact that Adam now called his wife's name " Eve," the " life ;" and that, too, while yet were echoing in his ears the sentence, " Dust thou art and unto dust shalt thou return." Before, when brought to him, he had named her after himself; he being named " *Ish* "—the " man," she was called " *Isha* "—the " maness," or woman. And why should he now, after the sentence of death, change her name to " Eve," the " living ?" Evidently because his faith has apprehended clearly the promise of life involved in the promise of the woman's seed to bruise the serpent's head, and thereby to restore the life which sin has forfeited.

Another evidence of faith comprehending the promise and referring directly to it, is the joyful cry of Eve over her first born—" I have gotten the man," as the Hebrew reads " I have gotten the man, the Jehovah :" and the naming him " Cain," the "Acquisition." Evidently with a clear and intelligent faith, she apprehended the promise that the Redeemer should be of the seed of the woman. True it was a sadly mistaken application of the creed, led astray as she was by the fond hopes and wishes of a mother. But this is only what occurs to the strongest and most intelligent faith of thousands of Christian mothers still, who rejoice over the " acquisition " of the highest blessing in the son of fondest hopes and highest expectations, and yet find him become an apostate and a murderer. Eve calls the first born Cain, " the acquisition," because she thinks him the promised Redeemer, and therefore calls the second born "Abel," the "vanishing"—supposing that he must come under the general law of the curse, "Dust thou art and unto dust shalt thou return." But, widely mistaken as was her application of the truth, her faith in the truth itself is none the less striking and remarkable.

A further evidence of the exercise of faith by these first sinners is found in the record immediately following that of the judgment upon them, implying that their faith found utterance in confession. "Unto Adam also, and to his wife, did the Lord God make coats of skins." This implied slaughter of the animals could have taken place for no other purpose than sacrifice. They were not slain for food: for the grant of the animals as food for man was not made till after the flood in the revelation through Noah. They could hardly have been slain merely to obtain their skins for clothing: for that would involve an altogether anomalous exercise of Divine wisdom and skill, and one in contradiction of God's usual method of providing for the attainment of his ends by the simplest means. There were other materials in abundance around them to serve the purposes of clothing, without the infliction of death upon the living creatures. The only solution of the statement that is natural and probable is, that the animals were slain in sacrifice; and that solution is abundantly verified by the subsequent history, beginning with the sacrifice of Abel. To these penitent believers, therefore, Jehovah appointed a mode of confessing their faith, by a worship that set before them vividly the great fundamental truth, just revealed, of the bruising of the heel of the Deliverer for their sins, in order to the bruising of the head of their destroyer. Nor can we conceive of anything more profoundly impressive to them than the witnessing the death of a creature for the first time in the world, in immediate connection with the preaching of pardon for their sins. "Looking upon him whom they have pierced," through the dying of the victim, and standing at the altar clad in the covering of the victim—thus was presented to them "Christ crucified," and justification by faith in his atoning sacrifice. That such was the nature of the transaction is made the more evident by the fact that they taught Abel, their child, also to bring "the firstlings of his flock and the fat thereof."

It is still further in proof of such an understanding of the gospel of the lost Eden that not only was a worship appointed to them, but a special place of worship, also, with the visible symbols of Jehovah's presence to accept their worship and commune with them.

In the very infliction of punishment upon them, there is a mingling of merciful consideration for the sinners, at their expulsion from Eden. As at the creation of man, so now, it is represented to have been a matter of consultation in heaven: "Behold the man is become as one of us, to know good and evil: and now, lest he put forth his hand and take of the tree of life, and eat, and live forever: therefore the Lord God sent him forth from the garden of Eden, to till the ground, whence he was taken." In addition to the reason of fitness and propriety, requiring that the use of the sacramental seals of the covenant should no longer be left to the sinner after the covenant is broken, a reason of expediency and mercy is suggested. As the fruit of the tree of life communicated the power of endless existence to his physical nature, the use of it can no longer be allowed to a creature doomed to return to dust; nor would its use be other than the infliction of a curse, in dooming him to live forever in his present sinful and sorrowful condition. It adds greatly to the force of this record to bear in mind that the tree of life that figures here, in the opening of the revelation of God, figures just as conspicuously again at its close in the visions of the Apocalypse. And, in the latter case, it appears that the right "to eat of the tree of life" is the special symbol of the eternal restoration in heaven.

Within full view of the garden, therefore, with its tree of life, Jehovah sets up his place of worship, to proclaim to Adam that a work of redemption is first to be accomplished by the woman's seed before he can be restored to his original glory and the right to eat of the tree of life.

Though banished from Eden, he is not banished either from the view of Eden or from the visible tokens of Jehovah's presence : into which presence he may come as an humble worshipper.   Though the record informs us, " so he drove out the man," it informs us, also, that " he placed at the east of the garden of Eden Cherubims and a flaming sword, which turned every way to keep the way of the tree of life."

Some commentators suggest that the reading of the original here may be " Cherubim and the gleaming as of a sword;" and that the intention may be to describe the brightness between the Cherubim, as the intolerable brightness of a sword flashing in the sunlight.   However it may be read, there is no doubt it means to set forth the fact that here, at the east of Eden, was set up that special symbol of Jehovah's presence which afterward was exhibited to Abraham and to Moses; which after the same manner " dwelt between the cherubim" on the ark of the covenant in the tabernacle and in the temple; which shot forth the fire to consume the first sacrifice at the dedication of the tabernacle, and again at the dedication of the temple; and which symbol was seen in the visions of Ezekiel, as the fourfold living creature, and in the visions of John in the Apocalypse.

It is, indeed, probable that the brightness between the cherubim at Eden may have assumed some special form of appearance to express the prohibition of the tree of life ; but its significancy was of the merciful presence of Jehovah, not, according to the popular impression, of a fierce guardsman, sword in hand, but as Jehovah to be reverenced and worshipped.

It was before this symbol that Abel brought his offering, and, by the coming forth of the brightness to consume it, he saw that " Jehovah had respect unto it." It was from this " presence of the Lord," that Cain " went out" when he became an apostate.

Thus when man the sinner is driven out of Eden and no longer allowed to " eat of the tree of life," it is not to utter hopelessness and irretrievable doom. Jehovah not only gives him ordinances of worship, as a nurture to his faith and hope, but sets up for him the symbols of his own presence to commune with him in the worship on earth. And in this worship of penitence and faith, under the new covenant of mercy, man is taught to keep perpetually before him at once the tree of life of the Eden lost, and the sacrifice of his Great Deliverer's sufferings to work out for him a title to eat again of the tree of life in the Eden restored, and that in his original nature as the compound being, both spiritual and physical, when the mortal shall have put on immortality.

It remains now only to complete this view by adding, that as there was a worship appointed before Jehovah's presence, there was also a special sacred time appointed for it ; so that in his cares in tilling the ground and his weariness from having to eat his bread "in the sweat of his brow," the worship should not be neglected. "At the end of days," says the Hebrew, Cain and Abel brought their offerings. When it is remembered that already the seventh day had been ordained of God, even before Eden : that we find the division of time into periods of seven days universal, though there is no mark in nature, as in the case of days and months and years, for such division ; and that subsequently the seventh day was thus specially reordained of God, there is no room left for doubt that this " end of days" was the end of the week—

the Sabbath day—on which Adam had taught his sons to come for special worship before Jehovah.*

From this brief and necessarily imperfect survey, in outline, of the Eden story, it is manifest that to these first sinners a gospel of salvation was revealed, containing, in germ, all the great distinctive truths of the Gospel afterward developed in the successive covenants of the " sundry times and divers manners," till the coming of the Son of God, and the close of the revelation with his Apostles. And it is manifest also that these first sinners, by virtue of that gospel, exercised godly sorrow for sin and faith in the Redeemer.

That Abel was a true gospel worshipper the Apostle expressly declares, saying, " *by faith* Abel offered unto God a more excellent sacrifice, and obtained witness that he was righteous, God testifying of his gifts." They worshipped in the immediate presence of Jehovah, according to his appointed ritual ; at his appointed times. In short, there and then began the visible Church on earth, composed of the same materials, antagonist to the same wickedness and apostasy from the presence of the Lord, with the same creed, in substance, exercising the same living faith, and separated as the same body of peculiar people, which has existed in the world ever since. And to this peculiar people, thenceforth through all the ages, and not directly to mankind at large, did Jehovah communicate " the lively oracles of God."

In order to apprehend clearly the truth of this general statement, we need only analyze and fix definitely in our minds the popular conception of the Church, as an existing fact, and compare it with this outline.

Setting aside technicalities, and aiming at the general popular conception of the Church, rather than a scientific description, we shall find these to be the elements of it:

---

* See Appendix, Note A.

First—As to the materials of the Church on earth; they are sinners under conviction of sin and misery seeking to flee from the wrath to come.

Secondly—These sinners with a gospel of salvation held forth to them and apprehended by faith, and thereby called to a new life.

Thirdly—These penitent believers constituting an organized community, under special covenant with God; with ordinances for nurture in holiness, and with laws and government to direct them in spiritual things, and to separate them from opposing powers of evil in the earth.

Fourthly—These organized penitent believers labouring to call in unbelievers, and having the manifestations of the special presence of Jehovah among them to accept their worship, bless them, and give them success.

Now compare this popular conception with the elementary facts just developed from the record of the Eden covenant—the evidences of conviction of sin—of a clear apprehension of the doctrines embodied in the promise,—" I will put enmity," &c.,—of the exercise of faith in the promise—of the confession of that faith in worship—of the place and time of that worship before the holy symbols of Jehovah's presence, and of the conflict immediately begun between the faithful and true worshippers and the false and apostate men who " went out from the presence of the Lord " :—and then will you see that it is not by the mere flight of a creative imagination, but by the processes of a very rigorous logic, that we have thus constructed from these fragmentary joints, found in this old record, the organism of the gospel creed, the covenant, the worship, and the visible Church of the lost Eden.

Nor think this a mere curious inquiry into the religious views of a fossil age. A large part of the confusion of ideas which unhappily prevails among us, concerning both the Church of God and the revelation of God in his word, arises from a failure to perceive that the Church began with the very first sinners of our race, and that the gospel began to be revealed also at the beginning of our race. The Bible, therefore, is the record of only one religion; the development of one and the same way of salvation; and is the history of one and the same Church from first to last. Therefore it must be literally true that "*all* scripture—all alike, is the inspiration of God"—and all "profitable for doctrine."

As it is impossible rightly to comprehend any author so long as we have utterly misconceived of his plan, his method of utterance, his scope and aim, so it is equally impossible to comprehend the Bible, so long as we have these vague ideas of it, as a history of different religions and of different degrees of divine authority. It is one gospel, developed through the successive covenants which God made, and in exposition of which he spake in time past by the Prophets, then by his Son and his Apostles.

And this view of it brings home very solemnly the Apostle's warning to us who enjoy its fullest and last development. If even under the inferior light Abel could exercise faith, what excuse can we plead? If under even that light, "every transgression and disobedience received a just recompense of reward, how shall we escape"?

DISCOURSE IV.

THE GOSPEL CHURCH VISIBLE SEPARATELY ORGANIZED ; ITS COVENANT CHARTER WITH ITS SEAL ; ITS CONSTITUENT ELEMENTS.

GENESIS xvii. 4, 7, 10, 11, 13.—Behold my covenant is with thee, and thou shalt be a father of many nations. And I will establish my covenant between me and thee, and thy seed after thee in their generations for an everlasting covenant, to be a God unto thee and to thy seed after thee. This is my covenant, which ye shall keep between me and you, and thy seed after thee ; every man child among you shall be circumcised ; and it shall be a token of the covenant betwixt me and you. He that is born in thy house, and he that is bought with thy money must needs be circumcised, and my covenant shall be in your flesh for an everlasting covenant.

ROM. iv. 11.—And he received the sign of circumcision, a seal of the righteousness of the faith which he had.

MARK x. 14.—Suffer the little children * * * of such is the Kingdom of Heaven.

SOME of you, my brethern, are perhaps ready to ask, on the suggestion of such a topic of discourse as this ;—" Is not our religion more plainly revealed to us in the New Testament? Why then this reference back continually to the dimmer light of the Old?" Plausible as seems the question, the fallacy of it may easily be detected by asking another :— " How shall we be able to understand the teaching of Jesus and Paul and Peter, if we study not the Old Testament to which they continually refer as containing the germinal truths of which their teachings are but the outflowering and the fruit?" And the question is specially pertinent as relating to this covenant with Abraham. The obscurity which so commonly exists in the minds of the people concerning the whole question of the visible Church, with the long train of practical questions growing out of it, arises in large part from oversight of this passage of Old Testament history. Here, midway between Adam and Christ, stands this transaction with Abraham, marking as distinct an era in the history of redemption as the covenant of grace with Adam, the first natural head of the race, and the covenant with Noah, its second natural head, guaranteeing the race from a second destruction by water. And has it ever occurred to you that, in all subsequent revelations, so much greater a prominence is given to this, than to the great covenants with Adam and Noah? The number of references to it are in the proportion of about one hundred to the covenant with Abraham, against some eight or ten to those with Adam or Noah. And still more remarkable than their number is the character of these references. For a thousand years, until the modification of the Abrahamic covenant by the setting up of the typical throne of David, the very title by which God is known is " The God of Abraham ;" and this covenant is made the ground of his dealing with the people of Israel. Nay, the very annunciation of the coming of Christ was hailed, in the song of Mary his mother, as verifying what " God spake to our fathers, to Abraham and his seed forever." And Zacharias, filled with the Holy Ghost, also sang that God is coming " to remember his holy covenant, the oath which he sware to our father Abraham." The very title of the first gospel is " The book of the generations of Jesus Christ *the Son of Abraham.*" The appeal of Peter to the multitudes after the Pentecostal gifts was an appeal to them as " the children of the covenant which God made with our fathers saying unto Abraham, in thy seed shall all the kindreds of the earth be blessed." Paul, in his most elaborate expositions of the gospel theology, sets out this covenant with Abraham as a great germinal part of the scheme. He sets forth Abraham himself as the great representative man, like Adam and Noah, standing as head and father of the faithful of all nations, when he received the sign of circumcision a seal of the righteousness of the faith which he had.

Now whence the prominence to the covenant with Abraham? The answer will be found in a summary statement of the record here taken in connection with the preceding and subsequent history. Anterior to this era the protracted period of human life—the life of one patriarch, or head, extending over many centuries—rendered it unnecessary, and, indeed, hardly possible, that either of the two divine ordinances for society, the state or the Church, should exist as organizations apart from this third divine ordinance of the family which was first of all appointed. Now that the contraction of the days of man on earth leaves no longer one natural head by precedence of age and paternal right entitled to govern the tribes descended from him ; of necessity states, governments, under chosen rather than natural heads must be instituted ; and, by force of the same fact, the body of the redeemed " seed of the woman " must be organized as a government also, distinct from the family. Hence it is that here, midway between the first gospel promise of a Redeemer in Eden and the glorious fulfilment thereof in the incarnation of the Son of God, stands the covenant with Abraham. It involves all that was involved in the covenant of grace with Adam, and the covenant of security to the race, and the line of descent in Shem, made with Noah ; but proceeds to organize the people which shall be gathered under those covenants into a visible body, distinct both from the family and the state, and separated from the rest of mankind. As to its component elements, the church had indeed existed from the first by virtue of the enmity put between the chosen and the reprobate seeds. But henceforth the chosen are visibly and formally set apart to become the special visible body of Messiah, among whom, and through whom, the covenant of grace shall have its administration.

Just as, in the history of creation, the light is the result of the great creative fiat of the first day; yet midway between the beginning and end of the creation stands the act of the fourth day, organizing the sun as the light bearer in the heavens for the illuminating of the earth; so though the elements of the Church visible began with the case of the first sinner and the worship of Eden, yet midway in the progress of the work of redemption stands this covenant with Abraham, organizing the elements into a visible Church of God; henceforth, under the very law of its being constituted the agent for the diffusion of divine light in the world. All subsequent covenants are but the further confirmation and elucidation of this.

That this account of the matter is correct will appear from a few general considerations—all that can be presented within the brief limits of such a discourse.

1. If we undertake to inquire into the origin of the visible Church, as an existing phenomenon, in its peculiar separate organization for spiritual purposes, with government, officers, ordinances and sacramental seals, we shall find that it has not originated at any period since the Apostles of Christ. If we ask them concerning its origin, they refer us back to Jesus Christ who commissioned them. Did it then originate with Jesus when on earth? No! for he claims that all his doctrines are but the developments of Moses and the prophets which he came to fulfil. Did it originate then with Moses? No, he declares that he came to this singular people, in Egypt, with

a message to fulfil and further develop a scheme previously revealed to Abraham, and found the covenant people already organized, to whose recognized heads, the elders, he presented his commission to be verified. But now, when we take a step further back in the inquiry, and come to Abraham, we find no longer any references pointing us still backward,—but here stands the peculiar transaction constituting him the "father of many nations" under an "everlasting covenant" with a special seal. Properly enough we conclude that we have now reached the source and origin of the phenomenon concerning which we inquire. And this the more especially that nowhere else, as we have traced the history backward, have we found anything like a divine charter, or covenant, creating this singular and evidently divine organization.

For surely no Christian can conceive that such a government, whose uninterrupted existence can be historically traced back at least a thousand years beyond that of the oldest governments in the world, could have been self-originated, or a mere accident, or incident in the world's history!

2. An examination of the terms of the transaction shows clearly that it must have been intended to record some new and peculiar relation to Jehovah, of this Abraham the believer, and his descendants and their households. The promise here to be a God to him and his seed could not have meant simply a covenant for his personal salvation; for this had been assured to him before when "he believed God, and it was accounted to him for righteousness." Nor can it mean to be a covenant of natural blessings to his natural descendants, for in the covenant are included the household, embracing servants and all; while, on the other hand, many of his descendants, as the families of Ishmael and Esau, had no birthright in this covenant. The Apostle Paul expresses it fully by declaring that in this covenant Abraham was "the heir of the world," and the representative of all who in all ages after

should exercise the faith of Abraham. If so, then the covenant to be their God, and to make them a blessing indicates a purpose specially to dwell among, and manifest himself to, this peculiar body, and, through it, to manifest his grace to the nations. In short here are all the elements of a definition of the visible Church ; and this is the beginning of that peculiar society as a separate visible body on earth.

3. Nor is this charter ever to be annulled. It is "an everlasting covenant." And though we grant that the term everlasting may, at times, be used in a limited sense, such cannot be the case here ; for its blessings are to reach to all generations of him who is the representative father of the faithful. Under this charter Moses may develop the theocratic commonwealth, and David the theocratic kingdom, and these may pass away again—but still the covenant charter is not annulled. Just as, under the covenant of grace, the great fact of justification by faith may be exhibited, now in the simple sacrifices of Adam or Abel or Noah, or now in the elaborate ritual of Moses, or now in the simple ordinances of the New Testament, without thereby annulling or even impairing that covenant ; so in the case of this great charter covenant of the Church. If the doctrine of a sinner's justification is not affected, as to its essential principles, by changes of the mode of presenting it, so neither is the doctrine of the Church by any modification of its forms under different dispensations.

This covenant with Abraham is, therefore, the divine charter of the visible Church as heretofore and still existing. There is no other charter found in scripture. This is the chartered, visible society, " the Church," in which " God set some Apostles, some prophets, some pastors and teachers," under the New Testament dispensation—for there was no other church organized in which to set them. On the contrary, the Apostle (in Romans iii. 29, and in iv. 11=17, and in Gal. iii. 7–9) expressly declares, that the New Testament Church of believers is the true successor to the covenant with Abraham. Nay (in Rom. xi.) he expressly argues that the rejection of the Jewish body, and the reception, under the covenant, of " all that believe" with Abraham, is only as the cutting off one set of branches from the olive tree and ingrafting others. It is still the same tree, but the currents of its life are partially directed to a new channel.

All this will appear still more plainly if we proceed now to consider the nature and significancy of the seal to this covenant. In some of the covenants made with men, Jehovah alone binds himself to perform, after the manner of a written covenant among men, simply to pay or to do on the one part. But in this covenant with Abraham, as afterwards with the Passover covenant, the transaction is of that sort in which both parties must bind themselves by signature and seal to the engagement. Accommodating himself to that habit of thought among men which regards their interests as more secure when not left to contingencies, or future questions of doubt about the construction of the promise, and therefore, close the transaction by solemn covenant, signed and sealed, behind which they need not go for evidence ; so Jehovah, in these covenants, not only binds himself but calls upon the beneficiaries of the covenant to enter into engagements with him, signed and sealed by an external act. The seal is so devised, also, as to express by symbol the nature of the blessings covenanted. With a view to that native tendency of a heart conscious of sin to doubts and confusion of ideas about the terms of salvation, he ordains that all the blessings promised shall be expressed in form of a solemn covenant, with an external seal to be attached, symbolizing the nature of these blessings, behind which covenant the doubting soul need not go to look for evidence of title to his favour. And he calls upon them, moreover, to come, generation after

F

generation, and affix this seal as a perpetual reminder of the terms of the covenant, and their engagement under it.

This is the origin and *rationale* of the two sacraments of the Church. They are ordinances of worship in which the minister, standing forth, as Jehovah's attorney, presents the instrument, and believers come forward and sign by affixing the appointed seal thereto. In the one covenant, made with Abraham as representing all the faithful, which organises the believers as Jehovah's peculiar body of people, they come for ward and covenant, on their part, to be his people, and to live as such by the aid of his Holy Spirit. In the other, made with this organized Church through Moses, he covenants to redeem them by vicarious atonement, and they covenant to rely upon that atonement for spiritual nurture here, and life hereafter.

But was not this seal annulled in the New Testament? Did not the Apostles resist strenuously those who insisted on continuing it? No, it was changed as to its form, but not annulled; just as the seal of the covenant to redeem the Church by vicarious atonement—the passover seal—was changed in form but not annulled. And in both cases the change of form involved no change of the ideas symbolized by the seal. As the sense of the passover covenant, expressive of faith in the atoning blood of the Lamb from a prophetic stand-point, in eating the flesh and sprinkling the blood, was modified to express faith in the atoning blood from a *historic* stand-point, by eating the bread, symbolizing the broken body, and drinking the wine, symbolizing the shed blood of the Lamb of God;—so circumcision, the seal of the covenant with Abraham organizing the Church, was changed—from the act symbolizing, from a *prophetic* stand-point, faith's longings and hopeful trust in divine power for the cutting off the sins · of the flesh—to the act of washing with water, symbolizing, from a *historic* stand-point, faith contemplating the divine power to regenerate and purify, given in the outpouring of the Spirit.

The opposition of the Apostles to the continuance of the old seal was, manifestly, not on the ground that there is no longer any seal, but that the seal has been changed in form, and therefore the old can signify nothing, or, if it is held to have any significance, must in that far derogate from the significancy of the new.

That, just as the Lord's Supper is simply a New Testament modification of the passover seal of the covenant through Moses to redeem the Church by his blood, so the ordinance of baptism is but the New Testament modification of the seal of circumcision appended to the covenant with Abraham organizing the visible Church; that this covenant is the divine charter under which the Apostles acted in modifying the form of the Church, when the Church of one nation is now to become the Church of all nations; that baptism and circumcision, as seals, both have the same import, however unlike as to external forms, and both symbolize the same truth of the Holy Spirit as the regenerator and sanctifier of Jehovah's people— these are facts that no careful and intelligent reader of the New Testament will call in question. If baptism is not the seal, there is no seal; and, consequently, no such covenant to express the relation of Christ to his visible Church, and of his Church to him, which is involved in the words, " I will be a God unto thee and thy seed after thee." But the whole course of the apostolic argument went to the point that, so far from annulling the old charter, the new order of things under the dispensation of the Spirit fulfills the old covenant; and its charter privileges are the more firmly established. The Apostle Paul expressly interprets the covenant promise " I will make thee a father of many nations," to mean that Abraham was hereby constituted the representative head of all who shall believe as he believed. The very silence of the

New Testament or its merely incidental reference to the
question of the organization of the visible Church, shows
plainly that the Apostles regarded that matter as already
provided for; and that the Church needed no new charter of
organization but simply a modification of form under the old
charter, to meet its new position in the history of redemption.

That baptism is understood to take the place of circumcision as the sacramental seal of the covenant which organizes
and perpetuates the Church, and is of the same spiritual significancy, is obvious from the fact that, both in the Old and
New Testaments, circumcision becomes the figurative expression for the work of the Holy Ghost in renewing the nature;
precisely as baptism becomes the figurative expression for the
regeneration by the Holy Ghost under the New Testament
dispensation. (Compare Deut. x. 16 and xxx. 6; Lev. xxvi. 41;
Rom. ii. 29 and iv. 11; Phil. iii. 3; Col. ii. 11–13). Nay,
more, the Apostle uses the two interchangeably as expressions
for the same spiritual idea, and expressly declares baptism
to be circumcision; so that, in every form of uttering thought,
the identity of the two, both in purpose and significancy, is
set forth.

Thus it will be perceived, that the marked peculiarity of
this Abrahamic covenant is in bringing into view the body of
the elect, as provided for in the covenant of grace with Adam,
not simply as the external manifestation of the ideal of that
covenant, but, at the same time, as an actual institute for the
calling and training of the people of God. From this time
forward, through the entire revelation, the visible Church is
set forth as an organized society, with a government established in it; externally called to the privilege of receiving
the oracles of God, and of being specially under the charge
of Jehovah as his peculiar body of people; the special beneficiary of his promises, and enjoying the special agency of
his Holy Spirit. It is not limited to those who are actual

believers. It is Jehovah's vineyard, well-hedged, indeed, but oftentimes having vines therein that produce only wild grapes. It is Jehovah's garden, well cared for, and well tilled, but in which there may be barren fig trees. It is the wheat field which the husbandman has carefully sown with wheat, yet in which the enemy sows tares to grow up with the wheat. It is a great net, as an instrument in the hand of Jehovah for gathering his people out of the great depths of a world of sin ; but the very operation by which he gathers the good must, in the nature of the case, gather the bad also. It is a sheaf of choice wheat in his threshing-floor, from which the chaff is yet to be winnowed. It is, in short, a body called out of the world, yet in which many more are called than are chosen.

This brings us now to the fundamental question of the *constituent elements* of the society organized by this covenant charter to Abraham. You will observe, that a principle common to all the covenants pertaining to the work of redemption, namely, the principle of family representation, stands out here with peculiar prominence. While the scriptures, everywhere, especially guard us against the error of supposing that the blessings of salvation, according to the covenant of grace, have respect to natural descent, or that men born again, are born " of blood, or of the will of the flesh, or of the will of man," or any other than " born of God ;" yet, on the other hand, special prominence is given to the fact, that in the out-working, in time, of the scheme of redemption, the children of those who are themselves parties to the covenants of God have a birthright to the privileges and the penalties of those covenants. Thus, by virtue of the penalty of the broken covenant of works with Adam, every child born of the race of Adam is born to die. By virtue of the covenant of redemption with Christ, as the second Adam, every mortal that dies must rise again from the dead. Under the covenant of grace with Adam, when there was to be a destruction of the race by water, God said unto Noah, "come thou and *all thy house* into the ark, for *thee* have I seen righteous;" and for the righteousness of Noah, even the apostate, scoffing Ham, is sheltered from the impending doom. Under the covenant with Noah, not to destroy again with a flood, every child descended from Noah to the end of time has a birthright in that guarantee promise. Under the covenant with David, his male offspring, in every succeeding generation, had a birthright claim to the throne of Israel, to which even their unfaithfulness could prove no bar; the reason assigned for not rejecting the unworthy apostates, as Saul was rejected, is—"the oath which I swear to David." You will perceive how, in several careful repetitions, that principle is made to stand forth pre-eminently in this covenant with Abraham. His children, in successive generations, are recognized as having a birthright, not only in its general privileges, but as born members of the great visible community which this covenant, as a charter, founds and organizes: and it is commanded that they be formally recognized as citizens by birth, by affixing, through their parents for them, their signature, and the seal to this covenant. And so intimate a part of the structure is this principle, that no matter what extent of meaning be given to the covenant, this principle must go into that meaning; and no matter what enlarged degree of development of the covenant, this principle must go into that development. Here, then, far back at the very root of the visible Church, and fundamental in its charter, we find the rights of our children to a place with us in the Church, as Christ's spiritual commonwealth. Just as really and truly are they born citizens of the visible commonwealth of Christ, as they are born citizens of the commonwealth of the United States, or of Great Britain. In both cases the exercise of their rights is held in abeyance for a time: in the one case, until

God's grace brings them to majority spiritual, and prepares them to exercise their rights as full citizens ; in the other case, until *nature* brings them to majority and prepares them, by years and intelligence, for the exercise of their rights as citizens. Indeed, the difference between the theory of the visible Church that makes its constituent elements individual believers only, and the theory, derived from the Abrahamic covenant, that the Church consists of believers and their children—its believers representing families—is precisely analogous to the difference between the Continental Jacobin theories of the state as composed of individuals only, who have surrendered certain personal rights, and the Anglo-Saxon theory of Britain and America, that the State is constituted of men as representing families either in *esse* or in *posse*.

To those, therefore, who demand of us, " where is the explicit command of the New Testament for the recognition of our children as members of the visible Church ?" it is sufficient response, if we choose to rest the question there—"where is the charter in the New Testament organizing a visible Church ?" If we find the original charter, in this covenant with Abraham, still recognized in the New Testament as the charter of the Church, then the inevitable conclusion is that the provisions of the original charter as to what are the constituent elements of the visible Church are also recognized, unless something expressly to the contrary is declared. The true statement of the issue in controversy is—" where is the command in the New Testament *changing* the fundamental constitution of the Church and excluding the children from it ?"

With this view of the case before us, we are prepared to comprehend the profound significance of the story how, among the few occasions on which Jesus manifested indignation and something like bitterness in the language of rebuke, one was that in which his disciples officiously interposed to thrust away from him parents coming with their children for his blessing. The disciples thought it an impertinence of parental fondness to be troubling the Master, in the midst of his labours of healing and teaching, with the little ones who could not appreciate his blessing. But " he was indignant," says the Evangelist, and said " Suffer the little children to come unto me and forbid them not, for of such is the kingdom of God." And after blessing the children, he turned in rebuke to his disciples—just as on another occasion, he turned upon the Pharisees their contempt for publicans, in the remark " the publicans and harlots shall go in before you " —and severely remarked to them " think you that children have no interest in the matter ? I tell you, unless ye become like them ye shall not yourselves enter the kingdom."

That " of such is the kingom of Heaven " in the sense of the Church on earth, which is his kingdom, may readily be understood in view of the foregoing argument; and, therefore, I pass by that view of the subject to offer a few suggestions, in conclusion, upon the significancy of the saying as relating to the real kingdom of God, the Church of the redeemed in heaven, of which the visible Church is a representative shadow.

And I desire the more, in this connection, to point out the grounds upon which those of us who hold firmly by the doctrines of the covenant, both of grace and of the Church's organization, rest our confidence of the salvation of our dead children, as part of the kingdom of God—because, from this point of view, we may more easily detect the fallacies of the three popular errors on this subject, arising, severally, from the three corruptions of the truth, viz.: that of Romanism, which makes their salvation depend upon their baptism,—of Rationalism, which makes it depend upon their freedom from the taint of sin,—and that of the popular perversion of the doctrines of grace which, assuming their salvation as a mere opinion, makes it an argument against those doctrines—especially against the points of original sin, and the election of grace—that these imply the damnation even of little children.

From what we have shown of the nature of baptism, as the seal of the charter covenant of the visible Church, you may at once discern the error of the Papists, which perverts that which is simply a seal of the covenant into a channel, and the only channel of the grace of the Holy Spirit; precisely as the Pharisees, whom John the Baptist and Jesus rebuked, made the old sense of circumcision, not a simple seal of the covenant of the external Church, but a channel, and the only channel of grace unto salvation. Assuming that baptism makes them Christians, instead of declaring their birthright in the privileges of the covenant mercy, both Papal and semi-Papal sacramentalists turn the children who die without this sacrament away from Heaven. Hence, also, the folly of the Papal and semi-Papal error of applying to the dying child the seal that has significance only for the child that, it is hoped, will live in the visible Church.

Rationalism, in all its forms, rejecting the anterior covenant of grace, of which this is a development, and denying the fact of the native sinfulness of the race as a race, for which sinfulness this covenant of grace was a provision, rests the *opinion*—for it can amount to nothing more than an opinion, —that the dead children are all saved, on the ground that, dying before moral action, they are not sinners, and need no regeneration.

The orthodox creeds of the Reformed churches all assert that " in Adam all die " spiritually ; and that, represented in him, every creature born of Adam is guilty before God, and born with a depraved nature ; but that the electing love of God hath purposed a restoration of part of the guilty race, and that part are by the grace of God, renewed, justified, and received into the kingdom of God. Popular clamour, led on by noisy demagoguism in theology, insists that such a theory excludes from heaven even the children who cannot believe and be saved, except it be such as, without regeneration, and by virtue merely of the election of God, are accepted into the kingdom of heaven. Hence the silly slanders, to the effect that Calvinists have written and preached of " infants in hell a span long." A preaching which none of the reporters, however, have ever themselves read or heard ; but only have it in most cases from some one, who heard some one else say, that he remembered to have heard his father, or some old man say, that his grandfather had heard it reported of some iron-sided Calvinist that he so wrote or preached ! And yet all this in the face of the notorious fact that the men who have written most of the words of consolation for parents bereaved of their little children, are those whom the creeds of the Reformation have taught to expound the gospel. To whom do English-speaking mourners go in their sorrow over their dead children ? To the volumes of Smythe of Charleston, or of Rice and Prime of New York, or of Macfarlane or Cumming or Harris of London, or of Russel, or Cuthbert, or John Brown, or Grosart, of Scotland,—Calvinists all of them, of the sturdiest stamp. Or if we turn to the great expositors of scripture—with the exception of a few divines, who, laying great stress on the covenant of God in Baptism, hesitate to say that he makes no distinction in this regard between the covenant children and the children of the heathen and infidels—we find, from Calvin himself forward—Sibbs, Willet, Henry, Scott, and their successors—all Calvinists—expounding the scriptures in this sense.

Nor is this a curious incidental fact merely. For it can easily be shown, that, on no other theory of the gospel than this of the Reformed creeds can any argument be founded to demonstrate, logically, the salvation of the dead children.

All other views of the matter can offer nothing better than the *opinions* of wise and good men. Such *opinions* may satisfy the curious, the speculative, or the thoughtless; but, in the dark hour of sorrow, " Rachel, weeping for her children, refuses to be comforted" with mere *opinions*. Faith must point to a divine rock on which the feet may be planted, as the waves of the tempest beat over the soul!

The Calvinistic creed, or more properly the creed of the Reformation, on this subject, reasons with the old epitaph on the grave-stone over the three dead children :—

> " Say, are they lost or saved ?
> If Death's by sin, they sinned for they lie here :
> If heaven's by works, in heaven they can't appear :
> Ah Reason, how depraved !
> Revere the sacred page, the knot's untied :
> They died, for Adam sinned—they live, for Jesus died."

But we will be told that this argument applies only to *elect* infants. For does not the confession of the Church of Scotland say " *elect* infants dying in infancy?" And is not that as good as saying, some of them are not elect ? True, but does it not seem curious to argue that if one says he has a number of choice lambs in his fold he therefore means to say that he has some that are not choice ? But, again, where is this clause found in the confession ? In the third article that treats of the elect and the non-elect ? No ! but in the tenth article, " of effectual calling." Having declared that the chosen of God are called by the Word and Spirit, and quickened by the Spirit, that they may answer the call—the question naturally occurs—" But how then with those who die before they can apprehend and accept the call of the Word?" The confession proceeds to declare that such are regenerated in virtue of the atonement, without the call of the word, by " the Holy Spirit, who worketh when and where and how he pleaseth:" therefore the infants elect are saved, just as adults are, by the blood of Jesus securing their gracious renewal. Strange that the very article that declares how infants are saved, should be cited as evidence of belief that infants are lost!

But why then use the qualifying term "elect?" Why not say "all infants dying in infancy are saved?" For two reasons very sufficient. First, it would have been logically out of place here, as introducing another subject than that of *how* the elect are saved, which is the topic in hand,—not *who* are the elect? which had been defined elsewhere. Secondly, the Confession makes no declarations,—being a confession of faith,—not directly, or by immediate inference, declared in scripture. And the scriptures being intended for those only who can understand them, and to declare to such the terms of their salvation, and the grounds of their hope and comfort, without gratifying curiosity,—nowhere expressly declare, in direct terms, that all infants shall be saved: while they do declare that the elect of God, adults and infants alike, shall be saved through the effectual working of the Holy Spirit. When the Bible stops speaking, the Confession always stops; just as, when the Bible speaks, the Confession fearlessly speaks, whether men will hear or whether they will forbear—nay, even though they mock at and malign it.

But does not this imply, contrary to what has been said, that the Bible does not teach the salvation of all the dead children? Not at all. For, while, in virtue of its great principle of reserve on all points of curious inquiry, it makes no such direct statement, yet it furnishes abundant grounds of comfort and assurance to the soul in sorrow earnestly searching for it.

What are the grounds of comfort? I can now only present them in suggestive outline, to guide such as desire to search the scripture for them.

The argument is threefold. From the analogy of faith.

From the nature of the future existence. as presented in scripture. And from statements of scripture directly in reference to this point.

First,—There is nothing in the grounds or conditions of salvation, as stated in the gospel, to interpose a barrier to our belief in the salvation of all the dead children. It is not on account of " works " which they could not do ; and though salvation is by faith, yet it is not for the sake of the faith as a work of the sinner. They may be saved, therefore, simply " by grace " as adults are, and therefore can sing with them the same eternal song " Worthy is the Lamb, who washed us in his own blood."

Second,—Neither is there anything in the method of salvation, by the work of the Holy Spirit in renewing, to contravene this belief. For though he works through the word in the case of those who believe, he works without the word also, saith the confession, "when and where, and how he pleaseth," and, therefore, may regenerate the infant without, as in the case of the adult, working through the word.

Third,—Neither is there any ground of difficulty in the sovereign electing love of God. For just as the effectual call, and the offer accepted by the sinner, proves him to be one of the elect ; so the call of the infant by Jesus, away from the trouble and sin to come, may prove it to be one of the elect.

Fourth,—Neither is there any ground for supposing the dead children excluded from heaven, by reason of the doctrine that they are of a guilty and depraved race ; since the guilt in any case is removed by the atoning blood of Jesus, justifying the sinner, and procuring the grace of the Holy Spirit ; and all for nothing in the saved moving him thereto, but only of his own free sovereign love ; thus putting the adult and the infant upon the same level as to claim for grace.

Fifth,—As there is no ground in the analogy of faith to *deny,* so there is, on the contrary, much from which to affirm, the salvation of infants dying in infancy. Thus infants dying because Adam sinned, also rise from the dead because Christ has risen. "As they have borne the image of the earthly, so shall they bear the image of the heavenly." As certainly as, by some relation to Adam's sin they die, so certainly, by some relation to Christ in his work as Mediator, every one of them that dies shall burst forth from the grave, and " the mortal put on immortality." If, then, by virtue of the relation to Christ, that half of the curse is removed which relates to their physical nature, why not infer that, on the same ground of sovereign grace, the other half is removed, which relates to their spiritual nature ?

Sixth,—And this seems, again, to receive direct confirmation by the Apostle's declaration in reference to the first and second Adam, " where sin abounded, grace did *much more* abound." For, if we count the aboundings of grace only in the numbers of adult sinners saved, this statement seems not to be realized. The aboundings of sin in every age, so far, exceed vastly the aboundings of grace. But it puts another face on the statement, when we conceive of the dead children as all called by Jesus Christ to himself. More than one-third of the race die under two, and more than one-half of the race under five years of age. If these are counted for the kingdom of heaven, we set out, in our estimate of the abounding of grace, with over half the race redeemed in infancy, and to these add the millions that, since Adam, have accepted the call ! And when we have conceived of the vast majority thus gathered out of two thousand generations,—then we may begin to catch the spirit of the Apostle's saying, " where sin abounded, grace did much more abound !"

Seventh,—This view is again confirmed by all those scriptures which describe the vast numbers of the redeemed in heaven. It is "a great multitude that no man could number." It is " out of every nation and kingdom, and tongue,"—and of course, therefore, out of some tribes that have not been evangelized, and who can be represented, therefore, only by their infants gathered in infancy. It is to be understood also, relatively to the number not saved, and to the whole number of the race ; and must, therefore, include the dead children.

Eighth,—To these general views must be added the argument from the scripture account of the retribution of the future for the lost. This retribution is generally described in a manner to exclude the dead children, since it is made to have reference to the moral actions of the doomed. The condemnation is on the ground that " they loved darkness rather than light, because their deeds are evil." Their judgment is " according to their works." Their retribution is the reaping of a harvest of evil action in life. " He that soweth to the flesh, shall of the flesh reap corruption." " What a man *soweth*, that shall he also reap." And so of multitudes of scriptures. A chief element of the retribution is to be the memory of sins done—none of which things can be predicated of the future existence of the dead children.

Ninth,—With the argument cumulating thus at every successive step of the view of the analogy of faith, and the direct statements of scripture concerning the nature of the future state, we come now to the express declarations of scripture touching children, and their relations to the everlasting kingdom. Even in the Old Testament, with its very limited statements concerning the existence after death, we find David saying of his dead child, " I shall go unto him, but he shall not return unto me." This must mean, I shall go unto him whither he is gone, into " His presence where is fulness of joy and blessings for evermore." Since there was no comfort in the thought that he would go to him in his grave, any more than in the like fact that he should go to Absalom in the grave. Besides, David indulges in no such truisms as, " I shall also go to the grave." And it is worthy of remark that

this hope of the salvation in this case, was of a child of sin,
who could have little ground of claim by reason of the faith
of his backslidden and apostate father. It is also of a child
that had not received the sacrament of circumcision, having
died before the eighth day, the time appointed by the law for
the sacrament, and therefore his salvation was independent of
the sacrament, contrary to the Papal notion.

So the poor Shunamite mother could say by faith " it is
well with the child," though she had left his corpse in the
prophet's chamber.

Tenth,—We find moreover, in the Old Testament, the same
special claim to the children, as peculiarly his own, which
Jesus sets up for them in the New Testament ; and the same
special indignation at the heartlessness which repelled them,
as incompetent to enjoy the spiritual blessings of immortality.
Saith Jehovah by Ezekiel (xvi. 21,) in his terrible wrath at
the horrible offerings of the children in idolatrous sacrifices—
" They have slain *my* children, causing them to pass through
the fire." Thus laying claim to them as his peculiar possession. So also in Jeremiah (xix. 4, 5) in reference to this
same cruel practice,—" They have filled this place with the
blood of innocents ;" and therefore he gives utterance to his
specially hot displeasure.

In the New Testament I need only refer you to the very
explicit declaration of Jesus, " Suffer the little children—of
such is the kingdom of heaven," which, you will find, the
more it is studied in connection with his indignation at the
disciples, and with the nature of the kingdom of heaven, in
its two-fold aspect, as the Church on earth and the Church
of the redeemed, the more you will be impressed with the
utter folly of supposing him to mean simply that adults must
be simple and artless like little children to enter heaven ;
or, indeed, anything short of meaning that, in the plan of
redemption, the children are specially provided for, both in

the kingdom on earth, the Church visible, and in the kingdom above, the redeemed Church.

Eleventh,—As putting the cope-stone upon this argument, thus cumulating at every step, I must refer, though it be in a word, to the express declaration, that in the vision of the great day, John " saw the dead *small* and *great*—in the sense of little ones and full grown, as well as of humble and high position—stand before God." And that he saw also, corresponding to this fact, " the *books* opened, out of which the dead were judged," " according to what was written in the books." " And *another Book was opened, the book of life :*" which can be understood in no other way so clearly, as in the supposition of three classes at the judgment,—believers and unbelievers, who were judged according to their works, out of the two books, and the little ones, who had done no works, were recorded in a third book specially appropriated to such —a book of life (see Revel. xx. 12).

Such are the general grounds of our faith concerning the children who die. I have discussed this question—though not of immediate connection with the great covenant charter and its provisions for the children who live, rather than the children who die—because of the favourable stand-point for such discussion secured by the exposition of the covenant and the nature of its seal ; and because the perversion of this seal has led to the cruel doctrine of Rome concerning the children dying unbaptized. Nor is the evil confined to the Church of Rome : but owing to the vague and uncertain views with which a Romanizing Protestantism permeates the popular mind, even many excellent Protestant Christians are led to misuse the sacrament of Christ by applying to a child, *because* it is dying, and going to the church above, the seal which recognizes its rights as living in the visible Church on earth, and as such has all its significance. I mean not to say that the seal of the covenant is not to be applied, irrespective of the question of life or death ; but only that the prospect of death should not be the special ground and reason for apply-ing an external seal which, primarily, contemplates the subject of it in the relation of a member, by birthright, of the visible Church on earth. And the use of the sacrament, in a manner to suggest the approach of death as a ground for its use, tends only to propagate and confirm the error among the Protestant masses, that the baptism makes the child a Christian ; whereas the baptism is but the solemn declaration officially that, under the terms of the charter covenant of the Church, the children of believers are born members of the visible Church.

Such, then, is the origin of this remarkable body, organized a visible government on earth separate from all other social organizations. This is the kingdom not of this world. Here it has stood for near four thousand years ; while all other governments coeval with its origin have not only perished, but the very records and traditions of them have almost passed from men's knowledge. Well might Jehovah speak of this kingdom as an everlasting kingdom ; and call him now Abra-ham, "the high father of a multitude." You perceive, therefore, brethren, that not only the gospel existed and was preached long before the incarnation, but the gospel Church also existed. And this peculiar spiritual government, into which you and your children are called now, is one and the same with that four thousand years ago. "The gates of hell shall not prevail against it." You may understand now, what has perhaps puzzled you before, why so little, comparatively, is said of the Church and its constitution in the New Testa-ment. It is not at all because the Church was not divinely organized, or that the question of the Church is a matter of indifference, as some would have it, and no essential part of the gospel of redemption ; but simply because there was no call to organize and give a constitutional charter to a Church in the New Testament. That had been done two thousand years before. Jesus came as a minister of that Church; became a member of it by his birth, and was formally recognized as a member of it, just as the children are now. His disciples were members of this same Church; and after the work of redemption was completed, instead of setting up a Church for the first time or even a new Church, they simply modified its forms of worship and government to adapt them to the new order of the dispensation of the Spirit. For, in the nature of the case, the ancient forms of worship having been those of a prophetic faith must now change into forms suited to a historic faith. And just as the government had changed from the patriarchal to that by the chosen elders, under the covenant with Abraham; so under the apostles such a modification occurred as suited the Church of all nations, now that it is no longer the Church of one nation. Therefore so little is said of the constitution of the Church in the New Testament. The mistake which so confuses men's views of this question of the Church arises, very largely, from that miscalled " *High-Churchism*," which is but just half *high enough;* since it refers the origin of the separate visible Church to a period just half way back in its history; and looks for the Church's charter, as a visible organized government, where there is none, but simply a modification of its ordinances and government to adapt it to a new phase of the work of redemption. "The Church of the living God, the pillar and the ground of the truth" is an essential element of the scheme of redemption, and has existed since men began first to be redeemed. And as a separated visible government, " though not reckoned among the nations," the Church began as soon as men began to organize states as distinct from family. *

---

* See Appendix, Note B.

SECTION II.

___

___

DISCOURSE V.

THE COVENANT OF THE CHURCH'S REDEMPTION ; ITS SEAL, AND THE SIGNIFICANCE THEREOF.

Exodus xii. 3, 7, 11, 14.—Speak unto all the congregation of Israel, say-ing, In the tenth day of this month, they shall take unto them every man a lamb according to the house of their fathers, a lamb for an house, &c.

And they shall take of the blood and strike it on the two side posts, and on the upper door post of the houses.

And thus shall ye eat it ; with your loins girded, your shoes on your feet and your staff in your hand ; and ye shall eat it in haste ; it is the Lord's passover. For I will pass through the land of Egypt this night, and will smite the first-born, &c.

And the blood shall be to you for a token on the houses where ye are : and when I see the blood, I will pass over you, and the plague shall not be upon you to destroy you, when I smite the land of Egypt.

Luke xxii. 15, 20.—With desire I have desired to eat this passover with you before I suffer. For I say unto you I will not any more eat thereof until it be fulfilled in the kingdom of God.

This cup is the New Testament in my blood which is shed for you.

I Cor. v. 7, 8.—For even Christ our passover is sacrificed for us ; there-fore let us keep the feast not with old leaven, &c.

Assuming, my brethren, that you are all familiar with the details of the story of the bondage in Egypt ; of Moses' call from the desert, his mission and message : of the wonders whereby he has at once visited judgment upon, and sought to bring Pharaoh and Egypt to submission and obedience,—I desire now to fix your attention upon the consummation of all, in the formal covenant of deliverance made here with this peculiar body of people, organized by the previous charter covenant with Abraham, as those of whom Jehovah is specially the God, and they specially his people.

If I take occasion frequently to remind you that the method of God's revelation is by a successive series of covenants, each a fuller development of the germinal, first covenant, and of all that precede it; this is, because I would have you hold fast the clue which should guide you to the right interpretation of the book, and guard you against most of the difficulties that have been raised with the record by many learned interpreters; who, with very obscure ideas of the Gospel revealed in the first, or indeed, in any of the covenants, and with little experience of its power, find mere learning and natural genius unequal to the task of rightly interpreting the oracles of God.

The summary of the historic facts here shows this to be a covenant transaction. On the part of Jehovah, a statement and exposition of a certain blessing of redemption from cruel bondage has been made, which statement here is put into the form of a covenant. And, as before he called upon Abraham to enter into the instrument with him, by an external act, affixing his seal thereto, and saying, " This is my covenant, every male shall be circumcised, and it shall be *a token* betwixt me and you;" so now, appointing the shedding and sprinkling of blood, he declares " The blood shall be to you for a token." This, therefore, is a covenant of a sacramental nature; and, after the method of the former covenant, a seal is appointed to be affixed thereto, which seal itself is formed to be a symbol of all the great truths and blessings stipulated in the instrument.

Looking backward, and comparing this with the previous covenants of Jehovah, we shall find this to embrace, and bring

out more clearly, the truths and blessings of those that preceded it. The enmity and struggle between the two seeds,
of his Eden covenant, here stand forth strongly, in the
hostility of Egypt to Jehovah and cruelty to his chosen.
The bruising of the heel, in the sufferings endured by the
chosen seed; and the bruising of the head in the overwhelming judgment upon Pharaoh. The theology of the sacrifice
of blood, revealed in Eden, now reappears in the blood of
the lamb slain and sprinkled. The promise of the covenant
with Noah, securing the descent of the blessing to the line
of Shem, here appears in the body of his descendants selected
as special objects of divine favour. The provisions of the
charter covenant with Abraham, organizing the descendants
of Israel as a visible Church, here appear actually fulfilled,
in not only a vast body of people, but that body organized,
as the congregation to which Moses speaks, and that too with
its elders already executing their office of rule; to whom he
came at first with his credentials from Jehovah, and to whom
as representing the congregation he now repeats the command of Jehovah.

And as looking backward, we find this covenant a further
development of all that precedes, so, looking forward, we
perceive that this again is, in turn, a germ to be developed
by those which follow it. In what we may call, by proper
restriction of the sense, its political aspect, the body here
covenanting with Jehovah is at once the numerous body of
his seed, through Isaac, fulfilling the covenant with Abraham
organizing them as a people; and at the same time, is the
germinal nation, which, in the covenant with David, shall be
organized as the typical kingdom of Messiah, representing
the future kingdom to be gathered out of all nations, in which
and over which, Jesus shall rule through all successive ages.
In its spiritual aspect, as a theological and ritual revelation,
we perceive at once that it is the germ of that great New

Testament, or new covenant, transaction between Jesus and the representative disciples which developed this to its prophetic earthly fulfillment ; and in view of which, on " that dark and doleful night," in Jerusalem, Jesus said : " With desire I have desired to eat this passover with you before I suffer ; for I will not any more eat thereof until it be fulfilled in the kingdom of God." And therefore, he modified the seal of this covenant, adapting the seal to the new aspect of it, as no longer *prophetic* but *historic*, by commanding " Eat this bread which is my body, and drink this cup, which is the new covenant of my blood shed for many ;" " And do this,—no longer by faith, in prophetic anticipation, but by faith historically,—in remembrance of me." So, accordingly, we find the apostle, under the new dispensation of the Spirit, declaring that in the new seal of the old covenant we still have held forth the same truths and blessings of the old covenant, " For Christ our Passover is sacrificed for us, therefore let us keep the feast (the Lord's Supper) not with the old leaven," etc.

The substance of the record here, is therefore, this : That as before Jehovah entered into a sacramental covenant with Abraham, by which his descendants, through Isaac, were organized into the visible Church of God, and this covenant has now, in the progress of four hundred years, had its fulfillment so far as that Israel has here become an organized body of two or three millions, but is suffering under cruel bondage : so he now enters into a special covenant to redeem it, as a peculiar people to himself, from this bondage ; constituting the whole as a typical representation of the great deliverance of his redeemed from the bondage of Satan. And as before, so now, he calls upon them to enter into the sacramental instrument with him by affixing, every one, the seal thereto. And he frames a seal, according to the method of all his sacramental covenants, which shall itself symbolize the great truths and blessings stipulated in the covenant, namely, their redemption, for the sake of vicarious atonement by blood.

These general facts lie so plainly upon the surface of the record, from the call of Moses to the close of this passover transaction, as to need no detailed exposition. I therefore pass on, directly, to the consideration of the great truths of this covenant, as symbolized in the seal affixed of slaying and eating the paschal lamb, and sprinkling the blood ; and the significancy for us of the whole lesson.

It is scarcely needful to remind you, that the blood shed in this sacramental act, betokens the same thing as the blood of the sacrifices ordained in the gracious covenant of the lost Eden : and offered by Adam and Abel and Noah and Abraham. That it holds forth the great idea of atonement for sin by the substitution of the life of the victim,—which " life is in the blood"—for the forfeited life of the sinner. But you may observe here the development of a new truth in the way of faith's application of that doctrine. It is the exhibition of the mode in which, and the conditions on which, the penitent becomes clothed with the rights of the substitute. This consists simply in sprinkling the blood—nothing else. " For when I *see the blood* I will pass over." The hyssop branch, with which the blood was struck on the door, is the simple emblem of the appropriating faith which applies the blood to the sin-stained soul. Hence David, under a deep sense of his sinfulness, cries " purge me with hyssop and I shall be clean." The unleavened bread which is to be eaten betokens the sincerity and truth with which the act is to be done. The bitter herbs so specially commanded are a significant reminder, not only of the sorrowful eating of " the fruit of their own doings," to which they were doomed, but also a warning that redemption by the sprinkled blood may be consistent with many a disagreeable cross and trial. Yea, and the very mode of the eating, with the staff in hand, loins girt, and sandals on the feet —" eating in haste"—is a significant reminder that though they are the redeemed of Jehovah, they are still pilgrims and strangers, as all their fathers were. That they have no abiding city here, but must be up and journeying from the land of Egypt and its bondage to a better country, even the land of which the Lord hath spoken to the fathers.

Thus suddenly we come here upon a gospel of full detail, which is henceforth to take the place of that more general and indefinite gospel of salvation by atoning blood which has hitherto been revealed ; and which, doubtless, has left to the faith of God's children many a dark puzzle, especially in the detail of how this salvation is to be applied to the case of the sinner.

Instead of a study, technically and in detail, of the significancy of the several truths symbolized in this seal, we shall probably attain more practical results, if now we consider the general significancy of the whole of this revelation in its practical application to our day in the Church, and personally to ourselves.

The great ideas here presented may be classified into two orders of truths: *First,* the objective truths, presented in the divine side of this picture, concerning God, Jehovah, and man's relation to him. *Second,* the subjective truths from the human side of the picture : viz., the effect of the divine truths coming in contact with the human soul.

And, in regard to both these classes of truths, we should ever bear in mind that these inspired histories of God's dealings with man and of man's conduct toward God, are unlike all other histories. For it is not simply as curious records that we read them ; or that we may find ingenious and fanciful applications of them to our case. " All history is prophecy," said Lord Bacon. But in a far stricter sense than he understood his own maxim, and yet in even a fuller sense, is all the inspired history prophecy. This is the history of a Jehovah, " the same yesterday, to-day, and forever ;" and of a human nature under the special administration of Jehovah, which is also the same thing substantially. under all the phases of its different ages and civilizations. Hence the subtle logic ever at work in the mind of all true believers, which almost unconsciously constructs a syllogism upon every promise suggested by the facts of the inspired history, and derives thence a conclusion concerning the method both of God's dealing and of the conduct of human nature toward God in the present, or any past, or any future age. It was the method of God's saints of old, and is of his saints still, to reason, that, God being unchangeable, he will therefore be likely to repeat in the present what he hath done in the past, and human nature being unchanged, it will therefore be likely to act toward God in the present, under like circumstances, just as in the past. It is this that makes the word of God the comfort and warrant of God's people, and a perpetual warning to those that love him not.

Bearing in mind, then, this principle, let us study the views here presented, first of the objective truths on the divine side of this picture.

The retributive justice of God is symbolized for us in all its terror, in this doom which impends, as a dark thunder cloud. over Egypt, and over all the houses unsprinkled with that blood. It is a true symbol of the condition in which the gospel presumes all to be to whom it comes with its provisions of atoning blood.

Nor is it easy to conceive of a symbol of doom more fraught with dreadful terror. This loss of the first-born—with all its heart-rendering sorrows—is worse than death itself to the survivors. Think of it! The hope—the pride—the joy of every family cut off at once, leaving none to sympathize with others, for each alike is absorbed in his own grief—when roused at midnight by the groans of the expiring first-born, he hears the wail ascending all around him.

And it adds aggravation to the woe, that all this could have been avoided ! For Jehovah's messengers have been warning them and afflicting them for weeks past, and demonstrating the power, while they urged the simple and reasonable appeal of Jehovah. And a further aggravation is that it is so just a recompense of reward. For, the sorrow that breaks the heart ever tends to bring out, as the fire brings out the invisible writing, those records on the tablets of memory which are unnoticed or forgotten in the day of brightness and joy. So was it with Joseph's brethren when sorrow came to bring out the remembrance and the confession, " we are verily guilty concerning our brother." And now, as each household gazes upon its dead first-born, think you there arose not visions of the murdered babes of the Hebrews, and the wails of the Hebrew mothers, that for long years gone have been crying, " How long, O Lord, how long !"

Is this a dreadful picture ? Yet it is but a type of what *must* be—a shadow merely of the wrath to come to all the unsprinkled soul's tenements in eternity. Ye that affect to think so lightly of death and eternity ! see here this shadow and gather the elementary ideas of what *shall* be, from what *has been*, already, under the government of God. Standing, in imagination, amid these complicated horrors in Egypt—the groans of the dying, mingling with the shrieks of the living, throughout a whole empire :—all earthly pomp and power levelled to mingle its unavailing cries with the lowest and meanest in a common woe—here see what it is for " God to whet his glittering sword and his hand to take hold on vengeance."

The grand failure of all the arguments, which men found upon the benevolence of God, against a wrath to come upon the ungodly, occurs just here : in that it proves too much, and therefore proves nothing. · If God's benevolence must exclude the idea that he will punish, it should equally exclude the idea that he *has punished :* and therefore leaves unaccounted for the wrath that has come, in the attempt to prove merely imaginary the wrath that shall come. The whole history of the world's sorrow and anguish flies in the face of this theoretic argument. The hell at which men scoff, as never to come, has already begun here on earth ; and but for the restraining hand of infinite goodness, preventing its full development, would have been completed long ago in a world of pure evil, with its natural consequence of pure torment, and anguish unmixed with any good or any alleviation.

But turn not away from the picture in disgust, as though it represented God acting unjustly and therefore cruelly in the infliction of this doom. For remember it comes not until after the most amazing forbearance and extraordinary pains to avert it. From the first they have deserved wrath, for their cruel crimes. Yet mercy has foreborne with them, and urged them to repent. The right arm of omnipotence is not now first bared to strike in wrath. It has been bared in mighty works of wonder to warn, before this. The gleaming finger of omnipotence has beckoned to them many a signal. The voice of reason and entreaty has pleaded, and warned them in vain !

Tell us, ye that adjudge this doom unjust and cruel—what man of you—nay, what holiest man on earth—having his hand armed with irresistible power, would have borne so long with the evasions, the falsehoods, and the insolence of Egypt? This is the thought that shall forever exclude the alleviation of the torment that might come from feeling that they suffered unjustly. This remembrance will recur of the forbearance of God—the warnings of God—the pleadings of God. There shall be none to play " Prometheus bound," and heroically struggle against a mere arbitrary almightiness, in that hell of which the gospel warns us !

2. A second great objective truth, in contrast with this, is

shadowed forth in this idea of a covenanted peopl redeemed by Jehovah, and their salvation secured by this very destruction upon their enemies. It is a truth which still further expresses to us the goodness of God even in his " strange work " of vengeance. Such is his love for them that, having by a former covenant organized them as a Church for himself, he now, to assure them, by another covenant binds himself to redeem them, and calls upon them to come and seal the engagement with him by sprinkling the blood, and eating the sacrificial feast. Nor, into that holy covenant was one of these doomed ones forbidden to enter, if he were but willing to avouch Jehovah.

3. But the grand central truth of all the objective truths. here, is shadowed forth in that blood of the spotless lamb shed and sprinkled on the door posts. It has a deep, mysterious meaning and finds its interpretation in the history of Calvary and the cross, far onward yet, even fifteen hundred years, in the history.

The blood-marked house is but representative of every soul tenement on earth, the dweller in which—made alive to the impending doom by the voice that cries from Sinai, " whosoever sinneth, him will I blot out from my book," and by the voice crying from the depths within—hath fled from under the dark thunder-cloud of wrath, to him who was lifted up on the cross. This blood is not only the central idea of this, but of all the revelations of God. The whole gospel is, in fact, summed up just here, " when I see the blood I will pass over." Blood! blood! this is the one cry of the gospel—the Alpha and the Omega of the gospel. All hope of the divine favour—all strength to resist and conquer sin—all power of a holy life comes from this blood. Is man redeemed ? It is because " we have redemption through his blood." Are any ransomed from sin ? " Not by corruptible ransom of silver and gold " are they purchased, " but by the precious blood of Christ as of a lamb without spot." Are these justified? "Being justified by his blood." Are these cleansed and made holy? "His blood cleanseth from all sin." Are they, as strangers and wanderers from God, restored? "Ye who sometime were afar off are now made nigh by the blood of Christ." Have they access to the Father's presence in prayer? It is because the High Priest hath gone before "sprinkling the blood." Are they arrayed in spotless robes to appear at the court of the Great King? "They have washed their robes and made them white in the blood of the Lamb." Are sinners cast off at last to eternal death? It is because "they have trampled under foot the blood of the Son of God."

Thus in the gospel revelations, all mercy, compassion, and grace of God, have their ground in that blood. All conviction of sin, all holy desire and emotion in the soul, all strength to overcome sin; as all hope and trust and peace and joy in the Holy Ghost, come from that blood. As saith the scriptures concerning the living creatures—"The life is in the blood"—So of the scriptures themselves we may say, emphatically, "the life is in the blood."

Let us turn now, in the second place, to the subjective truths of the application of the blood, shadowed forth here: and on the supposition that human nature then and now is the same, we shall probably find something very personal to us.

This blood, now, each one must apply for himself, sprinkling it on the door posts, or the covenant to redeem is of no avail as to him.

Endeavour then to transfer yourselves, carrying with you the knowledge gained by observation of the reception of the gospel among us, to that land of Goshen, lying in the full flood of light from an Egyptian vernal sun that afternoon, in strange contrast with the murky cloud, in sight yonder, over-hanging Egypt: and study the workings of human nature under this gospel message which Moses hath sent, through the elders, to all the people.

Deep earnestness is marked upon every countenance in Goshen, and hasteful energy upon every movement. At each door of the humble dwellings, in which preparation is making for a feast, the inmates are watching the father, or head, acting as a temporary priest. Solemnly he takes the hyssop branch, and, dipping into the vessel containing the blood of the lamb that has been slaughtered for the feast, he strikes it—this side the door, and that—and over the door. The solemn ceremony over, the preparation goes on. The lamb is roasted whole, not a bone broken: for the families of the nearest friends, sufficient to consume the whole, have united in the purchase and the slaughter, and will commune together in the sacrificial feast. The family, instead of preparation to retire to rest, as the shades of evening fall, are all, strange enough, preparing as for a journey. There are, doubtless, many uneasy thoughts—some nervous trembling, under the mysterious warning that every house unsprinkled with blood shall bewail that night, in bitterness, its first-born. For the Angel of death shall spread his wings on the night breeze, and touch with blight and withering the pride of every unbelieving household. And the terrible events that have been transpiring in Egypt have come to the ears of the people. Here are all the elements of the gospel warnings and of the threatened woe of which it warns. What think you, judging from what we see of the reception of the gospel message now, was the reception then, by the variety of characters that heard it in the land of Goshen? Let us analyze a little the congregation of Israel.

1. Here is one, representative of a numerous class, who, after all, looks on with stolid indifference at the preparation scene during the afternoon. Toil and trouble hath soured

him, or the enticements and temptations of his position under
the Egyptian taskmaster have made him very sceptical upon
the whole subject of the covenant with Abraham. It seems
very strange to him that if Jehovah had contracted to be
specially their God, he should leave them to such a lot. As
to Moses and Aaron, and their assurance of Jehovah's
remembrance of his covenant, and the wonders they have
been doing; all the good that has come of it has been to
irritate the taskmasters and double their labour. He will
buy no lamb: has other uses for his money; or has no
money; and, as to this new zeal about religion that has
seized the people and this new sort of worship, it seems very
absurd. They seem all to be getting ready in haste for departure, forgetting that the Egyptians may have something to
say on that subject. He looks on in moody silence, or scoffs
and jests at the blood sprinkling. He will sprinkle no blood.
But, as Moses has proclaimed *freedom* for you, is it not worth
trying?

2. This one again is no scoffer: he has great respect for
Moses and Aaron: admires their patriotic spirit and their
boldness in speaking to Pharoah; hopes they will yet worry
him into measures; yet thinks this new zeal about religion a
little excessive; and indeed can see no particular connection
between sprinkling the blood on the door, and the promised
safety from the very curious pestilence which, it is said, is
about to come upon the whole empire. He therefore sprinkles
no blood. The reasoning is not very logical, though that of
those who pretend they can accept only a logical religion.
For if Moses and Aaron are not from Jehovah, they are
terrible impostors, merely making trouble; and deserve none
of that respect which you affect for them. If they, on the
contrary, are from Jehovah, and recognized as such, why
acknowledge Jehovah's authority in the general and yet void
it in all the particulars?

But with the unbelievers and the critics, in their several varieties, who sprinkle no blood, we have less concern than with the various workings of faith in those who obey.

3. This one, we may imagine, though he obeys the call, sees not very clearly why it should be done, nor comprehends very clearly the meaning of the act. Yet he is thoroughly alarmed at the impending danger. And under the impulse of fear, together with a disposition to obey the commands of Jehovah, he sprinkles the blood. Very likely he will display unusual zeal and earnestness in doing it; and, to make assurance the greater, will be very punctilious in performing the sprinkling in the most imposing and solemn manner. Likely he will add to the act of sprinkling any very mysterious and impressive forms that he may have seen the Egyptian priests use, or some of the traditional practices of religion which have come down from his ancestors beyond the Euphrates—good old pious customs that Terah's family practiced, or which were favourites in Laban's household. In his mind the blood struck upon the door posts has the character of a magical charm to keep away spirits of evil and disease and death. Yet he has faith enough, with all his darkness of mind, to sprinkle the blood, and is safe. For the gospel nowhere tells us just what degree of error is compatible with salvation, if it be not error that keeps one from sprinkling the blood.

4. Or this one, again, of less superstition but of more restless and speculative turn, cannot drive from his thoughts the query of the scoffer "what good can that spot of blood on the door post do?" It rings in his ears and puzzles his thoughts continually. It almost tempts him to reject the whole thing as a visionary dream or imposture. But then his consciousness of many a short-coming and many a transgression makes him feel that if death should come he surely deserves it, and cannot escape it by anything he can do. With a very weak faith—nay seemingly, a doubting and self-contradictory faith—he sprinkles the blood and is safe.

5. Or here is a genuine child of faithful Abraham, who has sometimes obtained a glimpse of the great truth involved in the shed blood, and experienced, in view of it, inexpressible comfort and peace. But the weakness of the flesh, and the temptations of sin, and the harassing cares of life have overshadowed his spiritual vision, and hidden the light from his view. The remembrance of many a sin returns and sits heavily upon his conscience, and thereby darkens his views of the great doctrine of the atonement for sin. But still, at the command of Jehovah, through Moses and the elders, he prepares the lamb, and sprinkles the blood. Yet as the shades of night thicken, and all are waiting in anxious suspense for the blow of vengeance and of deliverance, imagination is busy, and fears and terrors, as dark spirits, rise from the depths of his soul. And now unbelief suggests in view of the array of past sins which memory parades before him, " can a little blood, sprinkled on the door post, blot out *such* sins ?" Can the mere acceptance of such a call and command from Jehovah purge the conscience of such guilt ? However this blood might avail for the sins of the poor wretch who under the burden of transgression cries out, for the first time, to Jehovah in his distress,— yet can it avail for one who hath proved faithless to vows, and buried out of sight his very covenant, under " a multitude of transgressions ?" O, thou of little faith ! Hast thou not listened to the promise ? He said not—" when I find a tenement wherein there is no sin, I will pass over." Nor—" when I find one who has, on the whole, not gone far astray, I will pass over." Nor—" when I find a strong and active faith like Abraham's, I will pass over "—but, " when I SEE THE BLOOD, I WILL PASS OVER."

Sayest thou, doubting soul,—" But I have no faith, and therefore have no ground of hope in that blood,"—Well, let us test that point. Go, then, wash off the blood from the door post, and risk the great crisis of the judgment night without it! Wilt thou? Not for all the kingdoms of the world and all the glory of them. And why not, if thou hast no faith in it that makes it availing for thee?

Sayest thou—"But I am unholy in affections, unfit for the society of the redeemed and the holy angels." Well, come, let us test that point also. Assume, then, thou art swept off with the corrupt, and vile, and godless ones of Egypt into hell! What wilt thou do there? How employ the time—or rather the eternity? In yearning after the Father's house? In efforts to proclaim the mercies and the faithfulness of the God of Abraham? In efforts to persuade the spirits doomed in the eternal prison still to love him and adore him? Then hell itself shall have become heaven! Shame upon thy doubts and fears, O thou of little faith!

6. Here is another type of faith. The strong, heroic faith, of the true child of Abraham. It relies upon that blood and nothing else; simply because, as memory recalls sins and conscience accuses terribly, faith still sprinkles the blood. The preparation being made with solemn cheerfulness and joy, as night draws on the holy supper is eaten with high discourse of the wonders of Jehovah's goodness in calling Abraham, at first, out from among the idolatries beyond the Euphrates, and binding himself in a covenant with him; His long suffering mercies to Isaac and Jacob, and Joseph, are perhaps, dwelt upon. His mercies, amid all the afflictions of Israel are recalled to mind. As the hour of judgment approaches, with staff in hand, and "feet shod with the preparation of the gospel," he is ready to move at a moment's warning. Nay, should he *see* the very angel of death approaching his dwelling, it could excite no terror in him; for such is the confidence in Jehovah's word. that he could calmly and exultingly point to the blood, and shout, "Passover; Passover"—for so hath Jehovah commanded!

7. And, finally, we may well suppose also that, in that

hour of the revival of Jehovah's true children, there may
have been the case of some poor apostate sinner of Israel,
whom the fears, or the allurements of Egypt have turned
aside from all faith in the covenant with Abraham to utter
carelessness and thoughtlessness in reference to Jehovah, now
awakened to great concern, through the general excitement
and concern of the people. On this afternoon, we may well
suppose the enquiry suggests itself, to many, under the warning of the angel of death about to come, will that blood on
the door post avail for any but Israelites who have stood fast
to the covenant? And the inquiry is heard from every
quarter, men and brethren of Israel, what shall *we* do? Is
it worth while for such as we—apostates—the very chief of
sinners—to prepare the lamb, and sprinkle the blood? Shall
those who have broken the solemn covenant of Jehovah with
Abraham be allowed to become parties to the new covenant?
If there were such, the answer from every true Israelite,
doubtless was—"Yes! Come on, and strike the blood upon
the door post. Though your sins be as scarlet, they shall
become as wool, by the sprinkling of this blood! Jehovah
goes not behind the covenant to search for proof against you.
He will remember your sins no more. For he looks only to
faith's seal to the instrument—saying, ' WHEN I SEE THE
BLOOD I WILL PASS OVER.' "

DISCOURSE VI.

THE GOSPEL OF THE SINAI COVENANT; ITS RULE OF LIFE TO
CONVICT OF SIN; ITS RITUAL TO TEACH THE TAKING
AWAY OF SIN; AND ITS SOCIAL ORDER MOULDED AS A
TYPE OF CHRIST'S SPIRITUAL COMMONWEALTH.

EXODUS xix. 3-7; xx. 1-17; xxiv. 7-9 AND xxix. 38-42.—Thus shalt
thou say to the house of Jacob, and tell the children of Israel: Ye have
seen what I did unto the Egyptians, and how I bare you on eagles' wings,
and brought you unto myself. Now therefore, if ye will obey my voice
indeed, and keep my covenant, then ye shall be a peculiar treasure unto
me; and ye shall be a kingdom of priests, and an holy nation.

And Moses came and called the elders of the people, and laid before their
faces all these words which the Lord commanded him.

And God spake all these words, saying, I am the Lord thy God, which
have brought thee out of the land of Egypt, out of the house of bondage.
Thou shalt have no other gods before me.

And Moses wrote all the words of the Lord. And he took the book of
the covenant and read in the audience of the people; and they said, All
that the Lord hath said will we do, and be obedient. And Moses took the
blood and sprinkled it upon the people, and said, Behold the blood of the
covenant, which the Lord hath made with you concerning all these words.

Then went up Moses and Aaron, Nadab, and Abihu, and seventy of the
elders of Israel; and they saw the God of Israel.

Now this is that which thou shalt offer upon the altar; two lambs of the
first year day by day continually . . . a continual burnt offering throughout your generations, etc.

DEUT. v. 2, 3, 22.—The Lord our God made a covenant with us in Horeb.
The Lord made not this covenant with our fathers, but with us, even us
who are all alive this day. These words the Lord spake unto all your
assembly in the mount . . . and he added no more. And he wrote them
in two tables of stone, and delivered them unto me.

DEUT. vi. 1, 4, 5.—Now these are the commandments, the statutes, and
the judgments; . . . Hear, O Israel; the Lord our God is one Lord; and
thou shalt love the Lord thy God with all thy heart, and with all thy soul,
and with all thy might.

DEUT. x. 1.—At that time the Lord said unto me: Hew the two tables
of stone, like unto the first, and come up unto me in the mount, and make

thee an ark of wood. . . . And he wrote on the tables according to the first writing, the ten commandments which the Lord spake unto you in the mount out of the midst of the fire in the day of the assembly, and the Lord gave them unto me. And I turned myself and came down from the mount and put the tables into the ark which I had made, and behold there they be, as the Lord commanded me.

GAL. iii. 17, 19, 24.—The covenant which was confirmed before of God in Christ, the law which was four hundred and thirty years after cannot disannul, that it should make the promise of none effect.

Wherefore then serveth the law? It was added because of transgression, until the seed should come.

Wherefore the law was our schoolmaster to bring us unto Christ, that we might be justified by faith.

FORTY-FIVE days after the covenant with its passover seal to redeem his chosen people, in connection with the last of the marvellous judgments upon the Egyptians, this body, consisting of two or three millions of people, is found, not on the borders of Canaan as they might easily have been within the time, but in an opposite direction. They have moved south-eastward to that waste desert around Mount Sinai, far southward in the peninsula between the northern arms of the Red Sea. How thoroughly they are here segregated, apart from the habitable world, and alone with Jehovah,—as indicated in the saying of the text, " I bare you on eagles' wings and brought you unto myself"—you may form some conception from the graphic picture of the scene of their present encampment by the American traveller Stephens :—

" The mountains become here more and more striking, venerable and interesting. Not a shrub or a blade of grass grew on their naked sides, deformed with gaps and fissures . . . Before us towered in awful grandeur, so high and dark that it seemed close to us and barring all further progress, the end of my pilgrimage—the holy mountain of Sinai. Among all the stupendous works of nature not a place can be selected more fitted for the exhibition of Almighty power.

" It is a perfect sea of desolation. The crumbling masses of granite all around, and the distant view of the Syrian desert, with its boundless waste of sands, form the wildest and most dreary, the most terrific and desolate picture that the imagination can conceive."

Such then was the spot to which they were suddenly transferred, as if on eagles' wings, from the exuberant fertility of Goshen to be alone with Jehovah. The scene and the circumstances of their isolation are important elements in the exposition of the great covenant transaction which now occurs between Jehovah and his newly redeemed Church. For so describing it as a Church, I but repeat the words of the martyr Stephen: " This is he that was in the *Church in the wilderness.*"

Beyond doubt, the strange jumble of ideas in the popular mind, and, indeed, in the minds of not a few learned critics, concerning the law given at Sinai, and its relation to the gospel and the Christian Church, arises, in large part, from overlooking the fact that this whole transaction is another covenanting between Jehovah and his " Church in the wilderness." Not, indeed, such sacramental covenant as that of circumcision, organizing the visible Church, nor that of the passover, covenanting for the redemption of the chosen body, but still a formal covenant providing for the spiritual nurture and growth in grace of the redeemed Church.

These loose notions—whether of the popular mind or of the Rationalistic interpreters—that the law given at Sinai is merely some vague moral precepts delivered to mankind at large, together with some semi-political laws organizing a Church, or, rather, something half Church and half state, and an elaborate ritual, with all of which the Christian Church has no particular concern—are the more surprising, since both the record, in the 19th chapter of the preliminary preparation for delivering and receiving the first revelation from

Sinai, and the record, in the 24th chapter, of what was done with it when thus received, most expressly declare that it was delivered to the Church, as Church, already organized; that the preparation for it was through a council or synod of the "elders" of the congregation; and after the delivery it was solemnly executed, as a covenant, between Jehovah and the Church. And *after* thus solemnly adopting, by covenant act, the first revelation, consisting of the ten commandments, with an exposition of the application of their principles to the intercourse between God and man in worship, and man and man in ordinary affairs, *then* "went up Moses, and Aaron and seventy of the elders," representing the Church, to a sacrificial feast in the presence of Jehovah in the mount, preparatory to the extended revelation concerning establishing the tabernacle of Jehovah their king among them, and the duties of the priests, his courtiers. *Then*, again, when the palace was prepared, "according to the pattern shown in the mount," Jehovah descended and took possession of it; and thenceforth, from that tabernacle, Moses received all the details of the Levitical law of worship; of ecclesiastical law to govern the Church; and of civil and constitutional laws for the government of the peculiar theocratic state established to be the type of Christ's spiritual and everlasting kingdom.

This simple reference to the facts of the successive revelations at Sinai, recorded in Exodus and Leviticus; together with the fact that in Numbers are recorded such ordinances as the incidents of administration, during the wanderings, gave rise to; and that Deuteronomy contains simply a summary of the previous ordinances made thirty-nine years afterward, with a view to adapt them to the settled state of the nation, now soon to take place, will be found to relieve much of the confusion of ideas on this subject. And a careful reading of the whole, under the light of this statement, will make manifest that Moses did not *organize* a Jewish

Church by revelation from Sinai, as the popular conception hath it, but found the Church fully organized with its government of elders, at the time of his call. For to these elders he came with his credentials (Ex. iv. 29) : to these elders he revealed the sacrament of the passover (Ex. xii. 21) ; and before these elders, in council or synod, he laid the message of Jehovah, and through them made preparation for the meeting of the congregation before the Lord at Sinai (Ex. xix. 7). And not only was the Church organized with elders to govern it, before the law at Sinai, but there were also priests already recognized in the congregation assembled at the mount, before giving the law (Ex. xix. 22, 24). Neither is it true that, by this revelation, given at Sinai, Moses organized the Jewish *civil* commonwealth, with its magistracy for secular affairs ; for he found a civil government organized, before the giving of the law. And it was not by suggestion of revelation, but on the suggestion of Jethro his father-in-law that the magistracy was appointed. This was done as a matter of common sense and natural reason, just as the magistracy of any other civil commonwealth is appointed. And, indeed, the careful student of Moses will discover, throughout his system of ordinances for Israel, that, though in both the Jewish state and Jewish Church Jehovah ruled as Head, being served by its citizens as their King, as well as worshipped by them in their capacity of Church members as God, still the distinction between that which is political and that which is ecclesiastical is kept up far more carefully than in most modern Christian states, and in the conceptions of many modern Christian people. So that, even were there any apology for the modern blunder of citing, as precedents for a purely secular government, the ordinances of a Theocratic commonwealth, established for the specific purpose of furnishing a type of the great spiritual kingdom of Jesus Christ, still there could not be found, in the Mosaic

'inances, either precedent or apology for most of that con-
ling of powers secular and powers spiritual which has so
often in modern ages brought both the Church and the state
to the verge of ruin.

You are ready now to ask—What then is the nature and
purpose of the Sinai revelations : and what place and relation
do they hold in the gospel system ?

The answer to this question is not left to our conjecture
or to mere ingenious inference. In much fuller detail than
in the case of any of the preceding revelations is the whole
matter expounded for us by the scriptures themselves.

This is a covenant transaction, and this law, so called,
constitutes simply the stipulations of that covenant. So it is
expressly declared of it, " The Lord our God made a covenant with us at Horeb." It was ratified formally, as a
covenant, when first received, the people being called upon
solemnly to swear it, after it had been written down in a book.
To give it still more solemn and venerable form the fundamental
truths of it were engrossed upon stone by the hand of Jehovah
himself. When, after this, the people violated all its solemn
stipulations, by the idolatry of the golden calf, Moses understood the covenant to be annulled, and therefore destroyed
the divine autograph of it. When they were pardoned
and their relations to Jehovah were restored, it was again
divinely written and deposited in the chest or ark, upon the
cover of which the throne of Jehovah's visible presence was
placed, hence called the ark of the covenant ; and thus it was
preserved to after generations as the perpetual reminder
that they were in covenant with Jehovah.

It was a covenant with this body of people, *as a Church*,
the body organized by the covenant with Abraham, and its
redemption guaranteed in the passover covenant. In speaking of the body as the Church we are but repeating, as I
have said, the words of the martyr Stephen in Acts vii. 38,

" This is he that was in the Church in the wilderness, w
the angel that spake to him in Mount Sinai with our fa*
who received the lively oracles to give unto us." And that
this is no mere figure of speech is plain enough from the
reference of this covenant back to the covenants with Abraham and the passover covenant, as fulfilled and further
carried out by this covenant.

It was a covenant with this Church as a *representative* body,
standing for the Church of all succeeding ages. Moses, forty
years after, when this generation that stood before Sinai had
all perished, expressly says to the next generation, " The
Lord made this covenant not with our fathers *but with us,
even us who are .all here alive this day.*" By parity of
reasoning the Church that stood at Sinai, thus representing
one, represented all succeeding generations. And, accordingly thenceforth in the succeeding ages, including that of
the Apostles, the inspired teachers regarded the Church as
still under this covenant. And you will observe how, under
the New Testament dispensation Stephen expressly says,
" Our fathers *received the lively oracles to give unto us.*"
That is, they stood there as representing us.

It was a covenant *wholly spiritual* in its significancy. Moses,
just as Jesus afterward, sums up its provisions in the generalization, " Love the Lord thy God with all thy mind, soul and
strength." And the Apostle expressly argues that, so far
from disannulling the previous covenant of spiritual blessings
with Abraham, as the representative father of all who believe,
and who thus constitute the true circumcision, it is intended
to include that covenant, and both confirm and develop more
fully its provisions of spiritual blessing.

As to the *end* and purpose of this Sinai law covenant, the
Apostle Paul not only leaves no room for uncertainty or
further need of exposition after his clear and elaborate exposition in the epistles to the Romans, the Galatians and the

Hebrews, but expressly answers the question,—" Wherefore then serveth the law?" in these explicit terms—" It was added because of transgression until the seed (promised in the Eden and the Abrahamic covenants) should come. Wherefore the law was our schoolmaster to bring us to Christ—*that we might* be justified by faith."

The substance of the whole matter, therefore, is this: That as the covenant with Adam, for the blessing of a divine human Redeemer to restore a part of the race through vicarious atonement, was more distinctly developed in the covenant with Noah, establishing the blessing in the line of Shem; and both these, again, more fully developed in the covenant with Abraham establishing the blessing in the line of Isaac, and organizing the redeemed body as a Church settled in a promised inheritance; and all three of these, again, more fully developed in the passover covenant, bringing out more distinctly the engagement to redeem this Church by faith in atoning blood; so now this Sinai covenant is a still fuller development, in detail, of all the preceding covenants, intended to teach and to produce a conscious conviction of the need of a vicarious atonement; the method of applying its benefits by faith for the pardon of sin, and purification of the nature; and the relation of the believers to their Redeemer, as king and head of an organized commonwealth.

With this general view of the nature and purpose of the Sinai gospel kept distinctly before you, these last four books of Moses—instead of presenting, as they may have done hitherto, a somewhat confused medley of precepts and promises, ethical, ritual, ecclesiastical and civil; and all of uncertain application to Christianity—will be found to assume a simple and natural logical order, each portion in its proper place, and perfectly adapted to its special end. First, a general code of ethics covering the whole ground of man's relation to God on the one hand, and to his fellows on the other (Ex. xx). This followed by a divine annotation on this general abstract code, illustrative of its application to all the practical relations of man in life, as worshippers of Jehovah, as social beings in civil society, and as members of a peculiar spiritual society (Ex. xxi.–xxiii.). This being received and formally adopted by covenant (Ex. xxiv.), then an extended revelation, expounding the construction of a typical palace in which Jehovah proposes to have "the tabernacle of God among men" (Ex. xxv. xl). This constructed and taken possession of by Jehovah, then an extended revelation, from his palace, of a ritual of worship which shall teach all the particulars of the application, by faith of the vicarious atone ient, and the purification of the life by faith which "works by love and purifies the heart;" together with certain modifications of the social and civil law already existing so as to mould the civil commonwealth itself into a prophetic testimony to the coming of a Redeemer and a type of his spiritual kingdom (Lev. i. xxvii). To which is added a brief historical account of the administration under this system in the wilderness (Numbers i-xxxvi); and then a summary rehearsal, after forty years, with certain additions and modifications needful to adapt it to the settled state upon which the people were then about to enter. (Deut. i-xxxiv).

I thus repeat the outline and order of this Sinai revelation here that you may have it distinctly before you preparatory to a summary analytical statement of the purposes aimed at in making this revelation.

These people standing at the base of Mount Sinai, are to be contemplated in three different relations, with reference to each of which these laws were given.

First, they stood as men representative of all men of the Adam race, and, like Adam, creatures owing duties to God and to his other creatures.

Second, as the chosen, organized, spiritual body under the covenant with Abraham, constituting them Jehovah's peculiar people, and him their God.

Third, as a social and civil organization which is to possess a country guaranteed to them as an inheritance for a special purpose.

Contemplated in the first aspect, they needed a moral law, or ethical rule of life, definitely pointing out their duties to God and man, in order that the comparing of their life with it may directly fasten conviction upon the conscience. Such a law of two tables they received, first as the foundation of all other laws which are but the detailed application of its principles. Its provisions are arranged with marvellous logical method, so as to be exhaustive on the subject of moral duty. Those concerning God, the invisible, begin with the invisible acts of the heart, and proceed outwards to the words and deeds of the life ; those concerning man, visible, begin with the outward deeds and proceed inwardly to the desires of the heart. The substance of the ten commands is, thou shalt worship God only ; in his appointed way only ; using his name reverently in worship only ; specially worship him at his appointed times ; worship and honour father and mother, his representatives, and at the same time types of all that earthly authority which he has delegated for social order; nor shalt thou injure thy fellow man either in *deed*, against his life, affections or property—in *word*, against his reputation —nor in *desire*, against anything that is his.

So perfect and exhaustive is this ethical code, few as its words are, and simple, that the human mind can conceive of no moral act, or impulse that comes not under one or other of its categories. Yet, in order to aid men in making the application of it to the practical duties and relations of life, its divine author vouchsafed to append a series of practical applications of it by way of general illustration, to questions of duty, social, civil, ritual, ecclesiastical — as contained in the twentieth to twenty-fourth chapters of Exodus.

Contemplated in the second aspect, as the chosen and organized spiritual body under the covenant with Abraham, they needed—not an ecclesiastical constitution organizing them, for that they already had ; nor a theological creed and ritual of worship, for that they also had already—but a further development of their ecclesiastical constitution, adapting it to their new condition ; and a fuller detail of their theology and ritual, in order to set forth more clearly, by its symbols, both the objective theology of redemption by atonement, and the subjective theology of that atonement, applied by the faith of the individual, to the renewal and purification of his nature. Such an adaptation of their ecclesiastical constitution they received, in various incidental precepts and enactments ; and such an expansion of the ritual, in the elaborate detail of Leviticus, with incidental precepts and enactments elsewhere.

Contemplated in the third aspect of a social organization to dwell together as a nation—they needed not organization and a political constitution, for that they already had. And had it been the purpose of Jehovah to leave them simply an ordinary civil community, with his church established among them, there would have been no revelation of civil law, save by way of illustrating and applying the moral law as before mentioned. They would have modified and changed their civil polity as experience and the counsels of wise statesmen, such as Jethro might suggest ; just as any other people under the guidance of natural law and reason may modify their civil laws. But it being the purpose of Jehovah to dwell among them, by his visible presence, and to constitute this political commonwealth a type of the great spiritual commonwealth over which he specially rules, as his people, and to be a perpetual prophecy of the coming Messiah, it was needful to introduce various modifications of their civil code with reference to that purpose. Hence those peculiar laws forbidding the alienation of their lands by any family, or the aliena-

I

tion permanently, of his liberty by any Israelite; hence the exceptional command to marry a brother's widow, contrary to the general law forbidding marriage within that degree; with all the modifications of rights of property and person which grew out of these. Hence the various ordinances making idolatry, consultation of evil spirits, false prophecies, etc., treasonable. Hence, in short, the whole of those peculiar principles of civil law in the Mosaic code, and in the administration under it, which have so often been perverted by being applied as precedents in ordinary civil governments; as though Jehovah had covenanted with these civil governments to dwell among them as their theocratic king; or, as though Jehovah purposed to make some one of these model governments of modern times a type and a perpetual prophecy of his coming to the earth. It is, manifestly, from this confusion of ideas concerning the spiritual import of the Mosaic civil institutions that men get the precedents whereby they confound together the spiritual and the secular powers;—though, even in the Mosaic institutes, these powers are carefully kept asunder, so far as they could be, under that peculiar theocracy—and by this confusion perpetually endanger both civil and religious liberty.

That the Sinai revelations did not organize a civil and political system, but only make some modifications of a common law system already existing, is manifest not only from the fact that no such civil and political system, as a system, is found in them; but from the further fact that, finding such common law usages among the people, as the *goel*, or blood revenge, and polygamy, descended to them from the patriarchal constitution, the law of Moses simply modified, restrained, and ameliorated their application. He made of the one a great gospel type, by instituting cities of refuge, in which the manslayer should be protected against the wild impulses of passion in the avenger of blood. In the other case he interposed legal forms to protect the wife from the passionate impulses of the husband. Jesus expressly declares, "Moses for the hardness of your hearts gave you this precept" of the civil law. He aimed to correct an abuse of a common law usage from the patriarchy; he did not first ordain divorce or the usage of polygamy out of which that common law of divorce originated.

But while, for purposes of analysis and exposition, we may thus contemplate the Sinai covenant as aiming to meet the three-fold aspect of the body with whom it was made, viz :— men, as men, as church members, and as citizens of a peculiar civil commonwealth; we must not forget that, in its great practical aspect, these divisions all merge together, and, practically, it is to be considered in its two-fold character of a law to convict of sin, and a gospel to teach the pardon and justification of the sinner by faith, and that a faith which purifies the heart. In this view it is, on the one hand, a law of commandments " exceeding broad, reaching to the thoughts and intents of the heart," with divine annotations showing the application of its precepts to every relation of man as a creature of God, and as a social being with relations to his fellow men. On the other hand, it sets before the convicted sinner, in fullest detail, the gospel salvation by symbols and types. The perpetual daily offering of the lamb upon the altar is its central symbol, and, around that ancient figure of the old covenants, is arranged, in eloquent symbols, the whole subjective process of salvation—faith, purification—consecration to Jehovah. It is *law*, but not antithetical to the gospel, or as contrasted with the doctrines of Jesus and his Apostles. It is law and gospel both. Nay the very law itself is grounded upon an evangelical motive, " I am Jehovah thy God who brought thee out of the land of Egypt "— who have redeemed thee, and entitled myself to grateful service and obedience—therefore worship me only; in the appointed way only; naming me in reverent worship only; worship at the appointed times; and render due worship to my representatives and the type of that order I have appointed for society; nor in deed, nor word, nor desire, do any injury to thy fellows. Hence, that which is most distinctively ethical in the Sinai revelations is yet distinctly evangelical in the ground and motive of obedience. And that which is ethico-ritual is intensely evangelical in all its forms and ideas—as you may readily see in Bonar's or Seiss' or any other popular expositions of the Mosaic ritual.

Our habit of conceiving of this ancient ritual as merely a dark and mysterious hinting at a salvation yet to be revealed, goes far beyond the Apostle's meaning in describing the law as "having a shadow of good things to come." He says this with special reference to the error of those who insisted on clinging to the ancient prophetic mode of presenting Christ crucified to a faith which had yet to look forward to Christ's first coming as we now look forward to Christ's second coming; whereas, Christ having come, and faith having to look backward historically, the symbols designed as prophetic speech of him are not only needless, but the use of them, after their purpose is accomplished, can only tend to obscure the view of Christ; and the desire to use them can arise only from the dangerous error of resting in the external symbol without penetrating to its internal spiritual sense. This is the clue to the interpretation of all that Jesus first, and Paul after him, had to say on the subject of the Sinai law; viz, that they had need to contend, perpetually, with men who saw not the real meaning of the law which they extolled so; and who would feed the people, not upon the internal kernel of truth, but upon the husks containing it, out of which they had suffered the kernel to drop and disappear from view.

It was not that the Sinai gospel was intended to veil the

.ruths of salvation, as from men who might not be able to appreciate and feel their spiritual power, that Jehovah choose to write it in these symbols projecting all their shadows toward the great central Cross. It arose from the nature of the case, and out of a reason in the very nature of the human mind. The gospel that instructs a faith which must look forward, prophetically, to a future not yet actualized, must speak through symbols rather than in literal language, in order to be comprehensible to the human understanding, which can neither conceive nor utter its thoughts of the future save in symbols, types and analogies. This you see even in the New Testament. All is literal enough so far as relates historically to Christ and salvation; but when it comes, as in the last book of the New Testament, to develop the future of the gospel kingdom and the second coming of Christ, precisely as in the Old Testament, all become symbols and types. The believers of the Old Testament age had, of necessity, to be taught by symbols concerning the first coming of Christ, just as believers now can be taught only by symbols concern ing the second coming of Christ. In ordaining that gospel ritual of shadowy symbols, Jehovah, in accordance with his usual method of revelation, accommodated himself to the habits of thought common among men. The saints guided by Moses were taught, in the prophetic language which they could best understand, precisely the same gospel truths which were taught the saints guided by Paul in the historical language which they could best understand. Having in literal terms, therefore, furnished a law of life to convict of sin, far more clear and in detail than any previous revelation, the Sinai Covenant proceeds also, far more clearly and in detail than ever before, not only to hold up as heretofore the gospel provision for sin in atoning blood; but the gospel instructions for the application of that provision to the conscience of the sinner by faith—the cleansing of the heart to which such faith leads, and the consecration of the life to the Redeemer. Thus the gospel according to Moses differs neither in creed nor practical religion from the gospel according to Jesus and Paul, but only in the language in which, from the necessity of the case, it had to find utterance.

The argument against the papal and semi-papal ritualism of modern times, which proposes by the authority of the Church merely to set up symbols in worship for teaching religious truth and assisting devotion, it will be perceived, runs much deeper than any mere reason of inexpediency or impolicy in matters of indifference. For the error of these modern symbols, as appendages to the ordinances of worship is, in principle, exactly the error of the Judaizers against whom Jesus first, and after him Paul contended so earnestly. It is the error of bringing back the cumbrous machinery absolutely necessary to meet the special difficulties of teaching a gospel whose great facts were yet prophetic, and of substituting this in place of that simple, direct, literal teaching which alone is necessary, and therefore alone is proper in exhibiting the great facts of the gospel now become historic. It is an attempt to force in symbols where there is no place for them, and therefore where the use of them can have no other effect than to encumber and hinder the communication of truth. Moreover the very attempt itself, and the zeal with which it is prosecuted, evinces clearly that those who make it perceive not the grand internal truths of the symbol and their significancy to the heart. That they are resting merely in the outward observance; admiring the outward shell, without penetrating to the kernel within; appealing to the imagination merely, and not to the conscience and spiritual nature of men. And besides this, the use concurrently of two methods so unlike in their nature of conveying truths cannot possibly result in any other effect than to blur, confuse and obscure the view of truth to the minds of the people; and, as a necessary consequence, to make them lose sight at last of the real spiritual truth altogether, and perceive only the symbol itself as appealing to the imagination. The mind having the advantage of directly contemplating a historical " Christ crucified " is, manifestly, not aided but hindered in its conceptions, by compelling it to use symbols, and thus look prophetically, and " through a glass darkly " at Christ crucified.

But far more conclusive than any considerations of philosophy and expediency, is the argument that there is no more authority in the Church for constituting a symbol, than for adding to the revealed truth of God. The true symbol must be divinely framed and constituted. It is no more left to the vagaries of human fancy, or to rest upon mere human authority, than the truths it was intended to teach. " See," said Jehovah to Moses, " that thou make all things according to the pattern showed thee in the Mount." Even Moses was not left to his own taste and discretion, in fashioning a single cord, or loop, or tassel of the Tabernacle and its furniture—the symbolic palace of Jehovah, and typical at once of Christ the Prophet, Priest and King, present and ruling in his Spiritual Kingdom. The authority of God alone can constitute a gospel symbol. And the claim to set up a symbol in gospel worship, which Jehovah has not set up in his word, is really a claim to speak as the messenger of Jehovah, and to come with authority to actualize a divine pattern revealed to him who sets it up. It is a claim analogous to that of Mohammed, Swedenborg, or of Joe Smith.

From this view of the gospel of the Sinai covenant, and of the symbols and types through which it was obliged, by the very nature of the human mind, to find its utterance, while " Christ crucified " was yet a prophetic instead of a historic fact—you may find your minds relieved of much of that obscurity which often exists, even among earnest Chris-

tian people, concerning the relation of this Sinai Covenant to
the Church under the present dispensation. An obscurity
which is specially unfortunate at a time when a treacherous
infidelity labours to subvert the faith of Christians in the
inspiration of this portion of the scriptures. The question is
continually raised as we press the obligations of God's law—
" But has not this or that enactment of the Mosaic code
been repealed by the coming in of the gospel dispensation ?"
And good men, labouring to run the line between the repealed
and the unrepealed, have suggested the maxim—" All that
is moral stands—all that is ritual, ecclesiastical or political is
repealed." No doubt, the principle intended to be uttered
by this maxim is true. But it is a singularly unfortunate
mode of uttering the truth. If I have correctly analyzed and
stated the nature and purposes of the Mosaic revelations,
then — *nothing that Moses ever enacted has been repealed,
any more than the things enacted by Jesus or Paul.* Many
of the Mosaic enactments, practically applying principles,
expired by limitation. As the leaves fall from the tree at
the change of the season, having fulfilled their office, so the
gorgeous foliage of the Sinai ritual of symbols fell away, so the
prophetic types of the Sinai ecclesiastical and civil ordinances
fell away when their functions were fulfilled. But the
Divine tree itself continued a living tree, with all its functions of life in exercise, according to the times and seasons
appointed for it, and leafed out again under the warm breath
of spring—even the reviving power of the Holy Ghost at the
opening of the dispensation of the Spirit. All the great
gospel truths and principles of the Sinai covenant still
stood, notwithstanding the fashion of uttering them changed,
and the concrete ritual and typical organisms which they
animated passed away. The eternal truths embodied in
that typical palace of Jehovah : in that one altar of sacrifice ;
in that altar of incense ; in the offerings appointed for them,

bloody and unbloody ; in that Theocratic kingdom and its laws of naturalization, purification and excommunication— all these, like the great Author of them, are "the same, yesterday, to-day, and forever."

Hence we need apply no cautious limitations to the saying of Jesus, " Heaven and earth may pass away, but one jot or tittle of this law shall not pass away till all be fulfilled." Even the very jots and tittles of its ritual pass away only because they have fulfilled their end in adapting the truth to the " sundry times " of the revelation of redemption. No one who is familiar with the reasonings of that great Apostle, whose specialty it was to be the Jewish iconoclast, and dash in pieces the narrow perverted ritualism of his age, but must be filled with admiration at the heights and depths of his inspired logic, when, planting his premises upon these old covenants with Adam, and Abraham and Israel at Sinai, and David, as the great gospel bonds in which Jehovah hath bound himself to secure the sinner's salvation—he proceeds to reason out the title of all that believe, irrespective of blood or nation, or age, to the benefit of those covenants as being represented in them. And with what majestic transcen dental generalization does he, in the epistle to the Hebrews, take the dead symbolism to which a contracted, unspiritual ritualism still clings, and re-animate it with the new, fully developed gospel truths, until it swells out again to infinite proportions. As in that vision of Isaiah, the year King Uzziah died, he saw the temple and all its symbols expand infinitely, until the golden throne of Jehovah, on the ark of the covenant, was lifted up to infinite heights and breadths ; and the temple expanded to the dimensions of the universe : and the visible symbol of Jehovah's presence on the mercy seat became the Jehovah actually filling immensity with His presence ; and the mysterious emblematic creatures that with their wings overshadowed the mercy seat, rose and expanded, and floated apart, veiling their faces, as one shouted " Holy !" and the other answered " Holy !" and then both in chorus sing " Holy is Jehovah, God of Hosts : the whole earth is full of His glory !" So these symbols of the ancient Sinai covenant, under the glowing logic of the inspired Apostle, again are re-animated for us, and rise and swell into proportions of infinite grandeur ; till tabernacle and smoking altar and flowing blood, and floating cloud of incense, become so many infinite transparencies blazing with excess of light, exhibiting to us the actual scenes transpiring in the inner temple of the spiritual universe. No ! No ! To the soul that has ever caught the inspiration of Paul's New Testament logic, this cold and cautious criticism that so narrowly inspects, and so sweepingly lops off the repealed from the unrepealed, till but a sightless stump is left, seems irreverent and almost blasphemous !

Brethren, this is the true spirit in which to study the gospel of this Sinai covenant. It is no curious and amazing history, merely, of how Jehovah once spake and covenanted with certain Israelites at Sinai. " Not with your fathers merely," said Moses, forty years afterward, " did he make this covenant at Horeb, but *with us who are all alive here this day.*" And said Stephen, fifteen hundred years afterwards, under this our own dispensation, " He spake in Mount Sinai with our fathers *who received the lively oracles to give unto us.*" It is no theory of mine, therefore, but the Holy Ghost's, that this Sinai law is our law. And just as truly was it with you and me, brethren, " who are all alive *this day*," that he made that covenant. It was to you and me that he spake these " ten words" of command, to show us our sin, and make us feel it. For you and me he appointed that ritual of atoning sacrifice to teach us, by its beautiful symbols, how the sin is to be taken away ; for you and me those typical purifications for sin and uncleanness and those signs and the cleansings of the leprosy; for you and me those cities of refuge, and that singular typical common-wealth with its curious laws and constitution. All this is just as really and truly the word of Jehovah to us, and as really deserving of our reverence, as though we had heard the voice of the thunders, and had seen the lightnings and the smoke and the shaking of the huge mountains, and Nature herself, half dissolved in fear, prostrating herself in reverent awe to attest the words of her Maker and Lord, as the word of the Almighty to men!

Say not within yourselves, surely, if we had lived in the days of these fathers of the Church in the wilderness, and seen all these wonders, we would have believed and have been saved. Alas, they who did see it, and who trembled at it, could soon forget it and be as rebellious as any of you; yea utterly neglected and despised it and miserably perished! And all that for precisely the same cause that leads you to neglect it now—"the same evil heart of unbelief!" With the Apostle, therefore, I quote, as a warning, the reasoning of the Holy Ghost, by David, from this very case: "To-day if ye will hear his voice, harden not your hearts, as in the provocation in the day of temptation in the wilderness. So he sware in his wrath they shall not enter into my rest."

SECTION III.

REDEMPTION AS REVEALED THROUGH THE SPIRIT OF CHRIST IN THE PROPHETS.

DISCOURSE VII.

THE GOSPEL CHURCH BY COVENANT TYPICALLY SET FORTH AS THE ETERNAL KINGDOM OF DAVID'S SON.

II Samuel vii. 1, 2, 4, 5, 16, 13, 20, 24.—And it came to pass, when the king sat in his house, and the Lord had given him rest round about from all his enemies; that the king said unto Nathan the prophet, see now, I dwell in an house of cedar, but the ark of God dwelleth within curtains. And it came to pass that night that the word of the Lord came to Nathan, saying, go and tell my servant David, thus saith the Lord, shalt thou build me an house for me to dwell in?

And thine house and thy kingdom shall be established forever before thee: thy throne shall be established forever.

Then went king David in, and sat before the Lord, and he said, who am I, O Lord God? and what is my house, that thou hast brought me hitherto?

And this was yet a small thing in thy sight, O Lord God: but thou has spoken also of thy servant's house for a great while to come. And is this the manner of man, O Lord God? And what can David say more unto thee? (I Chron. xvii. 17. Thou hast regarded me according to the estate of a man of high degree, O Lord God. What can David speak more to thee for the honour of thy servant). For thou hast confirmed to thyself thy people Israel to be a people unto thee forever: and thou, Lord, art become their God.

Psalm lxxii. 1, 8, 17 and lxxxix. 3, 4.—Give the king thy judgments, O God and thy righteousness unto the king's son. He shall have dominion also from sea to sea, and from the river unto the ends of the earth. His name shall be continued as long as the Sun: and men shall be blessed in him: all nations shall call him blessed. I have made a covenant with my

chosen, I have sworn unto David my servant. Thy seed will I establish forever, and build up thy throne to all generations.

LUKE i. 32.—Thou shalt call his name Jesus, and the Lord God shall give
unto him the throne of his father David : and he shall reign over the house
of Jacob forever.

ACTS ii. 30.—Therefore being a prophet, and knowing that God had
sworn with an oath to him (David), that of the fruit of his loins, according
to the flesh, he would raise up Christ to sit upon his throne ; he seeing this
before spake of the resurrection of Christ. He said on this wise (in Isaiah
lv. 3) I will give you the sure mercies of David.

THIS brief historical record of the vision of Nathan, the
covenant with David, announced through him, and David's
reception of the message, might well be selected to illustrate
what has already been said in a previous discourse of the brief
and fragmentary, yet wonderfully germinal and logical character of these Divine revelations. To the superficial reader
this seventh chapter of II Samuel, or its parallel passage in
I Chron. xvii. conveys little other impression, than that
David, now settled comfortably in his capital, gratefully
resolves to build a more befitting and attractive palace
for Jehovah whose vicegerent he is in reality. For unlike
Saul, his predecessor, who, as soon as the possession of a little
power developed the ambition and pride of his nature, sought
to rule in his own right, and to avoid Jehovah's prophet who
anointed him, David, once in power, gratefully remembers
the marvellous loving-kindness of Jehovah, and seeks more
and more to exalt him, as the real sovereign, in the eyes of
the people. Whereupon Jehovah, in return, vouchsafes to
assure him that the throne of Israel shall be hereditary in his
family forever. But while superficial readers, and indeed
many learned critics, see nothing profounder than this in the
story, no thoughtful Christian reader can fail to perceive
that this falls infinitely short of reaching the vast depths of
its significancy. For he cannot retrace a step backward in
the history, or advance a step forward, to ascertain the con-

nection and scope of the narrative of the vision, without seeing
that this shallow view of the passage gives rise to inexplicable
puzzles.   Why should David be so overwhelmed, and lying
prostrate, cry " O Lord God, what can David say more unto
thee ?"   Why this reiteration in various forms of the terms
" forever," as the only limit to the throne and kingdom
promised ?   What can he mean by the exclamation " Is
this the manner of a man ?" Or, as in the parallel place in
Chronicles—" thou hast regarded me *according to the estate
of a man* of high degree ?" And this the more especially if
we take the Hebrew reading of the first—" *Is this the law of
the Adam,*" and of the second—" *regarded me according to
the order of the Adam from above,*" as if its parallel is the
saying of the Apostle (I Cor. xv. 47) " The second man
(Adam) is the Lord from heaven ?" And then, too, the
point which seems to make the honour so overwhelming, and
one, compared with which all that Jehovah has done hitherto,
in raising him from the sheep-cote to a throne, seems a small
thing, is " thou hast spoken of thy servant's house *for a
great while to come.*"

Once the attention is arrested by these puzzling suggestions,
and the mind turned to the diligent search for the solution
of them ; by a comparison of scripture with scripture, this
remarkable place will be found to be another of those successive germinal centres from which a whole series of
revelations is developed—of like character with the covenant
of grace with Adam in the lost Eden : with Noah fixing the
blessings in the line of Shem : with Abraham organizing the
visible Church : with Israel in Egypt and at Sinai, developing
definitely, and in detail, all that before had been promised.
And this conception of the nature of the revelation once
obtained, then all details of the narrative swell into grander
proportions ; the vision itself and David's view of it are
perceived to be sublimely spiritual : and, still more, the

remarkable prominence given to this revelation through the whole series of prophets, forward to the close of the Old Testament,—its prominence in the angels' annunciation of Jesus —and its like prominence after the opening of the dispensation of the Spirit, in the arguments of the Apostles, all become intelligible enough to us.

Looking backward now, first to the occasion of this revelation, it will be perceived that the saying "The Lord had given him rest round about from all his enemies," involves something more than the mere restoration of peace after a long civil war, and after fierce struggles with foreign foes. The history, immediately preceding, records how David had recently taken this Jebus or Jerusalem, as the last stronghold of the Canaanitish nation, in the land of promise. And that taken, the original covenant with Abraham to give to the chosen people the land of Canaan as an inheritance, is at length completely fulfilled. Four hundred and thirty years, according to the Apostle's chronology, elapsed from the making of the covenant with Abraham to raise up, in the line of Isaac, that peculiar nation for whom Canaan should be the natural inheritance and the fulfillment of that part of the covenant, in the array of a nation of two or three millions at Mount Sinai, to enter into another solemn engagement with Jehovah. And so, again, another four hundred and thirty years have elapsed between the first coming of the nation from Mount Sinai to its inheritance and the full possession thereof by the united nation under David in the capture of this Jebus,—which becomes thenceforth so prominent, through all time, as the City of David, Jerusalem.

These words, therefore, "The Lord had given him rest," mark a great epoch in the history of redemption—even the complete fulfilment, in its temporal sense, of the covenant with Abraham concerning the peculiar nation and the land of inheritance. So David evidently regarded it. For now, with every preparation of priests and Levites for the holy office, and of special inspired songs of praise, he had brought up the ark of the covenant, and pitched its permanent abiding place in Jerusalem, with national singings and shoutings and dancings. Nor was it any mere holiday parade. The ark, with its visible symbol of Jehovah's presence, thus brought to Jerusalem, was at once the re-acknowledgment, by the nation, of Jehovah as their covenant king; their witness to the unity of the nation in the covenant with him; and their recognition of all their rights as derived from those ancient covenants to be his people and he their God.

The very terms of the inspired psalm sung by the mighty choir, as they bear the ark to the holy hill, show how the Spirit of God taught both David and the people to regard it. " Be ye mindful always of his covenant: the words which he commanded to a thousand generations: even of the covenant which he made with Abraham and of his oath with Isaac: and hath confirmed the same to Jacob for a law, and to Israel for an everlasting covenant: saying, unto thee will I give the Land of Canaan, the lot of your inheritance; when ye were but few even a few, and strangers in it."

Thus instructed as to the nature of the service they were engaging in, we may appreciate the spirit of that prophetic song in which, as the national procession with the ark and Jehovah's brightness on its cover, approached the newly won capital, they " lifted up the voice with joy " as the " voice of many waters" under the lead of Chenaniah, singing,—" Lift up your heads, O ye gates, and be ye lifted up ye everlasting doors, and the King of Glory shall come in."—And when the choir stationed under Heman or Asaph at the gate to receive the procession, shout back the inquiry " Who is this King of Glory?" the mighty shout of the glad myriads that follow answers back, in a voice of music that shakes Mount Zion, ' The Lord, strong and mighty—the

Lord mighty in battle—the Lord of Hosts, he is the King of Glory."

It is very manifest, therefore, that David, and, through the inspired writings of David, the people generally, fully appreciated the greatness of the epoch marked by the conquest of Jerusalem and the complete possession of Canaan. They expressly declare their recognition of the new era in the recital of the covenant with Abraham and its fulfilment at last, in the triumphal song as they carried up the ark. Another cycle of the history of redemption is completed.

And now looking backward and forward from this point, we discover that, on the one hand, we have the interpretation of all the mysteries of Providence in his dealings with the people since Moses, by way of preparing for this kingdom under David : and all the mysteries of his dealings with David, by way of training him, in the school of sorrow and affliction, to the heroic faith of Abraham as a preparation for the position he is now to occupy—a position analogous to Abraham's as the head of a covenant. On the other hand, looking forward we find here, in this revelation to David, through Nathan, the clue to the interpretation of all the prophecies that follow, of the coming of Messiah: and here also the starting point of that new style of thought and speech, and the new developments of the Eden promise of the seed of the woman, which characterize all subsequent revelations.

It was under this wide view of the moral position of Israel, after four hundred years of struggles and delays and failures, now in full realization of the promise fulfilled at last : and under the influence of the high and holy excitement of locating the ark in Jerusalem, and reorganizing its priests and Levites for perpetual service before it, that this idea of a permanent palace for Jehovah occurred to David.

It was, therefore, no mere question of æsthetics as applied to religion, nor any mere grateful impulse of desire to show

personal love for Jehovah. It is the profound reasoning
of one who sees a grand cycle of providences completed and
of promises fulfilled, and a new era opened. It comes of
David's reasoning with himself, that if the settled state, in full
possession of the promised inheritance, is indicated at last by
a gorgeous permanent palace for David, the king, in a permanent capital, then should it not be indicated also by a gorgeous
permanent palace for Jehovah, the real king, instead of this
mere tent which speaks still of travel and struggle and unrest?
Nay will not the people, in their admiration of David's palace
of cedar, lose sight of the great fact that Jehovah is the real
king, unless his palace excites similar attention?

It was in response to these humble and yet profound questions of how the ancient gospel, preached to the fathers,
should now be adapted in its forms to the new era of the
Canaan promise fulfilled, that this revelation through Nathan
was made. Interpreted in this light it at once becomes plain
and at the same time swells to a grandeur of view, and an
infinity of reach that at once exalts it as worthy to form the
germ from which to develop all the succeeding prophetic
revelations of Messiah, as a King seated upon an eternal
throne. Now we can understand why David was overcome
with ecstasy of emotion. Why he thought that all which
Jehovah had done for him in raising him to a throne was a
small thing compared with this new covenant promise. Why
he felt himself now exalted to the position of the Adam, in
that, like Adam and Noah and Abraham, he had been
selected to stand as the great representative and typical man,
and the starting point of a new covenant, in the grand series
through which the scheme of redemption was to be developed
to men.

The substance of the whole transaction here is this: That
the seed of promise in all the old covenants having now become a fully organized nation, and put in full possession of the

promised inheritance, Jehovah now enters into a covenant with David whereby the nation is organized as a typical kingdom, and the house of David appointed to reign through successive generations, as typical kings, until the great Antitype should come to reign over that universal spiritual commonwealth of which the kingdom of Israel is the type. This becomes, therefore, a new and additional development of the relations and office of the promised Deliverer to the faith of the church. Before, he has been revealed, in every age, as her Prophet, to reveal the will of God. Thus was he revealed in all the Theophanies of the Patriarchal era, in the Sinai revelations, and in the oracles of the Theocratic era. Before, he has been revealed, in every age, as her Priest. So he was revealed in all the varieties of the ritual of atonement by sacrifice. Now he is revealed also as her King, to rule his chosen people and conquer all enemies. And henceforth, while faith contemplates him none the less as Prophet and Priest, it contemplates him chiefly as coming in his Kingly office to gather out of all nations and all ages a great spiritual kingdom as the result of his prophetic and priestly work.

With this view of the revelation by Nathan and the covenant with David kept distinctly in mind, as you read the subsequent portions of the Old Testament, and even the New, you will find much of the obscurity removed which may have heretofore invested them.

Thus for instance, the numerous Psalms relating to the king and the eternal throne which otherwise are full of dark sayings, often made still darker by the theories of the critics for interpreting them in a " double sense," or for determining whether they are " Messianic Psalms," all now become simple and easy of comprehension, as the utterances of faith founded upon the covenant, organizing Israel as a type of the spiritual kingdom, and setting up David and his royal line as the type of the Great King to arise out of his line. `Indeed it will be found that this covenant seems to modify all the forms of speech concerning the Deliverer to come. And thereby the intelligent Christian may, without any special knowledge of Biblical literature, determine in many cases whether a psalm was composed anterior to this covenant with David or subsequent to it, by its very style of thought and expression concerning the coming of Christ. If before, the forms of expression correspond to the language of the ancient Saints, anterior to David : and if after this, a new style of language and thought is employed almost as distinct from the former as is the language and thought of the gospel of Matthew from that of Malachi or Isaiah.

This explains, too, the purpose and application of all those Psalms relating to the King who is to rule in righteousness, and the reason of that apparent confusion of time in which the references to the period of his reign is at first sight involved—seeming to shade off insensibly from the temporal into the eternal, and from the finite into the infinite. Just as the Lamb of the sacrifice ever and anon assumes the spiritual significancy of the Lamb of God slain from the foundation of the world : just as the mercy seat and the Cherubim and the brightness become the throne of Jehovah, with the living creatures, and Jehovah high and lifted up ; so, continually, David and the kings of his line merge ever, in the songs of praise and in the visions of the Prophets, henceforth, into the King whose " name shall endure as long as the sun, and his dominion from sea to sea."

Here is the explanation of what has, no doubt, often puzzled many of you : namely, how to separate in idea what seems to be said of David, in such Psalms as the twenty-second, and of Solomon in such Psalms as the twenty-first, forty-fifth, and seventy-second, from what is meant to be said concerning Messiah.

The difficulty of conceiving how David or Solomon, in any

given case, is a type of Christ is removed by calling to mind that, by this great covenant with David, he and the kings of his line are constituted types of the spiritual king, as Israel, ruled by Jehovah visibly present, is a type of the eternal spiritual commonwealth.

The right comprehension of this covenant with David explains to us also the importance of Solomon and the prominent place given him in the Old Testament. The question occurs to one reading the story of Solomon—How comes it that he should stand typically to represent Christ? True he was very wise and learned; but he was also very foolish and licentious. True he was inspired to write a portion of the scriptures: but so were others far less eminent than he; and even Balaam was inspired to utter one of the most glorious of all the Old Testament prophecies. True, he was the builder of the Temple which David proposed to build, and the splendor and magnificence of his public works mark his reign as the Augustan age of Israel: but David had gathered for him, by his toils and conquests, the wealth which he lavished, and David had organized anew the magnificent Temple service, all ready to be set in motion with the new Temple. True, his reign was a reign of peace, and filled the earth with the fame of the great monarch. But it was David whose statesmanship had re-organized the kingdom and appointed the whole system of administration. So far from being the greatest constitutional king of Israel, considered simply as a statesman, and politically speaking, Solomon was probably the worst of all the bad kings of David's line. He subverted the liberties of the people, and left the government ready to drop to pieces in the hands of his imbecile son. And yet great prominence is given to Solomon and his works as a marked era in the history of Redemption.

It was simply this covenant with David that gave Solomon his prominence as the executor of Jehovah's purpose revealed to David, for the remoulding of the national system into a type of that spiritual kingdom over which David's son shall reign.   Only as he stood first in the line of promise according to the covenant with David and as an inspired writer, did he differ from any of the kings who succeeded him.

You will observe that from this time forward the chief purpose of the prophetic teachings and revelations is to develop the nature, the functions and the destiny of this peculiar typical kingdom, organized by the covenant with David, under the administration of the great Founder and King typified in David's royal line.   The key note to which the harp of prophecy is attuned henceforth is " *Thy throne, Oh God, is forever and ever, a sceptre* of righteousness is the *sceptre* of thy *kingdom.*"   The fundamental form of the Church's theology is moulded in this promise of a coming King to administer a universal kingdom.   The Church gospel becomes a proclamation, as in Isaiah, " I will make an everlasting covenant with you according to the sure mercies of David."   As this conception of a spiritual kingdom to come is that with which the series of Old Testament revelations closes, so it is that with which the New Testament opens. Jesus has come to sit upon the throne of his father David, is the grand annunciation at the incarnation of the Son of God.

" The kingdom of heaven is at hand " is the first New Testament preaching.   This kingdom according to the covenant with David, as the kingdom of heaven and kingdom of God, was the grand subject of the preaching of Jesus during his personal ministry.   It furnished the charge, upon which he was tried and condemned, that he made himself a king.   He denied not the accusation, but said " my kingdom is not of this world."   It was this truth of his Kingship that, so far as his death was a martyrdom, he died to attest.   Nay, his enemies sarcastically poured contempt upon him by placarding it upon his cross " This is the king of the Jews."   The grand fact first proclaimed by the Apostles after his ascension and the outpouring of the spirit was, " Him hath God exalted to be a *Prince* and a Saviour." The last vision of him by mortal eye is as the " Lamb in the midst of the throne." And the last gospel that closes up revelation, comes from Jesus as " the root and the offspring of David."

In these days of very loose notions of the Church, and of its nature as a distinct spiritual government, the important fact seems to be too commonly overlooked that the doctrine of Jesus as a King, and the Founder of a government, constitutes the last and highest development of the mediatorship of Messiah, and the chief burden of all the prophets concerning him from the time of the covenant with David forward.

And while the modern theology seems to give a secondary place to the doctrine of the kingship of Christ, and the corelative doctrine of the Church as his separate and distinct spiritual kingdom on earth, the scriptures, on the contrary, give to the Kingship of Christ a prominence greater, even, than to his office as Prophet and Priest of the Church. In fact, in the scriptures, Jesus Christ is exhibited as the Prophet who reveals all and the Priest who redeems all, in order that he may be the King that rules all. So far from being a mere incident of the gospel plan, or a mere deduction from its theology that there should be such an institution as the Church for the benefit of believers, it is an essential feature of the scheme, to the development of which a whole era of revelation from David to Christ was devoted. So far from coming merely as a Socrates or Plato, to teach a doctrine which naturally leads its disciples to band themselves together for mutual benefit, Jesus Christ came as a Divine Solon, also to be a lawgiver and the founder of a government on the earth. The governmental element in this gospel scheme is fundamental in it, and was as carefully developed as its theology of atonement. Not more elaborately did Jehovah institute types and symbols in the successive covenants with Adam and Noah and Abraham and Israel, under Moses, to set forth to the view of faith the great truths of vicarious atonement for sin, of a peculiar people to be gathered for himself out of the fallen race, and of a regeneration of the nature; than did he institute special types and symbols in his great covenant with David, to teach that this people should constitute a peculiar spiritual commonwealth, with constitution, laws and ordinances, presided over directly by the Mediatorial King.

This view of the matter not only explains to us the position of David, as a great representative man like Adam, Noah, Moses and Abraham, in the history of redemption, but explains to us also why this aspect of the gospel blessing as an organized government, should be the prominent aspect of it at the opening of the New Testament; and why in the preaching of John Baptist, and Jesus, and in the current thought and speech of the people, the gospel blessings, in fulfilment of all the old covenants, should be spoken of as "the kingdom of heaven." The reason is that this had been the last and highest development of the covenant of grace up to that time. Relatively to the ancient covenants with Adam, Noah and Israel under Moses, this covenant with David and the prophetic teachings, which developed it constituted, as we would say, the "New Testament" of the ancient Church down to the era of the Evangelists. And just as we, while accepting all the revelations concerning the Covenant of Grace, naturally conform our thought and speech concerning it to the style of the Apostles from whom we have the last and highest development of it; so the Church of the era of John Baptist and Jesus naturally conformed their thought and speech to that which was their New Testament or last development of it; namely, the covenant with David and the teaching of the prophets under it. And all of these specially aimed to exhibit the governmental element of the covenant of grace and the kingly office of Christ. And in addition to this, the covenant with David was, in fact, a great step preparatory to the Incarnation, and the change of the Church of one nation into the Church of all nations. Nay, paradoxical as it may seem, the very overthrow of the typical nation and the typical line of David, by the power of heathen conquerors, was itself a grand essential preparation for this actual setting up of the purely spiritual commonwealth which should cast its lines across all nations and kindreds and tongues ; and the near approach of such a consummation necessarily gave prominence to that special phase of the gospel system. So that both the burden of the scriptures which stood to them as their New Testament, and the sayings of the times, continued to make "the kingdom of heaven" the uppermost thought when the gospel promises were the subject of consideration by the people. And, adapting his teaching to the wants of the time, Jesus, in all his discourses, his parables and private conversations, dwelt continually upon the theme of " kingdom of heaven " and the " kingdom of God."

Many and various practical lessons are suggested from this view of the prominence of David, and the special constitution of David and his kingdom as the type of the gospel kingdom— two or three of which, only, I have space left to notice.

In the first place, it is manifest that all those views of religion are very defective which ignore the churchly and governmental aspect of the gospel system ; and which seem to regard nothing else essential in the gospel than certain fundamental truths of theology and ethical precepts. Whereas the entire purport and scope of the last and highest developments of the covenant of grace, is to the effect that the man who truly exercises faith in Christ is thereby born into a community and made a citizen of the great spiritual commonwealth of Jesus Christ the King. And to ignore this feature of the gospel is practically to ignore not merely certain texts of scripture but whole sections of the scriptures. True, indeed, an unspiritual Formalism has perverted these teachings, and magnified the Church above all that is called gospel. But the same unspiritual Formalism has utterly perverted also the great doctrines of Atonement, justification by faith, and regeneration of the soul. And the perversions of the truth in the one case, no more than in the other, can constitute any apology for undervaluing or ignoring the truths which Christ has made fundamental. The No-churchism which recognizes no Divinely appointed Church government with its laws and ordinances, is scarcely less fatal to the truth of Christ, than the High-churchism which makes the authority of the Church, and obedience to the Church, the sum and substance of Christian faith and practice. While it is schismatical and sinful to stickle for the incidentals of the Church to the breach of Christian unity, it is none the less inconsistent with true and enlightened gospel faith to treat with latitudinarian contempt, as trifles, that which Christ hath ordained as part of the order of his spiritual kingdom.

In the second place, it is equally manifest that this great spiritual commonwealth which is the last and highest development of the covenant of grace; for the exposition of which, to the faith of the people, the kingdom of David was constituted a type, and which Jesus came to consummate; is a "kingdom not of this world;" nor is it capable of being blended with the kingdoms of this world; nor can its agencies and ordinances be properly used for the ends and objects of the kingdoms of this world; nor are its limits to be set in accordance with the limits of the kingdoms of this world: nor should its unity be marred by the strifes of the kingdoms of this world. Its powers are altogether distinct from those powers with which God, the Creator, hath invested the rulers of the world-kingdoms and commonwealths, however, in some incidents, they may have similar aims and ends. It is of the essential nature of this spiritual commonwealth, in which the Son of David reigns, that it recognizes no distinction of "Jew or Greek, Barbarian, Scythian, bond nor free," that it have no respect to civil and political divisions of human society; and that it allow no political strifes to mar its essential unity.

In the third place, it is manifest that every true believer in Jesus Christ is brought by his conversion, not only to new views of truth and a new practice of ethics, but unto new spiritual relations as a fellow-citizen with the saints.

And while he still owes the same duties of allegiance and obedience which he owed before as a citizen of this or that nation; and all the same duties as a man, to his fellow-citizens; he has assumed new relations, and become a citizen of a "better kingdom, even a heavenly;" he owes allegiance to Jesus Christ its head; and duties to his fellow-citizens, the saints which, though they are not to be enforced with pains and penalties, are none the less sacred and binding on the conscience. Nor is it treason any the less base to conspire with, "aid and abet" the king's enemies, when it is the spiritual, than when it is the secular ruler. Nor is it dishonesty any the less to fail to discharge the duties one owes to his fellow-citizens of the heavenly, than of the earthly kingdom.

It is in this doctrine of a gospel kingdom—a fully organized spiritual government, of which believers are citizens,—and not in the sense of any mere vague Platonic sentiment, that those constantly repeated injunctions of the gospel to "love one another" are founded. And every thing that tends to obscure this doctrine of the spiritual government, or misapply the holy agencies and ordinances to secular ends, tends in so far, precisely, to mar or destroy the holy communion of saints.

The Apostles Paul and Peter, and John utter no mere

common-places of sentiment, when they declare " Love that worketh no ill to his neighbour is the fulfilling of the law;" that we should " above all things have fervent charity among ourselves, for charity shall cover a multitude of sins :" and that the sum of all the message from God is that " he who loveth God shall love his neighbour also"—yea, " that we ought to lay down our lives for the brethren."

These exhortations are to a great fundamental Christian duty whose ground lies in the very nature of the gospel scheme of salvation, as organizing a community, a new social relation—a kingdom of which David's kingdom was set to be the type.

In the fourth place, you will perceive that the view here presented of the kingdom and Church of Jesus Christ as fundamental, and so important as to form the grand point to be developed in the last and most advanced of the series of Old Testament covenants, has a very important application to the peculiar tendency of our times in the direction of an organized and combined evangelical effort which ignores the churchly idea of the gospel, and proposes, by mere human wisdom, to contrive agencies for doing the gospel work of the Church. For manifestly this theory of Christian action involves more than any mere inexpediency. However unconsciously the error may be entertained, the theory involves fundamental error in theology. It ignores, as of no consequence, a great principle of the scheme of redemption, to the development of which an entire series of its revelations was devoted through a thousand years of its history; a principle which gave its peculiar phase to the teachings of Jesus. It implies an error, in regard to the Kingly office of Christ, analogous to that of all the ethical gospels in regard to his Priestly office ; and to that of the Rationalists in regard to his Prophetic office. It is founded upon the seeming assumption that, in regard to that phase of the gospel which implies a Church divinely founded and entrusted with the gospel agencies, it is a failure. Independent of the arrogant claim to substitute humanly devised gospel agents and agencies for those which Christ appointed ; independent of the claim to do by the popular suffrage of Christians what Popes and councils may not do in the spiritual kingdom ; independent of the impolicy of giving colour to the popular infidel cry—" the Church is a failure ;" independent of aiding Rationalism to subvert the gospel, by thus sundering what God hath joined together—the gospel truth, from the Church of the living God, the " pillar and ground of the truth ;" this tendency to human contrivings for carrying on the gospel work grows out of a fundamental and dangerous error of theology.

The doctrine of Christ our Priest is indeed the directly vital truth of our subjective theology ; and the doctrine of Christ our Prophet the directly vital truth of our objective theology.   But neither of these can be properly expounded, nor long maintained in their purity, if we ignore the doctrine of Christ our **King, and the Church his " kingdom not of this world."**

DISCOURSE VIII.

THE GOSPEL OF THE KINGDOM IN CONFLICT WITH AN APOSTATE CHURCH : AND WITH DESPONDING FAITH.

I KINGS xviii. 17–20, AND xix 1–4, 8, 12–14.—And it came to pass, when Ahab saw Elijah, that Ahab said unto him, Art thou he that troubleth Israel ? And he answered, I have not troubled Israel ; but thou, and thy fathers' house, in that ye have forsaken the commandments of the Lord and thou hast followed Baalim. Now therefore send, and gather to me all Israel unto Mount Carmel, and the prophets of Baal four hundred and fifty, &c.

And Elijah came unto all the people, and said, How long halt ye between two opinions, if the Lord be God follow him : but if Baal, then follow him. And the people answered him not a word, &c.

And Ahab told Jezebel all that Elijah had done, and withal how he had slain all the prophets with the sword. Then Jezebel sent a messenger unto Elijah, saying, so let the Gods do to me, and more also if I make not thy life as the life of one of them   *   *   *

And he arose and went for his life * * * And came and sat down under a juniper tree : and he requested for himself that he might die.

And he arose, and did eat and drink, and went in the strength of that meat forty days and forty nights unto Horeb, the Mount of God.

And behold the Lord passed by and a great and strong wind rent the mountains, and brake in pieces the rocks before the Lord ; but the Lord was not in the wind ; and after the wind an earthquake ; but the Lord was not in the earthquake ; and after the earthquake a fire ; but the Lord was not in the fire ; and after the fire a still small voice. And it was so, when Elijah heard it, that he wrapped his face in his mantle and went out, and stood at the entering in of the cave, and behold there came a voice unto him, and said, what doest thou here, Elijah ? And he said I have been very jealous for the Lord God of hosts : because the children of Israel have forsaken thy covenant, thrown down thy altars and slain thy prophets with the sword ; and I, even I only, am left, and they seek my life to take it away.

PART I.—THE GOSPEL OF THE KINGDOM IN CONFLICT WITH
AN APOSTATE CHURCH.

IT is not yet quite a century since the modification of the
commonwealth of Israel, under the covenant with David, was
completed. Four hundred and thirty years from the covenant with Abraham, and four hundred and thirty more from
the constitutions of Moses was that kingdom in building;
and yet within thirty years, after the completion of the modifications under Solomon, which set it forth as the typical
kingdom, it had fallen asunder in the unskillful hands of
Solomon's imbecile son.

The sad tale of the northern kingdom, from its separation,
is soon told. Wily Jeroboam, a refugee in Egypt, raised up
of God to be the scourge of the follies of Solomon, no sooner
found himself monarch of Northern Israel than, like many a
Royal " *Defender of the faith*," after him, he must take in
hand the religion of his subjects; and, tampering with God's
ordinances, modify them to suit his political interests. Fearful of the influence of the Temple at Jerusalem, if the people
continued to go up thither three times a year, and forgetting
to trust Jehovah, who had given him the throne, he proceeded
to set up a more convenient worship at Bethel and at Dan
within his own limits. And to make it attractive he modified
the *form* of worshipping Jehovah after the fashion of the
" advanced thought " and refined civilization of Egypt;
representing him by the Egyptian symbols of Apis—the
golden calves. But to conform sufficiently with the current
worship to ease the public conscience, he appointed holy
times, as well as holy places, different from those at Jerusalem. He set up high places of worship, in Samaria and elsewhere, as rivals of the temple at Jerusalem. He organized
a priesthood, also, for the new religion, selecting for the
office " the lowest of the people : " for such would give him

least trouble with their scruples, and would be bound to him by all the obligations of official creatures to their creator; so that he might rely securely upon their sycophancy, subserviency and loyalty to himself.

"What odds about the *form* of worship, if still we worship in substance the true God?" would Jeroboam argue against the scrupulous old Covenanters who stickled for the covenants of Abraham, Moses and David. "Why trouble ye the peace of the nation, when the government, reverencing religion as essential to virtue, and virtue to liberty, and, therefore, as in duty bound, aiming to promote religion—presents it in convenient reach of the people, and clothed in those decent and attractive forms which befit an advanced era of civilization? As to going up to Jerusalem three times a year—everybody knows that the worship at Jerusalem is a novelty of the David family, and that our venerated fathers worshipped, not at Jerusalem, but at Shiloh, and elsewhere, within the present limits of northern Israel. And as to these scruples about *changing* the *time* of the feast, what sane man can think it of importance enough to scruple about, whether a feast be in the seventh month, or the eighth month? True a prophet of Jehovah denounced Jeroboam and his altar, rending it with a word, and scattering the ashes: and palsied the arm of the king, fiercely thrust forth to seize him; but did he not restore the arm again at the king's request? and did not the impertinent prophet meet with bad luck on his way home—a lion seizing upon him and slaying him?"

And, reasoning after the manner of the modern no-churchism, that takes the Bible only for substance of doctrine, and claims that Jehovah's appointment of ordinances and times of worship—the priesthood of worship and the ritual of worship—is no bar to any little modifications that may make our worship more attractive and impressive—it is difficult to gainsay Jeroboam's argument. But, whether difficult or not, Jeroboam had the semi-infidel mob as the tribunal of judgment, and the power of the sword at his back to enforce his logic ; no marvel, therefore, if the scrupulous old Covenanters were triumphantly silenced.

In accordance with the uniform experience of all ages, the divine appointments once set aside, the Church, left without chart or compass, drifts further and still further from the truth toward utter apostasy. The modification of the forms of worshipping the true Jehovah by Jeroboam within less than a century, has led, under Ahab, to the worship of a false God, and the substitution of Baal for Jehovah. Ahab, seeking to advance himself by high political and commercial connections, has allied himself with the powerful house of Ethbaal, at once king of Sidon and high priest of Astarte, the supplanter and murderer of Phelles his predecessor. And now Jezebel, cousin german of the murderer Pygmalion, and of the Dido of Virgil's story, with all the stern, fierce fanaticism of her blood, rules over both Ahab and his kingdom of Israel. All the malignant energies of her nature have concentrated themselves in the purpose to blot out the very memory of Jehovah from her new dominions.

The splendid ritual of Baal, enforced by the example and patronage of her court—made fascinating to the mob by every trapping of magnificence—performed by a priesthood whose influence is unbounded—backed by all the despotic power of the fashion of Tyre and Sidon—the Paris of that civilization—has at last triumphed everywhere.

But suddenly Ahab is startled, in his capital, by an apparition. It is a singular, rough, unknown man from far across the Jordan, who, denouncing his corruptions of religion, abruptly swears, " there shall be neither rain nor dew for these three years, but according to my word." The prophet passes on before the incredulous king has seen the prophecy verified by time ; and, when the judgment begins to bear heavily, it is easy enough for Jezebel's court demagogues to persuade the poor people that their suffering all comes from the malignant old prophet; and thereby to embitter them all the more against Elijah and the prophets of Jehovah, as troublers of Israel. Of course the apostasy to 'Baal rapidly progresses. The rainless three years and a half, which smote the hills and valleys as with fire : the sky all as brass over their heads —the atmosphere a suffocating winding sheet, within whose folds life must gradually die out, is but too expressive a symbol of the spiritual drought and famine that has fallen upon the Church of God in Northern Israel.

But suddenly a strange rumour spreads among the suffering people. Nothing less than that the old prophet has dared to return from his exile : nay more, has dared to meet Ahab face to face : nay more, has challenged the whole priesthood of Baal to a contest before all the people on Mount Carmel ! And immediately the whole country is full of excitement. All sorts of people, for all sorts of reasons, resolve to be present ; and, in obedience to the summons of the king, immense multitudes throng the sides and summit of Carmel. The king and court, and the Baal priests, with all imaginable pomp and splendor, come to witness the final triumph of Jezebel's religion. And now Mount Carmel seems one immense living pile.

It is precisely the fit stage for such a drama. From its summit, as they look westward and northward, they see the Mediterranean dotted with the merchant ships of Tyre and Sidon, outward or inward bound, with the riches of the world; and Tyre and Sidon in all their glory—the grand strongholds of Baal. As they look eastward and southward, yonder may be descried, far off, the Sea of Gallilee gleaming in the morning sun ; and as the eye sweeps round to the southward, the plain of Jezreel, and Mount Tabor shooting up out of it ; and, southward still, Ramoth-Gilead and Mount Ebal and

Gerizim and Shechem, and Shiloh, and a hundred mountain tops and villages, around which hang a thousand hallowed associations and memories of the marvellous power and loving kindness of Jehovah to their fathers. Thus they stand as with two immense maps unrolled at their feet; on the one side the map of the kingdom of Baal, on the other side, of the kingdom of Jehovah.

Thus assembled—all curiosity and excitement—waiting impatiently the opening of the contest, and wondering what method the strange, bold prophet will adopt; till at length the old man attracts all eyes as, with his servant aiding him, and exhausted with the long ascent, he is seen threading his way up through the vast crowd. Curiosity is now at the highest pitch. What will he say or do? How will he bring on the conflict? Will he address himself to the king and court in the same bold style as before? So some anticipate; and they tremble for his safety; for the popular feeling is high, and at a word Ahab can turn upon him ten thousand human wild beasts. Or will he attack the priests of Baal, and demand of them the proof of the existence of their God, and, on the other hand, himself make a mighty argument for Jehovah? So others anticipate, and they are resolving to hear candidly, weigh the argument, and decide according to its merits. So man reasons; but the foolishness of God is wiser than men. Of what use to appeal to Ahab with argument and eloquence? Poor, cowardly, subservient tool of Jezebel, who dare not have an opinion of his own, save as she please? Of what use to argue with these Baal priests, bought up, by the dainties of Jezebel's kitchen, to work all manner of infamous imposture? Of what use to reason about and demonstrate the doctrines of Jehovah to these crowds of apostate Israel? Reasoning never demonstrated them into the belief of the Baal doctrines, and how shall reasoning demonstrate them out of it? Their darkness is not from want of light, want of proof, want of argument, but, simply, from want of conscience, and want of heart for Jehovah's service; and from dalliance with the absurd idea that they may somehow, for expediency's and popularity's sake, conform to the court religion without renouncing and dishonouring Jehovah.

Therefore, casting aside all these vain side issues and logical trifles, as he stands forth and the vast concourse is hushed into silence, the old prophet brings them squarely to the issue, with a single sentence whose tones thrill them as though Carmel shook under their feet, "*How long halt ye between two opinions?   If Jehovah be God follow him, but if Baal, then follow him.*"

"And the people answered him not a word." The single sentence is a shot point blank to the heart. Carried to its mark by the Spirit of God, the shaft quivers in ten thousand consciences—Baal is already defeated. All that follows of the proposed test and the altar, and the fire from heaven, are but the successive steps of the victor pursuing his vanquished and demoralized foe.

My brethren, forget not, as we pass along, that this scene on Mount Carmel is not merely historical of things that *were*. It is a grand representative picture of things that *are*, where-ever the gospel is preached. This congregation on Carmel is a representative congregation; and seldom does a sabbath congregation gather in the land, that, if analyzed, will not be found to consist of the same four classes of men as this on Mount Carmel. First, a very small minority, more or less bold to confess it, decided for Jehovah. Second, a larger minority thoroughly decided for Baal. Third, a much larger minority than either that do not know whether Jehovah is God or not. Fourth, the majority of all who do not *care* whether Jehovah be God or not. Allow me for a moment to imitate the man of God, and, casting aside all other issues, simply press home upon you the absurdity of this hesitancy and compromising in the great question of religion. For, in a very brief exposition of the case, I can show you that, of all conceivable positions and theories in reference to the gospel religion, this halting, hesitating, trimming between two, is the most irrational and absurd. Select, if you please your own ground on which to stand ; I care not ; for on any ground this halting is absurd.

Do you stand on the extreme verge of unbelief—not yet satisfied of the reality of Jehovah's existence ?—or of the immortal retributions of which his gospel warns ?—nay, rather disposed to think it all a delusion of priestcraft? Then to you, of all men living, comes home this question, " How long halt ye ?" For, of all men living, you have the least time to waste in hesitancy and debate and speculations of religion! If there be no life of retribution after this —no heaven—no hell—if the life here is the all of your existence, and you a mere bubble, or fire-mist flitting for an hour under the morning sun, and then vanishing—then why waste its brief moments in worrying speculations, in imaginary fears, and fretting under the restraints of an imaginary conscience ? Hurry, ye miserable wretches of a day, to eat and drink, for to-morrow you die ; you have no time to lose ! If Baal be God—if this world is the all of you, and its God the only God—then follow him fully while you may! Haste, to fill up your hours with all the pleasures you are capable of enjoying! Give loose rein to your animal appetites—wreak your little brutish malignities ! Why, your fellow brutes around you are getting the start of you while you are halting, delaying and restraining yourself; and before you have your share of happiness you shall die and rot and be no more !

Do you stand, however, far within this outer circle of blank unbelief, and hold the existence of Jehovah and immortality and retribution, yet hesitate about important details of the doctrines of religion ? But if you believe in Jehovah, and in immortal retribution, that finishes the question so far as concerns you personally. For, whatever debatable grounds you may imagine to lie within the vast compass of that creed of two articles, there is really none, so far as concerns the main question. If Jehovah exists with the moral attributes you ascribe to him, then not to follow him, involves all of disaster that an immortal creature can fear. And in a few days, death may come and settle the question for you forever. While you are amusing yourself with dancing the theological slack rope, the day of the Lord is drawing very near. Life is half spent or more, and you have not yet determined the preliminary points of salvation ! At that rate of progress, when will you have reached the main questions ? And if you have even reached, how long must you be in deciding it ? Yet you halt, and move at your ease, or rather move not at all, though while you linger judgment lingers not, and while you slumber damnation slumbers not !

Do you stand on ground far within this, and believe, not only that Jehovah is, and is the rewarder of those who follow, and those who follow him not—but, also, that Jehovah hath spoken to men his will ? Yet you halt to settle your doubts about certain points of doctrine in that teaching ? Then, how *long* halt ye ? Either these points are essential to your salvation or they are not. Take either horn of the dilemma. If they are fundamental, and must be solved before you can follow Jehovah, then how long halt ye ? After half a life time or more already spent with the fundamental preliminary questions all unsettled, can you afford to wait longer and be in doubt longer ? What if death come and surprise you before you have reached the great question to which these are preparatory ? Hasten, thou sluggard ! Arouse thee ! Say not, a little more sleep, a little more slumber ; when the sun of life is already in the meridian, or even already declining ;

or, though neither, may suddenly go down before the noon! And your day's work is not yet fairly begun! Nay, the day's work of yesterday, and many days past, lying undone!

Or will you take the other horn of the dilemma, and say these points about which you halt are not fundamental? Then, still greater the folly of halting upon these merely speculative points, while, meantime, the great question of life is yet untouched!

Thus it may be shown of every variety of religious sentiment, short of actual faith and following Jehovah, that this halting on this subject is the most irrational of all positions. If there be a Jehovah, follow him! It is the only consistent course. If there be a heaven, then the fact is infinite in importance and not to be debated as against any other fact. Resolve to win its glories! If there be a hell, then, in the nature of the case, there can be no other wise course than to resolve at once to shun its darkness and chains; its "weeping and wailing and gnashing of teeth." The undecided, halting soul finds no countenance in heaven, earth, or hell! From all comes the demand, decide! If Jehovah be God, follow him! If Baal, follow him. If reason be God, follow reason! and be guided by its dictates! If Bacchus, with his riot and revelry, be God, then follow Bacchus. If Venus, with her sensual charms, then follow her. If Mammon, with his clinking chest, then follow Mammon! Let the soul of man follow, and fully enter into communion with its God!

I may be addressing some more earnest spirit who feels that the cause of his hesitancy has not yet been touched. For he not only believes that Jehovah exists and hath spoken, but receives as truth all that he has spoken; and desires in his heart to follow him. Yet he is restrained by consciousness of unworthiness to be called one of Jehovah's people;

doubts whether he exercises the faith that is unto salvation ; fears his inability to walk worthy of so high a vocation, and for these, or similar reasons, still halts, when the call is, " Come, confess, and follow Jehovah." Yet to all such, the question of Mount Carmel comes home in all its force—" How long halt ye ?" This question is not one of ethical worthiness or fitness, it is a question of *salvation*, from a state of ruin supposed to be consciously felt. It is not a question of how much you can do, or have done to entitle you to accept Jehovah's offer to redeem you ! but simply, are you willing to let Jehovah do it for you ? It is not even a question of how much faith, or how strong faith, but simply whether you have a willing heart, and can say, " Lord, I believe, help thou mine unbelief." Therefore, there is no place for hesitancy or debate on a question whether your sinking soul shall seize hold of the arm reached forth, mighty to save,—whether your famishing soul will take the water of life freely. Halt not ! Hesitate not ! Venture on him, and, looking to him for light, for strength, for grace, for every thing, just " follow him."

But we recur again to these proceedings on Mount Carmel. " I only remain a prophet of Jehovah," continues the old man, " but Baal's prophets are four hundred and fifty men." It is the language of courage, and yet the language somewhat of modesty and sadness, under the consciousness that a man must seem to be not only in the wrong, but also self-opinionated and wise in his own conceit, who stands thus in antagonism to the current sentiment of his age. There is no wider mistake, in judging of men, than the popular judgment that these Elijahs, who brave the popular opinion, and defy the ridicule, the threats, the malignant speeches of a world in arms, must be men of great self-conceit. On the contrary, they are generally modest men, self-distrustful by nature. And, though as witnesses for the truth of Jehovah, they press forward, utterly heedless of the thick flying shafts of malice and defamation, and seem to be *iron-clad* men; yet their boldness grows out of their clear convictions of truth and their implicit reliance on the power of Jehovah to protect his truth. In all else these iron-clad Elijahs are men of like passions with other men; and in hours of darkness and despondency are assailed many a time by the doubt—"May not I be wrong, seeing that I only think thus and all the world think differently."

In this respect Elijah stands as representative of the true children of God in the midst of every crooked and perverse generation. And every believing soul has this experience— For think not that it belittles and degrades this majestic scene to say that, in principle, it represents the struggle in the soul of this humble man or woman, this Christian boy or girl, when the question is made of duty to obey what Jehovah says, and what this Baal-god public opinion says. Then comes in this overpowering sense of being in a minority of one, or two, or three, against the multitudes that do evil. Can I be right? Is it modest? Is it humble as becomes a Christian? for me to set up my convictions, against the judgment of so many, even of reputable Christian men and women who conform here to the court fashions of religion? This boy, with impulses strongly set to follow Jehovah fully, as he comes first in contact with the Baal maxims of the streets, of the shop, of the counting-room; this young Christian girl, with heart all aglow with her first love of Jehovah, when called upon to come down from the strict law of Jehovah—"Be not conformed to the world, but be ye transformed" to the indulgences of worldly pleasures and fashions; have the same struggle to make. Nor smile, my brethren, at the little things to which I bring down the application of Elijah's case. Remember, Jesus made this boy's and girl's case of importance enough to denounce a special woe against " whosoever shall offend one of these little ones." Neither is it any fanciful or defamatory analogy, which makes these Baal conformists in Carmel representative of the popular theology and ethics which passes under the name of Christianity with large classes of our nominally Christian communities. It is simply because our modes of religious thought now, differ from theirs on Carmel, who gave visible form and local habitation to their gods or dominant ideas, that we do not see Baal gods in just as numerous array in New York and London and in a thousand other cities, as in Tyre and Sidon of old. And the conflict is, in principle, just the same as Elijah's, when in a thousand forms of business or pleasure the earnest Christian conscience finds " I, even I only," regard this usage of trade contrary to the ethics of Jehovah, but here are four hundred and fifty of the most reputable men of trade who conform to it ! " I, even I only," regard this custom of society, or this maxim, or this indulgence as contrary to the letter and spirit of the gospel ; but here are Christian families of good report who conform ; yea, and four hundred and fifty prophets, that seem to stand high as religious teachers, who expressly justify it, or by their silence connive at it ! Is it modest in me to object ? Nay, may I not seem self-righteous ? Now, the only safeguard against temptation, here, is clear conviction of the truth and the ever present consciousness that, if right, then " they that be with us are more than they that be with them."

Let each party " *lay a sacrifice on wood, and put no fire under*," continues the prophet of Jehovah. It is no random choice of a test ; but precisely, the test to recall to these apostate Israelites the glorious truths of the past. " The God that answereth by fire, let him be God." It was the ancient and venerable sign of Jehovah's presence to accept the true worship of his saints. So had he accepted Abel's sacrifice, so had he appeared to Abraham in his offering. So had he shot forth the fire, from his throne on the Ark of the covenant, to consume the first sacrifice at the dedication of the tabernacle ; and again at the dedication of the temple. While, therefore, the prophet seeks a sign, he will have a sign which shall hold forth the truth of God to the minds of the people as the instrument of converting them from their apostasy.

" *It is well spoken,* " is the first utterance of the people. The prophet's astonishing question, " How long halt ye ?" has wrought effectually ; and the proposition for an answer by fire, awakens truths long dormant in their memories. Baal's priests have lost their control over the popular impulses, and, however unwilling, they can but accept the challenge, or expose themselves to the popular contempt. All their skill in priestly jugglery, and theological pyrotechnics, shall avail them little now, under the gaze of ten thousand eyes. Yet, in their desperation they must make a show of contest, hoping perhaps, that Elijah may at least make a failure, and leave the question where it stood before. And now while they proceed with their frantic rites, with many a mysterious ceremonial, and robes flaunting as they shout—" O Baal ! Baal hear us," the old prophet's soul is moved with mingled shame and indignation, that the children of the covenant—divinely taught through Moses and Samuel and David—should have descended so low, that base jugglers could have the assurance gravely to perpetrate such foolery before them ! Till, no longer able to restrain his contempt, he begins, with terrible sarcasm and bitter irony, to affect sympathy with them and to advise them. " Louder ! Louder !" he cries, " your God has too much to occupy him, since adding Israel to his dominions ! He is probably absorbed in a council about the vast affairs of Tyre and Sidon ! Possibly he is off on a hunting expedition—or gone on a cruise with the fleet, or a tour of inspection ! May be, he has been taking a frolic ;

and is drunk, and asleep—Louder! therefore till you wake him and compel his attention !"

This is but one of several instances, as you may see in the Psalms and Isaiah, and the other prophets, wherein the inspired men have used irony and ridicule against false religionists. No doubt this speech of Elijah to the Baal prophets would grate harshly on the sensitive ear of many of our modern will-worshipers, and even many of our liberalists in religion who have no scruples in making Moses and David and Paul, and their adherents, the subject of their sarcasms, would affect to be shocked that a man of God should be found deriding these earnest Baal priests, who are so *sincerely* endeavouring to get the ear of their God !

Ridicule is not the test of truth, as claimed by the Deists of the last century : for a Sir Matthew Hale or a George Washington could be made ridiculous enough by means of a fool's-cap and harlequin's coat put upon them, as robes of office. But, while not the test of truth, ridicule is, in many cases, the only logical method which can be employed to check the progress and stay the influence of religious impostures. It is one of the adroitest of the wiles of Satan to array, in very sanctimonious dress, pious lies, and impostures so preposterous as to set all reason at defiance ; and when they are assailed with derision—as such follies can only be assailed— to make a terrible outcry at the impiety of our treating sacred things, and holy convictions with levity. And especially are the phases of religious imposture which favour stage effect, and gorgeous show, and theatrical cant in religious worship, terribly afraid of such argument as Elijah's. Now it is a folly, scarce less than equal to that of the Baal priests, to undertake to reason out of men's heads religious delusions which reason never put into them. When men put their religious theories out of the pale alike of reason and scripture ; or, in other words, ignore, in the high concern of religion, all

that intelligence which distinguishes the working of the
human mind from the mere instincts and impulses of the lower
creatures ; are we to allow them to deceive the ignorant and
the impulsive without restraint, merely because they assume
the airs of sanctity and devotion ?   Nature has provided no
other means of managing a donkey than the lash.   When
Baal priests have the assurance to practice their juggleries,
no matter how earnestly they leap upon the altar, and cut
themselves, and how earnestly they urge their vain repetitions, " O Baal, Baal ! hear us,"—there is no other method
than Elijah's left us.   When modern Baal priests would palm
upon the ignorant and foolish their legends of winking
Madonnas ; of houses of our Lady of Loretto, that fly through
the air ; or of the liquefaction of St. Januarius' blood ; when
Mormon prophets come with their legends of an appendix to
inspiration dug out of a hill ; when self-styled spiritualists,
with messages from the other world, uttered through such
spiritual channel as bed-post, table-leg or bell-wire, by spirits
whose natures, if their prophets are to be believed, have
grown only the more senseless, earthly, sensual and devilish
from ceasing to tabernacle in the flesh ;—and attempt to
invest these fooleries with an air of extra sanctity and sentiment
—what is left for the prophets of Jehovah but to lay on the
lash of ridicule till the imposture is scouted by the people
whom it attempted to deceive ?   The current clamour of
impostors,—" We are ridiculed not answered "—is simply
another trick of imposture.   For, it depends entirely on the
nature of the case whether ridicule is not the only sensible
answer.   Such is the propensity of fallen humanity to
religious delusion, that he who should found a religion on
the denial that three times four is twelve, would, with plausibility and assurance enough, gain adherents.   But who could
answer the argument for such a creed ?   Not all the Arith-
meticians in America.   If men will ignore their own under-

standings, and put their religious imposture beyond the reach
of argument and proof, then the prophet of the truth must
needs crack his whip to keep the imposture in its place ; or lay
on the lash if it endangers the public safety.

While thus disgusted and wearied, the hour of evening sacrifice draws on.   And, for the same reason that he selected
the answer by fire as the test sign, the man of God now proceeds upon the principle of so working wonders, as most
effectually to impress the revealed truth of God.   "Come
away from the impostors and their disgusting jugglery," is
his command to the now wearied and disgusted people.   And
taking the twelve stones of an old altar, which must recall to
their memory the former days of the unity of the twelve
tribes, when Jehovah gave them their ordinances, he prepares
the sacrifice in a manner to exclude all possibility of suspicion
that any earthly fire was hidden there.   Then at the moment
for the evening sacrifice,—as another in the series of spiritual
mnemonics, whereby the old truths of the gospel of their
fathers shall be recalled to them—the man of God bows and
prays.   No pomp—no theatrical pageant—yet what holy awe
thrills the heart of the mighty congregation, as word after
word of the simple prayer conveys its volume of suggestive
thought!—"Jehovah, God of Abraham ; Isaac and Israel:
—Let it be known this day, that thou art God in Israel—
and that I am thy servant!"   He ceases.   The gleam, as of
a lightning flash from heaven, darts upon the altar pile : it
dazzles for a moment the myriad eyes that are fixed upon the
altar !   There is a hissing and crackling for a moment;—
the smoke as of a powder flash—and lo, sacrifice, wood, altar,
water vanish as an exhalation !

Awe struck, the astonished multitudes prostrate themselves
and with one voice, shout, as though Carmel itself had found
a voice of thunder in its depths, and a tongue to articulate
" Jehovah is God !   Jehovah is God !"   Baal's priests are

overwhelmed with confusion. Elijah, as directly commissioned to execute the law which both king and people had contemned, gives the order for their execution.

Remember, ye that now, fascinated by the seductions of the Baal god of this world, are striving to ease conscience, by professing reverence for Jehovah yet practically serving Baal; this part of the Carmel scene is also representative! Though the vast majority is with you now, yet the day of sorrow is fast approaching when you shall cry "O Baal! Baal! hear us," but there shall be no voice to answer, or power to save, from the doom of everlasting shame and contempt.

I must pass over the wonderful scene, of the prayer of faith, wrestling for the blessing seven times till the usual sign in nature appeared, in " the cloud big as a man's hand," For it would require a whole discourse to develop properly that wonderful illustration of the nature and power of prayer. I can only refer you to the key to the exposition of this whole matter of Elijah's sealing up the heavens, calling down the fire, and then the rain, given by the Apostle James; for the remarkable point made by the Apostle is that, in all these proceedings, it was not first by Divine revelation direct that Elijah either uttered the judgment of the drought in Samaria, or proposed the fire test in Carmel, or knew that the rain was at hand. He was, in all this, "a man of like passions with" the believers who pray for any special mercy. His spirit was moved to think he heard the sound of much rain, just as, sometimes, the hearts of God's children are moved to feel that the Lord will come, after three days, and revive them. The whole case is a literal illustration of what the Apostle Paul teaches us concerning prayer: namely, that we know not what to pray for, but the Spirit moving upon the soul, first inspires the desire and the petition: hence we receive the answer because God's Spirit moved us to ask. Men like Elijah get so near, and so familiar with

Jehovah, that, as affectionate children, they may sometimes presume, as it were, to say beforehand what the Father will do for his glory. And thus it appears that through all of these transactions Elijah's heart, moved by the Spirit, felt so sure of being sustained that he ventured to pronounce the judgment, propose the fire test and promise the speedy coming of the rain. And then he agonized in prayer that Jehovah would not suffer his own name or his prophet, to be dishonoured. Hence this teaching of the Apostle invests this story of Elijah with a new interest; by revealing to us the fact that the prophet was not simply working miracles, but, meanwhile, moving in a common sphere with all saints who pray.

The victory won, and all crowned with the blessing of the refreshing torrents, Elijah partakes in the general joy. As the glad thousands rush down Carmel shouting, Rain! Rain! and the trees of the forest, the birds—all nature sing, Rain! the prophet renews his youth. He desires to evince to the king, that the slaughter of his Baal prophets implies no hostile feeling to him: and if possible to win him over and strengthen him in the purpose of obedience, henceforth, to Jehovah, and the reform of religion. So, girding himself, when Ahab mounts his chariot to dash down to shelter himself from the rain in his palace at Jezreel, the prophet condescends, after the oriental fashion, to run before the chariot as *avant courier*. And, equally to the king's gratification and astonishment, the old prophet outstrips his fleet horses, in the race for the palace. There the man of God leaves him and retires to muse on the wonderful deeds and the loving kindness of Jehovah; full of hope doubtless, that the great work of restoration and revival, commencing with the court and the multitudes from Carmel, would spread, until Israel shall be redeemed from apostasy.

DISCOURSE VIII.

PART 2ND.

THE GOSPEL OF THE KINGDOM IN CONFLICT WITH DESPONDING FAITH.

"*And Ahab told Jezebel all that Elijah had done,*" *&c.* This brief summary, doubtless, covers scenes of tragic grandeur in the palace of Jezreel. We can readily imagine how, Elijah having left him, the king, rushes into the presence of his queen, who has, all day, eagerly awaited the issue of the singular gathering on Mount Carmel. Full of the excitement, he rapidly utters his report. "The old Tishbite has triumphed! He called down fire from heaven to consume his sacrifice! I saw it with my own eyes, and there was no room for deception. He has also called down this torrent of rain from heaven. The people, overwhelmed with astonishment and awe, fell on their faces and cried 'Jehovah is God!' Indeed the prophet left them no room for doubt. The multitude immediately became uncontrollable, save by Elijah. At his command, they seized upon the whole body of your prophets, and Kishon runs red with their blood. It will be, perhaps, safest to yield to the popular pressure. Elijah seems kindly enough disposed toward me. Strangely enough the old man has run, as the advance herald of my chariot, all the way from Carmel, keeping before my fleet horses at their best speed!"

But, as he thus rapidly runs over the story, suddenly, as if thunderstruck, his tongue palsies, his thoughts become confused, his mind wavers. At the mention of the slaughter of the priests, a death like pallor overspreads the queen's countenance for a moment—then a cloud of blackness gathers, and her eyes flash as the vivid lightning. At the suggestion of submission to the popular judgment, such a glance of ineffable contempt darts upon Ahab, that it transforms his very thoughts; and in a moment all appears to him in a new and opposite light. This is the Ahab, remember, whom the sacred history, in a single line, portrays, so expressively, as, " Ahab whom Jezebel his wife stirred up." And now the tempest waxes fierce, and the curses fall thick upon Elijah and his God. The very fires of hell have been kindled in her fanatical heart; and a famishing thirst for blood, in revenge for the blood of the priests of Baal. Rather would she the whole kingdom should have perished by the famine than have witnessed such a triumph for Jehovah. Nay the very thought of Elijah enjoying to-night, quietly, his proud triumph is to her insupportable; and that he shall quietly sleep upon it is perfectly maddening. In the eager impatience of her womanly desire for vengeance, she determines to spoil his feast, and send him a thorn for his pillow. And with genuine, womanly uncalculating passion, she hurries off a minister with the terrible message and oath, " So let the gods do to me, and more also, if I make not thy life as the life of one of them by to-morrow about this time." Of course, reasoning after the manner of men, this notice was the surest way to defeat her purpose! Yet how natural though paradoxical the picture!

As simply a specimen of human nature painting, there is nothing equal to the Jezebel of Scripture in all the circle of literature. The strokes of the pencil are indeed very few. It is an outline, with no filling up of the details, as in the tragic poets. Yet the student who will take the pains to gather from the record and study this outline, will find the Jezebel of Scripture stand out before him with more distinctness than the Medea of Euripides or the Lady Macbeth of

Shakespeare. The mere outline sets her forth with a power, and vividness, and a gigantic grandeur of wickedness, yet, witha', a naturalness that no human genius has ever equalled.

Meantime Elijah, in a glow of enthusiasm, is awaiting the result of the news at the palace. Who shall say what hopes begin to animate him, that the set time for the restoration of apostate Israel is now fully come? Ahab has evidently been deeply impressed and convinced if not converted. And why may not the indisputable proofs of the reality of Jehovah's power and presence which Ahab has carried to the palace affect the mind of Jezebel also, and break the spell of the Baal delusion? Nay, why may not the Lord use Jezebel herself as his instrument for turning the whole of her royal family, and Tyre and Sidon, to the true God? And, these turned, why may not all the surrounding nations be brought by so extraordinary a conversion to acknowledge Jehovah?

In the midst of some such dreams the messenger enters, announcing the terrible oath and the threat! And if it is a strange contradiction to send the message and thereby give him opportunity to escape, how much more strange the contradiction that the Elijah who has boldly faced alone the king and court, and the fickle, obsequious mob of Israel on Carmel, should now at the cursing of an angry woman, arise and run for his life? O ye who know something by experience, of the effect of high hopes suddenly blasted, and enthusiastic calculations suddenly upset by the stern logic of the realities of life as it is—ye may understand something of this strange inconsistency. It is one of the peculiar laws of the spiritual life, that when Jehovah has created in the soul some convictions of his purpose to bless, human nature at once begins to cover them all over with its self-created accretions, until the original divine creation can no longer be recognized. Then, when, in his all-wise providence, and in mercy to us, he comes to knock off these accretions from his own beautiful

creation in the soul, we at once conclude that Jehovah is
against us and hath changed from his purposes of mercy.
Jehovah has not told Elijah that Ahab and Israel, Jezebel
and Tyre and Sidon are to be converted to the truth; but
only that he will, for the present, withdraw his judgments and
send rain upon the famishing people. Reasoning from our
own tendencies to his, we infer that Elijah may probably
have become intoxicated with his success in the work of
reform, and in laying out plans by which Jehovah will proceed
with his work. And therefore, in the hour of disappointment
and temptation, his faith gives way. As if he now feared
that the malice of Jezebel could circumvent the very purposes
of Jehovah himself, behold this triumphant champion of the
faith on Carmel, now fleeing for his life! Yea, after crossing
the border into the southern kingdom—the dominions of pious
Jehoshaphat, where any prophet of God would be received
with honour—he dares not stop even there. Some spy of
Jezebel may follow him, and by some trick cause Jehoshaphat
to extradite him; and this is the more likely from the friendship that is growing up between Ahab and Jehoshaphat.
Onward, therefore, he rushes through the kingdom of Judah
to its extreme southern border on the desert. Nay even
there he fears he may not be secure; and leaving his servant,
proceeds still southward toward Sinai into the great desert
itself. For one whole day he pushes onward over the burning sands and under the burning sun, till nature is utterly
exhausted; and, says the record, " he came and sat down
under a juniper tree, and he requested for himself that he
might die; and said O, Lord God, it is enough; take away
my life, for I am no better than my fathers."

What is the matter with Elijah? What is the solution of
this paradox, that a man is running for his life and yet praying to die? It is, indeed, inconsistent enough, yet never was
painting truer to the life of a saint of God in darkness and

desertion. The clue to the whole mystery is that Jehovah has not said to Elijah "Arise and flee"—as before he had said, "Go show thyself to Ahab"--or "Arise, get thee to Zarephath." The record simply states that, hearing Jezebel's fierce oath, Elijah "arose and went for his life." Once the communication between Elijah and Jehovah is broken he is just as inconsistent and weak as any of us. Well did the Apostle James say "Elijah was a man of like passions with us." Here we see that he was. He is running away to save his life and yet praying, "It is enough; O Lord, let me die!"

There is no more common delusion than the notion that it is great evidence of piety to be willing to die. Often we hear that such a one, "was resigned to die," as proof conclusive of a converted heart. But from this place we may see that such desire may consist with actual disobedience. And, beside, the heart is deceitful, and there may not be the willingness that we suppose, when it comes to the crisis. There is a deep insight into the workings of the human heart in that old fable of the school books, of the labourer who weary, exhausted and disgusted with life, threw down his burden and prayed for death to come and relieve his labours; but when Death did come in answer to his petition, asking, "What is wanting?" the petitioner responded, "Nothing, save some one to help me raise my burden, that I may get under it again!" The readiness to die may not be as real as men suppose if put to the test. On the other hand, Christians often make the mistake of writing bitter things against themselves because they cannot feel willing to die, should God call them to-day. Whereas, all that this could prove, if anything, is that, probably, God does not intend calling them to-day. When the day comes for actual dying, then will he give the grace for dying. What we need to-day is grace to live. "Give us *this* day"—day by day—" our daily bread" is the method of God's dispensation of grace. Hence, how many a pastor has been surprised as well as comforted at finding the feeble, timid one of his flock, that at first shrunk back in terror from the thought of dying, able, when the day comes, to shout with triumph, " O Death, where is thy sting?" and endowed with a strength of faith that surpasses that of the most fearless.

Jehovah is compassionate to his weak and suffering prophet. " He knoweth our frame, he remembereth that we are dust." So, as the prophet lies there exhausted and unconscious, a heavenly messenger comes with the provision needful to sustain sinking nature, and, placing it within reach, arouses him saying, " Arise and eat." Remembering how Jehovah had miraculously fed him during his previous exile, we would suppose Elijah must at once understand the case, and recognize Jehovah's special presence. But, such is his condition of bodily exhaustion and of spiritual stupor, that he seems, at the first call, to be aroused only to consciousness enough merely to reach forth, as by a sort of instinct, and take the food. "He did eat and drink and laid him down again." But after a time he is aroused again and restored fully to consciousness, and to some reflection on his case, alone there in the desert. He seems not yet to perceive that he is out of the way of duty, and therefore is wandering in darkness.

Nothing could be more life-like than the views of this pictorial history of the spiritual darkness of a true child of God. Elijah is perplexed with regard to his vocation, and puzzled at the mysterious ways of Jehovah in seeming to stop the good work so gloriously begun on Mount Carmel. He feels badly, and begins now to study out some remedy for himself. Here he sits, an exile in the burning desert, feeling himself an outcast from God and the world. In spirit he is back upon Carmel, and sees the people reeling in the idolatrous orgies of Baal, as his priests announce that the

Jehovah prophet, after coming to disturb Israel, has fled. He is in the streets of Jezreel, and hears them resounding with blasphemies, Jezebel drunk with the blood of Jehovah's people whom his mighty work on Carmel has caused publicly to commit themselves. Ahab is again raging at the prophet that troubled Israel. All seems lost. Elijah feels badly, very badly. Utterly disgusted with such a world he will hide himself in the impenetrable solitudes of the desert. He will, by way of diverting his thoughts from the disgraceful degradation of the present Israel, go and hold communion with the glorious past of Israel's history. He will visit the very spots in the desert where his forefathers, led by the fiery, cloudy pillar, camped and worshipped. Nay, he will penetrate to the very Mount of God itself which smoked under the touch of Jehovah's foot, and shot forth the lightnings and reverberated the thunders, as he delivered to the awe-struck congregation his great law. There, amid such hallowed associations his drooping spirit shall certainly be revived and strengthened, and he will feel better.

Brethren, here you have the original principle so plausible and pious seeming from which developes most of the will worship that corrupts religion. It is in this effort of the soul, in its uneasiness and unrest under a spiritual cloud, to relieve itself by substituting the culture of imagination in religious worship, instead of the direct culture of the heart. It will substitute devout sentimentalism for communion with God through his appointed means of the word and ordinances. It is the blind instinct within them that impels men to some sort of worship, while the hardness of heart and darkness of mind keeps them from the spiritual communion. Hence the common mistake, when their religion fails to answer its end, of supposing that it is their circumstances in life which prevent their being Christians. It is, they think, the pressure of temptation from the world's fascinating pleasures ; or absorbing care from the world's rough business ; or irritability of spirit from the world's heartless and cruel usage. If they could once get to some retired cottage ; some community of pale sisters wholly devoted to God—or of self-sacrificing brethren—where they could renounce the world ; or if they could enjoy some impressive ritual whose beautiful prayers, and chants, with music resounding through " long drawn aisle and fretted vault," bathed in " dim religious light," which might raise their absorbed spirits on wings of devotion, then surely, they would at once grow in grace and make high attainments in sanctity.

The religion that ministers to this feeling evinces its profound knowledge of human nature and human weakness, but not a very profound knowledge of God's word, and insight into its principles of worship.

Well, Elijah strengthened in the physical man and refreshed, journeys on southward toward Sinai. And, doubtless, as he passes spot after spot in the desert, where once the camp of Israel and the tabernacle stood, he finds his mind deeply interested, his imagination active and his heart filled with emotion. But, alas, his spiritual man is as dark, discontented and restless as before. Still he is persuaded that it will be different when he shall have reached that great theatre of Jehovah's glory, Mount Horeb. He will go to the very spot where Jehovah stood and uttered his law ; and beyond question the sacredness of that spot will exalt his spirit as he touches it, and fill him with holy peace ! Thus onward, onward, for forty days ; fresh images arising before him every day ; here the little oasis, there the palm-trees—there the rock where his forefathers had camped and the pillar rested over the tabernacle, and Moses held a council with the elders —but still his soul is restless and uncomfortable.

At length, in the southern horizon, begin to loom up the peaks of the Sinai range, and then the lower Mount Horeb,

the Mountain of God.   As he approaches nearer they grow
more bold, rough and rocky, and put on the appearance of a
magnificent temple of worship reared by God for himself in
the eternal solitude.   And yet there is disappointment.   The
spiritual man is not refreshed as he expected.   Still he moves
on and begins to climb the dark, rocky heights ; but for all
that he can see, it is simply an immense piling up of porphyry,
granite and grunstein.   It is just like any other porphyry,
or granite.   Night draws on apace as he climbs ; soon he can
see no longer the mountain ridges and sand plains far below
him ; his thoughts are shut up to himself and the spot where
he stands.   He is alone, forsaken, an outcast from human
fellowship.   The enthusiasm dies out, and the physical nature,
sustained till now by the supernatural food, begins its cravings ;
and, with the growing lassitude dies out the spirit of adven-
ture and the desire to explore any farther.   A gloomy cave
in the rock opens before him, into which he casts himself for
shelter and rest ; and wrapping his mantle about him he gives
way to dismal forebodings.   Shall he now be left here to die
of exhaustion and hunger ?   For he has not the strength left
to retrace his long and weary way over the burning sands.
In a troubled slumber, perhaps, the word of Jehovah comes
to him as aforetime.   But, to his surprise and grief it is in a
tone of reproachful rebuke, " *What doest thou here, Elijah?*"
Strange implication ! that, after all his toil and laborious
devotion to come thus piously to the Mount of God, he should
receive this which is any thing but an approving welcome !
With a spirit yet unbroken and chafing under the reproof, he
answers back, reciting in a spirit of self-justification his devotion and his troubles, " I have been very jealous for Jehovah,
—Israel has cast contempt upon his covenant and ordinances
—murdered his servants—I am left alone, and hunted down
as a panting hart on the mountains."   Is it not time for thee
to visit vengeance for such sins ?   But instead of words of

commendation of his zeal, or of sympathy with his sorrows, he receives simply the command, " Go forth, and stand before Jehovah."

Elijah obeys the call, assured now that, like Moses of old, he shall witness the terrible majesty of Jehovah, as when he descended upon this mountain and it smoked at his touch. That would have suited his present frame of mind. He would enjoy beholding the terrors of the Almighty, after seeing the wickedness of Jezebel and of apostate Israel, and after thinking of the murder of his fellow-prophets. It would comfort him to feel that vengeance and power belongeth unto Jehovah. But, as creeping out of his hiding place, he stands erect in the murky darkness, a strange event suddenly breaks the awful silence. In an instant a tornado bursts forth, as if maddened by long imprisonment under the everlasting hills. It hurls the rocks, plunging, thundering, bursting down the cliffs. The clouds dash over the sky as the squadrons of a mighty army of cavalry in fierce conflict ; the sand-deserts seem aroused into a fury of passion and toss their curling billows to the sky as though an ocean of waters !

Elijah is filled with awe at the magnificence of God ; but alas, though he stands awe-struck, no voice of comfort and sympathy speaks to his darkened spirit. The tornado ceases as suddenly as it began ; and in a moment all is calm ; but Elijah is comfortless—*"Jehovah was not in the tornado."*

Suddenly, however, the solid mountain under his feet begins to vibrate, and now rocks as a skiff tossed upon waves of the sea. The rocks that just now were split by the tornado, seem ready to fall upon each other ; the sand-deserts undulate as the sea under a ground swell ; hills sink, valleys open, chasms yawn, nature seems in convulsions around him. Still more terrible is this view of the magnificence and majesty of God. But when, in a moment, all is still again, he stands in cold, comfortless silence as before. For all this brings no peace to his agitated spirit—*"Jehovah was not in the earthquake !"*

Suddenly a mighty fire gleams forth, lighting up the dark
cliffs, as though the heavens were on fire over his head. It
crackles and roars, as it swoops past him, and fills his soul
with still greater awe and dread. But still he is left standing after it passes in the same cold gloominess of spirit,—
"*Jehovah was not in the fire!*" All the terrific images of
Jehovah's greatness and terribleness, while they affect deeply
his imagination, have not touched his heart. So thousands
have found it since, who in their weariness and disgust with
the world, have taken to these Horeb pilgrimages, and
attempted through the imagination to rise to spiritual communion with God.

Tranquillity now reigns once more and the solemn stillness
of the sanctuary, as though Horeb, Sinai, mountain cliffs and
sand-deserts, aroused from their slumber are all lying in mute
awe and adoration at the feet of Jehovah. A "still small
voice" at length breaks the silence, and, though repeating
the question, "What doest thou here, Elijah?" yet, somehow,
now its accents seem to murmur softly in the very depths of
his soul. It is a tender, gentle, complaining voice, as that
which said in Gethsemane—"What, could ye not watch with
me one hour?" It breaks Elijah's heart. Abashed, confused,
humbled, he covers his face with his mantle; and though he
too utters the same words in response, yet how changed their
tone and spirit! It is in the accents of a subdued and humbled child—those wailing accents at once of penitence and
confidence, which never yet father, that was not a monster,
could resist. "I have been very jealous for Jehovah;" thou
knowest how sincerely I grieved at the dishonour of his name.
Israel,—poor children of the covenant—led astray by servants
of the Devil, has apostatised. Thy prophets, the witnesses
for the truth, have all been slain. No other voice than mine
remains to be lifted up in testimony for Jehovah. And me
they persecute to the death."

Elijah is now prepared for instruction, light and restoration. Indeed the marvellous events of the night have shown him how Jehovah judgeth, not as man judgeth, of the means to affect the soul. That his expectations of crushing Israel into obedience by the mere vengeful power of Jehovah's judgments, in shutting up the heavens from watering the earth, in commissioning the sword of justice—were all his own weak devices, not Jehovah's purposes, beyond what he had already done. The rush of the tornado in its fury; the rocking of the earthquake; the roar and crackle of the fire storm—all these had failed to subdue his own spirit. How then shall the manifestations of Jehovah's power and vengeance subdue the hard and rebellious heart of Israel? The soft accents of kindness and reproach had triumphed where tornado, earthquake, fire-storm, all had failed.

In accordance with all this is the lesson and instructions now given. First, " Go, anoint Hazael, king over Syria, and Jehu, king over Israel." Judgment must indeed come upon the apostates, according to my solemn oath and warning. But it befits not my prophets, the preachers of my gospel, to be the executioners and the men of blood. I will use Satan against Satan. Hazael and Jehu, men of blood, shall accomplish my mission of vengeance better than thou. " Go also, and anoint as thy successor the amiable Elisha, son of Shaphat;" for there is also a mission of love to Israel to gather out, comfort and edify mine elect in the midst of the work of vengeance. He shall go forth a Barnabas, son of consolation, as thou hast gone forth Boanerges, son of thunder. He shall " go forth eating and drinking" with the people, affectionately winning them to the gospel; as thou hast gone forth, " neither eating nor drinking," warning them of sin and calling to repentance.

And think not thou art alone—that there is no need of such a ministry to a nation of reprobates, that all are vessels of wrath fitted to destruction.   Thou art not alone ; for I have sealed as mine these seven thousand, who, like thee, have refused to bow the knee to Baal ; though unlike thee, they have not felt called upon openly to resist Ahab and Jezebel.

Now Elijah's eyes are, opened and his bands are loosed. The dark puzzle is solved ; all is clear enough.   With light heart and elastic step he takes his way backward toward Israel.   What though Jezebel is there, yet seven thousand of Jehovah's saints are there ; and the eternal shield of Jehovah is there to be a shelter over them and him ?

I must leave to your own deductions and reflections the varied and striking practical lessons which this story of the ancient gospel of the kingdom in conflict with desponding faith affords to every desponding child of God ; to every soul in darkness, vainly striving to devise the means of its own recovery, rather than by simply returning to God in penitence and faith ; and to every soul tempted to bitterness and un- charitableness.   " Elijah was a man subject to like passions as we are," saith the Apostle.   Let us not forget, brethren, that " we are men subject to like passions as Elijah ;" with yet far lower attainments in grace ; and, therefore, far weaker in the hour of temptation and trial.   We need, then, to " come boldly to the throne of grace, that we may find mercy and grace to help us in the time of need."

DISCOURSE IX.

THE GOSPEL OF PARDONING MERCY AS PREACHED BY THE
PROPHETS OF THE KINGDOM.

Isaiah i. 10, 18.—Hear the word of the Lord, ye rulers of Sodom ; Give
ear unto the law of our God, ye people of Gomorrah.   To what purpose is
the multitude of your sacrifices unto me, saith the Lord. * * *   Bring no
more vain oblations, incense is an abomination unto me ; the new moons
and Sabbaths, the calling of assemblies, I cannot away with ; it is iniquity, even the solemn meeting. * * And when ye spread forth your
hands I will hide mine eyes from you ; yea, when ye make many prayers I
will not hear, your hands are full of blood.   Wash you and make you
clean. * *

Come now and let us reason together, saith the Lord ; though your sins
be as scarlet, they shall be as white as snow; though they be red like
crimson, they shall be as wool.

"I PRAY thee of whom speaketh the prophet this ?   Of
himself (and his generation only), or of some other persons."
To answer this important inquiry, we need but analyze carefully the picture of the sins which the prophet sets before his
people, as preliminary to his glorious, full and free offer of
mercy.

First,—A marked feature of the portraiture, here drawn,
is that they are sinners under the light of Jehovah's special
revelations and appointed ordinances. It is now two hundred
and fifty years since what may be called the New Testament
of the ancient Church was given through David and Solomon;
the last form of the development of the old covenants. And,
under this new form, setting forth the typical throne and
typical kingdom of Messiah, prophet after prophet has been

N

raised up to expound and develop still more clearly the great scheme of Redemption. Schools of the prophets have existed since Samuel, sending forth teachers, to expound the gospel of the kingdom. And the very division and secession of northern Israel has, incidentally, tended to keep alive a spirit of zeal for the ordinances as adapted by David and Solomon to the settled state of the nation.

Second,—These sinners are such in face of every obligation of love and gratitude to Jehovah, arising out of peculiar blessings and privileges. To say nothing of the privileges which caused David to sing, " Blessed is the people whose God is Jehovah," and, " What one nation in the earth is like thy people, even like Israel ;" Jehovah, since David, has blessed them far beyond their deserts ; and the strokes of his chastisements have been far fewer than their crimes. Generation after generation, he hath continued to interpose his shield for their protection against all foes, and to cause their cup of joy to overflow.

Thirdly,—Yet in the midst of all these mercies, sin everywhere abounds. The public men and the people alike are corrupt. The moral perceptions of men seem blunted, until the gratitude of the very brutes is a reproach to these children whom Jehovah hath nourished and brought up. " The ox knoweth his owner, and the ass his master's crib, but Israel doth not know, his people do not consider." Corruption in the high places of justice abounds. The rulers are rulers of Sodom. Yea, violence and blood stalk abroad through the land ; and their popular vices are so debasing and degrading that not only their rulers are as rulers of Sodom, but their people are as the people of Gomorrah.

Fourthly,—And yet all this wickedness clothes itself in the garb of religion. The outward forms of worship are punctiliously observed. The wealth that has been coined out of the groans and tears, and blood of the oppressed, the weak, the

fatherless and the widow, is lavished on costly religious ceremonial. With great pomp the solemn feasts are observed ;
with great show of sanctity prayers are multiplied, and
sacrifices and oblations. But the worship is all a mere
phantom worship. No conscious presence of Jehovah gives
it power over the spirit. It is a sanctimonious masquerade
before Jehovah. Counterfeit, hollow voices, utter its heartless petitions, and shout its empty hallelujahs. There is no
eye of faith to look through these magnificent scenes of the
temple worship and see them, as the prophet saw them,—
when he saw " The Lord Jehovah high and lifted up, and his
train filled the temple," as it expanded to the dimensions of
the universe. No ear of faith discerns, in the sounds that fill
the temple courts, what the prophet heard ; as the reality of
which the outer temple worship is the symbol—the seraphim
floating above the throne and one singing " Holy!" the
other answering " Holy!" and then both in chorus shouting " Holy is Jehovah of hosts ! the whole earth is full of his
glory." ·

Brethren, it is one of the saddest and most solemn of the
warnings both of the word of God and of experience, that the
vilest of sins, and the worst of sinners, may be found within
the very enclosures of Jehovah's covenant. And that may be
the case, too, at the very time when the Church and Christianized community are most consciously admiring their own extra
piety, and with most imposing parade, attending very punctiliously upon the outward worship of God. It has been so
under every era of the revelation of God. Isaiah found in the
divinely constituted Church of God these rulers of Sodom and
people of Gomorrah ; and this even the prevailing type of the
religion of his day. It was in the divinely chosen Church, in
which were observed the punctilious tithings of anise, mint
and cummin, that Jesus found the men of whom he said,
" Ye hypocrites ! how can ye escape the damnation of hell !"

It was holy priests and elders, too scrupulous to enter a heathen governor's house on a holy day, that could yet, in midnight caucus, during the holy passover, plot the murder of the Son of God. It is within the circle of Christianized communities that the prophetic eye of the Apostle Paul discerns " in the last times," treacherous and corrupt seducers, " having the form of godliness, and denying the power thereof," that shall be guilty of every sin against God and man.

Let us not think, therefore, that it cannot be of such times as ours, in Protestant Christendom, that the prophet speaks. Alas, is not every day adding to the proof that neither light and knowledge, nor infinite obligation for distinguishing mercies, nor multitudes of fasts and festivals and holy days, and formal acknowledgments of Jehovah; nor yet immense wealth consecrated to the service of religion, are, any of them or all of them, any guarantee that there exists not high-handed wickedness, oppression, blood-thirst, utter decay of morals, and apostasy from the simplicity of the gospel? But, aside from the question, as it affects generally our age, and its moral and spiritual condition, let us not forget that this may be a very *personal* thing to *us*, and to our condition before God, whatever may be the condition of the age generally. Do you recognize any of the features of the prophet's picture as living realities? then of *you* speaketh the prophet thus. Whether you be a cold formal worshipper who have lost your first love, or whether thus living in sin without ever having come to Jehovah and assumed the vows of his covenant—of *you* the prophet speaketh this!

Having considered to whom he speaks, let us carefully consider, in the next place, what it *is* the prophet says to all such. Observe, it embraces three points chiefly. First,—a proposition to stop and reason the matter with Jehovah. Secondly, —the subject matter of the parley sin and its aggravations.

Thirdly,—the remedy for sin—its effectiveness, certainty and readiness.

1. " Come now and let us reason." The proposition is very suggestive ; both of the cause why men continue to live in sin ; and of the means and process whereby Jehovah would bring them back to himself.

The grand cause of the continuance in sin is that men will not *reason* of the matter. It is not that they do not know enough ; but they do not reason concerning what they do know. It is one of the mysteries of the human soul that, as Coleridge says, truth may become so true to us as to lose all the power of truth over our understanding, and lie stowed away as useless rubbish in the garners of memory. Just as sometimes a man of great wealth, from want of skill in applying wealth to its practical uses, may live in far less comfort than many a man of half his means. Just as sometimes a man may have vast knowledge ; be a walking encyclopœdia ; and yet, for all the practical purposes of knowledge, live the life of a fool. So men may have all knowledge of the gospel, and yet live practically atheists.

So too in morals, a man may not only apprehend fully, but feel strongly, the force of all ethical duties and obligations ; and yet live in self-indulgence and dissipation ; and in prac tical defiance of all laws of morality. Nor is it from want of certainty, as men sometimes persuade themselves, that they live on in sin, defying Jehovah's law and despising his gospel. Nothing can be more certain than that every man that lives must die ; and yet perhaps no one great truth produces less impression on men. They live just as if they are to live here forever.

Hence the gospel call comes ever as a cry of alarm to arouse men and arrest their thoughts, "Come let us reason!" "Awake, O sleeper, and call upon thy God!" Reason, as an immortal creature should reason. And the first process in a

sinner's conversion is this. Hence this is the meaning and
purpose of all gospel ordinances, so far as relates to men yet
unconverted. Christ arranges these ordinances and his
providences so that, "Wisdom shall lift up her voice in the
streets." Through his ordinances and providences he is ever
calling to every one, as he passes along the dusty highways
and crowded thoroughfares of life, and beckoning a halt,
" Ho ! thou man of business, with the quick step and restless
eye—a word with thee !" Is all this hurry of thine to get the
work done before " the Master come in such an hour as ye
think not ?" Ho ! thou man of finance—a word with thee !—
what is the state of exchanges ? What art thou taking in
exchange for thy soul ? The market is excited, perhaps, just
now ; for the great soul broker is in the market, buying up
largely ! But watch thou him closely. These are fancy stocks
of his—nay bogus stocks ; and sham certificates, beautifully
engraved indeed, but not a shilling of soul specie in all his deep
hell-vaults to redeem their treacherous pledges. Ho ! thou
old man garrulous with wise saws and modern instances, to
show how much better were the former times, than these. Is
it not rather a late watch in the night, with thieves prowling
about thee, while thou art discussing the degenerate times ?
Hast thou ever thought how much better even these times are
than the quickly coming eternities, to all who come to them
without the requisite provision ? Ho ! thou gay youth of
pleasure—and thou gay, fluttering creature of fashion, thinking only of the gorgeous assemblies for revelry. Is not the
entertainment growing rather dull ? And hast thou made
preparation of suitable court dress for the still more gorgeous
assembly at the marriage of the King's Son ?

Yes, " stop and let us reason together," is the first call of
all the gospels. Once men are persuaded to get out of the
crowd, for a private word with Jehovah, and the headway is
checked a little, then there is much hope. For the gospel of

Jesus seldom fails to gain its purpose once men will earnestly attend to its argument.

Are you then disposed to reason the matter with Jehovah? Well, the subject of which he would speak to you is sin. Does it seem to you to need apology, that he should call you aside to speak of so disagreeable a subject? Then the apology is ample. It is not that he takes pleasure in dwelling on such a subject. But because, in the essential nature of the case, this must now be the first point, in discussing the relation between God and man. For that relation has been disturbed. Sin has projected its dark, broad shadow between you and God. It is no dogma of theology, merely. Your own sad experience, every day, proclaims your soul in a state of disorder and disease. A curse has fallen upon it, which finds it's response in the aches, and ills, and pains, and sicknesses, and sorrows of life. Your existence here is a progressive death. "The moment we begin to live we all begin to die." And all this because of sin. Hence this must be the first thing to be settled. Indeed the awakened sinner who has begun to reason, no sooner attempts to speak to Jehovah in prayer, than this consciousness of sin casts a cloud over his vision, and silences his voice. The backslider finds this in the way of his return to peace and joy. The earnest Christian finds sin the obstacle ever interposing between himself and Jehovah. There is therefore no help for it; Sin *must* be the first subject of the reasoning.

But blessed be the name of Jehovah! Though he calls us to reason with him about sin, it is not to prove to us how justly he might damn us; but how this sin question may be arranged; if once we fully comprehend the greatness and guilt of it enough to desire it to be taken away.

How shall this be done? Not by palliating it! not by mitigating the enormity of it! No, but by fully, heartily, honestly admitting it, in all its aggravations ! " Though your sins be as scarlet and red like crimson." The critics tell us that one of the terms here refers to the outward appearance, glaring, attracting and fixing the attention ; the other, from a root signifying *double-dipped*, refers to the ineffaceable stain of sin upon the soul ; a stain that no rain, nor sunshine, nor dew can ever wash out, or bleach. The meaning is, however *aggravated* your sins may be.

What then, are some of the circumstances that aggravate sin ? For though every sin deserves God's wrath and curse, yet some sins, in their nature, and by reason of several aggravations, are more heinous in the sight of God than others. The prophet's picture of the sinners of his day furnishes us with the measure of these aggravations.

First, then, sins are aggravated, sins of scarlet,—when committed against special light and knowledge. It is a principle of common sense that the servant who knoweth the master's will, and yet disobeys, is worthy of more stripes than he who knows it less perfectly. The sinners to whom Isaiah preached, under the more complete revelation of the covenant of Grace, through the last covenant with David, sinned against clearer light, than the sinners to whom Moses and Joshua preached. How much more, even than these to whom the prophet is preaching, do sinners now sin against clearer light, who have in their hands the last and complete development of the New Testament covenant of grace—nay, and over and above this, the knowledge of the outworking of the completed scheme of grace, under his providence, through now near two thousand years !

And not only so, but most of those whom I address have not only this knowledge in their possession, but the calls of the gospel have been urged upon them by every conceivable motive, and every most potent agency. The voice of the pastor of their childhood and youth has plead. The voice of the sabbath teacher has plead. The voice of a father's authority and of a mother's love has plead. The voice of a brother, sister, husband, or wife or bosom friend has plead. O, if there be scarlet sins, from light and knowledge and motive disregarded, of whom could the prophet speak here more pointedly and personally than you?

In the second place, sins are aggravated and become scarlet sins when committed against special obligations of gratitude. Among men, no character is esteemed more base than the ingrate. When you would overwhelm one with the charges of a terrible indictment that shall fasten upon him the indignant verdict of men, you rehearse how you served him in the day of his distress and adversity; fed him in the days of his poverty; or stood his friend when malice assailed him, and all forsook him and fled; and yet, how he has turned upon his benefactor with malignity, or treated you with neglect and contempt. And why should it be held less an aggravation in him who plays the ingrate toward Jehovah, "from whom cometh down every good and perfect gift?" If so, then I pray thee, "of whom speaketh the prophet this," if not of you, who cannot recall an hour of life unmarked by some blessing from Jehovah? Mercies have showered upon you. Mercies to your country—mercies to your neighbour-hood—mercies to your friends—mercies to your family; personal mercies—and these of all classes—mercies temporal—mercies spiritual—mercies of providence—mercies of grace. Through the whole journey of life, from the cradle to the present hour, you have tread, at every step, upon mercies—strewn as flowers in your pathway, and their perfume fills the very air you breathe! And yet, perhaps, you have seldom thought of him; nay, worse, have treated his offers of pardoning grace with contempt, and set his holy will at defiance Verily, if there be sins of scarlet, such sins are these!

In the third place, sins may be aggravated, and become

sins of scarlet and red like crimson, from the social position of those who sin, or their relative position towards others, or their peculiar gifts and endowments which give them influence over others. This is on the score of the consequences of the sins, as well as of their intrinsic baseness. For such is the social constitution of our present state, that, in a high sense, every man is his brother's keeper; and is justly held accountable for the influence of his sins on others as well as on himself. We are the creatures of influence. We speak each other's words, we think each other's thoughts, we are moved by each other's emotions, we borrow each other's looks, we breathe each other's breath. The fashion of our moral existence is that of an infinite web whose centre is the throne of God and its circuit the universe. Each intelligent being is a mesh of that great web; and his every moral movement vibrates, as the stroke upon the water, wave following wave, inward to the centre, and outward to the circumference! The sins of men long dead thus live still, in their influence on men still living: and the sins of men in distant parts of the earth come vibrating over us on their mission of evil.

Now, in such a world, what must be the character of the sins of public men, and of magistrates in high civil positions? Does not the prophet justly describe them as rulers of Sodom? While the sins of men in private station—their revelries—their profanity—their contempt of Jehovah—are indeed great, yet their influence for evil is not so great as the same sins of men in exalted position. In the one case the sinful passions and lusts rage indeed, but rage, as the volcano of *Mouna Roa* rages, in the depths of its deep gulph, sending up their exhalations. In the other case, the sins are as the overflow of some Etna or Vesuvius carrying devastation and death, as the fiery flood rolls downward over the plain. What shall we say, therefore, of the sins of public official men? Of the sins of unofficial men, who by their gifts, their wealth, or their natural power of influence, are enabled to mould the thoughts and tastes of thousands? Especially what shall we say of the sins of masters of households, whose influence often extends to hundreds of servants? Of the sins of fathers and mothers, to whom God has given to stand as his representatives to their children? Shall such not feel that the prophet here speaketh of them—as guilty of the scarlet sins and red like crimson?

In the fourth place, sins may be aggravated as being committed against special covenants and vows; and thereby implying peculiar faithlessness and recklessness; on the principle common among men that, the breach of a solemn bond is more faithless than a failure to meet any other engagement. This was the special aggravation of the sin of those to whom the prophet preached. They were solemnly engaged by covenants with Abraham, with Moses, and with David, to be peculiarly Jehovah's people, as he to be peculiarly their God and Redeemer. In this regard, their sins were more aggravated than those of Sodom and Gomorrah, whose cry ascended up to heaven, and brought down the fires of vengeance. For beside the intrinsic wickedness of doing the deeds of Sodom and Gomorrah, these sinners, in so sinning, added the guilt of faithlessness to their solemn vows and the vows of their fathers.

It is this that gives their peculiar aggravation to the sins of such as have formally and publicly entered into the covenant of Jehovah, in our day. They add to the intrinsic guilt of their transgressions, this violation of solemn faith pledged. And on this account it is, that their sins are also the most hurtful in their influence, by bringing reproach on the religion of Jesus Christ, as a religion that hinders not its votaries from being faithless. Here again, as you contemplate the low standard of the Christian life—see you not the prophet speaketh thus of us?

Having reasoned thus of the matter, do you find that as you reason, your sins rise up before you glaring as scarlet? Does the despairing conviction come over you that the stain is ineffaceable? that the soul is *double-dipped* in transgressions that are as crimson? Are you ready to cry out, " Father, I have sinned against heaven and in thy sight, and am no more worthy to be called thy son !" Say you, " Behold I am vile, what shall I answer thee ;" " mine iniquities have gone over my head, they are a burden too heavy for me ?" Then Jehovah has somewhat more to say. If he hath broken he will bind up. He saith, " Stand not back for the enormity of your sins. Though they be as scarlet and red like crimson—never mind—they shall be as snow and as wool !"

On what ground, and on what security may such sinners rest? Simply this; that " where sin abounds grace much more abounds." By virtue of that atonement held up to view in every sacrifice at the altar, symbolizing the blood of an infinite Lamb of God, full provision is made for all sin—absolutely all—however great the aggravation. The law stands in all its force, " the soul that sinneth it shall die." But Jehovah hath, in the covenant of Redemption, provided for a substitution of life for life. The blood atones because " the life is in the blood."

And not only is provision thus made, in general, but Jehovah—to assure the faith of poor sinners who, seeing their sins in all their aggravation, begin to doubt, whether this provision may be efficacious in such desperate case as theirs—has vouchsafed to bind himself to pardon and justify *all* who rely on the blood. His word not only, but his bond is given, " When I see the blood I will pass over, and the curse shall not come nigh you !"

And, in addition to the teachings of the ritual of blood, stand all his pledges, not only to take away the sin but to

purify and renew the bad heart.   For so he teaches, in all
the ritual of the sprinklings and washings and purifications of
the temple service.

Such was the gospel of pardon as Isaiah would state it.
It was all-sufficient then, for the assurance of those whose
sins were as scarlet and crimson, that it was a remedy sure,
effective and ever ready to all who will reason with Jehovah.

You, my brethren, have still clearer assurance, though the
remedy remains precisely the same.   You have the additional
assurance that " the blood of Jesus Christ cleanseth from all
sin."   " He came to save sinners—even the chief."   You
have the bond of the New Covenant, pledging him " who
bore your sins in his own body on the tree " to " save all that
come to God by him."   If you will reason—then fear not to
cast yourself upon his pledge to make the scarlet as the snow
and the crimson as the wool.

SECTION IV.

REDEMPTION, AS TAUGHT BY JESUS, THE INCARNATE WORD.

DISCOURSE X.

THE OFFICIAL AUTHORITY, NATURE, LIMITS, AND PURPOSES OF GOSPEL PREACHING.

LUKE iv. 16-21.—And he came to Nazareth, where he had been brought up; and, as his custom was, he went into the synagogue on the Sabbath day, and stood up for to read. And there was delivered unto him the book of the prophet Esaias. And when he had opened the book, he found the place where it was written,

The Spirit of the Lord is upon me, because he hath anointed me to preach the Gospel to the poor, he hath sent me to heal the broken-hearted, to preach deliverance to the captives, and recovering of sight to the blind; to set at liberty them that are bruised, to preach the acceptable year of the Lord.

And he closed the book, and he gave it again to the minister, and sat down. And the eyes of all them that were in the Synagogue were fastened on him. And he began to say unto them, this day is this Scripture fulfilled in your ears

THE visible Church of God still continued to have its centre in the land of promise, and in the city of David. Its creed was nominally still the covenant of grace as last developed in the covenant with David. Its ordinances were still the old ritual of Sinai, as David and Solomon had adapted that ritual, to the settled state; and both creed and ritual had more fully been expounded by subsequent prophets. Prophecy had ceased, and there was no open vision for four hundred and fifty years. Synagogues, Rabbis and Scribes had taken the place of the schools of the prophets. Revolution had followed revolution in the state, and chastisement after chastisement to the Church; till now only a few fragments of the typical kingdom, just sufficient to preserve the line of promise, and these ruled by a foreign tyrant, remained in Canaan. The rest were scattered among all nations, there to "prepare the way of the Lord." The typical throne of David had been taken away, as a necessary preparation also for the construction of the new spiritual kingdom, soon to be gathered from all nations.

Among the people, Rabbis, Priests, Scribes and Elders, generally, prevailed a cold, narrow, unspiritual, heartless, formalism, which while outwardly magnifying the creed and the ritual, had utterly lost sight of the gospel contained therein; "teaching for doctrines the commandments of men." For a century, indeed, a general expectation prevailed, founded upon the prophets, of some great change about to come. The unspiritual conceived of it as a political revolution, and a literal restoration of the throne of David. The true children of God waited for it, as the consolation of Israel. Especially during the last thirty years have these expectations been more certain and definite among the true believers, since divine communications have again come to his people through Mary, Elizabeth, Zacharias, Anna and Simeon, announcing the speedy fulfilment of the covenant with David.

Such, in general terms, was the condition of the Church and the typical kingdom when first John the Baptist, and then Jesus, began to proclaim "the kingdom of heaven is at hand." And, at an early period of his ministry occurred at Nazareth the exposition of the divine authority, nature, limits and purposes of that gospel preaching, which is now to take the place, both of the visions of the prophets and of the ancient teaching by symbols and ritual, as the instrumentality in the Church for calling sinners and edifying saints. It was, indeed, in an obscure place, and under very humble circumstances, that an exposition of such intrinsic importance and dignity was given. But what place or circumstances more befitting the first exposition of the ordinances of a gospel whose glory it was that " the poor have the gospel preached to them ? "

It is in an obscure village, far north of Jerusalem, the byeword and scoff of its own province of Gallilee ; which province itself was the scorn and scoff of the refined metropolitans of Jerusalem. For the sake of its very obscurity it had been selected by the parents of Jesus, in his infancy, as a hiding place from the cruelties of the Herods. There had he grown up as the son of Joseph the carpenter, surrounded by poverty and ignorance ; and thence had he departed unnoticed about the opening of the ministry of John Baptist.

But strange news has lately come to this little village. Rumour hath it, that this son of Joseph the carpenter has suddenly become a great man—great enough to have attracted the notice of the great people in the capital city, Capernaum. Nay more, that, travelling from place to place as a Rabbi, he is eclipsing the fame of John Baptist himself. And now, that the much talked of Rabbi has at length actually come to Nazareth, crowds gather to the synagogue ; and with eager expectation are they waiting till the presiding elder, rising from his high seat, shall hand the book to the son of Joseph, inviting him to read and expound the word. " What place will he select ? What curious things will he say ? We will see now what this thing is that has so fascinated the great Capernaum people."

He begins to unroll the volume—It is the book of the prophet Isaiah. Nor does he unroll far from the end of the book till he finds the place ; it is the sixty-first chapter, among the last of his sublime predictions of the future glory and the new order of things in the Church when " the Redeemer shall come to Zion." He reads—" The Spirit of the

o

Lord is upon me, because he hath anointed me to preach the
gospel to the poor : he hath sent me to heal the broken-hearted,
to preach deliverance to the captives, and recovering of sight
to the blind, to set at liberty them that are bruised, to preach
the acceptable year of the Lord." All eyes are rivetted
upon him as he sits down to begin his discourse on such a
theme. And the curiosity becomes the more eager at his first
sentence—" This day is this scripture fulfilled in your ears."
But soon mere curiosity merges into wonder at the gracious
words, as he proceeds to develop the infinite meaning of the
glad message of the text, and to demonstrate how he himself
is the actual of the prophet's great ideal. How the typical
kingdom of David, for whose restoration they were longing, is
now to be fulfilled in the great antitype—the kingdom of God
on earth. And how, now, the prophets of the Church shall
go forth to preach this gospel. New views of truth begin to
burst upon them as he expounds the covenant of grace ; new
hopes of mercy as he dilates upon the love and compassion of
God ; new convictions of sin, as he dwells upon the sorrows,
the blindness, the slavery of sin ; new courage, as he expounds
the promise of the Spirit, to release from the captivity to the
law of sin in the members ; new fountains of emotion open in
their hearts, as he applies the Balm of Gilead ; new purposes and resolves, as he closes by proclaiming, " This is the
accepted time "—wait no longer—just here, just now—
"Come take the waters of life freely."

Brethren, " this day is this scripture fulfilled in your ears "
also : and so it is every day that you hear the gospel preached.
These are the words of " Jesus Christ, the same, yesterday,
to-day and forever." And, in these words, he sets forth to
us the significancy of these gospel ordinances, which he hath
appointed under the new covenant, as our means of grace, in
place of the ordinances of symbols and types and ritual which
had been the means of grace to his people under the old

covenants. We do well, therefore, to analyze carefully this prophetic statement, thus expounded and applied by Jesus himself, the minister of the sanctuary ; and whose personal ministry is the type of that gospel ministry which he established for the New Testament Church. For this statement will be found exhaustive, covering all the fundamental points, of the Divine qualifications and appointment of the office : its purpose and functions ; the manner of discharging them ; and the end to be had in view in preaching the gospel.

I. The primary qualification for the office is, "*the Spirit of the Lord is upon me.*" So was it said, in the ancient Church, not only of the inspired men " who spake as they were moved by the Holy Ghost," but of any man stirred up to any work by Jehovah. The Spirit of the Lord was upon leaders such as Gideon and Jephthah, and Sampson and Saul, impelling them to execute a mission for Jehovah, even though in some cases they gave little evidence of the Spirit's work of grace upon the heart. It is so still with the men who have this mission of Jehovah to preach and rule in the Church. This work is not therefore, one that every man, even with learning sufficient, should feel that he is called upon to assume, unless he has some other special call to the profession. If the Spirit of the Lord is upon him to this end he will find something *positive* in his experience. He will feel the pressure of the Apostle—" Wo is me if I preach not the gospel."

The error of our times and country, however, is not so much with reference to the original call and qualification for the ministry, as in regard to the continuance of the Spirit of the Lord, guiding and directing the true gospel preacher in his work. There seems to be prevalent a sort of Sadduceeism, whose conceptions fall far below the true extent of the Spirit's work. It is not all the truth, by any means, that the Spirit calls him to the work, and then leaves him to the best exercise of his reasoning powers, eloquence and learning in the discharge of it. The Spirit of the Lord continues upon him, guiding his choice of what to say ; for every true speech in the name of Christ, officially, is prompted by the Spirit, and accompanied by him on its errand to fashion the vessels of glory, or the " vessels of wrath fitted to destruction." The relation of the preacher of the New Testament is very close to the prophet of the Old Testament whom he succeeded. He has now, indeed, no further new communication to make from Jehovah, for the revelation is complete. Yet, though he look not to a vision of the night, nor listen for a voice from the unseen to syllable the words of Jehovah, he must reverently come to the oracle of Jehovah—his completed revelation—inquiring " What will Jehovah say unto this people?" And, getting his message he goes forth to proclaim " thus saith Jehovah." Nothing is plainer in scripture than that the true gospel preacher has the presence of the spirit of Christ upon him, in every official utterance. For saith Jesus, " Go preach, Lo I am with you alway." The Holy Spirit comes " to take the things of Christ and shew them unto him," that he may shew them unto the people.

II. Qualified thus, by the Spirit upon him, he is also specially " anointed," that is, commissioned, as for an official work— " to preach." Nor is there, perhaps, any truth of our holy religion which needs more to be impressed upon the minds of the people, and to be brought out in the consciousness of the Church, at this day. It is to be feared that, in the reaction from the general disgust of mankind with the arrogant claims of ghostly authority by a corrupt priesthood, Protestants are tending to the other extreme of ignoring the true divine authority of the gospel ministry. Because an unspiritual and formalistic priesthood—palpably without the divine qualification of the " Spirit of the Lord upon them,"—have yet been punctilious to the highest degree.in claiming the divine official commission, and themselves as the only authorized ministry,

men have learned to scoff at every form of claim to speak
with the authority of a divine commission, and to conceive of
the Protestant minister as simply one of the brethren chosen
to teach, and to care for that which the masses have not time
to care for.   Even many pious and earnest people, in this day
of Christian activity, seem to conceive of the gospel ministry
as merely another form of those agencies for doing good, common to all Christian men and women, such as the teaching
in the Sabbath school, the conference and social meeting,
the conversation of the colporteur, &c.

True, in a very important sense, every Christian is a propagandist singing ever " O that all would believe ;" for it is of
the essential nature of the new life that it makes " him that
heareth say, come." True, every agency for gathering in
sinners, and for Christian nurture is, in its place, all important.
But it must not be forgotten that, over and above all these,
" the Lord hath anointed " a ministry, commissioned, not only
as chief of all these agencies, but officially to speak for God to
men in the word ; to speak for men to God in prayer ; to
stand as Christ's attorney in the sacraments presenting the
covenant and receiving the signature and seal of his people
to it.   Not only is this public official utterance of the minister
different in kind from the similar utterance in the family, and
in the private gatherings of Christians " speaking often one
with another ;" but it differs also from his own private utterances, as the utterance of the judge on the street differs from
that of the judge on the bench.   This will appear further as
we proceed to consider,

III.—The function and purpose of his office.   It is " *to
preach the gospel.*" And, by virtue of the special anointing,
this preaching differs, in kind, from all merely human forms
of thought and teaching, however it may resemble them.   To
preach may be eloquent utterance, but that is not all, nor the
essential part of it.   To preach, may be profound reasoning ;

but that is not all, nor the essential part of it. To preach, is
to teach, but that is not all of it, though the primary end of
it. To preach, is to expound a book; yet not, as in the
schools, the book of a Plato who *spoke*, but of a Jesus who
speaks. It is to enforce an ethics ; yet not, as in the school
of a Socrates who moralized, but of a Jesus who *is* purifying
the heart by faith. It is to develop a great system of thought
concerning God and humanity ; yet not as received merely
from "holy men of old who spake as they were moved by the
Holy Ghost," but as revealed now by Jesus to the souls of
his people.

Preaching, then, is that peculiar official utterance, of one
divinely commissioned to speak in Christ's name. Saith the
Apostle, " We are ambassadors for Christ, as *though God
did beseech you by us*, we pray you, *in Christ's stead*, be ye
reconciled to God." It is authoritatively setting forth the
divine terms of reconciliation. Just as his Master and the
Great Type of his ministry, so the preacher " speaks as one
having authority and not as the scribes."

But some one is now ready to ask—" Is not this re-assert-
ing the old priestly assumption, by divine right to dominate
over the conscience ? And will not this carry us back to the
priestcrafts and tyrannies of ghostly authority ?" I answer,
candidly, so it will ; unless he who claims this authority is
carefully restricted within the sphere of his commission. If
he is allowed to claim and exercise such power as inherent
in him personally, by virtue of some indelible grace of holy
orders, and not because the Spirit of the Lord is upon him to
this end ; if he is allowed to transcend the limits of his
commission, and, deliver authoritative opinions on any other
questions than of the reconciliation to God through Christ;
if the people make him their infallible judge in cases of
dividing the inheritance, or their guide in determining to
which Cæsar they owe allegiance ; that is the peoples' affair,

not the gospel's. The guarantee against priestly domination lies not in denying the divine authority of the ministry, and thereby denying any true gospel preacher. It lies in the careful restriction of his authority within the limits set to it in his divine commission. For, you will observe, in the next place, that the commission here confines him to a very special and narrowly limited sphere. "The Lord hath anointed me *to preach the Gospel*." In this office he is to "know nothing but Christ Jesus and him crucified." His sole business, officially, is to proclaim, "Jesus Christ came into the world to save sinners, of whom I am chief;" and to expound and enforce the terms of reconciliation. As the discourse of the ambassador, outside of his special official sphere—of politics, finances, morals, literature,—is not to be taken as of any higher authority than the opinions of any other man equally intelligent ; so when the ambassador of Christ discourses, outside of his commission, concerning science, physics, metaphysics, politics, ethics, national affairs, civil and military, his discourse is of no higher authority than that of any other man, equally intelligent. Nay, his opinions are of even less value than other men's, since he can know little of these matters, if true to his Master's work. And if he undertake, officially, to speak of such things when he stands forth to speak in the name of Christ he is simply an impostor, seeking to gain currency and confidence for his opinions under false pretences. And if the people submit to the imposition, quietly, the result will soon show itself in a ministry with no Spirit of the Lord upon it, and a Church with no Spirit of the Lord in it. And though without the Popish form of it, yet, in reality and in substance, there will be priestcraft as artful, ruling over as thoroughly a priest-ridden people, as ever disgraced the great Roman apostasy.

The *Gospel* is that for the propagation of which the Church has been constituted a spiritual commonwealth, with its offices to bear rule and to preach. By. divine authority, in like manner, the secular interests of the world, as the great theatre of the gospel's operations in gathering God's elect, have been committed to Cæsar. And never are these powers confounded that the confusion is not rebuked by leaving the Church, on the one hand, to spiritual death, and the state to the decay of liberty on the other. But when, in the true spirit of the divine commission, the Church, with a single eye to her divine *charter* and mission, and her ministry, under a deep sense of their official responsibility, "preach the gospel," then the work of Christ goes forward, conquering and to conquer, whether the world-powers frown or smile.*

IV. Not only is the preacher's office of divine appointment, but also the method and manner of discharging the functions thereof. "To preach the gospel *to the poor*." It is this feature that distinguishes the system of instruction appointed in the gospel from all those humanly-devised schemes for the instruction and elevation of mankind which have made illustrious the world's benefactors. Though its subject matter is the profoundest that can occupy the human mind; though all other knowledge is but ancillary to this knowledge; though its truths, at all points, expand from the finite to the infinite; it yet cites as the evidence of its divine origin, that "the poor have the gospel preached unto them." The originators and expounders of all other systems of thought seek out only the more gifted, the intelligent and the refined, to be made trophies of their skill in the work of enlightenment. But Jesus Christ comes proclaiming himself "able to save to the uttermost"—even to the uttermost extent of degradation and ignorance. Nay, while his system excludes none—high or low—he rejoices, saying, "I thank thee, O father, that thou hast hid these things from the wise and prudent, and hast revealed them unto babes."

The meaning of all this is, that the method of preaching

---

* See Appendix, Note D.

the gospel must be adapted to the humble in spirit, and to the capacity of the uneducated ; making the instruction of the wise and prudent incidental, rather than primary. It proceeds upon the assumption that, "Not many wise, not many noble, not many mighty are called." There are, indeed, *some* such called ; for Christ excludes none. But when called, it is incidentally, by means that are adapted to the capacity of the masses, rather than by any excellency of speech and words of man's wisdom, specially appointed for the conversion of the wise, the noble and the mighty. And it is the grand peculiarity of the gospel faith that is unto salvation, that it is precisely the same faith whether as existing in the heart of the poor unlettered peasant, or of the mighty man of science. Its great truths are equally adapted to suit the humble powers of thought and limited capacity of the one, and to exercise, to their uttermost, the loftiest intellectual powers of the other, and fill to their fullest the largest capacities. The gospel adapted to the poor is equally adapted to the great ; while the gospel that aims only to meet the capacity of the wise and great is adapted to the spiritual wants of neither. Its message is to "the poor in spirit," to "the meek and lowly in heart;" to "the weary and heavy laden." And while its truths transcend the reach of the loftiest gifts ever bestowed upon the natural understanding, and its stupendous problems have a length and breadth and depth that transcends the compass of human reasoning, yet they find an interpreter, in the bosom alike of the peasant and the philosopher, which expounds them to the apprehension of a soul conscious of sin and desirous of salvation. This gospel comes as a bread of life to the hungry soul, and as a water of life to the thirsty soul. It is, therefore, no more a marvel that the poor and unlearned, alike with the great and learned, should understand and use it, than that the poor and unlearned with little knowledge of the chemistries of philosophers should, yet, as readily as the philosophers, understand how to appease their physical hunger with bread, and quench their physical thirst with water.

While, therefore, the schools send forth their disciples with the command—" Go forth, apply the powers we have disciplined and the knowledge we have imparted in extending the domain of thought, and in elevating the standard of learning. Seek to be illustrious, as scholars and philosophers, and worthy the plaudits of the wise and intelligent of your race," Jesus Christ sends forth his disciples, saying—" Go, with the Spirit of the Lord upon you,—sanctifying all your gifts and attainments,—and ' preach.' Preach,—not learning, philosophy, ethics, political economy—but ' the gospel.' And fashion your gospel, not to the æsthetics of the refined, with stilted rhetorical step; not to the whimsical demands of the caviller with learned air; not to the exactions of the scientific sceptic with profound philosophic phrase. Aim at the capacities of the masses; the poor in spirit, poor in learning, poor in taste; and, whatever the schools may think, the gospel from your mouth, ' made the power of God unto salvation' shall certify your skill ' as workmen that need not be ashamed.' The two grand requisites, therefore, of the preacher's office are: First, that he preach the gospel—nothing else; second, a gospel addressed to the capacity of the masses of the people. The force of all this will appear more clearly as we proceed, next, to consider :—

V. The prophetic catalogue of the purposes and ends of this gospel preaching. For this catalogue will be found to embrace the entire purposes of this office, and all that the soul needs a gospel for.

First, the gospel comes " to heal the broken-hearted." It assumes that it comes into a world full of sorrow; where " man is made to mourn." That as " sin has entered," projecting its dark shadow; " so death." including all forms of

sorrow, " by sin." Physical suffering with its sorrows ; for
the death begins to work from man's birth, in aches and pains
and sicknesses. Mental suffering ; for the death worketh darkness of the understanding, proneness to error, dulness of
perception, and all the weariness of mind that flows from
them. Sorrow of heart ; for the death worketh all manner
of loss of friendship, loss of confidence, loss of affection, loss
of friends, near and dear, with all the agonies of bereavement
and of sympathy with suffering. But, worse than all, sorrow
for sin ; growing out of the consciousness that all these other
sorrows come from the estrangement of the soul from God ;
and are but types of that eternal sorrow which shall follow as
the just penalty of sin, still conceiving and bringing forth death.
And even when faith " hath laid hold of the hope set before
us in the gospel," this sorrow continues to be the portion of
God's children in such a world. The temptations too strong
for us, and the sins that do easily beset us continually break
the grasp of faith on that hope. The tears of sorrow ever
dim the eye of faith. Now it is the distinguishing glory of
this gospel preaching that it has the balm of Gilead to apply
to these broken hearts. It comes to those mourning, as they
look upon him that their sins have pierced, to assure them
that the blood from the pierced side " cleanseth from all
sin ;" for he hath made propitiation for our sins with his own
blood. It comes to comfort the people of God in their afflictions with the assurance that the afflictions come neither by
chance, nor because he is angry with them ; but because he
sees it best for them ; and " the light affliction that endureth
for a moment shall work out a far more exceeding and eternal
weight of glory." It comes to assure the hearts broken by
bereavement that these strokes are not in anger ; " for whom
the Lord loveth he chasteneth." That they sorrow not as
those without hope, for " they that sleep in Jesus will God
bring with him." Not a sorrow—that is a godly sorrow and

not the mere sorrow of the world that worketh death,—but this gospel has its balm for the wound. O, it is not the applause of the thoughtless and light-hearted world that is music to the ear of the true gospel preacher; but the glowing heart utterances of some poor broken-hearted sinner pointed by him first to Christ; of some child of God, desponding and broken-hearted with the troubles that have made the world all darkness, and even shut out the light of God's smile from the soul—from whose spirit he hath chased away the darkness; of some broken-hearted father or mother or household, whom he has found refusing to be comforted because death has come and the loved ones are not, and has enabled them to say, " The Lord gave and the Lord hath taken away, blessed be the name of the Lord." To the preacher whose heart has listened to the music of their grateful blessings on him, all the adulation of the frivolous multitude—all the applause of literary and rhetorical critics, is as the sound of empty brass and a tinkling cymbal. The giddy, the thoughtless, the hardened in sin, the unstricken souls, need not be surprised that the gospel preaching has no fascinations for them. Its aim chiefly is at the wants of earnest souls, broken-hearted for sin, or by the consequences of sin.

Second, the purpose of the gospel is to preach " *deliverance to the captives.*" For it assumes that men must perceive the sin and sorrow to be not merely their misfortune but their fault,—that they are lying under sentence as " condemned already " and awaiting execution.—No man can reason intelligently concerning his present condition and relation toward God without the conviction that he is in a state of condemnation,—that his present estate is that of a condemned criminal in prison, awaiting the full infliction of the just penalty of sin. Hence the inquiry is forced upon such an one—Is there no way in which, consistently with justice and right, this penalty may be removed? Hence all the religions which men have devised—however varied in degree of intelligence, refinement and purity—are religions of dread—of bloody sacrifices and rites—of priests atoning at altars. All seem, more or less clearly, to recognize this conviction in the human soul of a penalty for sin, a guilt to be removed by atonement. Now the gospel comes to satisfy this inquiry "How can a man be just with God?" by showing how Christ crucified may righteously be accepted of God in place of the sinner's eternal crucifixion; and how "the Lamb of God taketh away the sin of the world." Not merely procures the *pardon* of it, in the sense that God, though still offended, agrees to waive the execution of the penalty : but "*taketh away* the sin, so that it shall be blotted out and remembered no more. Nay more, that the sinner may stand before God as righteous, being arrayed in the righteousness of his substitute. For Christ, the Sinless One, hath borne our sins in his own body on the tree," and is become "the Lord our righteousness." Such a gospel meets fully—and such a gospel only can meet fully—the demands of a sinner's own convictions of the just and necessary deserts of sin, under the perfect administration of a righteous God. Meeting those demands it brings the captive soul out of the condemned cell singing, "There is therefore now no condemnation to them that are in Christ Jesus? Being justified by faith we have peace with God."

A *third* purpose of this gospel preaching, and indeed a necessary preliminary to the foregoing, is "*the recovering of sight to the blind.*" For it is one of the effects of the death, that has caused the sorrow of the race, that it has also caused total blindness of the spiritual vision. The gospel, therefore, assumes that, whatever variety of intelligence may be found among the children of men, whether by reason of original endowments or by attainments, yet all are alike in darkness and in ignorance of any true soul knowledge, or of any consciousness of the truth that is unto salvation. A Saviour who meets the case, therefore, must be not only an atoning priest, but also an enlightening prophet, as well. Hence the gospel comes pointing the soul to his wonderful instructions of what man is to believe concerning God, and what duty God requires of man. To this end he became himself a preacher of this gospel of the kingdom. To this end he sends his Holy Spirit to reveal his truth unto babes. " No man knoweth the Father save he to whom the Son shall reveal him." All that natural religion can gather out of his works concerning God, is of little avail to instruct a blind and guilty soul. But the true gospel preached to him, with " the Spirit of the Lord upon it," shall cause the light to shine into the heart, as flashed the light upon the murky chaos, when the " spirit brooded upon the waters, and God said, let light be !"

A *fourth* purpose of the gospel preaching,—which at once places it beyond all comparison with any merely human teaching—is "*to set at liberty them that are bruised.*" Without the holding forth to a sinner the Kingly office of his Saviour, and his power to deliver from the galling slavery of sin, the salvation would be incomplete. For of what avail to him to be enlightened in the knowledge of the truth, and even to be pardoned for all the past, if left in his conscious impotency to struggle with the inherent sinfulness of his heart kept in active eruption by the temptations of a sinful world without ? Of what avail to let the light break in by opening his cell, and to proclaim the pardon *for a reason*, and reprieve from the sentence, if the pardoned criminal shall be left lying there helpless with the shackles upon him still galling him ? But it is the glory of the gospel to be not only a pardon and a light but also a *power*, " the power of God unto salvation." It not only, as the ethical schools, points to the way of virtue and happiness saying, " this is the way, walk ye in it,"

but it saith, "rise, take up thy bed and walk" to the
helpless cripple, or "stretch forth thy hand" to the man
of the withered hand, with the word of command imparting
a divine power, that restores his spiritual strength to the
poor cripple, and sends him on his way " leaping and glorify-
ing God." To him conscious of his impotency its glorious
assurance is " my grace is sufficient for thee." Thus every
phase of the sinner's condition is provided for; nothing,
absolutely nothing, is left undone, that he needs.

And hence the *fifth* and last distinguishing feature of the
gospel preaching. That, wherever its voice comes presenting its scheme, just then, and just there can it "*proclaim
the acceptable year of the Lord.*" For it can say just here,
" and this day, is this scripture fulfilled in your ears." These
blessings of grace which the gospel preacher proclaims are
not a beautiful theory which men may sometime hereafter test
by application of its principles; not something involving a
long discipline and preparation. It is a present offer. Now
is its accepted time: *now* is always its day of salvation. It
is intended to be applied on the spot. There is no need of
waiting, for *all* things are ready. Jesus Christ is present
here and now, in this preaching, to verify its truths and
fulfil all its pledges. You wait not to get rid of the sin, but
come to him to take away the sin ! You wait not to provide
a fit dress—purity of character enough to stand before God
—but come to him and receive the wedding garment—even
his righteousness. You wait not till you have more light;
but come to him to give you light. You wait not to test
whether you have moral power to keep your resolutions and
vows; but come to him, and implicitly trust him for the power
and all the grace to enable you to live in newness of life.
Nay, you wait not for more faith or stronger faith; but come
just as you are with all your darkness and doubts, crying
" Lord I believe, help thou my unbelief." There is nothing

to be waited for, but every thing to impel you to seize upon the offer while it is the acceptable year of the Lord. No gospel preacher can ever state the case and then leave you to decide to-morrow. To-day is the day of grace! To-morrow may be the day of doom! To-day, as you come, with your sorrow and darkness and weakness, he can confidently assure you, because, he can point you to the Lamb on Calvary atoning for you—"Able to save to the uttermost all that come." To-morrow he may have become to you "the Lamb in the midst of the throne," before whom the universe trembles with terror!

Such, brethren, is this great inaugural discourse of Jesus at the institution of his new order of ministry in the New Testament Church under the last and highest development of the covenant of grace. A ministry that unites in it the functions both of the priest and the prophet of the ancient Church. It is a priesthood that officiates not indeed at a visible altar, but stands pointing to the great sacrifice "offered once for all" and, therefore, not to be repeated; and proclaims, not in the prophetic language of type and symbol and ritual, but in the literal language of great historic fact, that God hath accepted the one great offering of Christ crucified, in that he raised him from the dead and seated him at the right hand of the Majesty on high. It is of the order of the prophet: yet not of one receiving his messages from the visions of the Almighty or in prophetic ecstasy, but from the completed revelation—the perpetual oracle—to go forth and say " thus saith the Lord Jesus." Its messages are but still clearer statements of what priests and prophets taught, and to the same purpose, of healing the broken hearts, proclaiming deliverance to the captives, the recovering of sight to the blind, the setting at liberty the bruised—the acceptable year of the Lord.

And in this review of the Saviour's exposition of the ancient prophet, I may say to you, in a somewhat special sense—" this day is this scripture fulfilled in your ears." I proclaim, therefore, "the acceptable year of the Lord." If there be one poor broken-hearted sinner, who has followed me with earnest attention, through the review of the gospel message; to such I say this Jesus, this gospel is intended for you. He hath come to heal the broken heart to-day if you will accept this proffered Saviour! If there be a poor, broken-hearted child of God, prostrate under the heavy stroke of affliction, and crying in terror "deep calleth unto deep at the noise of thy water-spouts! All thy waves and thy billows are gone over me,"--then for you this gospel is a personal message. He hath come to give thee "a song in the night," and kindly to remonstrate with thee, saying, "Why are ye fearful, O ye of little faith." "Hope thou in God, for thou shalt yet praise him." If there be any soul labouring under the sense of guilt, and trembling under the terrors of the law that proclaims—"The soul that sinneth it shall die,"—this gospel is intended for you. He comes this day to invite you, "Come to me and I will give you rest." "There is no condemnation to them that are in Christ Jesus." If there be any soul seeking the way of life, yet groping his way in darkness, this gospel to-day is intended for you. He comes to ask that you take his hand and be led by him, saying "I will lead the blind by a way they know not." Nay, if there be one whose soul longs for this salvation, but finds faith so weak that it is ashamed and afraid to offer such a faith; this gospel, to-day, is to assure you and encourage you to come—saying, "A bruised reed he will not break, nor quench the smoking flax." If there be one afraid to covenant with Christ because of a sense of impotence to keep his vows, from so often having broken them; this gospel is intended for you to-day. He comes to assure you, I will never leave thee nor forsake thee. Venture boldly, but venture wholly. "Rise take up thy bed and walk!" Yes! "this day is this scripture fulfilled! This is the acceptable year of the Lord."

DISCOURSE XI.

THE GROUND OF OUR SALVATION NOT ETHICAL BUT EVAN-
GELICAL : AND LIES WHOLLY IN THE INFINITE DESIRE
OF FATHER, SON AND SPIRIT TO SAVE SINNERS.

LUKE xv.   Then drew near unto him all the publicans and sinners for to
hear him.

And the Pharisees and Scribes murmured, saying,—This man receiveth
sinners and eateth with them.   And he spake this parable unto them, saying,—What man of you, having an hundred sheep, if he lose one of them,
doth not leave the ninety and nine in the wilderness, and go after that
which is lost, until he find it ?

I say unto you, that likewise, joy shall be in heaven over one sinner that
repenteth, more than over ninety and nine just persons, which need no
repentance.

Either what woman having ten pieces of silver, if she lose one piece, doth
not light a candle and sweep the house, and seek diligently till she find
it ? &c.

And he said, A certain man had two sons ; and the younger of them said
to his father, Father, give me the portion of goods, &c.   Son, thou art ever
with me, and all that I have is thine.   It was meet that we should make
merry, and be glad ; for this thy brother was dead, and is alive again ; and
was lost, and is found.

SUCH a breadth and depth of thought have all the utterances of Jesus, that a single paragraph furnishes more than
theme sufficient for an ordinary discourse.   Yet it is well for
us occasionally, to select as a theme for our meditations an
entire discourse, and seek to gather the wider views of truth
which are suggested by the analysis of an entire argument,
and a summary view of the bearing and relations of its several
parts to each other, and to the whole system of doctrine.

Indeed, in this way only can we properly apprehend and appreciate many of the great truths which he taught; since their full force can be perceived only as we contemplate at one view the truths developed by his argument in combination, and the grand results of his reasoning.

This fifteenth chapter of Luke contains a whole discourse of Jesus, consisting of three parables, all of them directed to the exposition and illustration of a great distinguishing principle of his gospel. A principle which in all ages has been a "hard saying" to the wisdom of the world; but which was specially inconceivable to the cold, narrow casuistic formalism into which, at the time Jesus appeared, the Church of God had apostatized under the covenant of grace, as developed by the covenant with David, concerning the typical kingdom of God.

The occasion which suggested the great subject of this discourse was the objection of the religious leaders of the Church that one claiming to be the Messiah of the covenant, should be run after so, by the masses of the ritually vile and contemptible; and that he should familiarly associate with such in utter disregard of that spiritual quarantine, which they deemed so essential to prevent the contamination of the holy from intercourse with publicans and sinners. They had often before, with plausible hypocrisy, urged this objection to destroy his influence with the better classes of society; and, even if honestly urged, it was chiefly a question of ritual. Yet, as in this case the objection was an outgrowth of the fatal error into which they had fallen, subverting the very central truth of the covenant of grace, he thinks it worth while to put the cavil to silence by exposing the entire misconception of the scheme of redemption on which it rests; and by bringing out in all its amazing fulness, the great principle upon which alone salvation is possible to any. For, as he proceeds to show, salvation is all of grace. The ground of selecting its objects is not any reason of ethical and ritual merit in them. It lies wholly in the love of Christ in seeking lost sinners ; of the Holy Spirit through the Church finding and renewing sinners : and of the Father who, in consequence of the work of Christ and his Spirit, receives and is reconciled to sinners, who are all alike undeserving, and hell-deserving sinners.

If the thoughts of this discourse are transcendently sublime, not less is the mode of presenting them transcendently simple and beautiful. In justification of his course he enters into no profound metaphysical discussion, adapted specially to the capacity of the learned cavillers, drawn from the nature of the covenant of redemption and the peculiarities of the theology revealed under it. So he might have done ; but having regard rather to the capacity of the poor publicans and sinners who, by reason of the discouragements from the religious teachers, have been led to think that religion is not a subject comprehensible by such as they ; he proceeds, by his favorite method of the parable, to present the whole matter of salvation something after our fashion of pictorial histories for the children, to aid their conception of the marvellous things of which they read. He presents, as it were, a magnificent panorama of redemption, a series of pictures exhibiting the attitudes and movements of all the parties to the infinite transaction. First, the picture of a scene in the great sin wilderness ; the shepherd, with uncalculating sympathy for the lost sheep, leaving the ninety and nine to go after the straying one ; and in the foreground of the picture is Christ the Great Shepherd joyfully leading back the lost sheep ; while, floating in the azure sky above, are the joyous faces of angels manifesting their glad wonder at his success. Next, the picture of the house-scene and the woman, his Church animated by the Holy Spirit, and employed by the Spirit as his instrument, with like uncalculating interest for the lost one

of her treasure, eagerly searching for it; and in the fore-
ground is the Spirit-moved woman gladly holding forth the
recovered treasure; while over her again are the faces of
sympathizing angels, glad at her gladness.   Next, the home-
scene of the Infinite Father, as the result of the foregoing
seeking and recovering of the lost, coming forth, in the full
yearnings of paternal love, to receive to his bosom the strayed
child that was "dead and is alive again;" while the angels
gather to the old home from which he strayed, with holy
rejoicings to welcome back the lost one found.   And as
incidental to this are introduced views from the human side.
First, of the successive stages of the soul's progress in
straying. Second, of morose Pharisaism in contrast with the
rejoicing angels—standing coldly off refusing to go in and
partake of the general joy.

If we wished to analyze, in detail, this wonderful exposition
of the grand principles of redemption, no other method could
be more logical, exhaustive, and beautiful, than simply to take up
in detail the successive pictures of this series, and discuss,
First, on the divine side, the work of Christ, the Mediator,
seeking the straying souls and the principles and motives
from which he acts.   Second, the work of the Holy Spirit
through the Church with her ordinances; and the principles
and motives from which he acts.   Third, the Father's act of
amnesty and reconciliation in consequence of the work of
Christ and the Spirit; and the principles and motives impelling him thereto.   Fourth, the sympathetic interest of the
holy universe of intelligent beings in these great transactions.
Then on the human side, Fifth, the view, or rather the
series of views, of the wayward soul in its straying, and the
process of its restoration to the old heaven home from which
it has strayed.   And sixth, the picture of cold ethicalism in
its selfishness and self-righteousness, carping at this danger-

ous, unethical enthusiasm over a miserable, thriftless, worthless sinner.

The limits of a single discourse, however, are too narrow for such an exposition in detail. Let us seek, rather, in a more summary method to gather the general doctrines of the argument of Jesus, from the three parables. This we may do by a consideration of the three general topics which the argument of the three parables expounds and illustrates :—

First. The principles and impulses on the divine side, which prompt and govern the work of redemption.

Second. The principles and impulses which, working in the soul, lead to its redemption.

Third. In contrast with these, the principles and impulses of that ethical gospel of the casuistic Scribes and ritualistic Pharisees, which it is a chief aim of Jesus, in this discourse of the three parables, to expose and rebuke.

I.—The obvious meaning of the whole argument is, that, in the first place, as before the eye of God and all holy beings, the whole world lieth in wickedness alike ; that ALL have gone astray ; that there is none that doeth good ; and therefore the very conception of any meritorious party, as contrasted with the wrath-deserving publicans and sinners is utterly absurd—-It is another form of stating the great truth in which the entire gospel theology finds its starting place ; that all men, by reason of a vast spiritual apostasy at the very origin of the race, are fallen, by nature, and lie in an estate of sin and misery. Any theory which ignores this fundamental fact cannot possibly lead to a right comprehension of the revealed gospel of God. Yet—while declaring man utterly depraved and lost, the whole head sick and the whole heart faint, all wounds and bruises and putrifying sores—the gospel has no sort of sympathy with the morose, cynical philosophy that scoffs at the littleness of man and his baseness, and asks sneer-

ingly, " What is man that Thou shouldst be mindful of him
or the Son of man that thou visitest him?"   It recognizes
him, base as he is, as originally made for a higher condition,
and even yet capable of a glorious destiny.   Accordingly,
Jesus here represents all the holy universe as interested for
him.   Seeking sinners, finding sinners, receiving sinners,
rejoicing over sinners is the grand idea of all heaven, and, in
heaven, is the fundamental conception of redemption.   The
mediatorial work of Christ was to go after sinners straying
and stumbling on the dark mountains.

The office of the Holy Ghost through all the ordinances of
the Church is diligently to seek for the sinner as for lost
treasure.   The Infinite Father's heart yearns for the
straying sinners as over his lost children, debased as they
may have become, and rejoices over their return.   And all
the holy beings that, as " ministers of his that do his pleasure,"
are full of sympathetic concern for the lost ; of sympathetic
interest for their restoration ; and of sympathetic joy over
their return.

The attitude of God the Saviour toward man the sinner, is
not that of an Infinite Ruler chaffering about terms of amnesty ˙
—The scheme of the theology revealed from heaven is no
commercial calculation of profit and loss to the universe, of
saving or of leaving to perish.   The God whom it reveals is
not an infinite political economist, working out the problem of
what souls it will cost too much to save, and the saving of
what other souls will require little sacrifice of the majesty and
stern demands of justice.   Jesus transfers the whole matter
out of the sphere of the cold, calculating ethical reason, into
the sphere of the heart moved by the natural impulses and
sympathies and affections, whose forces are not to be estimated
by the measures of reason and expediency.   So he here
represents every aspect of the work of salvation.

The Mediator who undertook to procure salvation ; the

Holy Spirit who applies the benefits of his mediation through the ordinances of the Church; the Father who, thereby, is reconciled and receiving back the straying soul—all are actuated by motives that are analogous to the natural affections and their impulses, rather than analogous to the cautious ethical judgments of the reason. And, so far from seeing, in this, anything of danger to the stability of God's eternal law of righteousness, and therefore jealously watching the movements of infinite love in favour of the apostate race—all the holy beings in the universe are looking on with sympathetic enthusiasm from the lofty eminences of their holiness, and the return of any one sinner of all the guilty race, crying: "Father, I have sinned" spreads joy and high gratulation through all the mansion in heaven!

This is wonderful, surpassingly wonderful, to mere human conceptions; and to the ethical philosophy of this world seems a most dangerous view of religion. All Scribedom shudders, at seeing thus brushed away the elaborate ramparts of casuistic cobweb which it hath erected to fence in purity and holy respectability from the contamination of publicans and sinners. All Phariseedom shrinks in horror, " as the kingdom of heaven suffereth violence " under the preaching of such a gospel, at the thought of soiling the sky-pure blue of the hem of its garments, and of the shocking rumpling of its showy phylacteries, in the press and jostling of the vulgar crowd of the accursed.

And yet, if our limits permitted, it might readily be shown that in thus describing the impulses that move all heaven for the sinner's salvation, Jesus hath by no means carried us beyond all analogies of nature, or reasoned contrary to all natural analogies; and that it is the Scribes and Pharisees who, absorbed in their casuistic and ritualistic abstractions, have forgotten nature and common sense. Nay, but it needs no argument and defence from us. Jesus himself, with a divine subtlety of logic, has construed the argument by the very selection of his analogies in the parables. The all-absorbing zeal of the shepherd to recover the lost sheep that is oblivious of the ninety and nine that are not lost; the like zeal of the woman, that seems to make little account of the nine pieces in her eagerness to recover the lost one; the yearning of the father's heart and his all-absorbing joy at the recovery of the lost son, as if he had no other son all the while;—all these are pictures of very paradoxical things, and curious problems in human nature which it would puzzle reason to solve by its rules of ethics, propriety and expediency. And yet every body knows that they are most natural things,—beautifully natural, and true to the life as heart pictures! Somehow, whether there is any reason and propriety in the thing or not, the natural men and women of earth,—the shepherds, the housekeepers, the fathers and mothers—will feel a concern about the straying sheep, the lost money and the wayward son, that seems to make them comparatively heedless of that which is all safe in possession. Somehow they will rejoice more over the one found than over the ninety and nine, the nine, or the one, not lost! And their good friends and neighbours will, somehow, sympathize more with their joy, in recovering the lost than in their contentment with what is not lost—yet all this they will do in utter disregard of the astute reasonings of the philosophy of expediency, the acute theories of the economists, and the staid dignities and proprieties of the worldly-wise sages! The one sheep that has strayed from the fold will occupy more of the thoughts and engage more of the earnest attention than all that have not strayed. The misfortune that causes the loss of the tithe of a man's property will be felt by him more keenly than all the enjoyments of the possession that still remains to him. He will feel, and his friends will feel, a keener sense of joy over the recovery of the lost. The father's thoughts will go after

the son that has wandered ; the son far off exposed to danger
from shipwreck and the battle field ; the son whom calamity
has overtaken; and his return in safety, or his relief, will
cause a joy not felt towards the sons who have been ever with
him.   Every day we may see the illustration of the principle
of the joy among the angels over one sinner that repenteth.
See, when one child of this large household is smitten, and is
fighting the death battle with disease, how the one monopolizes
for the time being, all the attention, as if there were no other
unsmitten children in the house.   All the thoughts, all the
heart anxieties, of father, mother, brothers, sisters, concentrate upon the sufferer as if every life was bound up in
this one life.   Nay, the interest spreads to the whole circle
of friends in the neighbourhood, and a thousand anxious
inquiries and earnest sympathies crowd in from every side.
And now, as the indications are that the fight is won, and
death baffled, what joy begins to well up out of the heart of
father, mother, brothers, sisters, and to overspread every
countenance !   What joyous congratulations from friends
everywhere !

Need I remind you how in these days of dreadful carnage
and suffering on the battle field, all the interest of the family
concentrates upon the noble son who has gone forth to the
toils and dangers of war.   And how after the battle, as the
whole country waits in breathless expectation for the news of
victory or defeat, one could not tell, on visiting that family,
that there was any other being in the universe about whom
they felt any special concern, until the question of the safety
of the absent son is settled ?   And when the word comes
that all is well with him a joy fills their hearts that seems to
exclude all joy over the other sons that have remained in
safety.

Now Jesus, selecting his analogies in a manner to bring
out this principle of human nature that is so indisputable as

a fact, whether it square with theoretic reasoning or not, simply transfers the whole matter of salvation to the same sphere, as analogous to these natural impulses. He might, doubtless, of his infinite knowledge have suggested to the learned scribes reasons of infinite force, why Christ and the Spirit and the Father, and the holy angels in sympathy also, felt this special interest in lost men. Perhaps it is because there was something special in the case of man, as a new order of being in the universe, a compound order of animal and angel which caused all heaven to feel an interest—first, in his creation, then in his trial, and then in his recovery after his fall. Man may have some mysterious importance of this sort from his peculiar relations to the universe. We have in Scripture mention of three occasions in which the angelic orders evinced sympathetic joy. The first was on the occasion of the creation of man and his world. " Then the morning stars sang together, and all the sons of God shouted for joy." The second, the occasion when the Son of God became man. " A multitude of the heavenly host was with the angel praising God, and saying glory to God in the highest, on earth peace, good will towards men." The third is the occasion mentioned by Jesus in this discourse. " There is joy in the presence of the angels of God over one sinner that repenteth." From collating these three occasions we would be led, naturally enough, to the inference, that there is some high mysterious importance attached by the universe of purely spiritual beings to the calling into existence of this new and peculiar order of being, the compound creature man; a creature not after the angelic order of a separate, individual, immaterial existence, but capable, through the connection of his spirit with matter, of communicating the power of an endless life to a whole race of beings propagated from him. Hence possibly the concern at the failure of the experiment in his trial; and therefore the joy and praising God at the near completion of the scheme for his restoration; hence the special joy at every instance of the success of that scheme in the repentance and return of the sinner.

But Jesus enters into no such high argument. He is preaching to the capacity of the poor, the publicans, the sinners who comprehend little of theology. Therefore he simply illustrates by a fact in the sphere of nature, that all alike comprehend the certainty and force of; that the natural feelings of the heart run not according to the cold abstract reasonings of men. And then explains the relations of God to sinners, under the gospel, as coming within the sphere of the unbidden impulses of the heart and natural affection rather than of the cold reasonings of ethical philosophy and natural religion.

II.—Incidental to this great pictorial theology on the divine side, is the pictorial series illustrative of a soul history, in the outworkings of the gospel plan. First, is presented the scene of a quiet home, the result of industry, thrift and economy under God's great law " in the sweat of thy brow thou shalt eat bread." And earth now can furnish no nearer a resemblance to that original home of the race in Paradise from which man fell. But, strangely enough, there is seen one standing, as the central figure of the picture, amid all its scenes of comfort and peace, with every mark of dissatisfaction and impatience. One idea is dominant in his mind—the idea of independence. Ambitious of being his own man, buoyant with many illusive hopes, he somewhat arrogantly demands, " Give me the portion that falleth to me " that I may do as I will with my own, and goes forth to be " lord of himself, that heritage of wo."

I must leave each one of you, brethren, to answer for himself, as we pass rapidly in review these pictures, how far this is your soul history.

A second picture now presents itself. Instead of the quiet

home, behold the hall of gayety and revelry, radiant with light, peopled with crowds of pleasure-seekers. The wine cup sparkles ; the dance wreathed in circles of glorious fascination ; music charms the senses ; wit, jocund rep rtee, song, beguile the hours. In the midst of the scene we recognize the youth of the former picture ; yet how greatly changed. The natural excitement and glow of youth has given place to the unnatural, feverish excitement of the madman, with disgust for the present, eagerly grasping at the future and the unattained. Every countenance indicates effort to think and feel, this is pleasure, while the inner consciousness gives the lie to the profession.

Let those who crowd the avenues to fame and pleasure, judge for themselves how far this is a life picture.

A third picture presents itself. The splendid hall of revelry is in the back ground, all gloomy and deserted. The brilliant lights are extinguished ; the garlands faded ; the stage scenery is removed ; and the stripped machinery exposes the coarse pullies, the dirty ropes, the greasy lamps, the rough boards, that moved and supported all the gay pageant. And here in the foreground sits a skeleton-like figure, with eyes unnaturally strained in search of food. We recognize in it the youth of the first picture ; and the man of pleasure in the second. Ragged and friendless he is gazing enviously upon a lean herd of swine, as they devour the rough pods of the carob tree. Yet it is plain that, under all the desires of the physical nature for food, there are other thoughts troubling him. There is a consciousness of self-degradation, of utter, incorrigible folly, of self-loathing and self-condemnation. There is a struggle, as between midnight darkness and flashes of light. Memory recalls glorious recollections, and despair dashes the hopes inspired by memory : till at length assuming the courage of a man he seems, to resolve " I will arise and go to my father."

This picture presents the whole gospel theory of man's natural condition, even as he himself must see it when he comes to himself. A being constituted as he is, even while he is straying away from God, must feel in his nature, if he will heed it, the gnawings of an unappeasable hunger. For "man cannot live by bread alone." Hence this perpetual restlessness and discontent, even when "all the kingdoms of the world and the glory of them" have been obtained. These souls are hungry. They are trying to feed on carob pods which are no true soul-food, only husks that the swine do eat. Hence those passions that render life miserable. This envy is but the sore hunger casting its malignant, selfish glance at the imagined soul-feeding of others. It is famine glaring upon the food of others, the sight of which only rasps and tortures the hungry soul the more! This cynical moroseness, and this remorse, are but the sore famine, turning in to prey upon the famished man's own flesh. And so of all other passions. Hence saith the gospel prophet, "The wicked are as the troubled sea which cannot rest, whose waters cast up mire and dirt. There is no peace saith my God to the wicked." This is the gospel explanation of the phenomena of human nature in its restlessness and passions. And man is not far-sighted enough to see what is the matter with him, till, under the impulses of the Spirit, "he come to himself." Then, as he begins to be rational, his dreadful condition breaks upon him and drives him to Christ for help.

Once more the canvas moves. The scene of the first picture in part reappears, the blessed home. But on the fore-ground of the picture appears a wretched-looking, emaciated man that totters and averts his face in shame, as he stretches forth his hands beseechingly. We recognize him as the same who has figured in different aspects in each of the views. Coming towards him with out-stretched arms of welcome appears the father from whom he so rudely separated in the first view.   The figures dissolve as we gaze upon them, and lo! the old mansion becomes lighted up, and there is a glad gathering of friends, and all the symbols of rejoicing over the lost one found.

Brethren, can you testify to the truthfulness of this picture also ?   If not, then as you follow this series of pictures to the conclusion, no more conceive of the gospel call as simply a cold ethical command ; and of obedience to it a mere cold calculating resolve to reform, which resolve shall be executed at some convenient season.   Endeavour to enter into the spirit of this soul-stirring picture of Jesus ; give that hungry soul of yours a chance ; and if you feel "I am perishing with hunger," arise, just as you are, and go to your Father ; and, with uncalculating child-like affection, rush to his arms, and spring within the blow of the rod of justice.   Then " shall there be joy in the presence of the angels of God " over you also !

III.—Having thus expounded the spirit and principles of the theology of salvation on the divine side, and on the human side, Jesus proceeds to expose and rebuke the ethical gospel of the Scribes and Pharisees, by exhibiting in contrast with all these noble and generous evangelical views of Christ, the Spirit, the Father and the holy angels, and of the rescued sinner, the reasoning and spirit of the representative man of the ethical gospel.   For we need not care here to enter into any learned enquiry with Jerome, Tertullian, and other fathers, whether the historic original of the younger son be the Gentiles, and the historic original of the older son, the Jews.   No matter to whom primary reference is made as the original of the portraits—if there be any such primary reference at all—" the word is spoken unto us," and paints our times just as truly.   It was spoken in reference to a revival of religion which interested the masses of the people, while it aroused the murmurs of unspiritual formalists.   And when-

ever the like thing occurs—whether in the awakening of the
masses, or the awakening of a single soul, giving rise to the
same objections—then of that thing Jesus is here speaking.

The canvas moves, therefore, once more, and, throwing
the illuminated home into the back-ground, presents, in the
fore-ground, the representative of staid and proper formalism
greatly excited; but with any other feelings than sympathy
in the general joy.   Hearing the news, and observing the joy
which it occasions, he is indignant, and will not go in.   As
in the previous pictures we have inside views of the whole
gospel scheme; so now we have the outside view of the whole
matter, as viewed objectively by world wisdom, which has
never yet experienced its saving power.

And the more carefully we analyze the picture, the more
wonderful will its life-likeness impress us, as a portraiture of
a phase of religion, and indeed a family of religionists, who
appear upon the stage whenever the work of divine grace
manifests its power among the publicans and sinners, and
whenever the shepherd rejoices, and the woman rejoices, and
the father, with all the angels, rejoices over the lost found.   I
have space to present only the general peculiarities and
phases of the antagonism to the gospel symbolized by this
elder brother.

The same fundamental theory of religion represented by
this elder brother, with its ethical gospel and its hostility to
evangelical faith, may exist, and in fact always has existed,
under two somewhat opposite phases.   One, the gospel of
Formalism, with its ethics of " days and weeks and months
and years;" with its penances and prayers-sayings; with
its charitable works of merit and its punctilious ritual observances.   The other, the gospel of Rationalism, with its elaborate rules of ethics; of obedience to the laws of human nature;
with its spiritual insights to guide to all truth of natural
religion; with its special reverence for the dignity of human

nature, in the higher and purer specimens of it. Thus it was at the time of Jesus' appearing. Phariseeism and Sadducceism, however at war between themselves, yet uniting on the common platform of an ethical gospel, made common cause against the doctrines of the new kingdom of God. Thus it continued to be during the ministry of Paul in a different field. The ritualistic " Jew required a sign ;" the rationalistic " Greek sought after wisdom ;" while both alike were hostile to a scheme of salvation by grace, which was " to the Jew a stumbling block, and to the Greek foolishness." And the great burden of the Apostle's masterly argumentations is the defence of " salvation by grace not of works, lest any man should boast "—against the ritualism which insisted on the merit of ceremonial observances, on the one hand, and the rationalism that scoffed at the unethical character of his gospel on the other.

And, in every age since, these have been the true dividing lines between the religions of all Christendom. Since the great Reformation—itself a grand struggle of the revived gospel of Jesus, first against the ritualism which had stifled its voice for ages, and then against the rationalism which, while rejecting the spiritual despotism, despised the doctrine of salvation by grace, even more than the ritual dogmas of the priestly despots—the whole field of religious thought has been subdivided between these three general forms ;—of Phariseeism with its ethics of ritual as the ground of a sinner's claim ; Rationalism or Sadducceism with its ethics of natural religion and its pretended obedience to the whole law ; and Spiritualism with its gospel of saving the lost by the direct interposition of divine love, without works of merit, but simply because Christ loved us and gave himself for us : because the Spirit loves and seeks out and renews the lost sinner ; because the Father " so loved the world that he gave his only begotten Son."

And, perhaps, at no period of the world's history have these three systems been fighting the battle more vigorously than at this day. Alas, I ought to say perhaps, that never have the two great antagonists of the gospel been more vigorous in their fierce hostility to this gospel of grace for publicans and sinners, or more subtle in the arts whereby they would destroy its power in the world; while the gospel itself seems to have become enervated, its triumphs checked, and its champions disposed to make terms of capitulation, and give up the strongholds of truth!

Nay, to give more definiteness to your conceptions, I may remind you that you may see this conflict going on within your own circle. If you examine the matter a little, you shall find the religion of all the men and women of your acquaintance dividing into these three great *churches*. Not according to the ostensible denominational lines of distinction, at all, but by lines of division running across all these lines. Of one division the Papist leads the van; but in his wake follows a long line of ritualists, gradually shading down to a few simple forms held in connection with the true gospel faith. Of another division the devotees of " the advanced thought "—who have discovered that the gospel of Christ is a laggard no longer to be borne with as a dead weight upon their march; and, almost abreast of the main advance, Unitarianism—falsely so calling it *nihil-arianism*—marches, with its long line following; not tapering, but spreading its ever-widening skirt over numerous phases of religious thought in all churches, Popish and Protestant alike. Of a third division, the most earnest of those in all churches who contend earnestly for the faith once delivered to the saints, as the foundation of the gospel offer to the publicans and sinners, lead the van; and these followed at different intervals—according as their zeal is strengthened and quickened by the knowledge which Christ has prescribed to direct Christian zeal- by the various sections of those whose hearts are touched by this gospel for publicans and sinners.

Now nothing can be conceived more exquisite than the skill with which Jesus paints this representative man, as a general portrait, equally life-like, of either and of all the phases of this ethical religionism, whether ritual or rationalistic, whether openly infidel or covert under great apparent zeal, for the publicans and sinners.

The chief lines of the character are : First, his calm, cool spirit of inquiry, which carefully avoids any contamination from the joyous excitement that reigns in the house. " He would not go in." He is one who does not allow himself to feel joyous from mere infection of sympathy, even with friends who are all hilarity. The emotions, on his theory, are not to be allowed to gush wildly from the heart, but made to behave themselves in the most marvellously proper manner, by being allowed to exhibit themselves only—after reason has carefully considered whether it is fit occasion—according to rule. " He heard music and dancing, and he called one of the servants, and asked what these things meant ?"

Second, his grave attempt to investigate the ethical fitness of things, first, by reason ; excluding, as of no account in the matter, all impulses of affection. Instead of rushing in at the news to share the general joy, he stands without in silent dignified rebuke of the fanaticism. He will first weigh in the balance of sober reason these emotions ; and, of course, the unbidden unreasoning emotions of the heart will weigh very little in such scales.

Third. With all his cool deliberate emotionless power of judgment, " *he is angry.*" How paradoxical, and yet how natural and true to the life ! For in all ages alike has this paradox exhibited itself, that the grave philosophic men of ethics and the stately and dignified men of rituals, alike, while so cautiously avoiding all impulses of the gospel *love*, have yet uniformly indulged very freely the impulses of anger toward the evangelical faith. While treating the impulses of enthusiastic love in the heart as fatal to any well-balanced judgment in religion, they seem altogether unconscious that the opposite emotion of anger can in the least disturb the delicate balance of their ethical judgments. Nothing is more remarkable in the history of the conflict of evangelical faith with its two great antagonists, than the fact, that in proportion as the former is earnest and sincere in its zeal for the salvation of publicans and sinners, does it rouse the anger and malignity of its antagonists. The calm ethical philosopher, whose spirit is unruffled as the sleeping waters on all other topics in the domain of truth, becomes most unphilosophically angry when the subject is " the truth as it is in Jesus."

The stately devotee of the ritual, while he can patiently endure, even with a half-forgiving smile, any and every form of rationalistic, semi-rationalistic, or unearnest dissent from his apostolical authority, yet can seldom refrain from anger when the dissent comes from the disciples of an earnest evangelical faith. Pilot and Herod here make friends over the condemnation of Jesus ; and the grave philosopher can sneer just as malignantly, and the grave ritualist curse, just as heartily as common men.

Fourth, his contemptuous refusal to acknowledge as of the same blood with himself and part of the family, the humbled sinner who cries " father I have sinned." " This thy son " saith he—not my brother—" which has devoured thy living with harlots." The significancy of this, and its truthfulness, few of you need to have pointed out who have witnessed the ridiculous affectation of exclusive ritualists. I pass on therefore to the more important errors represented.

Fifth, his argument against the ethical justice of thus receiving back the erring sinner—" Thou hast killed for him the fatted calf." The principle of his argument is precisely the same which is involved in all the scoffs and sneers and learned reasonings of ethicalism in all ages.   On the one hand the injustice of bestowing the reward of everlasting life upon the utterly undeserving.   On the other hand the inexpediency of it ; for what shall become of virtue in the world, if heaven is not the reward of virtue ?   " Shall we not continue in sin that grace abound ?''   Nay, sin the more to have it abound the more ? And the answer of the true gospel is precisely the same in all ages.   In the first place, as to the justice of the thing.   If put upon that ground none can be saved, for none deserve it ; all have sinned.   But if Jesus Christ have satisfied divine justice for all that let him represent them, then justice is magnified and the law made honourable.

And as to the danger to virtue from salvation by grace without works, Jesus prefers to risk his government on the love of the souls won by his love to obedience.   And besides, the provision which he has made for their pardon and justifica-tion, as righteous before God, includes also a provision to secure their newness of life,—those to whom there is now no con-demnation, because in Christ Jesus, " walk not after the flesh but after the spirit."

Sixth, his self-righteousness and selfish exacting spirit. " Lo these many years do I serve thee, neither transgressed I at any time."   And all this perfection boasted of while in the very act of offering insult and violence to every impulse of a father's heart, by rebuking, as ethically wrong, his joy over a son restored : is this no sin ?   I have not space left to dwell upon this very remarkable feature of all ethical religion ; its self-righteous assumption to rebuke the justice and fitness of the loving impulses of the Infinite Father ; its assumption to itself of a perfect integrity while in the very act of putting wrong and contempt upon God ; its commercial spirit that seeks to pay its own way into God's presence and favour, yet relying chiefly upon driving a sharp bargain, to gain the maxi-

mum of glory for the minimum market price ; its substitution
for the humble petition, " God be merciful to me a sinner,"
and the plea " Make me, all unworthy to be called thy son,
only as one of thy hired servants ;" the exacting demand—
" I have served thee many a year,"—" Give me a kid that I
may make merry with my friends !"

Seventh, not less worthy of note is the effrontery and
ingratitude and falsehood upon which the representative of
the ethical gospels founds his argument.   " Lo these many
years have I served thee and thou never gavest me a kid !"
And all this in face of the fact that the father, before the prodigal departed, had " divided *unto them his living*"—doubtless
assigning to this one his full half of the estate with the understanding that he is to be sole heir—since saith he " all that I
have is thine !"   Yet all this is nothing !

And is not this the very falsehood and ingratitude that
underlies all these legalistic claims to eternal life ?   They
uniformly forget, in their zeal against the injustice of salvation wholly of grace—irrespective of the works they boast of,
that God has already rewarded very fairly and fully their
moralities, their charities, their abstinence from the sensualities
of the prodigal.   " Where is the reward and encouragement
of all our self-restraint and virtuous acts, and charitable
deeds," say they, " if after all, publicans and sinners shall
enter heaven, merely on accepting the offer."   Jesus answers
all such, saying, " Verily I say unto you, ye have your
reward."   If God's power is to be measured and determined
upon the principle of " a fair day's wages for a fair day's
work," then hath he not already fairly paid ?   Hath he not
fairly " divided the living" between you and the prodigals ?
Ye men of all the virtues, moralities and respectabilities, have
ye not been all the while enjoying his estate in the life that
now is ; and all the comforts which his generous hand strewed
around you ?   Have not men honoured and trusted you, as

the reward of your integrity, thrift and economy ? Have not men applauded and idolized you because of your wise philanthropic deeds, or your distinguished intellectual attainments ? And yet, on seeing the sovereign grace of God bestowing his kindness on publicans and sinners, ye say, " We have served him and have received nothing." Is this your lofty integrity ; your fair dealing toward God ? Will ye take the full and generous wages for the service in the life that is, and then demand a monopoly in the life to come also ? Shame on such integrity !

How wonderful this portraiture of the cold, calculating, self-justifying gospel according to ethics !

But not less wonderful is the profound and annihilating response, with the re-utterance of the great truth he had before been illustrating through the three parables of his discourse : " Thy brother was dead and is *alive again*." It is not a case to be measured by your ethical calculations ! It is a case of life and death, that arouses every holy impulse of the heart. Ethical philosophy will do very well in the sphere of the natural ; but how shall it undertake to settle the terms and the price for a resurrection from the dead ?

Brethren, this is our short answer to all the scoffs and sneers, whether rationalistic or ritualistic, that malign us as enthusaists and fanatics, because we preach a gospel to publicans and sinners, and find our souls stirred by its success. Thy " brother was *dead* and is alive again." The scoffers have their scoffs simply because of their profound ignorance of the true condition of man before God, as vile and guilty and condemned already—" dead in trespasses and sins;" of the true nature of that power which raises him to newness of life ; of the true nature of the emotions in the soul thus rescued as a brand from the burning. If there were nothing more serious than the occasional aberration of a fine, noble, ingenuous nature, then all our zeal would indeed be fanatical. But this conversion of a sinner is a mighty work of the power that first called light out of darkness ; a wonder of mercy in raising a dead soul out of an eternal hell, to restore it to an eternal heaven ? Surely "It is *meet* that we make merry and be glad thereat !"

DISCOURSE XII.

THE AWARD OF THE JUDGMENT TO COME TO BE MADE ON PRINCIPLES NOT ETHICAL BUT EVANGELICAL.

MATTHEW xxv. 31–46.—When the Son of man shall come in his glory, and all the holy angels with him, then shall he sit upon the throne of his glory; and before him shall be gathered all nations; and he shall separate them from one another; as a shepherd divideth his sheep from the goats and he shall set his sheep on his right hand, but the goats on the left. Then shall the king say unto them on his right hand, Come, ye blessed of my Father, inherit the kingdom prepared for you from the foundation of the world: For I was an hungered, and ye gave me meat; I was thirsty and ye gave me drink; I was a stranger, and ye took me in; naked and ye clothed me; I was sick, and ye visited me; I was in prison and ye came unto me.

Verily I say unto you, inasmuch as ye have done it unto the least of my brethren, ye have done it unto me, &c.

SUCH is the wonderful conclusion of the wonderful discourse which Jesus delivered, privately, to his disciples as they sat on the Mount of Olives, the day before his betrayal. It is a discourse embodying more real knowledge of the way, and to what end men live, of the law of existence under which men live, and of the final results and eternal destinies of humanity, than is to be found in the tomes of all the unevangelical schools in the world. And such is the logical unity of idea which runs through its lofty generalizations, binding all its varied views of the relations of humanity into one vast argument, that the power of the whole is concentrated upon this peroration of that judgment to come, which shall reach back, and take fast hold of, all the impulses and activities of the life that now is.

In answer to their inquiries, "When shall these things

(the destruction of Jerusalem) be? and what shall be the sign of thy coming and of the end of the world?" he narrates prophetically, the events which shall precede and the circumstances which shall attend the beginning of the work of judgment which is to close up the old dispensation with the approaching destruction of Jerusalem, its centre ; and also the events which shall precede and the circumstances of the judgment— of which the former is a type—that, shall close up the next, and last dispensation, with convulsions which shall shatter the great temple of nature itself and leave not one stone upon another.

By his favourite method of the parable—that logical two-edged sword piercing to the soul, at the same time through the imagination and the reason—he develops the relation of all life under this last dispensation to the judgment which is to follow it, and, at the same time, in order to compel men's attention to these principles, through their powers of associations he devises a system of spiritual mnemonics that hangs his lessons of judgment to come, here, for the husbandman, on the fig-tree by his garden wall, where he walks at evening, here, for the household in the apartments of the servants ; here, for heedless and impulsive youth, and for all the thoughtless pleasure-seekers, amid the brilliant scenes of the marriage festivities, and rejoicings ; here, for the eager calculating men of business, amid the bustling activities of trade and finances, and on the tables of the money-lender in the exchange.

This life, as relating to the ministers left in charge of his Church, is symbolized as that of the servant faithful to execute the orders of the absent master, with an eye ever watching his coming ; or of the unfaithful servant, forgetful of his duty, and of the day of reckoning. The inner life in the souls of christian people is set forth as that of virgins waiting for the coming of the bridegroom—all alike asleep from his long delay ; but some, thoughtful to have oil in their lamps ready to join the torch-light procession; others, thoughtless, having none. This inner life, as also developing itself in outward activities, is symbolized as the life of servants, factors with entrusted capital, who shall render it back with great increase, and receive honour and applause; or without increase and receive shame and everlasting contempt.

Having in this amazing generalization presented the prophetic history, not only of the destruction of Jerusalem, but of the signs which shall distinguish the whole subsequent life of humanity, and its relations to the life to come, the divine teacher finds a peroration not unworthy the grandeur of his high argument. With the easy, unlabouring movement of an infinite mind, he presents the scenes of the judgment which shall close up the last, as the judgment upon Jerusalem closed up the previous dispensation. And this in a manner not only to burn them indelibly into the imagination, but bring their infinite truths within reach of the humblest human understanding.

The hour, betokened by all the previous signs of his coming, suddenly bursts, unanticipated, upon the living generations. The hand of the Almighty lets go its hold; and the beautiful universe drops into general chaos. The sun is turned into darkness; and the moon into blood; and the stars fall from their places. The elemental fires burst forth; the heavens as a parched scroll roll up: and lo! behind the rolled up screen, the " Son of man is come in his glory !" Spirits hoary with the revolutions of eternity attend him with reverent awe; and the sons of God, who shouted for joy at the birth of Time, are here to stand with Him at Time's infinite grave. The Son of man is come now, as a king and judge, to mount his glorious throne of judgment. At his command the archangel sounds the trumpet for the opening of the assize, and summoning the earth to give up the imprisoned dead, and the sea the dead that are in it. The sharp summons echoes through all the wide domain of the world. " In a moment, in the twinkling of an eye" the living change the mortal for the immortal; and ringing through the sepulchres of the earth and the deep caverns of the sea, the summons pierces the dull cold ear of death. It disinherits them all. The earth heaves; its charnel houses rattle, its tombs burst. The sea is stirred to its depths, and its surface hidden by the myriads of the sleepers rising from it. The air is alive with spirits, rehabilitating in the spiritual bodies which have sprung from the natural bodies as their germ. They gather in innumerable array—all the generations which the stream of time has swept into the grave—re-awakened and re-invested around that "throne of his glory!" They stand under the heart-searching eye of Omniscience, trembling as the leaves of an aspen forest in the twilight, with the struggling soul emotions of hope and fear, of confident assurance or trembling apprehension, of glad expectation or remorseful despair.

" And he shall separate them from one another, as a shepherd divideth his sheep from the goats." It needs but a single glance of the judge's eye, in this court, to discriminate the real character of every one of this " great multitude that no man can number." The decision depends not upon evidence of facts, but evidence of consciousness anterior to the facts. The quibbles and arts of the special pleader are unknown at this bar, for they avail nothing to delude the judgment of far-seeing Omniscience. The black guilt of the soul that never uttered itself in word and act, or that hid most securely from the keenest scrutiny of human skill, is laid bare, in all its deformity, to the instant glance of the judge. And as he sees so he divides : and by a line of separation that crosses all lines hitherto run between men. It divides between those of the same household, of the same circle of friends, of the same neighbourhood. It puts a father on the right, and a son on the left ; a mother on the right, and a daughter on the left ; a sister on the right, and a brother on the left ; a wife on the

· right, and a husband on the left : a servant on the right and a master on the left ; a peasant on the right, and a prince on the left.

With a smile that lights up the universe, the Royal Judge invites the one part, saying, " Come ye blessed of my Father, inherit the kingdom prepared for you." It seems to them as a dream. They speak of their unworthiness of this unbounded mercy; but are reassured. Joy transports them. The trial is ended; their destiny is fixed beyond possibility of further change; the prize is won; and the crown of everlasting joy is on their heads.

But who shall attempt to conceive of, and describe the horrors of the multitudes on the left to whom, now turning, he saith, " Depart, ye cursed, into everlasting fire, prepared,— not for you, but—for the devil and his angels,"—with whom ye took part. They remonstrate and plead now ; but it is too late. It is finished with grace, " stretching out the hands all the day;" it is finished with wisdom's earnest argument, " lifting up her voice in the streets and in the chief places of concourse ;" it is finished with mercy pleading with, and weeping over the despisers of grace. Justice hath raised its sceptre and begun a new reign, that knows no interposition of " One mighty to save ;" and that therefore must endure for ever. Their groans, and wails, and threnes of despair avail not now, even to have " the rocks to fall upon them, and the hills to cover them, from the face of him that sitteth on the throne." Not a ray of hope alleviates the melting sorrow. The farewells are no blessings ; for farewell hath lost its meaning ; since there can be no hope of welfare thereafter. Terror sits enthroned on the brow of the King, and, there " remaining now no more sacrifice for sin," must remain there forever.

Contemplating with wonder and awe the appalling grandeur of this scene, we are ready to ask on what principle is this verdict rendered, of infinite joy on the one hand and infinite woe on the other? What heroic deeds of infinite glory have these done, to merit that welcome, "Come ye blessed of my Father?" What crimes of infinite blackness have these done? What guilt inexpiable, and of ineffaceable stain upon the soul, sends these away, under the terrific sentence " Depart ye cursed?" The whole turns upon this principle simply, as its pivot.—" I was hungry, ye gave me meat ; and ye did not. I was thirsty, ye gave me drink ; and ye did not. I was a stranger, ye took me in ; and ye did not. I was naked, ye clothed me ; and ye did not. I was sick, ye visited me ; and ye did not. I was in prison, ye came unto me ; and ye did not."

But how can such a test have application to all these myriads of all ages and generations ? Since only an obscure portion of one generation had ever seen the King, as the man of sorrows, hungry, thirsty, and friendless? Yes, but then " inasmuch as ye did it not unto the least of my brethren ye did it not unto me." In this he speaks not of the personal Jesus in the flesh, but of the representative Jesus, standing as head of that great enterprise of founding and gathering a kingdom for himself out of the wreck of " the works of the devil ;" and regarding every poor soul, called by divine grace to join him, and become a fellow-citizen of the saints, as so being one with him that what is done to the disciple, because he is a disciple, is done unto the Lord. Hence the profound significance of his saying to Judas and his fellow Apostles when complaining of Mary's waste of the ointment that should have been sold and given to the poor, " The poor ye have always with you." They stand as my representatives conti- nually, and give opportunity to test your love for me : therefore grudge not to their Lord the single offering, to him personally of a grateful heart anointing him for his burial. What ye do unto the poor, the very least of my brethren, is done unto me.

"Yes"—now joins in with us the delighted legalist—"that is just what I have always maintained concerning the nature and rewards of true religion. Precisely as I have held, so Christ here makes the whole of religion to hinge upon good works of charity to the poor and the suffering. What comes now of this theory that preaches ever of a new heart, and holy affections, and faith, as the essence of all religion?" "Yes"—chimes in the amiable worldly moralist and philanthropist—"and while you have been wrangling about your creeds and worships: your doctrines of atonement and justification by faith and regeneration; about your liturgies, and sacraments, and forms; I have been feeding and clothing the hungry and naked poor, and visiting the friendless and the prisoner. Nay, not content with individual effort, I have organized charitable societies of men and women, that have proved far more effective and useful, every way, than these churches. Is it not, after all, just as I have maintained—no matter for beliefs and creeds where a man can show his charitable deeds. "He can't be wrong whose life is in the right?"

But be not so hasty in the interpretation of these sayings of the Divine Teacher, as though they were the mere word chaff which the superficial sport with on the surface, dropping out into the unseen depths the weighty kernel of truth, of which the words are but the husks. Such hasty interpreters have failed utterly to see the profound depths of the vast argument from which Jesus is now concentrating the essence into this peroration of judgment. They forget that these are the words of the King, and relate to "the kingdom prepared from the foundation of the world;" developed as to its materials, through all the ages of the world, under his leadership, labours, suffering and superintendence; and now to be completed and constituted his eternal kingdom. And, therefore, nothing that is said here has relation to acts except as they bear upon the interests of that kingdom, and their relation to him as King thereof. They overlook the very essential peculiarity of this test—" Inasmuch as ye did it to the least of these my brethren, ye did it unto me."

You will perceive that, in this regard, the test to be applied to the life at the day of judgment is thoroughly evangelical. Christ makes himself the great turning point. " To me," saith he, " is your allegiance due ;" and as done unto me have all these acts their peculiar value. So that the question " what think ye of Christ ?" is substantially the test question of the judgment. And the six acts specified have their moral and spiritual value not intrinsically, but as exponential of the state of thought and feeling in the soul concerning Christ.

What comes then of thy boasted good works thou legalist? Of what value thy deeds of holiness, Christ the King and his kingdom not being in view in the performance of them ? When thou shalt stand up before the great King and say, " Lord ! Lord ! have I not done wonders of goodness—my acts of piety, are they not known of all men ? My marvellous charities, behold, are they not written in all the newspapers ?" Then shall the King say.—They were done unto men, and have their just reward in the praise of men : they were done for the sake of self-gratulation or to obtain the luxury of praise in the newspapers and have received their reward. Not being done unto me, and with an eye to the honour of my kingdom, they have no value in this inquest. " Depart from me, I never knew thee—thou hast never known me !" And in surprise and terror shalt thou pass to the left hand.

And thou, amiable world-moralist, so much to be loved and applauded of men for thy noble-heartedness and generosity ; for thine acts are indeed praiseworthy, as springing simply from the amiable impulses of thy nature, instead of the cold

calculations of self-righteous legalism. But alas! if thy
deeds are done only as unto men, from the natural impulses
of humanity, whatever may be their value otherwise—how
can they be of any account in this inquest of what has been
done as unto Christ? These amiable qualities of nature
cannot be accepted in lieu of the affectionate loyalty to
Christ! There is this fatal lack of one thing yet, in all
thy gifts of bread to the hungry, and drink to the thirsty,
and clothing to the naked—that all are given *not as unto
Christ!* How shall accomplishments of mind and heart or
deeds of thy life atone for the crime of neglecting such a
God and Saviour?

And thou, noble model-man adorned with refinements and
moralities of life. What though thou followest after stainless
honour; shrinkest from all meanness, as from the leprosy;
shunnest all unjust gains; livest the patriot and philanthropist, striving to ease the wounds of tortured humanity and to
exalt the masses above the clouds of ignorance?—Nay, what
though thou aspirest, with noble ambition, to rise thyself and
bask in the sunshine of all attainable knowledge and truth?
Why, for any of these, or all of these, shalt thou expect to
pass unchallenged by the Son of man, the King from whom
thou hast stood aloof; nor done any of thy noble acts, nor
made any of thy lofty attainments with reference to him?

The test of judgment, therefore, is thus plainly seen to be
thoroughly evangelical in principle.

But another is now ready to ask. Is this not a somewhat
loose inquisition into the obedience rendered the King? A
very slight review of the grand results of a life? Is this
then *all?* Is it only these six acts of charity that shall be
brought out, for and against a man, in the great day which
tries the issues for eternity? Is then, this book of God's
remembrance filled up with entries of the most ordinary acts
of common humanity; which nature would teach a savage to

do ? Acts of value scarcely sufficient to be entered as items in a tradesman's daily journal ; and certainly of no higher importance than to be entered, aggregately, as " sundries " in his ledger ?

This inquiry grows, again, out of that narrow and shallow literalism in the interpretation of the word of God, which, forgetting that spiritual thoughts can be conveyed only in the language of analogy and approximation, catches at the mere words—the husks containing the thought, and manipulates and tears at the husk till the thought is dropped out and lost. So the enemies of Jesus, when on earth, blundered continually concerning his meaning ; as when he spake of his kingdom and of himself as a king ; or when he spake of the temple of his body ; or when he spake of himself as " the living bread which came down from heaven." And so even his disciples accepted too literally his words, and supposed they might sit, one on his right hand and the other on his left, in the kingdom of God. But such error here is, at once, made manifest even from a careful study of his words.

The mistake here arises from taking this enumeration of acts as a random list of any six, as specimens, out of a thousand acts that might have been named. Whereas it will be found, on careful study of them, that, with divine skill, Jesus here exhausts all the categories of heart testing acts, in this six-fold classification ; and that the six things which, on superficial glance, appear to be loosely cited specimens out of the numberless acts of the merest charity and humanity, recognized as duties by the veriest savage, constitute, perhaps, as severe a test of gospel faith and Christian character as is to be found anywhere in the Scriptures.

You will observe that the six things here set forth are peculiar, in that they cover the six phases of human misery ; and that every human affliction that arises may be referred to one or other of these six categories—hunger, thirst, nakedness, sickness, friendlessness, and restraint of liberty. They embrace the six germinal elements of all necessary consolations of human life—meat, drink, clothing, health, human fellowship, and the social privileges of freedom. They embrace the six things which it is the great aim of all human activity to enjoy, and of all human care to avoid the loss of The labours of life, in all its phases of occupation in the field, in the work-shop, in the pursuits of commerce, in the pursuits of learning, are directed to the securing of meat, drink, clothing, health, friends, freedom ; and to avoiding the sorrows of hunger, thirst, nakedness, loss of health, loss of friends, or loss of freedom. So that Christ hath here most wonderfully grouped, in exhaustive classification, at the same time, all human desires, all human calamities ; and, therefore, all phases of temptation to human nature.

Now in each of these states of calamity he assumes himself to have been, representatively, in his brethren of the kingdom ; and to have passed under the eye of every one of the great multitude gathered around his judgment throne ; and the test he applies to every one is "How didst thou act,— cherishing Christ, or neglecting him ? for Christ, or against him ?" Or, in the fuller statement of the point, Christ hath founded a kingdom on earth ; and hath set on foot a contest with the god of this world with his world kingdoms ; he hath associated with himself in the work those his brethren, the redeemed ones, as fast as snatched from the burning. In the prosecution of his enterprise, every form of human calamity is encountered ; and he will make it the test, what part each one took in the conflict, whether sympathizing with and aiding him, or coldly neglecting him ; and this as evinced by the acts of the life. For though he reads the heart, and needs not the evidence of overt acts for himself, yet it is meet that his brethren, who can judge only from the acts, shall see the propriety of the award.

Words give utterance to the thoughts and feelings of the soul, but may be false reporters; deeds attest the honesty of the words; and affliction shows the sincerity of deeds. Therefore a true test of a man's spirit must embrace the test of what affliction he will endure, or what loss he will suffer to sustain in affliction, as well as the evidence of the deeds or the words. For any cause will find friends enough to aid it, by both word and deed, while it is prospering and running with the popular current; but when it is struggling, and buffetting the waves of affliction, and needs sacrifices to sustain it, then none but its true friends will stand fast. There is, therefore, a divine philosophy in this statement of the test that seems so artless and simple at first sight. It can be neither evaded nor counterfeited; it can be applied alike to every rank and condition of men; it fairly attests the real state of the heart before God.

O! if Jesus had made his test, as some would have it, a question of orthodoxy of forms of belief; then every sound-headed student of theology, who logically drew forth from the word the grand system of doctrine embodied in it; every skillful logician, who had transfixed the assailants of the system on his keenly pointed dilemmas; every fierce and bloody defender of the faith who had " proved his doctrine orthodox, by apostolic blows and knocks," would pass triumphantly to the right hand. But the multitude, to whom carefulness about meat and drink and physical comforts had left no time to weigh these nice distinctions; the unlearned and ignorant without capacity to consult or comprehend the learned faculties and systems of Divinity; the children of poverty and sorrow whose heart burdens were too great for the free play of the understanding among these high arguments; all these would have been excluded. The kingdom of Heaven would then have become a university of learned dogmatists only.

Or if the test, as others would have it, had been the frames, feelings, excitements, and convulsions of the inner man only; then the self-confident rabble of enthusiasts would rush forward from the cells of the hermits, from the cages of the mad-house, from the noisy halls of fanaticism, even from the revelling places of the drunkard, and the bloody dens of the holy inquisition; all pleading the holy frames and deep convictions of their souls. Every visionary, every dreamer, every self-deluded prophet and false Christ, every self-righteous Pharisee, every malignant, fanatical Jezebel, would have rushed at once to the right hand; and the kingdom of heaven would become an eternal bedlam.

Or if, as still others would have it, the test of judgment had been devised to measure the intrinsic value of the offering or the greatness of the labour done, or of suffering endured, how many a selfish miser or self-indulgent Dives would have been glad, on a death bed, to compromise the matter by the gift of untold treasure that could no longer minister enjoyment, in exchange for a title to admission to that kingdom? How many in high station would willingly undergo all labours, and put their kingdoms and empires all to labour, for the sake of that title? How many would cheerfully undergo all penances and self-mortifications and tortures, as atonement to offer for a life of wickedness, on that day of trial?

But "to the poor the Gospel is preached;" and with reference to the poorest is the test devised on that day. Had it been any thing beyond a bit of bread, a cup of water, a sick visit, how large a body of the truest, and stablest of Christ's friends must fail to stand the trial?

It may be asked, however, in the last place, if this test can possibly be interpreted as universal; seeing that it seems to refer to ages of suffering and persecution? How shall Christians in the ages and countries of the Church's prosperity prove themselves whether they be ready to abide the test of judgment, since only rare and exceptional cases of suffering for Christ can fall under their notice ?

This difficulty is apparent only, not real. For a little reflection will satisfy you that the test is equally applicable whether to a suffering Church in ages of persecution, or a working Church, in days of peace and prosperity. By the very nature of the Christian life, causing "him that heareth to say come," as well as by Christ's special command, every Christian, and the Church of Christ are, essentially, propagandist. While, therefore, in the one case, the test is what one will *suffer* for Christ, or how far he is in sympathy with those that suffer ; in the other case it is what one will *do* for Christ, and how far he is in sympathy with every effort to call sinners and edify saints. And in this work he shall have full opportunity to minister to the wants of Christ's brethren. For it should be distinctly understood that propagandism— the missionary work—is an essential development of the spiritual life. Christ assumes that every man who is Christian enough to pray, will pray "Thy Kingdom come !" and of course will labour earnestly for that which he prays for. And in view of that feature of the spiritual life, Christ appointed among the ordinances of worship in his kingdom the " collection for the poor saints " as a means of grace. And Paul thanked God for his unspeakable gift in giving this grace to the Church of Macedonia, for the saying, " thanks be unto God for his unspeakable gift," was in allusion to their degree of piety as evinced by their gifts to the poor.

The obscurity which may exist in your minds touching the application of this test in our age arises very largely from the fact that our usages and methods of providing means in support of Christ's Kingdom have separated that provision too widely from our acts of worship ; so that the test which Christ arranged for his people, in their worship, has been practically removed from them. Instead of the contributions for the support of the gospel being the spontaneous offerings of hearts in which "faith worketh by love," and from purely devotional impulses, in many cases funds are received from the state, raised by compulsory tax: in others, largely, from endowments which the mistaken forethought of Christian people have laid up in store to support the gospel among their children, as if afraid to trust the power of God's grace to confer faith and love enough upon the children to support the gospel for themselves. And even where the contribution is voluntary, the giving is separated from the worship, both in idea and in fact, and laid upon the wealthy as any other claim in ordinary business transactions. Thus the gifts are not the tests of faith and love in those who give, while the humble poor of Christ's flock have, in the worship, little or no opportunity of exercising the grace of fellowship at all. Nay so entirely has this great idea of Christ's appointment in the worship of the Church, been lost sight of, that to many the collection at worship is becoming positively offensive, as unsuitable to the sacredness of public devotion. And to observe the dislike to frequent collections among many good people might almost suggest the painful suspicion that the nature of their business transactions during the week was such that the sound of money in the house of God on the Sabbath awakened disagreeable associations. When our present usages shall give place to more of the simplicity of the gospel, in this regard, and a nearer conformity to Christ's order in his Church, then will the outward prosperity and success of the Church become more truly exponential of the degree of faith and real piety which animates the people. And then will be seen and felt, in all its power, the significance of Christ's choice of this peculiar form of a universal test at the judgment.

Let it not be supposed, however, that this application of it is the only one for the Church in this age. I have made special reference to this application, simply because the usages of the churches, at present, seem calculated to obscure in the minds of the people the principles of this application. In all conditions of the Church, it will be found that, in some form, one or other of these six evils is the temptation to stand aloof from Christ and his cause. Though not literally in fear of hunger and thirst, yet, because of their eagerness to provide for, or enjoy, the luxuries that minister to appetite, men have neither time nor heart to attend to the call of the gospel. Though not fearing suffering from want of clothing, yet innumerable luxuries of fashion and dress prove a snare to the soul. Though not literally to be made a stranger by casting in the lot with the people of God, yet it involves, perhaps the loss of one's rightful place in the affections of the godless family, or in the esteem of godless friends. And so of many other forms of these temptations. The world still loves not Christ and his precepts, and therefore " they that live godly in Christ Jesus must suffer persecution."

The walks of business are full of maxims of trade and usages openly at war with the spirit of Christ's precepts. The world of fashion and pleasure is equally ruled by tastes and maxims and usages contrary to the precepts of Christ. And the Christian who stands manfully for Christ will find some inconvenience, some loss, and much scorn. Christ brings his judgment into close companionship with these every-day issues, and will demand whether you were ready to endure the cross for his sake, or stand by those faithfully who had to endure hardships for his sake.

But I cannot dwell upon the various forms of applying Christ's test. I have aimed to show from the connection that the test here enunciated is designed to reach back and cover our life under the whole gospel dispensation ; that it is a test thoroughly *evangelical* requiring works simply as the outgrowth and the evidence of a living faith in Jesus Christ

in the soul; that the test is absolutely universal in its reach
even to the thoughts and intents of the heart; that its peculiar form renders it equally applicable to a suffering, or to
a peaceful, working Church.

And now, brethren, I must leave you to make your own
application, personally, of the great truths here taught by
him who is our King and who will be our Judge.   Remember
that this is a very present matter with every one of us personally, since it is the every-day impulses and acts that now
distinguish our life which shall then be tested; and a few
more days, or years, at best, will settle the issue.   "He
that is unjust shall be unjust still; he that is filthy shall be
filthy still; and he that is holy shall be holy still."   The
testimony in the case shall be sealed up then for the verdict
of that great judgment.   If we would receive the welcome
"Come ye blessed of my Father" in that dread day, then
it behooves those of us who have been left in charge of the
Master's house to be faithful in executing the trust, ever
watching for his return, that he find us neither sleeping at our
post, nor acting a faithless part.   It behooves you who watch
for the Bridegroom that you may go into the marriage supper
of the Lamb, to see to it that, though you may from the long
delay be sleeping, you have the oil for the lamps, even his
grace in your hearts.   And not only so, but this inner life in
the soul must have its full and proper outworking in the diligent use of the several talents entrusted to you.   For only
with this spiritual life in the heart, evincing itself in the
diligent employment of the five, or the two, or the one talent,
will any be ready for the great assize, and its great test.
Beware how, resting on false grounds of hope, ye go confidently forward undeceived into the King's presence, saying
"Lord, Lord, have we not prophesied in thy name, and done
wonderful works," only to hear him say "depart from me
—I never knew you."

DISCOURSE XIII.

THE DIVINE TRAGEDY OF EARTH, HEAVEN AND HELL. HUMANITY IN ITS ESSENTIAL ATTRIBUTES TO INHABIT ETERNITY.

LUKE xvi. 19-31. There was a certain rich man, which was clothed in purple and fine linen, and fared sumptuously every day. And there was a certain beggar named Lazarus, which was laid at his gate full of sores, and desiring to be fed with the crumbs which fell from the rich man's table ; moreover the dogs came and licked his sores. And it came to pass, that the beggar died, and was carried by the angels into Abraham's bosom ; the rich man also died, and was buried ; And in hell he lifted up his eyes, being in torments, and seeth Abraham afar off, and Lazarus in his bosom. And he cried and said, Father Abraham, have mercy on me, and send Lazarus that he may dip the tip of his finger in water and cool my tongue, for I am tormented in this flame. But Abraham said, Son, Remember that thou in thy life receivedst thy good things, and likewise Lazarus evil things ; but now he is comforted, and thou art tormented. And beside all this, between us and you there is a great gulf fixed, &c.

THE identity of doctrine, and the logical coherency of this with the judgment discourse, concerning the relations of the present to the future life, appears so plainly in the Lazarus of this parable, as Christ representing himself in one of his brethren,—an hungered, athirst, naked, sick, friendless,—as to need nothing more than a simple reference to it, without further explication.

Jesus had been warning of the importance of a wise use of earthly goods ; of the antagonism between the true worship of God and the worship of riches ; and of the danger of covetousness. In answer to his solemn warnings " the Pharisees who were covetous," it is said, " *derided* him." As though judging it useless to reason with men determined not to be

enlightened and convinced, he seeks another avenue to the
heart and conscience through the imagination. For while the
gospel appeals, in chief, to the reason and understanding of
men, it appeals also to the imagination, to the passions, to all
the powers of the soul. Therefore, as by some divine acous-
tics, he places an ordinary world scene in such a focus that
the monotonous buzz and din and commonplace of the life
that is, comes echoed back, in terrific thunder tones, from the
endless vistas of the life which is to come.; and at once confirms and illustrates his previous argument, by presenting this
great tragedy of earth and heaven and hell; showing how the
mortal humanity reaches onward, and becomes the immortal
humanity inhabiting eternity.

I propose a brief critique on this divine tragedy; and to
gather from its *dramatis personæ*, its scenes and its dialogue,
the general truths which Jesus here inculcates.

" *A certain rich man was clothed in purple and fine linen
and fared sumptuously every day.*" This is a chief personage of the tragedy. That is an important error of interpretation here, which supposes that his sin consisted in being rich,
wearing fine clothes, or living sumptuously. The gospel
gives no ground for the too common impression that the rich
man will go to hell because he is rich, and the poor man to
heaven because he is poor. Nor, while enjoining " modest
apparel," and " the adorning of the inner man of the heart,"
rather than the outer man, does the gospel countenance that
sort of piety, which consists in the style of one's eating and
material of his eating, on Fridays or any other days; in the
cut and colour of one's coat, or the fashion of head dress; in
the tone of one's voice, the phase of one's face, the manner of
one's speech or the air of one's bearing. It is not even charged
that he became rich by unfair means. He was probably a
young man, since he speaks of five brethren, and of his
father's house—a moral man, being a Pharisee; and a nomi-

nal member of the visible kingdom, recognizing Abraham as his father.

It is far more important, brethren, for you to bear in mind, that Christ says nothing against this one of the heroes of this tragedy, except simply to paint him as one in full enjoyment of everything that the world has to offer, in contrast with the other earth picture which follows. Especially is this important to any of you who imagine that the warnings of the gospel apply only to the drunken, the profane, the licentious, the infidel, and not to you who " are not far from the kingdom of God." This man of the divine tragedy, for aught we can see, was just as moral, according to the world's standard, and as respectful to religion as any of you.

" *And there was a certain beggar,*" &c. In perfect contrast with him who had everything the world can give, is this picture of utter misery in the lack of all things ; concentrating in one case all six of the evils of the judgment test, hungry, thirsty, naked, friendless, sick, and—though not literally in prison—yet by the leprosy or other loathsomeness, excluded from the companionship of man as really as if in a prison. And, as we infer, sustained by a heroic faith, he bore it all without a murmur against Providence, or even a complaint against the rich man, saying, " even so Father, for so it seemeth good in thy sight."

Such is the view of the contrasts, as the present life exhibits them. Now the scene of the tragedy changes to the next life, and there again presents them in still wider contrasts, yet contrasts entirely reversed.

" *And it came to pass that the beggar died, and was carried by the angels into Abraham's bosom.*" Speaking, as he was, to Jews, he could convey no loftier conception of heaven than that it is the place where Abraham is ; and speaking, as he was, to people whose usage was, not as ours to *sit* at meals, but to recline on couches—the head of each person next below reaching to the breast of him above at table—(as at the last supper John it is said "leaned on Jesus' breast at supper") he could not more aptly express the second place of honour at the celestial table than to say, he was in Abraham's bosom. Thus he that was esteemed unworthy a place even among the servants at the rich man's table on earth, is transferred to the very highest place, save Abraham's, at the festive table in heaven !

It is specially worthy of note, how Jesus here, as the gospel elsewhere, ever symbolizes the immortal state to us in figures and forms gathered from the best and loveliest things that belong to the mortal state. The communion of friends together, in breaking bread at each other's table, is among the purest of earthly pleasures ; and, hence, that furnishes a favourite figure in the scriptures for the expression of what is spiritual joyousness and high privilege. The sacrament of the Old Testament covenant was cast into this form of a supper—so of the same sacrament in the New. The promise of Jesus to the believing soul is " I will come in and sup with him and he with me." And John permitted, in his visions, to gaze in upon the redeemed in glory, found them waiting for the marriage supper of the Lamb. So here Jesus, when he would describe the life to come for us, sets it forth as a communion of friends together at a glorious celestial feast with Abraham, the father of the faithful at the head of the table.

This is the glory of the heaven of Jesus, that it is a human nature heaven. And, to one who has truly entered into the spirit of his teachings of immortality, it is nothing short of blasphemous, to hear men coldly talk of the "immortality brought to light in the gospel," as but another mode of presenting the beautiful speculations of the schools concerning it ; and of Jesus and Socrates and Plato as co-ordinate teachers on this point. For what though Plato had demonstrated immortality—which he did not do, but only surmised it? of what practical use his immortality of a spirit, ushered naked and shivering into eternity, even when proved? What care I to be told of an immortality stripped of everything but mere existence? What joy to me in the thought that, after the present existence, I shall be dashed as a splinter from the wreck of Time, to float, vibrating and tossing on the ripples of the illimitable ocean of eternity? One shrinks from the thought of an existence that has nothing in it in common with the present. But it is a different matter, when Jesus tells us of an existence beyond death that is not severed at all from any thing that is pure and holy and beautiful in the present life ; of an eternal manhood, of which this is the infancy ; of an eternal harvest, of which this is the seed time ; of an eternal treasure house, into which shall be garnered for us all the precious jewels gathered out of the rubbish of earth and lit up by the beaming smiles of God Almighty, the sun thereof ; of the whole family gathered from the scatterings of earth under him " of whom the whole family in heaven and earth is named" —A family whose oldest children heard the echoes of the song of the morning stars when time began, and whose youngest children shall have heard, in the flesh, the sound of the arch- angel's trump, proclaiming that Time shall be no longer ! A family embracing patriarchs and prophets and apostles ; and the noble army of the martyrs ; and all the holy and good who have ever lived, with all the good, and pure and dear of the friends we have ever known ! Then, then, the immortality is attractive and to be longed for " with ardent pangs of strong desire !" Such an immortality is fitted " to comfort those that mourn and to heal the broken-hearted." For it enables us to follow our departed, in thought, to the assembly with Abraham, and to feel that, instead of wandering lonely through an illimi- table desert of eternal existence, they are with friends who care for them, and with Jesus who loves them, even with God

"who wipes away all tears from their eyes." We can, with
joy, now reason—what though,

> "A brightness hath passed from the earth,
> Yet a star is new born in the sky;
> And a soul hath gone home to the land of its birth,
> Where are pleasures and fulness of joy!
> Where its thirst shall be slaked with the waters that spring,
> Like a river of light, from the throne of the King;
> And a new harp is strung, and a new song is given,
> To the breezes that float o'er the gardens of heaven!"

The immortality, according to Jesus Christ, is no mere
shadowy, metaphysical existence, but the carrying over death
of everything sinless that pertains to humanity here.

The earth itself dies not; for the holy memories of it die
not; its purer and nobler affections die not; its holy thoughts
die not. They pass on, over death, imperishable as the soul
itself, to constitute the elements of its heaven. For the eternal
life, as Jesus teaches, actually begins here. "He that
believeth on the Son hath (not shall have) everlasting life."
And, of course, the consciousness belonging to the eternal
life here must go on with the soul, over death, as the consciousness of infancy goes on into manhood.

Such is the infinite contrast between the Lazarus lying at
the rich man's gate, with the dogs for companions; and the
Lazarus exalted, next to head, at the celestial table, with the
multitude of the redeemed doing him honour!

It is specially worthy of note, also, how Jesus seems ever
to select the very humblest people for the high places of distinction in his kingdom. This is the case in, perhaps, every
one of the few instances in which he appeals to that principle
so universal in human nature, the love of eminence and distinction. I recall now only three of these cases. One was that
of the poor widow that, timidly and half-ashamed, dropped her
two farthings into the treasury among the ostentatious gifts of
the wealthy; of whom he declared she had excelled them all.

Another was the case of the humble woman whose heart, bursting with gratitude led her to make the offering of her beautiful trinket, the alabaster box of ointment—all she had to offer; of whom he declared that fame should perpetuate her memory, "wherever this gospel shall be preached." The other is this case of Lazarus, who had not even the two farthings to give, and by reason of his infirmity, had nothing that he could do for the Master, except, with heroic faith, to suffer without murmuring; of whom he declares, he is exalted to the second place of honour in heaven.

Ye humble ones of Christ's people ! here is encouragement and comfort for you. You ask " What can I, a servant do, in my low station of poverty, to evince my faith and love." " What can I, a timid and shrinking girl do ?" "What can I, an over-taxed mother do, whose world lies wholly within my own dwelling ?" " What can such as we do ?" "O, if we were high in station, blessed with wealth, influence, office in the Church, then could we evince to the world how sincerely we love Jesus! But our want of opportunity to test our faith makes us sometimes doubtful whether we really believe and love him or not!" But any of you have a better opportunity than Lazarus had ; and yet he won the second place ! The measure applied by Jesus Christ is not the amount and value of the thing done, nor the extent of your sphere ; but the perfection with which you fill your sphere, whether it be large or small. Nay though your sphere be narrowed by poverty and suffering down to your very self, you may, by suffering aright, gain a higher place than many that can do much. What he will have is the devoted love of the heart, which may be evinced equally by great acts, or by small acts. The Queen on her throne, filled with gratitude for some great act of kindness and blessing, evinces the love for the great benefactor by a royal gift, it may be of the half of her kingdom. But the little child, whose heart your kindness may have won, just as clearly and beautifully evinces the love of its little heart by thrusting upon you with overflowing generosity, all the prized toys which it deems too precious to allow any other to touch! Just so with the gifts which evince love to Jesus. Indulge in no day-dreams of what you would do in another and larger sphere ; nor impatiently thrust yourself into spheres of doubtful fitness. Just where you are, and as you are, discharge the duties of your station, with a loving and trusting heart, looking to Jesus. If this simple principle were comprehended, we would have less of that ambitious looking for " a mission" which has exposed religion to reproach ; and a solution of the problem of " woman's mission." For then " feed my lambs"—a mission great enough for Peter, would no longer be thought not great enough for woman !

Now comes another infinite contrast, infinitely sad—" *The rich man also died.*" The riches avail nothing to save him from the last lot of the beggar ! The lines of their existence, though infinitely divergent, cross each other at death as a point common to both. Think of this, ye that serve Mammon as your master. Of what avail all that Mammon can do for you, after a few days of treacherous enjoyment. Will the stately mansions and the broad acres that surround them, make Death more chary of approach to their lord ? Will fine linen cool the fevered blood ; or purple sooth the aching frame ; or sumptuous fare tempt the languid appetite once he hath breathed upon you ? Will your garnered " bonds " buy the medicine that shall :

> " Minister to the mind diseased,
> Pluck from the memory the rooted sorrow,
> Raze out the written troubles of the brain ?"

Will your gleaming silver tempt Death to restrain his hand, when, " he hath bent his bow and made ready the arrow to the string ?" May your yellow gold ascend, before you to the high places of heavenly justice, as sometimes it hath ascended to high places of earthly justice, and bribe the pen of the recording angel to erase, or make no record of your deeds of sin ? Of what use then this carefulness and zeal in the service of Mammon, that leads you to neglect and contemn the service of God ?

" *And was buried.*" This is not said in the case of Lazarus, who probably was thrown aside as a loathsome carcass from the sight of men. But in the vain effort to keep up distinctions even after death, the rich man's body was probably escorted with solemn pageant to its burial. And, doubtless, out of his vast wealth a splendid monument was reared to tell the story of his virtues, and, possibly, like many of its kind, a lying monument at that. But his true monument he hath reared for himself, as we shall see a little farther on.

" *And in hell he lifted up his eyes being in torment.*" Here large numbers, who affect great admiration for the amiable teachings of Jesus, shrink back declaring, " this is a hard saying, who can hear it ?" The chief of these objectors may be classified into three ; those who deny that the scriptures mean to teach a retributive torment ; those who deem such a doctrine inconsistent with other fundamental truths of revealed theology ; and those who reject, alike, the inspiration of the scriptures and the retribution.

As to the first of these classes, who profess to accept the scriptures as of inspired authority and yet deny that they teach the doctrine of a hell, it must be confessed there is nothing to encourage an argument with such. For if the acknowledging of the scriptures, in the plain common sense meaning of their words, does not settle the question, it is difficult to conceive how such a truth can be expressed in human language at all. We need not stand upon the terms " hell " and " fire " and " Tophet." If these are offensive to " ears polite," then find smoother terms if you please. The question is not of words, but of ideas and principles.

Whether this scene is properly named "Hell," or "Hades," or "Sheol;" still it is a place where a soul is in "torment," "afar off" from Abraham's state of bliss, and crying out in anguish. So that the idea of a place of intense unhappiness, separate from the place of bliss after a man dies, and this growing out of something that had existed before death, is still left, though your criticisms have utterly rooted out the term "hell," or substituted for it the smoothest and most delightful of euphemisms. Nor does it affect, in the least, the principle, whether the parable is taken as narrating a real or a fictitious case; since Jesus Christ, whose "truth is stranger than fiction," would employ to illustrate his doctrines only that fiction, which is truer than truth, in the sense of having been specially created for the exhibition of some great principle. The real objection to the modern method of first applying a patent critical machinery to the words of inspiration, to squeeze out of them, before using, everything offensive or contrary to some new theory of theology, ethics, or philanthropy that has been first constructed outside. the sphere of inspired ideas, and then brought to the bible to be *underpinned* with texts, is not so much that it overthrows this or that doctrine of the gospel, as that it accustoms the people to trifling with the divinely inspired rule of faith. When the people are taught by one biblical critic that "hell" does not mean hell, but some poetic fiction; by another that "Holy Ghost" does not mean "Holy Ghost," but a metaphysical figure of speech; by another that "wine" does not mean wine, but water filtered through grape sauce; by another that "slave" does not mean slave but an apprentice or a hireling; by another that the saying, "All scripture is God-inspired," does not mean inspired in any sense that guarantees the scriptures against absurd, mistaken or legendary statements; how shall they do otherwise than conclude that, from the uncertainties of its meaning, the bible is utterly worthless as an infallible rule of faith?

Besides it seems utterly useless, if one had a taste for it, to argue the reality of future retribution, with such as profess to accept the inspired scriptures, and yet deny this doctrine.

For even after we have reasoned from indubitable premises, with mathematical certainty, to our conclusion that there is a hell, that conclusion must be expressed in language ; and it is beyond the ingenuity of man to find language more definite and less subject to perversion by criticism than that in which scripture has already expressed the same conclusion. But they say the scriptures do not mean that, though they say it. So these amiable theologians and critics might just as properly turn to the audience to which we have demonstrated that—

> " There is a death whose pang
> Outlasts this fleeting breath
> And O eternal horrors hang
> Around this second death "—

and gravely caution them against alarm at our conclusion ; that we did not mean what we *seem* to mean, that after the death of the body the soul may be unhappy ; that manifestly we used poetic figures of speech, and allowance must be made for poetic license ! In what language could we express the future retribution for sin ; or in what greater variety of method and connection, than Jesus and his inspired agents have already done ? And if these critics may say that Jesus and his inspired agents did not mean what they said, but something else—why not also say that, when we thus express in language the conclusions to which the most inexorable logic may drive us, we do not mean what our language conveys, but something entirely the reverse ?

Of that very amiable class of theologians who deny retribution on the ground that such an idea is utterly repulsive to their conceptions of the love of God, as everywhere declared in the gospel, there is space now only to say that their conception of the gospel is simply a caricature of the gospel; less rude, it may be, but not less wide of the truth than the fierce and wrathful gospel of the most malignant fanatic.

The gospel preached by Jesus, is no monotone of " love," " love !" It is no cradle song of lullaby to soothe a babe to sleep with. It is no strain for the compass only of the gentle rebeck, or " lute, or soft recorder." It is a many-sided, many-voiced strain to fill the mighty compass of that great organ, the human soul ; to sweep its infinite diapason, and awaken, alike, the deep thunder tones of an accusing conscience ; the loud wails of penitential sorrow ; the subdued tones of loving but trembling faith ; and the lofty notes of the holy ecstasy of "joy unspeakable and full of glory !" It is Jesus Christ who wept over sinners, saying " O that thou hadst known !" who proclaims " the terrors of the Lord" and flings " the arrows of the Almighty." Remember it is the same Jesus who spake the parables of the lost sheep, the lost treasure, and the father yearning after his poor prodigal, in the previous chapter, that speaks this parable of the rich man in hell lifting up his eyes in torment.

Of that class who reject the scriptures, and who, on principles of mere Deism, scoff at retribution, there will be occasion to speak further on.

"*And seeth Abraham afar off and Lazarus in his bosom.*" They who, from bitter experience, know anything of the pangs of a joy just within their reach, lost beyond hope of recovery ; of high expectation suddenly dashed to pieces, just as about to be fulfilled; of arriving at the station after long and weary absence from the loved ones at home, only to see the train, homeward bound, gone just out of reach—need not be told that this is one of the darkest lines of this picture of a lost soul. To be doomed, amid all the agonies of hell, to

see for ever Abraham afar off and Lazarus in his bosom, is
what must sting most keenly.   O, if that existence might be
an eternal oblivion of all that is holy and pure in pleasure,
and an utter unconsciousness that any thing better than this
state of torment existed in the universe, it would alleviate
half its horrors !   If instead of a division by " a great gulph
fixed," across which the doomed may look, it were an infinite
wall erected, with foundations deep laid in the depths of hell,
and its battlements overtopping the battlements of heaven—
then the soul might at last sink into comparative apathy, from
never conceiving of anything better than these horrors;
verily, this touch of the divine pencil throws a deeper darkness even over " the outer darkness," that shrouds the
" weeping, and wailing and gnashing of teeth !"

We come now to the dialogue of the divine tragedy
between hell and heaven.   First Hell speaks ;—

" *Father Abraham, have mercy on me and send Lazarus.*"

This is the only case of prayer to saints recorded in scripture ; and he did not get what he prayed for.   Alas, this
poor soul is ready now to plead his Church relation, and, being
within the covenant with Abraham his father, to set up that
as his claim to salvation.   It was the current error of his
time.   John Baptist had occasion to warn men against it,
saying, " Think not to say within yourselves, we have Abraham for our father."   Jesus had occasion to remind the
dignitaries of the Church, "If ye were Abraham's children
ye would do the works of Abraham."   Paul had afterward
continually to argue that only " they which are of faith, the
same are the children of faithful Abraham."   And, to this
day, one of the greatest obstacles to the true gospel in the
heart, and one of the most delusive errors, is this same propensity to rely on being in the true Church, as the chief title
to sit down with Abraham, and Isaac, and Jacob in the kingdom of heaven.   But while to be in the true Church is all-

important, that is not because, being there, one is secure of heaven.

On the other hand, how many a pastor has found with profound grief—when called to the death-bed of some poor reckless apostate from his birthright in the Church; who all life long has been ashamed of his relation, and joined with the scoffers to sneer at it—that now, when earth is fading from his view without, and nature dissolving within, he is ready enough to catch at that, as a sinking man catches at the straw; and relates the story of his birth as a member of the Church, the recognition of it in his baptism, and the prayers and godly instructions of pious parents, as some ground of hope for him still! Remember, ye on whom the vows of God rest; however you may now be ashamed of them, and scoff at the call to fulfil them, the day is coming when you shall in like manner be ready enough to acknowledge them; but alas too late! If you are wise you will call now upon your fathers' God, and the God of your mother, and ask that their prayers for you may be answered.

Heaven responds:—*Son, Remember, that thou, in thy lifetime, receivedst thy good things, and likewise Lazarus evil things, but now he is comforted and thou art tormented.*"

In this response is set forth substantially that great principle which is positively asserted, or more or less directly and distinctly assumed in every paragraph of the gospel. And not only so, but it is a principle embodied in the very constitution of the human soul—That *justice requires* a retribution after this life; at least in so far as to rectify the obviously imperfect dispensation of rewards and punishments here. For, as men see how on every hand wickedness goes unwhipped of justice; how dishonesty, falsehood, meanness, dishonour stalk abroad, and tread under their feet, oft-times, purity, truthfulness, benevolence, honour, fidelity; how the brute law of "*might makes right,*" becomes the law of man's rule over

man ; how " the wicked spreadeth himself in prosperity as a
green bay tree, and is not in trouble as other men, nor
plagued like other men ; " while men of integrity and virtue
have " waters of a full cup wrung out to them," until they
wail in their despair " I have cleansed my heart in vain and
washed my hands in innocency, for all the day long have I
been plagued, and chastened every morning ;" — they are
obliged to feel, that, if a just God rules the affairs of men,
there must be a high court of appeal, where these unjust
awards of earth shall all be set right.   In this aspect of the
question, they who deny future retribution not only contravene the revelation of God, but insult the ethical instincts and
universal judgments of mankind."

Heaven continues: *And besides all this, between us and
you there is a great gulf fixed: so that they which would
pass from hence to you cannot: neither can they pass to us
that would come from thence.*"

Aside from the judicial view of the matter, there is a reason,
in the natural order and eternal constitution of things, why
the rich man and Lazarus cannot spend their eternity
together.   While the bible holds forth heaven and hell in
the forensic aspect of the awards of a judgment, it no less
clearly exhibits them as the natural and necessary results of
the life on earth.   So that were there no coming of " the Son
of man in his glory ;"   no setting up of his throne of judgment ; no trial and award, no inquest into the deeds of the
present life, heaven and hell must follow, nevertheless.   For
those two estates in the future stand to the present in the
relation simply of a natural separation of the evil from the
good, which in this present state are *unnaturally* mingled
together.   Hell began on earth when sin began ; but, in
virtue of the great mediatorial enterprise of Christ to gather
out of the doomed race a body for himself, the hand of Infinite
Mercy suppresses the outbursting of its fires to give time and

opportunity for Christ to " see of the travail of his soul and be satisfied." Hence the Apostle speaks of our universe as simply " kept in store, *reserved* unto fire against the day of judgment, and perdition of ungodly men." And, since the work of redemption is finished, they speak of all the period that follows, as the " last time," indicating that at any time now, the period may arrive when the Mediator having no further use for it, the original sentence may be executed, and the *unnatural* give way to the *natural* order, of the good to itself and the evil to itself. In accordance with this theory of the race, as a race, is all the teaching concerning the case of the individuals of it. " He that believeth not," saith Christ, is *condemned already*, and the wrath of God abideth on him. On the other hand, " He that believeth, *hath* everlasting life "; the estate of heaven is already begun in his soul. Every man carries within him here the germs of his heaven or hell. The grace of God nurtures the one, keeping it alive to the day of deliverance ; the mercy of God restrains the other from bursting forth until the day of doom. The gospel theory leaves, really, no place for the cavils against the injustice of punishing a man eternally for the sin of a few days on earth. For, according to this theory, the sinner, remaining unchanged by the grace of God, and without the new life, goes on into eternity just as he is, to sin on, and therefore to suffer on for ever. He suffers here because he is a sinner, though, on account of the restraining mercy of God, he only partially suffers the consequences of his sin. He goes on a sinner and, therefore, to suffer, in an estate where mercy ceases to interpose, but where the full consequences of his sin follow it forever. Hence it is represented as the decree, after the present estate, " He that is unjust let him be unjust still, and he that is filthy, let him be filthy still, and he that is holy, let him be holy still."

Thus, also, the relation of the present to the future life is set forth by the Apostle as the natural relation of seed time and harvest. "What a man soweth that shall he also reap. He that soweth to the flesh, shall of the flesh reap corruption; and he that soweth to the spirit, shall of the spirit reap life everlasting!" By the same law, therefore, under which kind produces kind, and by which he that soweth wheat shall reap wheat, and he that soweth tares reap tares,—shall he that soweth sin, during the present seed time, reap the harvest of sin throughout eternity.

Bear in mind this very solemn view of the life here, as simply the elements of heaven and hell commingling; the heaven suppressed by the antagonist workings of sin in the members; the hell suppressed by the hand of God's mercy restraining it. Remember, too, that the condition natural is that of condemnation; and the new life in the soul the beginning of the everlasting life. Let not the fact of the junction of the two estates of life and death under the social conditions of the present life deceive you into the belief that there is little difference between " him that believeth," and " him that believeth not." When, of God's grace, that intimate friend of yours is led to believe in Jesus, leaving you in unbelief, then, and there, this separation begins. A narrow chasm at first perhaps ; you still join the hand of friendship across it. But it will go on widening and widening, till, after death, it spreads " a great gulf, fixed," infinite and bridgeless !

It is on the ground of this second argument, in the response of heaven, that we meet the class of scoffers at the scriptural doctrine of retribution before-mentioned. We will set aside that view if you please ; or even admit, for the sake of argument, the validity of your reasoning against the justice of eternal retribution. But " *besides* all this," independent of the question of the justice of the thing—by the natural and necessary order of the universe there is a " great gulf.

fixed," between the evil and the good in the future state. And what though you have overthrown the judgment seat of Christ in the gospel, and scoffed the whole theory of reward and punishment out of the faith and the memory of the world, —wherein will you have bettered your condition? The evil nature within you still exists; and unless you are to perish as the brute, must continue to exist for ever. If you scoff at the gospel theory of a change of nature by a divine regeneration here, as absurd and unphilosophical, it is equally unphilosophical to conceive of any such change there. So that, on your own showing, here is a nature full of passions, and evil passions at that, passing on, stripped of all that held the passions in check on earth, into eternity, an inextinguishable, intelligent, conscious being. Now what else can follow than some such estate as Jesus describes by these tremendous types? Follow, in idea, the men that surround you here, embodied in the flesh, as they pass into that existence, and tell us wherein the gospel exaggerates the picture of what must be their future estate. Follow this sensualist, whose only notion of enjoyment, or capacity for it, is of that happiness which he has in common with the brutes, that comes through gratified sensations. But now the link is rusted away which bound his spirit to the flesh, and thereby furnished that channel of pleasure through the senses from a material world; and he rushes, a naked, shivering spirit into a realm where there are no longer any senses to minister, or objects of sense to furnish pleasure! Follow this Shylock, whose only conception of happiness is of gold hoarded up, and to whom a loss by some speculation or accident brings the pangs of hell even here on earth—follow him as his spirit dashes into eternity, stripped of all his wealth, to wander an immortal beggar! Follow this creature of envy and jealousy, whose spirit burns with the smouldering fires of hell, if a rival gets the start of him in popular esteem, as he passes on to an eternal state in which the infinite gulf is fixed between the good and evil; across which he must gaze forever at the crowned victors in the race for true glory! Follow these, or any one of a score of characters that might be cited, into their immortality, and tell us what fitter figures Jesus could have used to describe it, than the eternal " wailing and gnashing of teeth!"

Yet this is not all; for it presents the mere negations of pleasure. And moreover it takes into the account only the self-action of each individual. But conceive of these spirits now all existing together. To aid the conception imagine the vile, depraved and reckless of the earth, even as they are in the flesh, all gathered to themselves. Empty out upon some island of the sea, all your prisons, with all the " hells " of your populous cities; all the haunts of licentiousness and crime; all the dens for the plotting of dishonesty. Let there be no virtuous men to move among them. Let it be the place where law with its threats comes not; where the usages of respectable life with their restraints come not; where the philanthropist with his appeals comes not; where angels and ministers of mercy come not; where the restraining grace of God comes not; and hope of amendment comes not; and death comes not, nor the fear of retribution after death. Let all the fierce wickedness that is in them work itself out in a carnival of every lust and revelry of every passion! See you not that these figures of the scriptures for such a state of existence, instead of being rhetorical exaggerations are but the feeblest approximations of finite language to the expression of infinite ideas of terror.

Here is the fundamental fallacy of all those scoffs at the gospel theology, as if it were responsible for the existence of the hell from which Jesus comes to redeem men. Hell is, in idea, altogether anterior to the gospel theology. It would have flamed none the less fiercely though Jesus had never come with the gospel remedy. Whether the gospel be trustworthy or not, there can be no doubt that the germinal fires of hell do exist already in the nature of man. And though the scoffers of these "last days" should triumph, and crush out of the world's thought every conception of a gospel, still these passions are alive in the human soul, and this depravity, with its inevitable sorrow; and so long as the soul exists must exist with it, save by some divine interposition such as they scoff at. Will men never learn that scoffing at the proposed remedy does not stay the disease? What though you demonstrate the quackery of the panacea that claims to be a sure antidote for cholera? that stays not the still tread " of the pestilence that walketh in darkness!" What though you loathe the remedy which science has compounded for your sick bed, and cast it from you? That gives no ease to your aching joints or fevered brain! What though in your peevishness, you strike down the arm of your physician, as he comes to hold over you the shield of his skill and ward off the thick flying arrows of death? That checks not the advance of the king of terrors to lay his cold hand upon you and claim you as his prey! Now the gospel is simply a remedy and Jesus Christ the great physician whom you must accept, or else let the disease of your soul work out the agonies of the second death.

Silenced by this argument, though it has failed to silence our scoffers yet in the flesh—changing the plea—Hell speaks:

" *I pray thee therefore, father, that thou wouldst send him to my father's house: for I have five brethren: lest they also come to this place of torment.*"

Next to his own torment is the agony of the thought that the brethren, who followed his godless example and were led astray by his evil influence, should come to suffer with him, and thereby increase his torment.

I have before said that he had reared his own true monument in life. So does every man that lives. For an influence, for blessing or for cursing, is ever going out from him, and the results will gather in upon him in the eternity to come. Men see not the operation of this principle in the present life; for if they did there would be less of that ambition to be known as ringleaders in wickedness, drawing followers after them to sin; and less of that sort of merriment that finds its sport in leading one, tenderly reared in seclusion, to swear his first oath, to engage in his first revel, to do his first act of open contempt for God and religion. What if the world's ambitious heroes, panting for blood and carnage, and for the adulation of sycophants, lived under such a law here, that they should see in this life the real monument that they have built for themselves? What if, instead of pyramid of brass or Parian marble, inscribed with its lying words, erected over them dead, their real monument were erected visibly around them yet living? What if around and over such an one as a centre, were reared a huge hollow pyramid of all the bones which his ambition has scattered to bleach and moulder; with the myriads of skulls facing inward to grin horribly down upon him; with all the blood which his cruelty has shed perpetually drizzling and dripping as moisture from the horrid walls; with the sighs of all the hearts which his faithlessness has broken moaning through the crevices, as moan the winds of autumn; and ever and anon, the despairing curses of all the ruined howling over it, as howls the tempest in its fury?

Yet analogous to this is the commemoration of the present in the future life; and this supposed monument is the type of the position of the evildoer, in eternity, with respect to his life here. Every man is building, day by day, his monument to commemorate his life on earth throughout the endless ages. And when death shall tear away the unseen screen

T

that now hides the seen from the unseen, he will behold his work all finished.

I need only suggest to you the solemn lesson which this cry of agony should have for godless fathers and mothers, who shall be held even more strictly responsible for the five children than he for the five brethren. If they pervert that authority whereby they stand in the place of God to their children during infancy, and the unbounded influence which they exert on all the subsequent life, and thus not only lose their own crown, but, so far as they can, tear the crown from the heads of the children God has given—what imagination shall depict the agony of the prayer for eternal separation, in that world, from those whom they loved here !

Heaven responds :—" *They have Moses and the Prophets ; let them hear them.*"

They are without excuse, even though influenced by the evil example of their dead brother ; for they had all necessary means of knowing God's will ; his warnings of the inevitable doom of sin ; and his kind invitations to them to accept the generous atonement provided to take away the sin of the world. O brethren, if Moses and the Prophets were gospel enough to leave them without excuse, then what excuse for those who, on the back of Moses and the Prophets have all the wonderful revelations of Jesus and the Apostles ! Recall, I pray you, the reasoning of the Apostle, " If the word spoken by angels (messengers), Moses and the Prophets, was steadfast, and every trangression received its just recompense of reward : ' How shall we escape if we neglect so great salvation ?' And again, " He that despised Moses' law died without mercy ; of how much sorer punishment, suppose ye, shall he be thought worthy who hath trodden under foot the Son of God ?"

Hell speaks :—NAY, *father Abraham ; but if one went unto them from the dead, they will repent.*"

Here is one of those marvellous portraitures of a universal, in an individual case, at a single stroke, which so distinguish the bible paintings of human nature under the calls of the gospel. " If one rose from the dead ;" if the proof were made clearer ; if there were more certainty of these things ; if these doctrines were not so puzzling or the rectitude of God's dealings were more manifest ; if our circumstances were more favourable and our temptations not so great ; in short, if God had done something else than he has done, or his gospel were, in some manner or other, different from what it is—then surely we would be Christians.

Heaven responds finally :—" *If they believe not Moses and the Prophets, neither will they be persuaded though one rose from the dead.*" This sentence is very commonly read as intending chiefly to assert the sufficiency of Moses and the Prophets, as a rule of faith, which truth has already been asserted in the preceding response ; and is taken as the foundation for discourses showing the fullness of the evidences of the Old Testament revelation, and therefore of the New Testament also. But the point of the response, evidently, is directed to the fallacy of the appeal just made ; and to assert that the difficulty in the way of sinners is not want of evidence, but want of heart, in themselves. While it indeed asserts, by implication, the perfect sufficiency of the evidence for Moses and the Prophets, it means also to assert that no matter though this evidence were stronger, the result would be all the same. For in fact it matters little to unbelievers whether the proof be sufficient or not ; since they have never attended to the subject enough to know whether it be so or not. They are *insincere* in the plea of want of proof, want of harmony in the doctrines, and want of consistency with the ethical reason. For even though such were the fact, they have never examined the matter enough to know it.

I have already transcended all proper limits of a discourse, or I should undertake to justify most fully this charge of the insincerity of the unbelief and cavils of men at the gospel. I must content myself, however, with a general remark or two for the special benefit of such of you as may sometimes be tempted to feel that, if the religion of the gospel be true, then it is strange that so large a part of the world have doubts about its evidences, and difficulties with its doctrines.

Just make the experiment of analyzing this crowd of un-believers, and estimate how many of them have ever gone into the question far enough to know whether Moses and the Prophets, Jesus and the Apostles, are worthy of belief or not. Set aside first the great crowd of the ignorant, the stolid, the sensual, the brutish who mock at hell without proof; and indeed, have neither the capacity nor the intelligence on the question of religion, to comprehend the force of an argument. Evidently more proof could do them no good ; for of what use to bring more proof to men who have never considered the matter enough to know that the evidence is defective and that more proof is wanting ? At once now you have cleared the field of ninety-nine hundredths of the unbelief in the world.

Now set aside, next, the class who disbelieve from mere affectation ;—the youth just home from college, supposing he has circumnavigated this great ocean of science from the beach of which Isaac Newton claimed only to have skipped stones, as a child ; and, in proof of his attainments, obtrud-ing his difficulties with religion on distressed mother and sisters. Or that class of minds which, in this regard, never grow old, but have a passion for the display of their origin-ality by not believing what people generally believe. For what proof can be devised that shall convince affectation ? And now we have again greatly thinned the ranks of unbe-lief. Next, set aside the really learned and gifted sceptical men of the secular professions, who will honestly tell you that their scepticism arises in large part, perhaps, from their ambition, while students, to rise in their profession, or the absorbing pursuits, after they have risen, which have never left them time to examine the question. For of course it is of no use to send Lazarus from the dead, to affirm the truth of Moses and the Prophets, to men who have not had time to know what Moses has said; nor time either, nor inclination to listen to Lazarus unless he come with some important case of worldly business. Now you have left, on the field controversy, none save the few who have written learned books and constructed elaborate arguments against Moses and the prophets. And of these I have space to make the suggestion, only, that he who examines them will find that in every case where the plea of difficulty and want of proof is put in, the conscious or unconscious insincerity of it is evinced either by the palpable ignorance of the inspired writer's real meaning, or by their application to scripture of principles of evidence which common sense applies to no other writings; and which if applied to any other ancient history, literature, or philosophy, would make a *tabula rasa* of all the record of the thoughts of all past ages.

But this critique on this divine tragedy has already, I fear, been extended beyond the limits of your patience. Carry with you the infinitely solemn truths which it has developed, and make, for yourselves, the obvious application of them to your daily life : remembering that Jesus aims here to present to you this every day-life on earth as it will be contemplated, at no distant period, from eternity, without the opportunity then to change the results.

DISCOURSE XIV.

JOHN xix. 15—37.—The chief priests answered, we have no king but Cæsar. Then delivered he him, therefore, to be crucified. And they took Jesus and led him away. And he, bearing his cross, went forth into the place called the place of a skull which is called in the Hebrew Golgotha; where they crucified him and two others with him, on either side one, and Jesus in the midst, &c.

But one of the soldiers with a spear pierced his side, and forthwith came there out blood and water * * * And another scripture saith, they shall look on him whom they pierced.

JOHN iii. 14, and xii. 32, 33.—And as Moses lifted up the serpent in the wilderness, even so must the Son of man be lifted up.

And I, if I be lifted up, will draw all men unto me. This he said signifying what death he should die.

A thousand years of preparation, as we have seen, gathered the material, under the covenant with Abraham, for the construction of the typical gospel kingdom by the covenant with David. Through another thousand years of wonderful vicissitude has this typical kingdom stood, until now not only the faith of Jehovah's saints but the instincts of the Jewish masses are eagerly anticipating the immediate rise of the kingdom which it foreshadowed, and asking " when shall the kingdom of God appear?" And yet the coming of the great Antitype to " sit upon the throne of his father David," and to establish his kingdom from sea to sea that " all nations may flow unto it," has only accelerated the decay of all spiritual life out of the typical kingdom, and accelerated its movement toward its utter and final apostasy. " He came unto his own, and his own received him not." But their very passion in rejecting him is used as the instrument whereby, through his death, the work of redemption shall be finished; whereby the scaffolding of types and shadows shall be taken away, and the finished scheme exhibited in all its perfection and glory.

As the germinal truths of the covenant with Abraham sprang forth, flowered and fruited, and then shed their fruit to germinate anew in the covenant with David, organizing the typical kingdom; so now, these truths, having again sprung forth, flowered and fruited, must shed their fruit again to germinate anew in the true spiritual kingdom which it typi fied. "The hour has come" that "the corn of wheat fall into the ground that it abide not alone, but bring forth much fruit." And wonderfully does Jehovah accomplish the fulfillment of his promises and purposes by causing the very wrath of man to praise him! On this memorable Friday morning, the 9th of April, as preparatory to the great act which sets up the spiritual kingdom, the Church of all nations—the sub ject of all types and symbols and prophecies—behold the culmination of the apostasy of the typical kingdom of David! The official representatives of this typical kingdom, with a representative mob of the masses at their back, are here around a heathen judgment seat clamouring for the blood of the Son of David! And, as the unwilling heathen judge, irritated to contempt and bitterness by a clamour that he despises but dares not resist, yields up the innocent victim, arrayed in mock royal robes and crown, cries out in scorn and derision, "What! shall I crucify your king?" — the maddened nation shouts, "WE HAVE NO KING BUT CÆSAR!" The very Church of the living Jehovah officially utters the blasphemy, that there is no spiritual kingdom—no saviour King for the throne of David! No king but Cæsar!

Brethren, does it seem inconceivable to you that the visible

Church of God on earth can become so utterly faithless and apostate ? I tell you nay, such must ever be the result, in greater or less degree, from any similar dropping out of the gospel spirit from the doctrines and forms of the Church. First will come the Erastian inability to perceive any longer the distinction in kind between the spiritual kingdom, its government and obligations, and the kingdom of Cæsar ; then, naturally enough, the spiritual kingdom is cast aside as an unnecessary appendage and a clog to the gospel ; then the gospel King and Priest rejected, and the shout " no king but Cæsar."

The very greatness of the fact that " Christ died and rose again according to the Scriptures"—upon which fact the whole system of revealed theology turns, as upon a pivot— may so absorb our attention, in reading this story, that we may overlook the illustrations of the doctrine of Christ crucified, which the very record of the incidents indicates a purpose to furnish us. You will observe that the Evangelists do not merely record the great fact that Jesus was crucified, as the Scriptures had foretold. They present the fact before us in an amazing word picture. And, as the skilful artist, in painting some vast object out of the range of ordinary thought, surrounds it on the canvas with ordinary objects,—men, dwellings, animals and trees,—as relative measures, whereby we may gather by comparison, some notion of the vastness of the central object : so these inspired painters, in presenting the dying Son of God, set him forth, not in solitary grandeur and vastness, but surrounded by human objects—by the play of human passions, the outbreaks of human wickedness, the gush of human sorrow—as if to enable us at a glance to perceive the immeasurable grandeur in which the Man of Sorrows towers above those merely human conceptions.

Let us endeavour to transfer ourselves back to that memorable Friday morning in Jerusalem, and study the scenes which are enacted there, after this formal act of apostasy by the representatives of the nation in shouting, "No king but Cæsar!" We shall find in them rich lessons of instruction, both on the human, and the divine side of the gospel system.

Attracted toward the court by this shout, "No king but Cæsar," we find the judge just in the act of yielding, under the popular cry, "If thou let this man go, thou—art not Cæsar's friend;" for he dreads the utterance of such a charge, however absurd, in the ears of the irritable Tiberius, his master. Therefore he gives sentence as they demand; but "he took water and washed his hands before the multitude saying, I am innocent of the blood of this just person."

Singular paradox; a magistrate innocent of the blood of one whom judicially he murders, while declaring him just in the same breath! No, no! Pilate, think not with water to wash off that stain of blood from thy hands. For, falling upon the official hand that pretends to weigh justice in the balance, its stain hath struck too deep for any water cleansing. The untitled, powerless, private man, forced by the mob to deeds of cruelty, might perhaps with the tears of ingenuous sorrow wash out the blood spot! But thou art imperial Cæsar's legate, Pilate. Thine is the strong arm of the law, flashing its gleaming sword, by God's ordinance, in the defence of innocence, as well as in vengeance on guilt. Thy gorgeous ermine is full wide to shelter in its ample folds this torn and bleeding lamb that the fierce dogs of bigotry are thus savagely pursuing. With all thy pompous pretence to dignity and chivalrous Roman honour, thou art but a miserable pedlar in blood! Baser than Judas whose narrow soul thought thirty pieces of silver a worthy price, thou art selling him over again for a worthless smile from these ecclesiastical bloodhounds, whom every manly instinct of thy nature loathes and abhors! Thou art a poor coward, Pilate, that thou fearest such a mob, with the strong arm of Cæsar to defend thee, and the broad shield of eternal justice to hold before thee! No, Pilate, no! Not all the waters of Jordan that washed leprous Naaman clean; not all the waters that ever gushed from the rills of Siloam; not all the tears of sorrow that shall flow through eternity for thy sin, shall ever wash off that stain of blood!

Yet how common seems this mistake of Pilate, that the unrighteous judgment of an official, given under pressure of strong temptations from personal consideration,—either of desire to win popular favour; or avaricious hankering after gain; or the impulses of partisan malice or party obligations may be atoned for, by giving the innocent the benefit of one's personal convictions and professions as an off-set against the damage to him of one's villainous official deed; and that it is enough to perform a little penitential handwashing for the filthy job done to popular order! How little do men seem to comprehend the solemn truth that, as in the Church, under his revealed law, God hath appointed his ministers to be his representatives, and will surely punish the corrupt and unfaithful servants, so in the state, under that natural law which he hath revealed to all men alike. "The powers that be are ordained of God;" and will likewise be held accountable to God. That the magistrate, called by the public voice to office, is in his sphere, "the minister of God for good," to the upright citizen, and the minister of God, "a revenger to execute wrath upon him that doeth evil." And every curse threatened against official unfaithfulness in the Church, lies with all its force, in the other sphere also, against the magistrate who misrepresents and caricatures God's essential justice. Ye cowardly hand-washers! If ye have not the manly courage to breast the billows of popular fury, and make your official voice heard above all the howls of the mob, then why thrust yourselves into places to which, obviously, God hath not called you? If Tiberius, moved by the popular clamour threaten you, then tell Tiberius and the mob, "we ought to obey God rather than men," and go into exile with a clear conscience for your companion. To the sort of men whom God calls to represent him, the passion of Tiberius and the curses of the mob are sweet music compared with the accusings of conscience! Beware how ye make light of bartering justice, either for the popular smile, or for place, or for gold. If by a righteous Providence ye be not driven to Pilate's doom of exile, and suicide, like Judas; yet, be assured that, amid the curses of the ruined, the wails of the heart-broken and the moans of the murdered ringing in your ears, ye shall wash, and wash in vain at that blood-spot throughout eternity!

And, on the other hand, when public virtue hath come to such a pass, that the clamour of the mob, instead of the covenanted law, must find utterance through Pilate on the bench; or, that popular sentiment regards Pilate's use of his official authority for personal ends either of avarice, ambition or passion, as a venial sin of natural infirmity, that a little handwashing may atone for; then may we know that the day of political doom is nigh such a people, even at their doors; for now, "judgment lingereth not and damnation slumbereth not." The judgment upon such a people hath in fact already begun.

We follow, where the mob has led the way with its victim, through an eastern gate of the city; and find here gathered upon and around a curious skull-shaped hillock, a motley crowd, all intensely excited, as they gaze at the scene transpiring on the summit: Beginning first our study of the ordinary and relative figures of the picture, our attention cannot but be attracted by the movements of scribes and lawyers—public opinion manufacturers—gathering each around him a little knot of listeners, delighted with the familiarity of the great men, and eager to hear what they will have to say. They discuss the various rumours of plots and treasons concocted by this Jesus: the positive testimony of the witnesses that he threatened to destroy the temple ; and his blasphemous confession that he claimed to be the Son of God. They horn and re-horn the condemned on their merciless dilemmas, after this fashion ; either he can deliver himself from death and will not ; or he would deliver himself and cannot. If he can and will not, he perishes justly, for his stubborn wilfulness. If he would do it but cannot, then he dies justly as a blasphemous impostor, who has falsely been claiming to be the Son of God. And the simple crowd gape with wonder at the learned men, and are surprised they never had thought of so obvious a truth before. Busy among the crowd too are holy priests and Pharisees, moving with unwonted condescension and familiarity among the common herd ; seemingly heedless of the rumpling their fringed borders, and their enormous phylacteries, in their zeal to have the people duly instructed in the merits of the case ! And they have occasion to use all their zeal ; for the people are easily swayed from one extreme to the other. It was only on Monday last that, as Jesus approached the city, they gave him an ovation which Governor Pilate himself might well have envied. Never had Mount Zion and Moriah echoed with more hearty Hosannahs. And beside, among this crowd are many whom Jesus has healed of disease, or whose friends he has healed ; and they feel grateful to him. And to many also his words have a strange fascination. Such impulses brooding in the hearts of the people may burst forth at any moment if there be exciting cause. And as the deed now done is incongruous, alike with the spirit of the Roman and the Jewish law, any tumult which may cause inquiry at Rome may prove disastrous both to Pilate and the Sanhedrim.

All these matters, however, are duly cared for. Hour after hour bears witness to the skill and strategy of these holy dignitaries of the Church. The infection of the official logic, wit and raillery becomes general. Louder and more wide.

spread are the shouts of laughter at the drollery of the mob jesters, as they wag their heads, and hurl the keen shafts of their satire. Ah! thou temple destroyer, and temple rebuilder! Try thine Almighty hand now! Thou omnipotent Messiah of the prophets, display thine omnipotence? Thou saintly truster in God; let us see if God will deliver thee! Till shuddering, at the worse than brutal ferocity of the human wild beasts, we shrink back as from the opened portals of hell.

We observe another of these relative objects of the painting, yonder in the back ground. It is the multitude of women who have followed him out of the city. Motionless and terror-stricken they gaze and listen with horror at the cruel yells, and though with instinctive modesty, they shrink back from the noisy crowd and stand afar off, yet, as by some fascinating spell, they are bound to the spot. Among them we may suppose moves neither pompous Pharisee nor witty official, nor astutely reasoning lawyer. The heart and the understanding of woman—save when she is utterly abandoned of God's Spirit, as some tigress Jezebel—while she contemplates suffering, is a poor theatre for the success either of the studied wit of the official or the keen logic of the lawyer. The intuitive aversion of her heart to cruelty annihilates the heartless jest; and the stubborn dogmas of her unanalyzing but unerring judgment, dashes in peices the flippant logic that pretends to justify barbarity and bloodshed. If she cannot argue against cruelty, she can yet weep over it. Nor shall stately smile of high official, nor solemn pomp of Pharisee, nor brilliant logic of lawyer ever change the conviction of her very heart of hearts, that wanton mockery at the agonies of the suffering is not un-manlike and un-godlike. They stand and weep, and wring their hands. It is not the utterance of a true faith in Jesus; but the deep natural sympathies of a womanly heart.

Within this outer circle, and nearer the centre of the knoll
is another of these relative objects, illustrating the singular
contrasts of humanity brought in contact with the wonders of
the gospel. It is a little cluster of military men, sitting as
calm and unmoved as if lounging at some Roman outpost.
Four of them seem to be intent upon a game of chance ; the
stake being a beautiful homespun robe without seam, evidently the work of delicate fingers, as a gift of affection.
Under the stony eye of the soldier we detect the hyena glance
of the gambler, as the successive throws of the dice indicate
hope or despair of winning the prize. But how does amazement fill our hearts, as the thought occurs of the old prophet's
complaint who seems to wake from the dead, after a thousand
years, and wail over the scene,—" They parted my garments
among them, and upon my vesture did they cast lots." The
insignificant toss of a Roman soldier's hand is executing the
eternal decrees of God, and registering the description that
marks the stripped owner of this robe as the Messiah to whom
the prophets bare witness?

Raising now our eyes, we behold a fourth of these relative
objects of the picture. A sight at which cruelty itself may
well shudder ! On two upright posts, with horizontal beams
near the top, hang suspended two victims, after a fashion
which could have been devised only by a demon. Through
each hand, extended to the horizontal beam is driven a spike
crushing through that delicate congeries of nerves and muscles which marks the hand, so evidently, as a work divinely
fashioned. Through the feet a similar spike is driven, nail-
ing them together to the upright post ; and thus the victim,
left no other support than a small projection on which he sits,
hangs quivering, and, in the writhings of his agony, lacera-
ting the torn hands and feet more and more.

They both justly suffer the same penalty of crime ; but
with far different spirit, as is obvious by their look and

behaviour. He on our right almost extinguishes our sympathy in our cold shudder at the fierce malignity of his nature.
The effect of the intense suffering draws out to the surface,
as it were, the wormwood and gall of a spirit long used to
crime against society. He is an enemy to mankind, and
mankind an enemy to him. It but adds to the fierceness of
his hatred, to find himself at last a helpless victim. As the
nails lacerate under the nervous twitchings of his writhing
body, and the intolerable pain causes him to cry out, the
lurid fires of hell seem to light up his eye. He curses the
world, curses himself, curses God. And as he curses, turning a fierce glance upon the uncomplaining sufferer at his
side, he joins in the fiendish sport of the mob, and cries,
" Ah, thou saintly Messiah, come down from thy cross and
take me down." True to the life this horrible picture of the
self-righteous sinner! " If I *am* a robber, still I am not one
of these saintly pretenders! I never pretended to be what
I am not." See, here, you that make this self-righteous
boast to keep you at ease in sin, see here the style of your
religion in that dying hour to which you put off the gospel
call! Men are apt to die just as they have lived!

To our left hangs the other, in outward appearance at first
sight not unlike this blasphemer. But we readily discover
him to be the reverse in every indication of character. The
naturally harsh and fierce demeanour has been subdued. He
struggles to bear his torture without a murmur. A calm
serene joy seems to have suddenly settled upon his spirit.
Where suffering abounds some felt joy much more abounds.
Now his eyes are raised to heaven as in thanksgiving;
and tears fill them, as he whispers his gratitude. He has,
a little while ago, heard the sufferer at his side in the
midst of the scoffs and jeers, praying " Father forgive
them, they know not what they do." And the conviction
at once flashed upon his soul that one who could thus

pray must be more than man, and is sure enough the Saviour Messiah! With the heroic faith which such a conviction evinces—a faith that could penetrate through all the darkness that now overhangs the man of sorrows, and discover in him still Christ the son of God, he breathes his simple petition, " Lord remember me when then comest into thy kingdom." And at once he receives the assurance, " To-day shalt thou be with me in Paradise!"

Ye, that are trusting to the dying prayer for the remission of sin and acceptance with God, note this case closely, and you will discover that it offers you no encouragement in your procrastination. There is one case recorded that none may despair and say, too late! But that case, remember, is not of one who has all life long been warned, and yet has spurned a thousand calls? Nor is it probable that a poor halting, procrastinating, double-minded sinner, who puts off till death the great work of life, will be able to exercise such a faith as the poor thief in the agony of death.

At the foot of the central cross we find a fifth of these relative objects; one every way calculated to arouse all the sympathies of the heart. It is a group of four; three women all of the same name, and a young man of beautiful figure and manly countenance; mild and gentle in look as a lamb, yet determined, bold and unyielding as a lion. He is facing boldly the derision and scoffs of the mob; and his heroic faithfulness and attachment to his suffering friend seems to compel for him the respect and regard even of that brutal crowd. For, down in the depths of human nature, lies hid an instinctive respect for the man that stands by his friend in spite of all hostility and hate. It was not probably, because he had more faith than the other disciples that John stood here when all had forsaken him; but rather that the manly and sympathising soul of John could not endure the thought of leaving the poor old mother to stand there heart-broken alone. For one of this group is Mary the mother of Jesus.

For eighteen hundred years Art, in all her forms, has laboured to give expression to the sorrows of Mary, yet, though hers is a human grief,—the gushing forth of a sorrow that has gathered to bursting in a human heart,—Art has never reached the desired goal. Poetry has lavished all its epithets and symbols of grief; Music has contributed every conceivable note of its scale. Painting has employed all its most touching lines of sorrow; Statuary has chiselled the softest and saddest outlines of which the marble is expressive —And yet, which of all has so perfectly suggested all the depths of the sorrow to our imagination as the evangelist John who stood at her side when, at one stroke of the word painting pencil, he says, " *Now there stood at the cross of Jesus, his mother*." What Art or eloquence of speech can add anything to that conception ; such a mother witnessing such a son, in the agonies of such a death ?

Thirty years ago, the old man of God in the temple uttered the prophetic words, " yea a sword shall pierce through thine own soul also." But it is not difficult to understand that to the daughter of Eli filled with glorious memories of the past history of her people, and of still more glorious hopes of the future kingdom of Messiah, all this should be taken as merely some strong figure of speech. How should it be otherwise when to her, a youthful maiden, as the last of the line of David, Jehovah's own angel had declared, " Thou art highly favoured among women." And, educated as she had been in the oracles of God, as interpreted by her age, it is not wonderful that she should, in the ardour of youth and hope, indulge in the loftiest expectations of the power and glory of her son as the Prince of the house of David. That she should in her dreams see, in the brilliant prospective, the array of a saintly conquering host; and gorgeous palaces and untold splendours, and Jesus her son, "fairest of the sons of men," standing as the author, the centre, the ruler of all? True she must have read in the prophets much to dash such expectations. For, amid all their peans of glory there came up ever the wail of the "man of sorrows, acquainted with grief." But how should she understand such prophecies when the whole learning and wisdom of her age passed them by as insignificant or to be understood only in a figurative sense?

What a wreck of fond hopes! What a dashing in pieces of splendid visions! As she now sees the Royal Son of David in the hands of his enemies, hanging in agony, an outcast from earth and heaven! I fancy the words of the youthful John fall powerless on the dull ear of her faith, as he tries to comfort her. He doubtless tells her, "despair not yet; Jesus told us last night at the table—Let not your hearts be troubled; believe in God and believe also in me. It is expedient for you that I go away." But you, children of affliction, who have hung around the death agonies of a child: ye know by experience, how dull the ear of faith is then! How, when even the departing ones assure you, "it is *expedient for you* that I go away," you cannot comprehend the lesson. Have ye had also something of Mary's glorious experience fifty days after this, when the amazing out-pouring of the Spirit demonstrated how expedient it was that Jesus should go away?

We direct our attention now to the great central object of this gospel word picture. And the first incident that we observe, beautifully connects him, as human, with these human objects around him. Aroused by the moans of the poor heart-broken mother at his feet, from the deep thought which appears to absorb his mind, he seems as one making final arrangement of his earthly affairs preparatory to his departure. Turning his eyes, all full of human kindness and sympathy, to the sorrow-stricken mother and the young friend at her side; his countenance lights up almost with a smile at the thought, that one of the twelve has proved himself worthy of trust in any emergency. The noble young friend that no danger could deter from standing by the son, will never desert the mother in her old age and helplessness! As Mary and John both look up with earnestness, seeing that he will speak, Jesus saith in the simple majesty of heart language—to Mary " Behold thy son !"—to John " Behold thy mother !"

Let it console you who ofttimes come to the throne of grace with a heavy heart, because of the impenitency, the dangers or the suffering of this son, this daughter, this husband, brother, father, mother—that you come to a Saviour who can sympathise with you in all the tender solicitudes of these dear relations. Nor are your little domestic sorrows beneath the notice of so exalted a King. Say to him in faith—" Behold my son !"—my mother, my husband, my brother, my father, my daughter ; and you shall not go away unblest.

Now, as if done with all earthly cares, he drops back into those mysterious contemplations and inward throes which manifestly absorb his soul. It is this awful absorption of spirit, amid all the agonies of the flesh, that at once distinguishes the central victim as at an infinite remove from all mere human sufferers. He is " treading the wine press alone ; of the people there is none with him." And as now we attempt to scrutinize the pale countenance, there is an overpowering awe and majesty in its calm contemplative communion with some inward grief that utterly baffles and repels us from the task. There is such an apparent unconsciousness of external pains, while every nerve and muscle of the bodily system is on the rack of torture, as fills us with amazement. We discern in a moment that the acutest penetration can never gather from the external countenance here the infinite emotions that prey upon the soul within. All the genius of the dramatist is here at fault. The pencil of

Raphael, or the chisel of Phidias, drops from the discouraged hand of the genius that dares the attempt. Hence no truly enlightened Christian soul ever looked upon a picture of the crucifixion, however exquisite as a work of art, without the impression, how infinitely short the picture falls of presenting the Jesus of his soul's ideal : nay without an instinctive shrinking from it as a profane mockery ! Genius can paint or carve Jesus the man bearing his cross, or the cross bearing the man Jesus : but only as genius may paint or carve the thieves on either side of him. But genius can no more paint or carve the Christ on the cross bearing the sins of the world than it can create a world. All the externals here fall infinitely short of expressing the struggle of his mighty soul in conflict with principalities and powers.

And, therefore, it will be found that, just in proportion as a man is drilled into an adoration of Jesus through the outward image of him, will the true idea of Jesus as an atoning sacrifice for sin drop out of the consciousness of his faith. And just in proportion as the Church magnifies the importance of the external ; parading everywhere the cross, the crucifix, the painting of the scene on Golgotha, just in that proportion do the great spiritual truths of the cross drop out of the consciousness of the Church ; and her worship become a mere soulless, unspiritual symbolism, appealing to the imagination rather than to the spiritual depths of the soul.

It is now high noon—the sixth hour—twelve o'clock. Behold, as we gaze, there are indications of inward agony as from a burdened conscience ! A change passes upon that calm countenance ! A strange, mysterious change ! It is the expression of one agitated at the thought of sin ; and an awful mysterious struggle is going on in the soul ! Is then this sufferer, that even Pilate declared to be a " just person," conscious of some transcendent guilt, unknown to all save himself ? How suspicious—just as foretold by the prophet—

begin to arise in our sinking hearts! "Surely he is stricken, smitten of God and afflicted." It may, possibly, not be virtue suffering with heroic fortitude because supported by a clear conscience. It is possible that man could find no fault in him, yet God sees and his own conscience feels, a terrible pressure under some guilt of immeasurable enormity.

Nature, as if in sympathy with our dark mysterious suspicions, lays off her sunshine and cheerfulness, and "from the sixth hour there is darkness over all the land till the ninth hour." As the anguish of him on the cross grows more terrible, deeper and darker becomes the gloom, till the noisy, profane mob is awed into silence. Terror begins to reign in the stoutest hearts. Many steal away at the beginning of the darkness back to the city; others follow as the darkness thickens: those that remain stand fixed to the spot by the fascination of their very terror. For three long hours the struggle goes on in that mighty soul: till even faith begins to fear the worst—that the sufferer will sink under the crushing weight and die under every visible token of God's displeasure.

But as it approaches the hour of evening sacrifice—suddenly all are startled by the strong cry from the sufferer, whom they supposed too feeble to utter anything above the low murmuring wail of the dying. The words ring as though the Psalmist prophet had come forth from the sepulchre of the kings to rehearse his wail: and it echoes back from Mount Zion—" *Eloi! Eloi, lama sabachthani!*—My God! my God, why hast thou forsaken me!"*

---

* Dr. Bushnell, who, after regaining somewhat the lost confidence of the Christian public by his able discussion of the " New Life " and "Christian Nurture," seems to have fallen into an almost insane hate for the doctrine of Christ's atonement as expiatory, and declares that, rather than believe Luther's justification by faith, the " Article of the standing or falling church," he would see the church fall—strangely enough dares to say, in a

It is the true type of every believing prayer that ascends to the ear of God. "My God," still!—"Yea though he slay me, yet will I trust in him." That appeal to the Father's heart is never in vain. And now it is heard. Deliverance comes

discourse of "Christ and his salvation," that this utterance of Christ on the cross is merely the interjectional cry of "*one just reeling out of life*" and to be understood not literally but as the hyperbole of anguish; since God did not forsake him, or regard him as suffering to satisfy divine justice.

This is an amazing instance of reckless dogmatism on the part of one who affects such a horror of dogmatists! And it illustrates the straits to which absurd theories of theology, reared outside the Scriptures are reduced, when brought to be forced in upon the Scriptures to secure for them the character of Christian doctrines. Dr. Bushnell is, manifestly oblivious of the fact that Jesus, in this cry, is quoting the opening words of that wonderful twenty-second Psalm, which prophetically narrates of Messiah how, "All that see me laugh me to scorn: they *wag their heads saying, he trusted in the Lord that he would deliver him; let him deliver him.*" How "the assembly of the wicked enclosed me; *they pierced my hands and my feet.*" And how "*they part my garments among them and upon my vesture cast lots.*" Does Dr. Bushnell mean that real anguish in its death agonies utters itself in poetic quotations? or that Jesus was only acting tragically in his death? He, indeed, expressly asserts that Jesus uttered what was not true, in crying thus—a mere exaggeration. And yet Dr. Bushnell writes a volume on "Vicarious Sacrifice," pretending to receive the doctrine.

So also in saying that he was "reeling out of life." Dr. Bushnell seems equally oblivious of the fact that Jesus said, "I have power to lay down my life and to take it up again," and that the Evangelists declare that so far from "reeling out of life" with those words on his lips, Jesus evidently became calm again; thought of a prophecy not yet fulfilled—viz. "In my thirst they gave me vinegar to drink," and therefore said, "I thirst;" that when he had received the vinegar he bowed his head saying "It is finished;" and then, so far from being exhausted, he cried with *a loud voice*, uttering the prayer of calm, joyous faith, "Father into thy hands I commit my spirit;" and thereupon "dismissed his spirit."

Surely the man who can so recklessly set aside the plain statements of Scripture, is not to be trusted as a guide to report for us the statements of the Protestant fathers touching the atonement! Dr. Bushnell has a right as against the Christian world to range himself with Theodore Parker in theology. But he has no right to pretend to teach atonement, and under "false pretences" lead men to disbelieve and to scoff at it.

to the mighty soul. The light of peace illumines his countenance! And Nature, in sympathy, resumes her cheerfulness.

But before passing on, with this climax of the agony on the cross fresh before us, let us contemplate the significance of this darkness and this despairing cry. Especially would I call upon all who pretend to accept the Evangelists as God-inspired, and yet deny that this suffering is in expiation of divine justice, to explain to us these amazing phenomena. For, be it remembered, these are not puzzles of the sort that trouble them concerning the doctrine of atonement. They lie not back in the sphere of the Infinite among the counsels of eternity, but in the outer sphere of the visible universe, and, therefore, are susceptible of explanation on some conceivable theory.

Explain to us, then, on any theory that denies the great principle that "he was wounded for our transgressions and bruised for our iniquities, the chastisement of our peace being laid upon him:" that "he bore our sins on his own body on the tree:" that "we are justified by his blood:" and that "by the righteousness of one the free gift comes upon all men to justification of life:"—Explain these amazing prodigies of nature darkening over him without, and the hidings of God's face darkening his soul within!

For, according to all that we know of the laws of human nature,—dying only as a martyr for truth, or even tragically to exhibit suffering in order to awaken and call forth the sympathy of a "new life," and lead it, in sentimental harmony with God, to suffer at the presence of sin in the universe,—Jesus should have, at least, died calmly and even joyfully. Heretofore he has manifested in all things unmurmuring submission to the will of God; and, seeing that Providence has ordered this time and manner of his death, why should a good man fear it, and agonize in spirit under the infliction of it? Even Socrates died without terror and mental suffering.

Still more than this, Jesus had none of those oppressive doubts that must trouble even a Socrates, assured of the justice of his cause—those doubts of having purity of character sufficient to bear the scrutiny of the immortal, as of the mortal judgment seat. Not unfrequently these doubts, at the approach of death, project their dark shadows into the chambers of the soul and bring out the writing hitherto unnoticed which memory has traced on its walls, recording many a sin. For Jesus had "no sin upon him, neither was guilt found in his mouth." Neither could Jesus have been overwhelmed with the uncertainty about immortality, which troubled even Socrates, that he should despond so in his death and cry "My God! why hast thou forsaken me?" For nothing could be surer or more real than his conviction of an immediate transfer of him the homeless one to the mansions of his Father's house.

Surely, it will not be pretended that the mere physical agony caused his spirit to break down, and despondency to overwhelm his soul, while we see the two men on either side of him enduring the same physical agony—one, with proud, defiant scorn, cursing and joining in the jeers of the rabble ; the other with holy peace of mind praying " Lord remember me when thou comest into thy kingdom."

We find no solution of this agony and despondency therefore either in the moral, the intellectual, or the physical nature of the man Christ Jesus. And the question still recurs, why should Jesus the leader and model of so many thousands of martyrs, and saints of high attainments in the new life, be, in his death, so different from them all? Why should David, with death staring him in the face, sing " the Lord is my strength, I will not fear what man can do," and yet Jesus wail in Gethsemane—" O my Father, if it be possible let this cup pass!" Why should Shadrach and his friends walk cheerfully amid the flames of the fiery furnace, with " a fourth form like unto the Son of God" walking with them, and yet the Son of God himself in this fiery furnace of affliction have "his visage so marred above any man's?" Why should Stephen, with the crushed bones grinding through the quivering muscles and nerves of his body, under the barbarous stone-blows, be able to cry, with the delight of a child, "Behold I see the heavens opened and Jesus standing on the right hand of God," and gently breath the petitions, "Lord, lay not this sin to their charge,"—"Lord Jesus, receive my spirit"—while Jesus himself moans in agony at the prospect, and wails the hidings of God's face in the crisis? Why should Paul exultingly say, "I am now ready to be offered, and the time of my departure is at hand: I have finished my course, henceforth is laid up for me a crown of glory"—while Jesus in loneliness of agony complains "What, could ye not watch with me one hour?" and, in view of the conflict with death, "Sweat great drops of blood," and now in the hour of dissolution cry, "My God! My God! why hast thou forsaken me?"

Brethren, there is no explanation of all this, short of a practical denial of the whole story, as anything more than legend, save in the explanation which the scripture gives of it, and which it is, indeed, the purpose of Old and New Testament alike to give us. This cross is the great altar which all the altars from Adam to Ezra typified. This victim is the Lamb of which every victim offered, under every revealed worship was a prophecy; and of which, indeed, every victim that smoked, through all the ages on the altars of heathenism was an unconscious prophecy. This transaction, in the outer sphere of the natural, is but the infinite truth presenting its finite side to our comprehension, that God's justice must be magnified in the infliction of the sentence "Thou shalt die" for sin, while God's mercy provides and accepts the substitutes in the sinner's stead. In this act the instinctive con-

sciousness of universal humanity—save as rationalistic theo-
rizing freezes out the soul instincts of humanity—receives the
satisfaction of its longings for an expiation for sin, that may
at once meet its ethical sense of right and its hope of the
divine favour. To this act that we are contemplating as the
grand centre, all the revelations and worships and mighty
wonders of all previous prophetic teachings looked forward ;
and all the revelations and worship and mighty wonders of
the succeeding apostolic teachings look backward. Nor can
any one, with intelligence enough to discern between mere
critical jugglery and honest common sense, and between solid
manly logic and " glittering generalities," read the Titanic
demonstrations of Paul in Romans, Galatians, and Hebrews,
without perceiving that to tamper with this simple story of
" Christ crucified " in its plainest common sense meaning,
is, just in the same degree, to filch away the very heart and
substance of the scriptures, and leave them a hollow sham, or
miserable wreck of old wives' fables !

But if we accept fully Paul's great idea that God is " setting
him forth, a *propitiation*, through faith in his blood, to declare
his righteousness for the remission of sins that are past,
through the forbearance of God," then we have the solution
of these mysteries. We can see why, at this amazing scene,
Nature should veil her face in terror, and, at its close, rise
reverently from her seat, dropping her sceptre, to do obeisance
to her departing Lord. We can see why still a deeper darkness than Nature's veils the light of God's countenance from
the sufferer; why "he is stricken and smitten of God and
afflicted." It is not, as we might have dark suspicions it is,
because he is paying the penalty of his own sin—but because
"he is wounded for our transgressions and bruised for our
iniquities." He is " bearing the sins of *many*," for, in him
are represented now all the sins of all the myriads which
shall constitute the body of the redeemed that are to sing
" he hath washed us from our sins in his own blood."

We return for a moment to the closing scene. The agony of the desertion is over, and the light returned. It is now three o'clock, the hour at which every day, for two thousand years, the sacrifice, typical of this, has been celebrated. As at twelve o'clock he had arranged his personal human affairs, preparatory to his departure, giving Mary his mother in charge to John; so now he seems absorbed with the thought of his official cares, and to inquire if all things written in Moses and in the Prophets and in the Psalms concerning his death have been fulfilled. There is yet one prophecy—" In my thirst— they gave me vinegar to drink." He cries " I thirst;"—and wonderfully is the prophecy fulfilled. There was no vinegar near to suggest it, but under a momentary impulse of com- passion, " one of them *ran and took a sponge and filled it with vinegar*, and put it upon a reed and gave him to drink." Again like the dice-throwing soldiers, the enemy is uncon- sciously registering the marks of Messiah. Everything now accomplished he announces, " It is finished !" and then calmly but with loud voice saying, Father, into thy hands I commit my spirit"—he departed amid the groans of agonized nature that rent the rocks; opened the sepulchres; and—to mark it as no ordinary earthquake—rent the hanging vail of the temple !

The frightened mob rushes away frantically, wringing their hands as they press into the city. The Roman soldiers, how- ever alarmed, must stand to their post. Their captain can only exclaim in mingled terror and astonishment—" sure enough this must have been the Son of God !" The women who loved and revered Jesus still stood afar off in amazement: they have no terrors of conscience to drive them off; and they are held fascinated to the spot.

As the evening shadows lengthen, behold, there comes for to the deserted hillock a squad of rough soldiers to finish the death work, and take the bodies away, out of regard for the tender scruples of the holy Pharisees about allowing the bodies

to hang beyond sundown on the gibbet. They roughly break
their bones and thereby hasten the death of the two thieves,
who might otherwise have lingered a day or two. To their
surprise the victim on the central cross seems already dead.
But the Roman soldier under orders must act very surely.
So to make sure, one thrusts his rough iron spear into the
victim's side to pierce his heart, and there comes forth blood
and water. It puts beyond all chance of dispute hereafter
that Jesus died; and rose from the dead and not merely from
a swoon!

But this singular incident—one provided for in neither
Roman nor Jewish executions—recalls to us the strange prophecy, " they shall look upon me whom they have pierced!"
" and the house of David and the inhabitants of Jerusalem
shall mourn." And our thoughts started in the direction of
the thoughts of the dying Jesus, to know whether " all things
are now accomplished and the scripture fulfilled," there seems
to gather around the deserted Calvary in the twilight a prophet chorus singing in the ear of faith his death, as gathered
the angels to sing his birth.

Zachariah takes up his plaintive elegy. " Look how they
have pierced him, and mourn. Awaked thou hast, O sword,
against the shepherd, and the sheep are scattered. They
weighed his price, thirty pieces of silver, and cast the thirty
pieces of silver to the potter in the House of the Lord!"
Micah takes up the strain,—"They have smitten the Judge
of Israel with a rod on the cheek." Daniel, as beating *time* to
the music on his great prophetic drum—" Seventy weeks are
accomplished"—the exact seventy times seven years—
and, behold, Messiah is cut off, not for himself, but to
finish transgression, make an end of sin; to make reconciliation
for iniquity and bring in an everlasting righteousness."
Isaiah's voice, many-toned as the organ, now wails, " He is
oppressed and afflicted, yet opened not his mouth. O, thou

despised and rejected of men, a man of sorrows and acquainted with grief! Yet it pleased the Lord to bruise him. He shall see of the travail of his soul and shall be satisfied; because he hath poured out his soul unto death, and is numbered with the transgressors; and bears the sin of many, and makes intercession for the transgressors." David, as if new depths of penitential sorrow are awakened in his soul—re-echoes the wail "My God! My God; why hast thou forsaken me? They have pierced my hands and my feet." Old Elijah, with spirit softened, comes to "speak of his decease now accomplished at Jerusalem." And Moses with him declares —"Behold the prophet like unto me"—Behold the true blood sprinkled at last under the covenant promising "When I see the blood I will pass over!" Jacob—"The sceptre hath departed from Judah, for Shiloh hath come. Behold him whom I saw at the top of the ladder, now descended to its foot on his mission of grace." Abraham, rejoicing to see this day, cries, "God hath provided the lamb, on the very mount Moriah—The Isaac is laid upon the altar, but no angel stays the father's hand." Adam with wonder declares the heel of the woman's seed is bruised—and terrible is the bruising; but thereby hath he crushed the serpent's head. Beautiful Eve mingles with the moans of Mary his mother, her joyous maternal song—now sure enough, "I have gotten the man, I have gotten the man—the Jehovah!"

Yes! Not a line, not a syllable of all that God hath spoken, at all the "sundry times" and in all the "divers manners" hath failed in this wondrous scene of the lifting up and the piercing on Calvary.

Brethren, I dare not even enter upon the great practical lessons here, save only to suggest the blessed lesson to you, from the manner in which this great central fact of Christ's death is here presented, surrounded by these relative human objects, and the play of these human passions answering back

to the amazing voice of God that speaks in this death. It is
the story of a "Jesus, the same yesterday to-day and forever;"
and of a human nature just the same also to-day as yesterday.
As you look on him pierced, and mourn that your sins pierced
him thus—Remember you look to him who could pray with
it all—"Father forgive them." If there is one of you who feels
himself a poor, cowardly, Lord-denying Peter, and weeps
bitterly as he seems to look upon you ; remember his gracious
message—"Go tell Peter to meet me in Galilee"—the kind
test "Lovest thou me ?"—and the grace that made Peter so
lion-hearted on the great Pentecostal day to say—not "woman
I know him not"—but to charge in the teeth of the excited
ten thousand, fierce and blood-thirsty in the streets of Jerusalem—"Him being delivered—ye have taken and with *wicked*
hands have crucified and slain." Nay if there is here a poor
Judas whom conscience charges with having betrayed and
sold the master, only come weeping like Peter—go not away
in despair to death—but come look upon him. There is no
such difference between denying and betraying, that Peter
may be saved and Judas not!

If there be some heavy-hearted father or mother or brother
or sister here, bowed down with sorrow for the hardness and
impenitency of this child or brother or sister, who hath forgotten all the vows of infancy and the teachings of childhood—
Fear not that your humble heart-troubles are too unimportant
for the great King. You have a High Priest who can sympathize with you ; one that, even amid the agonies of his cross,
forgot not these tender ties of nature, but said "behold thy
mother !" Come boldly with the burden and cry in faith—
"Jesus Saviour behold my child—my brother—my sister"—
and your cry shall not be in vain.

If there is one among you procrastinating the offer of grace
—and secure in the hope that when death comes he will accept
it—remember him who wasted his dying breath in jeers and

curses at Jesus. But on the other hand, if there be some aged sinner who feels it is now too late, then be encouraged with him on the cross, to cry " Lord, remember me !" and even yet obtain the assurance of his favour.

He was thus lifted up to " *draw all men* unto him," without respect to birth, or age, or moral character. The very gamblers who played for his robe ; the very mob that shouted " he saved others, himself he cannot save "—the very soldiers that pierced his hands and feet, and he that pierced his side, so far from being given over, were selected to prove how he is " able to save to the uttermost." For remember his last command runs " Go preach my gospel—beginning at Jerusalem."

SECTION V.

DISCOURSE XV.

THE APOSTOLIC STATEMENT OF THE TERMS OF SALVATION.

ACTS xvi. 29-31.—Then he called for a light; and sprang in, and came trembling, and fell down before Paul and Silas, and said, Sirs, what must I do to be saved? And they said, Believe on the Lord Jesus Christ and thou shalt be saved.

To the student perplexed by some curious anomaly in nature, or principle of philosophy; to the physician perplexed with some case for which his reading furnishes no parallel nor suggestion of a remedy; to the lawyer weary with looking for some precedent to settle the principle of the case in hand; how gladly comes the information that such a problem, such an instance, or such a case, has come before some great master of human knowledge, in these departments severally, and has been clearly and indisputably settled. Why should it be less a matter of gladness to you, my brethren, so deeply concerned in this question of salvation, and often so uncertain about it, under the various theories of men concerning it, to be told that the great question has been authoritatively settled and in a form precisely to meet your case, whatever it may be? That there is a decision not merely of the abstract principle, *in thesi*, as the logicians would say, but on a case actually occurring. Not a decision either, under some of the

v

ancient covenants with an incomplete development of the gospel salvation ; but twenty years after the last of the old covenants had given place to the new covenant in Christ's blood ; twenty years after the completion of the scheme by the death, resurrection and ascension of Jesus ; and given by a man to whom, after his ascension, Jesus had appeared personally for the special purpose of commissioning him to speak for him, in declaring the terms on which he will be the Saviour of men.　Not a decision, either, founded upon the case of some one peculiarly related to the scheme of salvation, as one of the chosen people, under special covenant, but upon the case of one wholly outside the covenants—a Gentile like you —and as worldly-minded and unbelieving as hitherto any of you have been.

You are perhaps ready to ask however—" Is not this a peculiar case, and out of analogy with mine, seeing that here was a miracle wrought in shaking open the prison doors and shaking off the fetters—whereas now there are no such miracles to convert men."　I answer no : the miracle here is but an illustrative incident in the case, and does not at all remove it out of the sphere of ordinary experience so far as relates to saving the soul.　For you will perceive that the miracle, so far from converting this man, left him frightened indeed, but as worldly-minded and full of concern about his official responsibility as ever ; yea so utterly atheistic as to be ready to commit suicide.　It was after the miracle was all over, and, as its result, had driven him to the verge of suicide, that the calm, kind words of the Apostle brought him to himself.　And now as the result of these kind words, taken in connection with all he had heard before, he was convinced, convicted of sin, and, in agony of conscience that made him tremble and prostrate himself, he asks, " what must I do to be saved ? "

It is a very common error that the miracles of the New Testament history were the great means of the conviction and conversion of men under the New Testament ministry. And this error involved in them is that which at once exposes the imposture in all these legendary miracles of modern saints and prophets wrought to convert heretics and infidels. A miracle never converted anybody: never was intended to convert anybody: never could in the nature of the case, convert anybody. For a miracle, that is, an act in the sphere of the natural which no power but God's can do, is simply the seal which God puts to the commission of those whom he sends to speak in his name, in order to verify the commission and to distinguish them from impostors and false prophets. It is analagous to the seal which is put upon the commissions and other public papers issued from the clerk's office, or the secretary of state's office ; and bears the same relation to the gospel preached by these commissioned men, that the seal of the office on the paper, bears to the commission and instruction contained in it. Nicodemus stated the logic of the matter precisely—" Rabbi, *we know* that thou art a teacher come from God, *for* no man can do these miracles which thou doest *except God be with him.*" Hence, when men claim to have wrought a miracle, we naturally ask—what revelation from heaven does this miracle attest the commission to deliver ? And so, when men claim to speak a revelation from heaven, we naturally ask—" where is the miracle that attests your authority to speak from heaven ? If the claim is to work miracles without any message from God to us, we know at once that it is an attempt to counterfeit the seal of the office in heaven. If a claim to make revelations without the miracles to attest it, we know at once it is the trick of an impostor and false prophet. Hence you find Jesus ever appealing to his mighty works as the attestation of his authority to speak God's words. And yet to such as curiously demand simply to have the miracle—" the sign "

—without caring to hear the message of God, he says " an evil and adulterous generation seeketh a *sign*, but there shall no sign be given."

In order to see that a miracle, in the nature of the case, is not a converting power, just imagine that it were our office, as ministers, on the Sabbath day to work miracles before you instead of preaching the gospel. The first exhibition of our power—say in raising some dead man—would indeed excite and frighten you—drive some of you, perhaps, to suicide, as this jailer. Others would go away talking of the wonder and filling the world with the story : but none of you thinking of your sins and the need of salvation ! The next Sabbath the same wonder repeated would not alarm and excite so much ; the following Sabbaths less and less ; till at length, the act of God's power in raising the dead would affect you just as little as those daily acts of God's power which keep the sun punctual to the moment every morning, and the moon and stars in their places.

This case therefore is, notwithstanding the miraculous inci- dents that precede, precisely the case of any one of you, who, in the ordinary way, have been led to accept the proposition that God is and that Christianity is true ; and moved by some call of the gospel entreating you, " Do thyself no harm !" have been led earnestly to ask " what shall I do ?" And, whether it be the case of a worldly mind, that never thought of it before, or of some one long familiar with the subject, and often aroused before,—or of some real Christian in darkness and doubt about his personal acceptance with God —here is your case made and decided, by one expressly authorized to decide it. And if you can comprehend the meaning of the terms of this short answer, " Believe on the Lord Jesus Christ," then you know all that is essential to be known in order to be saved.

For have you ever noticed the singular tendency of the

mind of this great inspired logician Paul, to *pack* the whole sum and substance of the gospel, whether as a theology or as a practical experimental truth, into one brief sentence or even clause of a sentence? As the mathematician glories in his science, which can often express in one brief formula, with a few signs, great propositions and facts which it would require pages to develop and utter in ordinary language, so Paul seems to delight in generalizations that express the whole gospel in one simple formula. As a theology, he expresses it all in two words, "We preach Christ crucified." As an epic history, in the sentence, "Jesus Christ came into the world to save sinners." So here as an experimental fact—"Believe on the Lord Jesus Christ,"—this is the whole of it. So that if you can comprehend two simple ideas into which analysis resolves the sentence, and accept them, you may be saved. These propositions are—First,—the object of belief—"The Lord Jesus Christ." Second,—the subjective act of the soul involved in the word "Believe." Assuming that you are in earnest enough, in asking the question, "What must I do to be saved?" to look at these two propositions from the practical and experimental standpoint, I propose to assist you in getting at their definite meaning by developing their significance in the plainest words, and by the simplest analogies and illustrations I can find; and reasoning, not theoretically, but simply upon the plainest principles of common sense and human nature.

As to the proposition, the object of the belief—"The Lord Jesus Christ"—I may assume that all of you have already some tolerably distinct conceptions of its meaning. The instructions of the fireside, of the Sabbath-school, the public worship, and even the ordinary social conversation under which you have grown up, give you greatly the advantage of the jailer in that respect; and have brought you naturally and almost unconsciously, to the same point, to which the earthquake brought him, namely, the conviction that this "Lord Jesus Christ" whom these ministers preach, and Christians talk about, is a divine being. You have also, perhaps, comprehended something of the profound truths of theology which are embodied in this title—for the title is a theology. You understand how as "Christ," he is the anointed and commissioned mediator between a holy God and unholy men. How as "Jesus," so named at his birth when he became the Son of man like ourselves, he is "the Saviour" of his people from their sins. How as "Lord," he is Head and Ruler not only of all things in heaven and earth generally, but, in a special sense, Lord of a peculiar body of people whom he redeems out of the lost race of men. And that, in fulfilment of all these titles, he came to earth, taking our human nature in conjunction with his divine nature ; lived a life of holy obedience to a law of which he was not the subject but the ordaining authority ; died the death of the very guiltiest of sinners, as an atonement for the sins of those he would redeem ; rose from the dead and ascended to the throne in heaven, thereby demonstrating that he was indeed the "Christ" appointed of God to be the mediator, and that this sacrifice was accepted of God ; and that the way is now open for the return of all who had rebelled against his authority, and by their sins had forfeited all claim to the divine favour. And that this willingness of God to receive sinners was further demonstrated, in sending forth the Holy Ghost, by whose divine power the sinners should be made willing and enabled to return to God. Supposing the knowledge of these facts already sufficient to enable you to comprehend them when thus summarily stated, I pass on to the second of these propositions, with which you probably have more difficulty.

The inspired direction is simply "Believe." There is a preliminary inquiry here which usually suggests itself to worldly men,—" Why believe ?" they say, how does that answer the inquiry, " what must *I do ?*" When the ministers of the gospel, instead of telling me to do anything, say " believe on the Lord Jesus Christ ;" what relation has this idea of the " Lord Jesus Christ " to the idea involved in the question of something to be done to secure God's favour ? If you would tell me what duties should be done—what prayers—what reform of life—what acts of holiness, must be done, I could then comprehend it as an answer to the question " What must I do ?" But instead of saying do these things, which constitute true religion acccording to the teachings of the gospel, you say nothing of doing, but only " believe,"— " believe on the Lord Jesus Christ !" Now, why is Christ held up to the thought rather than Christian duties in the acts of life ?

Without going into the depths of theology for an explana-tion—as I have promised not to speak theologically—we may find reason enough why Christ should thus be held up to your thought in the depths of your own consciousness, if you are in earnest in asking " What must I do ?" For any sort of analysis and observation of the state of mind which leads you to ask earnestly, will show that Christ is precisely the object to meet the wants of that state of mind.

Thus, in the first place, one of the reasons which induce you to ask for instruction in the way of salvation is the trouble you find, in your attempts to approach God in prayer for the pardon of the sins of which you are conscious, of conceiving of the Being to whom you speak, definitely enough to feel that your communion with him is a reality, and that he hears you and answers. You labour, as preliminary to any utter-ance, to have some notion of him to whom you speak. And as you endeavour to conceive of an Infinite Spirit, filling immensity with his presence, how everything seems to become confused and dizzy, till at last it seems to you as if you are speaking to mere vacuity; and naturally enough your thoughts and desires have no outflow, for all seem to come back upon you. Your thought refuses to convey the message which the heart would send. In this trouble, finding you cannot pray, save in some mere form that you feel is not true prayer, you come to us, saying "What must I do? I cannot pray." We answer, "Believe on the Lord Jesus Christ." And why? Because, in Jesus Christ God is presented to you in a form that your thought can conceive of, and that your heart's affections can go forth unto, though you see him not; just as they can go forth to the friend, father, or mother far off out of sight; as you sit down and write your thoughts to them, until it seems almost like speaking to them face to face. As Tayler Lewis somewhere says of the bible, that it is the Infinite Mind which comprehends all the finities, turning a finite side to finite men, that they may comprehend and commune with its thought; so we may say of "Jesus Christ," "God manifest in the flesh," that he is the infinite God presenting his finite form to us that we may conceive of and commune with him. "The same yesterday, to-day, and forever," that simple gospel story sets him before you so clearly and definitely, that, as you would speak to him of your sins and soul-troubles, you may be assured it is the same compassionate son of man, a "High Priest that can sympathize with our infirmities;" and you can talk to him as man talks to his fellow. See you not then how appropriately we say to you, "Believe on the Lord Jesus Christ" when in that state of trouble about praying, you come to us asking, "What must I do?"

Unitarianism, indeed, charges us with idolatry in praying to God as clothed thus in the form of humanity. But how can Unitarianism provide for this conscious want of every earnest soul that, burdened with a sense of sin and helplessness, tries to pray, save by treating the earnestness and heart feeling as fanaticism, and confining religious experience to

mere cold speculative thought of God? Suppose we grant
that a few of the more etherial spirits, by long training, can
rise to the heights of conceiving of God as a pure infinite
spirit, definitely enough to speak their heart utterances to
him and commune with him? Yet what is to become of the
vast masses of unlettered, untrained men? Of the poor unintellectual peasant? Of the little children? Of the broken-
hearted sufferers—in no frame of mind for subtle reasoning
and laborious effort to conceive of God? All these need just
as truly as Channing, or Ware, or Parker, or Emerson, to
have a God to whom, in their troubles and darkness, they can
go and pray. Tell them of the Jesus Christ, of whom they
can all conceive as the son of man, the man of sorrows, the
lover of the poor and the little children, and they can all pray
just as really as the profoundest philosopher. They can
readily be taught, especially under the leadings of the Holy
Spirit, that their thoughts reach his thoughts and find sympathy there. It is as our dying boy unconsciously and artlessly
illustrated it. After reading in the Sunday-school book the
story of the little boy in sorrow for his dying mother, who,
having heard the story of Jesus, conceived the idea of writing
a letter to Jesus and leaving it in a stump in the lonely woods,
where Jesus might find it;—said our boy, " It may seem
foolish in a boy like me, six years old, to feel so, but I could'nt
help wishing like the little boy, that I might write a letter to
Jesus and ask him to help the doctor to make me well, or else
to take me out of this dreadful suffering." We said, " why,
poor boy, we have a shorter way than that of asking Jesus for
what we want;" and were about to explain to him by some
simple analogy, but his thoughts recurring immediately to
what he had seen, with so much wonder and childish delight,
at the telegraph office—a question sent to one of the family
a thousand miles off and answered in a few minutes—his eye
sparkled through the tears as he asked, " How? could you

do it by telegraph?" Struck with the analogy, we could but reply " Yes! that is more like it. In everybody's heart the earnest wish for blessing from Jesus strikes a chord that reaches to the heart of Jesus, and he answers back to our hearts in the same way."

If the illustration seem childish and simple, it may only the more aptly suggest to you, who have felt this trouble, in the approach to God in prayer, how the things "hidden from the wise and prudent are revealed to babes!" and why it is that we meet such soul trouble as yours with simply holding up Jesus Christ to your thought.

But you find also a second difficulty that leads to this inquiry. That is, a surprising degree of darkness and ignorance on the whole subject, as experimentally applying to your case, however clear you may have supposed your general theoretic knowledge of the gospel to be. Like Bunyan's pilgrim in the Slough of Despond, you know nothing of the way of escape save that you must not not get out on the side next the City of Destruction from which you are trying to flee. Hence pastors are so often surprised that those whom they had trained so carefully in gospel knowledge should seem in such utter darkness, when the self-appropriation of their knowledge is to be made. This consciousness is, indeed, implied in the question " What must I do?" We answer again, " Believe on the Lord Jesus Christ"—why? Because Christ is specially revealed as the Prophet who by his teachings and spirit, meets that very difficulty. Having once obtained the conception of Jesus before alluded to, you can in no way so readily get the knowledge you want as by prayerful study of his own teachings of the way of salvation. You will now find with what wonderful simplicity he teaches. How, as a mother teaching the little ones by pictures and comparisons, so he by constant analogies and figures from the external world—conveys the ideas of this work in the sphere of the internal and spiritual. And once you realize that the gospel is not a story of what Jesus once said, merely, but of what he is *now* saying to you, and desire that, by his Spirit, he will enable you to understand experimentally his sayings, you will wonder that you should have been in darkness so long about that which is so plain.

A third difficulty which leads you to make this inquiry, what must I do?—is the greater consciousness of sinfulness now than you ever felt before. Though ready enough, heretofore, to acknowledge yourself, generally, a sinner, you had no such conception of your guilt and unworthiness before God as now. Your very efforts at reform, fixing your attention upon your sins, it seems to you that, with all your efforts to be good, you are every day getting worse and worse. It is this experience that leads to the common request, " Pray for me, I am such a sinner I cannot pray." And this enters largely as an element into the reason for asking—" What must I do?" Again we answer—" Believe on the Lord Jesus Christ." And why? Because, to meet this very difficulty, he is revealed as your Priest, making atonement, and thereby taking away sin ; and, by taking it away, releasing the conscience of its burden and the soul of its terror in approaching God. And once you apprehend clearly as a great reality, personal to you, that in this life of Jesus he obeyed for you, and that in his sufferings and death, you were represented, and your sins atoned for, then you begin to feel the force of the Apostle's saying—" Being justified by faith we have peace with God through our Lord Jesus Christ." And now you can approach God as a reconciled father.

There is still a fourth element of trouble in your experience which leads you to ask—" What must I do ?" You discover now, in a sense never realized before, your helplessness and your want of strength and self-command to keep your resolutions to lead a holy life. You find with Paul, " When I would do good evil is present with me." Before, you have relied upon your strength of character and your ability, if you only once determined on it, to lead a holy life. But now the habits of sin are so strong that you cannot but feel—" What though all the sins of the past were pardoned, and I assured of it by a voice from heaven ! still, if left here just as I am in a world full of temptations to sin, before another day passed I would be again covered with sin, and guilty before God." Hence you are afraid to trust yourself, when urged, in obedience to Christ's command, to confess him before men. You have so little confidence in your present purposes of holiness that you fear you will disgrace such a profession, and therefore hold back. And in your dissatisfaction and despair you ask, " What must I do ?" Once more we answer, " Believe on the Lord Jesus Christ." And why ? Because he is held up to your thoughts, in the gospel, as not only your prophet to teach and your priest to atone, but also your king to subdue your spiritual enemies and to rule himself in your heart. As the result of his work of atonement he has secured for you the Holy Spirit to create anew, to give sensibility to the conscience, and strength to the spiritual life. His gospel is not only a teaching of God, and of the forgiving love of God, but the " power of God unto salvation." It exhorts you, feeling your weakness and assured that you shall find grace to help you in time of need, instead of giving way to the power of sin, to feel that you can do all things, Jesus Christ strengthening you.

You may now begin to see why we hold up Jesus Christ simply, before the inquiring soul rather than direct him to do this and do that, under the rules of a Christian life. We do not mean that the newness of life of holy obedience is any the less important, or that it need not follow. The principle of the gospel is that you shall serve and obey not by rule, nor for reward, nor from mere fear ; but from the same principle on which you serve and obey the mother who has won your willing, uncalculating service by her love to you. Jesus Christ is willing to risk the ethics and the obedience of his people, after they thus accept him as the remedy for their troubles, on their sense of gratitude and love for him who loved them and gave himself for them. And, on the other hand, you perceive that the reason why we hold up Jesus Christ as the answer to " What must I do ?" is not from any pressure of theological dogma, but because it is precisely the direction which provides the remedy, with marvellous fitness, for the conscious wants which lead to the question.

If now you can understand the other term of the direction— " Believe "—which expresses the subjective act of the soul, in thus contemplating the object Jesus Christ,—then you have the whole of it.

But here again you feel great difficulty. You feel conscious that it must mean something more than simply to believe intellectually that Jesus Christ was and is ; as you believe that Cæsar, or Paul or Luther was and is. What is then this peculiar believing on the Lord Jesus Christ which is unto salvation ?

Here, again, let us take the simplest, common-sense method for ascertaining the significance of a peculiar, technical term that we are in doubt about. Your method, in ordinary cases, when reading an author who uses a term the meaning of which you do not know and have no means, as the lexicon, at hand to enable you to determine it, is to note carefully the connection in which the word occurs ; and, as you pass on, to note also its connection in a second and third and fourth occurrence. From the notions gathered out of the connection at one place compared with those gathered in the others, you construct for yourself the definition of the term. Let us apply the simple principles to any one of these inspired authors, and see what is the meaning of " believe" here.

We take the gospel of John. On the very first page we find, " He came unto his own and his own received him not." This you can readily comprehend ; for you know, from your own case, the state of mind and feeling denoted by saying you " receive" one who comes : the feeling of pleasurable satisfaction with which, when the announcement from the door is of a favourite friend, you " receive" him. Also you know the feeling, in the contrary case, when, though treating the visitor with all courtesy, still you in your heart " receive him not." Well, the evangelist proceeds, " But to as many as *received* him, even to as many as *believed on his name*, he gave power to become the sons of God." Here, then, we have discovered at least a part of the meaning of " believing," for the author puts it as synonymous with " receiving" Christ. And if after you have become acquainted with the Lord Jesus Christ as we have been contemplating him, we announce to you that he is here to call on you, do you receive him, with pleasureable satisfaction, analogous to that with which you welcome a friend ? If so, then, in so far, you " believe on the Lord Jesus Christ."

We turn over a leaf of the author, and reading on, we find, " As Moses lifted up the serpent in the wilderness, even so the Son of man shall be lifted up, that whosoever"——— Now, as the analogy recalls to our minds the scene of the dying Israelites, lying scattered on the hot sands of the desert, and hearing the proclamation " look upon the brazen serpent that Moses hath raised on the pole and you shall not die," we see, therefore, that the rhetoric would require the writer to continue the figure and say that whosoever " looketh to him lifted up shall not perish, but have everlasting life." But instead of " *looketh*," it is, " *believeth* on him, shall not perish." Hence you discern that " believing" is a synonym, again, for that eager, longing look which a dying Israelite would cast toward the serpent on the pole. And nothing can exceed the force and beauty of that figure. You have observed the power and eloquence of a look, often exceeding all power of speech. You have seen it in the speechless dying man, as he tries to communicate his heart's desire without words. You have felt it, as a child, and especially as a parent, when the little one at your knee, coveting some favourite object, as the fruit on the shelf, yet fearing to ask, lest it be chilled with a " no"—that most chilling of all responses to a child from one that loves it —casts that look of desire on the coveted object, and looks, and looks again, but dares not utter a word. If now the child would boldly ask for it in words you could refuse ; but you have more than the ordinary nerve if you do not break down, at last, under the appeal of that eloquent look, and respond to it by giving the object of desire, or kindly explaining and apologizing if it cannot be given. Well now " believing" on the Lord Jesus Christ is just that look of desire as the soul, in the troubles I have described, sees Christ thus set forth in the gospel. If you can recall how you felt, as a little child, while you timidly plead by a look when you could not, dare not, utter the wish ; and perceive that your present wish for salvation is like that,—then this is " believing."

We turn over another leaf, reading on and find, " Ye will not come unto me that ye might have life," and again on the next page, " No man can come to me except the Father draw him," and in immediate connection, " He that believeth on me hath everlasting life." Here, again, we discover that, in accordance with all the preceding, " believing" is synony- mous with " coming," and the state of mind implied in coming to one for relief—involving at once trust in his ability and willingness to relieve, and earnest desire for the relief. And so we might go on through the whole New Testament. It will be perceived that this " believing" assumes as its very start- ing point the ordinary belief, historically, in Jesus Christ as a

Saviour: and upon that element superadds the heart impulses of joyful acquiescence, desire and confiding trust in him as a friend. While these all, again, resolve themselves into simple willingness to have him as our Saviour from sin, and our Lord.

But one of the very things, perhaps, most difficult of belief of all the things in the gospel, is just this conclusion, to a soul yet in darkness and conscious of the burden of sin. And therefore, in conclusion, it may be important to confirm all that has been said, by proving to you, after the same fashion of reasoning as before, that this is all, absolutely all, that is implied in the terms of salvation stated by the Apostles. That there is no such consideration of good works to be offered; nor any such amount of penitence, and such strength of faith, to make one worthy, as men will insist on making a part of the condition of salvation. This proof can be made very conclusive by a brief examination, in comparison with the terms offered to the jailer, of all the forms of stating the terms found in the gospel.

Of these forms of statement there are three classes. First —literal statements. Second, representations of Christ's work in his miracles by analogies. Third, by figures of speech. The chief of the literal statements of the terms seem at first sight to be somewhat various and even contradictory. In one case the condition is " repent ;" in another " believe ;" in another " repent and believe ;" in another " repent and be baptized ," in another " believe and be baptized;" in another " repent and be converted ;" in another " whoso confesseth me, him will I confess ;" in another " if thou confess with thy mouth and believe with thine heart;" in another " whosoever shall call upon the name of the Lord shall be saved ;" in another " whosoever will, let him take of the water of life freely." But you will find that, on a thoughtful examination of these various statements, they are all merely different expressions for the same act of soul, according as that act is viewed on its different sides, and from different points of view. Repentance is the soul, after an apprehension of Christ's goodness, contemplating its sins; faith is the soul, after an apprehension of its sinfulness and helplessness, looking from its sins away to Christ; conversion is the outer expression of this faith and repentance in the acts of the life, turning away from sin to Christ. Any soul that truly repents, believes; any soul that truly believes, repents; any soul that truly believes and repents, "converts" from sin to Christ, as the natural result. So "confessing Christ" or being "baptized" —which is Christ's appointed way of confessing him—are the outward expressions of the internal penitence and faith of the soul, and imply of course the reality of that feeling which they represented. So "calling on the name of the Lord to be saved" implies the penitence which creates the desire to be saved, and the faith which trusts in the Lord Jesus for salvation. And all, in their last analysis, mean the same as "whosoever will"—wishes truly—desires truly—to have Jesus as a Saviour. And it is in confirmation of all that I have said, to find that our view of the terms of salvation, as set forth by the Apostles, so beautifully harmonises and explains all these different expressions of the terms found elsewhere in the gospel.

A second method of exhibiting the terms on which Christ receives sinners is by the record of his similar acts of grace, in the outer sphere, by his miracles of healing. You will find in the record of his miracles some striking external analogy to every feature of that soul-trouble which you experience. And, doubtless, it was for this purpose that the record of so many cases was made. It could not be, as some seem to think, merely to record for us the proofs of his divine authority to teach, for, after relating to us how, at his word, the dead arose from the grave, and, at his command, the winds hushed their howling, and the sea stilled its raging, what other proof could we want of his divine authority? For what other purpose then this careful record of all the incidents of so various cases of healing, than to illustrate, for those in spiritual darkness, how he restores sight to the blind; to illustrate for those conscious of their loathsome spiritual disease how he heals the leprosy of sin; to illustrate by healing the withered hand, or the poor cripple, how he restores the soul that cries what must I do? from its sense of utter helplessness. And so through the whole list of spiritual troubles. These miracles are all so many diagrams, as of the mathematicians, whereby Jesus will aid our minds to apprehend, and comprehend, those great spiritual truths, which otherwise so confuse us.

Now, turning to any of these cases you find that the same great truth as to the terms of blessing is set forth. The condition is only that, desiring the healing and believing in his power to heal, they come and gratefully accept the gift. Nay, in many of these cases, it is specially illustrated, how it is not for the sake of the faith, or in reward of strong faith that he grants his grace. Both Matthew and Mark record for us, how when in the coasts of Tyre and Sidon, outside the limits of the Church, he met with a case of very strong faith in a poor heathen woman. It was an anxious and sorrowing mother who brought her little daughter possessed of a devil, and fell in agony at his feet, crying, " Have mercy, O Lord, thou son of David!" For in some way she had been led to the knowledge of the ancient covenant and the belief that Jesus is Messiah. He tried her faith by that severest of all tests the national prejudices against any claim of foreigners to superiority,—saying "I cannot bestow gifts intended for the peculiar people of God as yet upon Gentiles; I cannot take the children's bread and cast it to the dogs." But the mother's heart, full of the one great idea, the suffering child,

forgot all prejudice and insult; and with that irresistible
logic of a mother-heart, as it were, cornered him with his
own argument, "Truth, Lord, it is wrong to take the children's bread for the dogs; but may not the dogs pick up the
crumbs that the children let fall? And wilt thou not let a
heathen dog, but still a broken-hearted mother, have this
crumb as thou art passing? The Saviour's compassionate
heart could not resist the appeal. But, making an exception
in her favour, cried " O! woman great is thy faith! Go along,
go along, and let it be as you say."

Now if this case of strong faith stood alone, you might
perhaps feel afraid to trust the gospel assurance, when you
think of your feeble, doubting faith in comparison with this.
But, as if to prevent that mistake, and to prove to you that
" he will not break the bruised reed nor quench the smoking
flax;" in the very next chapter but one, is told the story
of the poor father who came with his boy similarly suffering,
while the Saviour was up in the mount of transfiguration and had
his faith all wrecked, by the failure of the disciples, from want
of faith, under the worrying of the Pharisees, to heal the boy.
As Jesus comes down, at length, the poor father kneels and
cries " Lord, if thou canst have mercy on my son;" and, with
the natural impulse of the father, rehearses all the details of
this desperate case—so desperate, he thought, the disciples
were not equal to the task. Seeing his darkness and doubt,
Jesus tests his faith also, saying in effect, the " if" is not with
me but with you.—"If thou canst believe, all things are
possible to him that believeth." The poor father, seeing
that all depended on belief, burst into an agony of tears,
crying, "Lord, I believe," but, as if fearing he had gone too
far, takes it back, in the petition, "Help thou mine unbelief." But Jesus pitying him, who had no faith in his own
faith, took just what he had to offer, and healed his boy just
as he had healed the woman's daughter. O, if you are standing

back because you fear that though you desire Jesus to be your Saviour, you have no faith or so feeble faith—then you need not fear to press your claim on such a Saviour, who shows such compassion. If you dare not say, "Lord I believe;" yet pray "help mine unbelief," and venture on him fully.

I can only allude, in conclusion, to the third form of expressing the terms of salvation, as a final and conclusive proof, that the only condition is involved in the Apostle's statement as I have expounded it. Indeed it needs nothing more than an allusion, since these figures seems to be so graded as to express assurance of acceptance from the highest to the lowest degree of the energy of faith, and that the lowest will not be rejected. Thus you are told to "Flee from the wrath to come," to the "strongholds," as one having the energy to hasten swiftly, vigorously. But if you plead "I have no energy of faith to flee," then the gospel saith "come to Jesus," even though you must creep as the poor lame man, or grope your way as the poor blind man, and that shall be taken as faith. If still you plead "I am utterly impotent, unable to move, so as to come in any way," then, saith the gospel, "stretch forth thine hand and "receive" the Lord Jesus for he is nigh thee; and that shall answer as faith. Nay, if you still plead, "I cannot stretch out a hand, for the very arm hangs powerless as that of the poor man in the gospel," then saith the gospel "Look to Jesus," for "he that looketh upon him lifted up shall live." Nay more yet,—If still you plead, "I cannot look, for alas the hazy film of spiritual death is over my eyes, and all is darkness," then saith the gospel, "Poor sinner, if nothing else, lie still just as you are, and "submit to the righteousness of God," allowing Jesus to throw the robe of his righteousness over thee, and that shall answer, for ' WHOSOEVER WILL ' may take him for a Saviour."

Brethren, I have finished what I proposed, and I leave it now for you to say, whether, according to every principle of experience and consciousness, these terms of salvation could be fuller, freer, or more precisely adapted to the state of soul for which they were intended, or a more complete answer to " what must I do."

And here again to-day, in the name and by the authority of Jesus the Master, I say to every soul in earnest and troubled with the consciousness of sin, " Believe "—" only believe" not opinions, but on a personal Saviour—not a creed, but on a Christ—" Believe on the Lord Jesus Christ, and thou shalt be saved."

DISCOURSE XVI.

I Timothy i.-15.—This is a faithful saying and worthy of all acceptation, that Christ Jesus came into the world to save sinners, of whom I am chief.

The simplicity and comprehensiveness of this saying, as a summary of the Christian creed, has been justly applauded. Said the elder Alexander, after teaching theology forty years: " The longer I live the more I incline to sum up all my theology in the single sentence, " Christ Jesus came into the world to save sinners, of whom I am chief."

Nor let it be supposed that this language of the Apostle, even as a summary of objective theological truth is meagre and defective. For a thoughful analysis of the passage develops these propositions as contained in it.

1. That men are *sinners* is the fundamental fact upon which the whole gospel proceeds, and to which it all refers.

2. They are sinners in a sense that they need, not merely reformation, cultivation, elevation by a Socrates ; but *salvation* by a *Jesus*, that *saves ;* and therefore must expiate sin.

3. The Jesus that saves must needs be also *Christ* the " anointed," appointed—commissioned of God as Mediator, and therefore be divine.

4. The " Christ" must needs " *Come into the world* " thereby becoming Son of man, as well as Son of God.

5. This view, as objective truth, logically self-consistent and accordant with first truths, commends itself to the rational understanding as *faithful*—" reliable "—" believable "—to be confided in as truth.

6. Also, as subjective, experimental truth, it commends

itself to the heart and conscience of universal humanity, as *worthy of joyful acceptance.*

7. The practical result of its acceptance is a humility out of which springs the profoundest conviction that this gospel is able to save to the uttermost. For each feeling himself chief of sinners, because knowing more of his own heart than of other people's, conceives that a gospel that met his case can meet any case.

But I conceive, brethren, that neither the peculiar power of this Apostolic summary, nor the key to its interpretation, lies so much in its brevity and comprehensiveness, as in the glowing fervour which pervades it, as the grateful heart-utterance of personal experience. As one snatched from death's door, unexpectedly to enjoy the pulsations of a new life and health, gratefully attests, and feels that he cannot over-estimate, the skill which warded off from him the deadly assaults of disease—and enthusiastically urges that all the sick should try his physician ; so the Apostle here says in effect—" I whose case was so utterly hopeless—I a blasphemer and a persecutor of his people—now, a sinner saved by grace, stand a monument of his infinite power and goodness. Who can doubt the reliability of a gospel that saved me ? Or who can hesitate to try a remedy that met successfully such soul diseases as mine ?"

Without therefore going into an exposition, theologically, of the points shown to be involved in the Apostle's summary, but looking rather to his earnest commendation of it, as worthy the confidence and glad acceptance of all, I propose simply to show any of you, who have not accepted it, that this gospel view of man the sinner, ruined and helpless, and of Christ Jesus as the Saviour suited to the case, commends itself to your understanding as entirely reliable ; and is worthy your glad acceptance ; and that Jesus is ready to accept you, however great a sinner you may be. In order that you may the more readily comprehend my argument, I shall gather the elements of it from your own knowledge of facts, and your own conscious experience.

1. " *Came to save sinners.*" As just stated the peculiarity of the true gospel of Christ, and that which distinguishes it, at once, from all gospels of mere human device, is that it assumes, as its fundamental fact, that men are sinners ; guilty sinners under wrath ; helpless sinners, in a state of utter ruin. " He shall be called Jesus, for he shall save his people from their sins," was the word from heaven that heralded his coming. " The Son of man is come to seek and save that which was lost," and, " I came not to call the righteous but sinners to repentance. They that are whole need not a physician but they that are sick,"—this was his own formal declaration of the purpose of his mission. And in his wonderful discourse in defence of his conduct in mingling with publicans and sinners, against the Pharisees, the point of his argument was to shew that saving sinners is the grand enterprise which interests all heaven. That the mission of the mediator was to search for straying sinners ; and the mission of the Holy Ghost was, through the Church, to search for lost sinners, as for lost treasure ; that in consequence of this, God the father received back with joy the prodigal sinners, and the holy angels, full of sympathy with the enterprise of infinite love, rejoiced over the lost sinner found. That no being in the universe, outside of hell, but ethical religionists of the Pharisee order, did not rejoice at seeing such love to lost sinners.

If, as some in our day will have it, Christ Jesus came merely to teach and to set an example of virtue,—that would imply that darkness, and ignorance only was the trouble with men. If, as others will have it, he came merely to have them pardoned ; that would imply simply thoughtlessness, frailty and errors of judgment. But when it is declared that

Christ Jesus came to save sinners; that implies a state of wreck and utter spiritual ruin.

It would, indeed, seem superfluous, at first sight, that one should undertake to demonstrate to men that they are sinners, in a world such as this,—so full of sin and its curse,—and whose inhabitants so universally seem ready to admit that they " err and go astray like lost sheep." And yet unbelief on this very point lies at the foundation of most of the infidelity and contempt for the gospel that everywhere prevails. The gospel according to Channing, of the dignity of human nature; the gospel according to Renan, of the sentimental and transcendental oneness with God of human nature ; and the gospel according to Owen and Holyoake of the mere animalism of human nature, all alike reject the gospel idea of a Christ Jesus—Saviour—because all alike ignore the gospel doctrine of man a sinner, in the gospel sense. And for precisely a like reason, differing only in degree, many of you who do not scoff with the devotees of either of these gospels, at the doctrines of atonement for sin, yet your minds are in darkness and doubt on the whole subject of the doctrine of atonement and of the Holy Spirit, simply because, though you make the general admission that all men are sinners and you among them ; yet you have not clearly apprehended that they are sinners in the gospel sense. Not comprehending the nature and extent of the disease, you can not, of course, comprehend fully and clearly the nature and extent of the remedy. And therefore while from the impressions of early education you are not disposed to deny the general statements of the gospel, you cannot avoid the secret feeling that the case is overstated ; that the gospel does not accord with your consciousness in those strong statements of the " death of trespasses and sins ;" the " carnal heart enmity against God ;" and the heart " desperately wicked," &c.

Come then, let us reason together of this matter—looking for the elements of our argument, not among the dogmas of theology which you profess not to understand, but down into the depths of your own spirit.

By way of removing obstacles, and getting upon a common ground of argument, let me first premise a few things which the gospel does *not* imply in saying that Jesus comes to save sinners.

It does not imply, in the first place, that the state of ruin is complete and final as that of " the angels that kept not their first estate." According to the gospel, what specially distinguishes the estate of ruin in the present life is, that it is a ruin merely in progress. The sorrow that sin brings as its curse is mingled here with the tokens of a mercy and love that forbears because the Christ Jesus has interposed, and is yet carrying on his work of saving sinners.

The state which is to follow this is that in which the sorrow which the sin brings with it is no longer alleviated by the tokens of mercy and of purposed restoration. This gospel, observe, says he " came *into the world*, to save sinners ;" but he goes not into hell to save sinners. The *virus* of the spiritual death has been taken into the system, and the death stupor only is upon you here ; from this he comes to arouse you.

Hence you will observe the wide difference between the gospel view of the ruined and depraved condition of humanity, and the cold, cynical contempt for the littleness and meanness of man expressed by the infidel philosophy, that recognizes no higher estate from which man fell, nor higher estate to which he may be restored again. While the gospel describes you as a soul in utter ruin, it recognizes the fact that the ruin is of a temple originally glorious ; while it represents your moral nature as a chaos, without form and void and darkness upon it ; at the same time, all the elements of a beautiful *cosmos* are hidden within the chaos; and when God who " called the light to shine out of darkness" hath shined into your hearts the process of reconstruction shall begin, and go on until a holy God shall pronounce it good. While the gospel represents your spiritual nature as a desolate waste; it is yet the desolation of a wasted Eden, over which the fierce storms are breaking in their fury, but the germs of a beautiful life are sleeping in its soil, which the warm breath of God can call out again in due season. This gospel does not mean to deny, then, that there are germs of its original greatness still in the soul : that its power of moral perception is still there ; and its romantic admiration for that which is noble and manly and God-like is still there, even in its " death of trespasses and sins."

Nor does the saying, " came to save sinners " imply on your part a vivid consciousness of the utter alienation from God involved in this sinful estate. On the one hand, the standard by which the gospel measures acts of obedience to God may be much higher than yours ; and on the other hand, you may be unconscious of the real extent of your ruin, measured even by your own standard. You may be but another illustration of the Apostle's other saying, " If our gospel be hid it is hid to them that are lost, in whom the God of this world hath *blinded their eyes*," &c.

With these limitations of the meaning of the gospel in saying you are a sinner so ruined and helpless as to need a divine Saviour ;—let us look now for the evidence confirming that saying within these limits.

In the first place, if you accept the gospel story at all, then the fact that such a being as Christ Jesus should speak of you in such terms as he does, is at once very strong presumptive evidence that there must be something dreadful in your condition. For of all teachers that ever spake, Jesus is the last that could be supposed to use terms of exaggerated harshness, or of rhetorically overstating the character and condition of men on the side of evil. The tenderness of feeling that wept over a city full of malignant enemies, saying, apologetically, " O that thou hadst known:" the love that amidst agonies inconceivable, could pray for those that were inflicting the agonies, and plead, apologetically, " They know not what they do," " Father forgive them," would surely prevent him from using terms harsher than the facts warrant, in setting forth your condition before God. If, therefore, it seem to you that his statements go beyond your consciousness and moral judgments in this case, does not that rather argue that his moral standard is higher than yours, and his spiritual insight deeper and more piercing than yours, and his knowledge of your condition better than yours ?

Now, in addition to these considerations, when you proceed thoughtfully to consider the facts of your own consciousness and the movements of the moral nature within you, they will be found to confirm all that the gospel says of your estate of sinful ruin.

Beginning with the most palpable of your inner consciousness, I would remind you that, whatever may be your theories, you find yourself here in a world full of trouble and sorrow. And such is the constitution of your moral nature that you cannot avoid associating in thought, the existence of the evil with the existence of sin as the cause of it. Nor can you avoid the impression of some sort of moral disorder in the relation of men to the infinitely Good Being who, as reason teaches you, must govern the universe of men. And, as matter of fact, moreover you find that the greatest of your own sorrows, such as arouse your soul to its depths, never fail to develop in you a consciousness or at least a suspicion more or less definite and distinct, which connects the sorrow as a judgment back with some sin done as the cause of it, and of which it is the penalty. It is the propensity of men universally, whether enlightened or ignorant, thus to associate sin and suffering together as cause and effect. Of course we except from the rule the mad dreams of genius, such as those dark atheistic vagaries of Shelley that conceive of the universe as under the rule of a malignant being delighting in the infliction of pain, and also the artificial moral natures of men run mad with their own theories of no sin in the universe.

Another palpable fact is that you are surrounded by a world full of wrong; of men that do wrong; of men that applaud men that do wrong: yea whose hero-worship is at the shrine of monsters of wrong-doing. Nor can you hide from yourself the fact—however partial to yourself in your moral judgments—that you partake of the common nature, and are oftentimes a wrong-doer also. And that all this wrong-doing is against God's order—and the proper order—is also an instinctive impression of your nature; however you may thank God that you are not as other men in the extent of your wrong-doing. Yet like all other men you feel the tragic impulse of your moral nature giving forth its judgments that this transgression and disobedience should receive a just recompense of reward. You find also an inarticulate logic of the moral nature inferring that somehow there must be vast moral disorder, in the present state, under which so much wrong goes unwhipped of justice. And, withal, an occasional suspicion that your own future may yet bring the reckoning, and a conscious dread at the thought of it, if "judgment is laid to the line and righteousness to the plummet."

Now in all such impressions and impulses you are but finding attestations to the gospel saying of "Christ Jesus came into the world to save sinners." And in that very shyness of feeling which you may detect in your own heart at the thought of coming into the presence of God even now, and that shrinking back from the thought of death, you attest the fact that you are conscious of sin. For if innocent, and not a sinner, what has innocence to fear in all the realms of God, go where it may? Or, if merely frail and erring, why should mere frailty and error be afraid of a Being whose benevolence is written all over the works of his hands? Or why should a soul not conscious of impurity, and a conscience untroubled with guilt, shrink as you find yourself shrink, even now, from coming into the more immediate presence of a Holy God, though it be only in thought to commune with him?

Still more palpable facts of consciousness attest the disorder in your spiritual nature. What means this paradox, which you cannot have failed to notice—the infinite disproportion between your moral impulses and conceptions, and your ability to realize them? Why are these better aspirations always thwarted by some inertia of will that leads you ever to lag in the execution, or some jar of the passions with them, or some opposing impulse just on the theatre of action? That somehow your own judgment is set at derision by the lawless appetites and passions which it ought to govern? That your prudence is not equal to the task of restraining your impulses to do evil; and yet often interposes its restraints upon the more generous impulses of your nature to do some worthy or noble deeds? You boast of your reason and intelligence, which can be led only by logical arguments and indisputable proof to convictions that the gospel is worthy of acceptance. You boast of your determined will, that can restrain you from sinful indulgence. You boast of your practical judgment, as the guide of your life. But why is the reason and intelligence so often outwitted by the plea of appetite and strong temptation? Why does the strong will display its power chiefly in overruling your conscience? Why are the practical judgments set aside, so often, in the thoughts, and the acts of the life so wholly given up to the things which reason must teach you are unworthy to be the chief concerns of an immortal creature,—"things that perish in the using?" Why do you, a being gifted with the strong will and the practical wisdom, allow yourself to become the servile creature of the mere shams and shows of life which your loftier sentiments revolt at, and your profoundest convictions condemn as unworthy of you?

See you not that this whole moral and spiritual nature within you is in a state of hopeless disorder? Just attempt for an hour to watch, as one watches the processes in a bee-hive, the workings of thought, emotion and conscience; and how plain is it that all within is a disordered wreck. Whatever the philosophers may teach you of the laws of association of thought, to what small extent can the operation of any law be discovered, especially when you would make God and your relations to him, and the utterances of your conscience, and your condition morally and spiritually the subject of thought. How impulses, as it were from without, whose source no law can trace, rush in and break up the train in defiance of all laws of association. How suggestions base, impure, impious, wild, unaccountable, make the soul as very bedlam! As well attempt to trace the laws of harmony of the sounds from some worn-out and broken musical instrument upon which half a score of rollicking children are beating! One that makes the attempt in earnest will indeed be ready to accept the theory that the human soul is but a wrecked and broken harp, its strings all passive, save as struck by wild demons in their infernal freaks; until the Holy Ghost, whose aid was procured by him who saves sinners, retunes the harp and draws forth by his divine touch the heavenly music which it was originally framed to make to God's glory.

And still another most palpable proof of the moral ruin of your soul may be found in your experience touching those very impulses and powers within you, which the humanitarian gospels flatteringly cite to you as evidences that our gospel overstates the case. These higher and better aspirations of which you are capable; the immortal fires which slumber within you; and the powers of high spiritual life which give so much dignity to that soul that the gospel of Paul pronounces fallen and depraved.

Granted all! But alas, what should be more humiliating to you than to find that these noble impulses and aspirations have, somehow, a dead weight upon them which they cannot lift. That these immortal fires are, somehow, ever smouldering and smoking, never blazing forth! That these powers of a high spiritual life are, somehow, so shackled that they never can actualize themselves in lofty action, and realize the noble ideal that flits before you! Your will is strong enough—but then do you will according to conscience? or, even if in accordance with conscience, is the will obeyed? Somehow you do not execute what you will to be done! With the Apostle, you find a law in your members, that when you would do good evil is ever present. And at times, perhaps, you have almost cried with the Apostle, " O, wretched man that I am, who shall deliver me from the body of this death?"— though you did not reach in your experience his answer of deliverance, " I thank God through Jesus Christ my Lord."

This soul of yours, somehow does not obey the strong will! All the currents of habit set in against the will; the volcanic fires of passion burst out and overflow, in disregard of its authority! If you doubt it, then just will once to serve Jesus Christ; and see how much respect your will can command. You will see how the world and its interests set your will at defiance—nay you have seen it. How base motives creep in, and you cannot expel them! How you resolve to cast off the world with its pomps and vanities, and find them mock your efforts! How you try to flee from these evil suggestions and thoughts, and find yourself as a man trying to run away from his shadow! How you resolve to control your evil thoughts, evil tempers, and evil habits, and rise to the true ideal of spiritual character, and yet the wild thoughts and fierce tempers and lawless habits seem to chase you, and grin at you in derision!

Indeed, can we conceive of any aspect of human nature more affecting than this capacity for noble and lofty conceptions, with an utter powerlessness to execute them? So may you have seen some poor sufferer with the body utterly palsied and powerless to any effort, even the movement of a muscle, or of the tongue itself, while yet the intellect is unimpaired, and its powers evidently in full play within. There lies the poor sufferer on his bed; the eye still gleaming with intelligence, but the tongue powerless to utter it; the strong will in full play, yet not a muscle will obey its behest; the powers of intelligent conception actively at work within, yet not a motion to signify their existence, which can be inferred only from the anxious and beseeching eloquence that speaks from the eye. If you have ever seen the case, it was more affecting and distressing to you than the death itself which would release the spirit from the dead body.

Now very analogous to this is the case with these immortal spiritual powers within you, helplessly chained to the moral body of sin and death. What more affecting proof could be offered of the spiritual ruin in the soul than a spirit with such faculties and capacities bound fast to a moral corpse and crying: "Who shall deliver me from the body of this death?"

So far from any contrariety to the gospel statement, the existence of such impulses and faculties in the soul, without power of realizing themselves in act, is the very strongest confirmation of the gospel view that the soul is all in a state of disorder and disease, a wreck lying in its ruins, incapable of being restored except by the Christ Jesus who comes to save sinners. Thus the argument from the facts of consciousness cumulates at every step in proof that the gospel assumes rightly that you are a sinner in this strong sense of helplessness and ruin.

You will observe that I have not even alluded yet to facts, in that still wider field of argument, concerning those low, brutal instincts and mere animal appetites and passions which have so powerful a sway in your soul; and which your own moral judgments at once condemn as unworthy of your nature, and making you odious in the eyes of all pure and holy beings. I have avoided that field of argument, and chosen rather the evidence from those very phenomena on the ground of which you may think the gospel overstates your case. And I wish too to avoid raising any incidental questions of dispute, or unnecessarily arousing your pride, or exciting in you suspicions of the fairness of the argument. But, even thus narrowly confined, is not the proof conclusive that the saying which represents you a lost and ruined sinner, is one so much in accordance with your own knowledge and experience, as to make it to your rational understanding a " faithful " saying, one entirely reliable and to be confidently believed.

And now if on the back of all these natural experiences, you have been moved upon by the Holy Ghost, as I have no doubt you have been, more or less powerfully ; —if he hath awakened your conscience to new sensibility, opened the blind eyes of your spiritual vision, that you may behold something of your guilt and misery, and of the holiness of his law; and if he hath enlightened the understanding in the knowledge of the truth, then will you need no further argument to confirm it as a faithful saying that you are a sinner, guilty and condemned, as well as helpless and ruined before God, and be prepared to comprehend the argument from experience showing that the other gospel statement of Christ Jesus as the Saviour suited to such a case is also a " faithful saying " commending itself to your implicit belief.

2. But, whatever may have been the degree of your con-

iction of sin by the Holy Spirit, you may readily comprehend
en from the natural experiences of consciousness which I
ave been describing, what I shall now say, in brief outline,
of the adaptedness of the Saviour, Christ Jesus, as held forth
in the gospel to this spiritual condition of man the sinner.

He " came into the world." He took the human nature
upon him, to this very end, among others, that these sinners
might be able to comprehend the love of the Being against
whom they sinned ; and with their finite conceptions commune
with him.   He came, the " brightness of the Father's glory
and the express image of his person !" yet so veiling the
dazzling brightness that you might look upon him.   The
infinite in him puts on the measure of the finite to hold
converse with finite minds.   Christ Jesus is the love of God,
the mercy of God, the holiness of God, the sympathy of
God for man, all embodied for you in the form of a fellow-
being, to encourage you to approach God for the settlement
of this sin difficulty ; that you may speak to him as man to
his fellow, and tell the story of the soul disorder and soul
troubles, with the conviction that he generously sympathizes
with you and is ready to help you.   Nay, Christ Jesus comes
expressly in the character of a teacher, a prophet sent from
God, to expound for you the causes of this disorder in the
soul and to point out the remedy.   Need I tell you that, in
this whole aspect of the gospel's Christ Jesus, you find your
case precisely met ?   That all this exactly suits the darkness
of mind, and indefiniteness of conception, which has overwhelmed you when you endeavoured to conceive of God
definitely enough to speak of him; and the vague, dreamy
floating of the thoughts when you tried to pray, until all idea
of God seemed to vanish and you found yourself talking to
nothing ?   That this view of him, presents him as now saying
to you just as truly as he *said* to those who heard him in the
flesh those simple instructions of the nature of his kingdom and

the terms of forgiveness? And that you need no longer listen to the mere opinions and theories of learned scribes as they speculate of sin and its remedy : but have one to direct you who " speaks with authority and not as the scribes ?"

And so with the gospel view of this " Christ Jesus," coming to render a life of perfect obedience to that law to which he was not, as other creatures, subject, but as the representative of the great body of whom he is the head ; and then as the guiltless one to make atoning sacrifice for the sins of the world to take away the sin, and have it remembered no more ; thereby enabling the sinful creatures to stand, as represented in him, guiltless before God, and clad in his righteousness. Need I point out to you how precisely this meets that consciousness of sin that makes you dread the presence of God ? How, as that deep sense of guilt would frighten you away, Jesus Christ meets you to show you how, incorporated with him, you can suffer the penalty of your sins to roll over upon his innocence, and not merely be passed over and sentence remitted, but " *taken away*," as though it existed not. And how, therefore, you can approach God with all the innocent confidence of a little child and be adopted as his child ? Thus satisfying at once your sense of moral justice by showing you that the penalty has been paid for you, while he assures you of the love of God who gave his only begotten to die for you.

And so again with the gospel view of the " Christ Jesus," as securing also by his death the power of the Holy Ghost, from on high, whereby those that accept him as a Saviour are " created anew in Christ Jesus unto good works." That power that restores the disorders of the soul ; renews the will ; gives it strength to keep the disorderly passions in subjection, imparts vigour to the better nature, to maintain the struggle against the passions and lusts in the soul, and to live the life of grateful consecration to him. Need I point out to you how precisely adapted is such a Saviour to the necessities of that ruined and disordered soul which we have been describing? How accepting this offer you may go boldly forward, feeble as you are, feeling you " can do all things Christ Jesus strengthening you ?"

Thus even so far as the testimony of your inward experience goes, you can see that this gospel saying, both as to your disease and the remedy for it, is one that carefully studied must commend itself both to your logical nature as true— " faithful," in the sense that it is worthy of belief—and also commends itself to your heart as worthy of your glad acceptance. And having thus shown you, that independent of any testimony of others, this remedy is reliable, I may with the more confidence refer you to the universal testimony in its favour of those who have made the actual experiment, which testimony is uniformly with Paul, " this is a faithful saying and worthy of all acceptation." The conviction of the innumerable thousands, living and dead, who believe this gospel to be of God, is founded mainly upon their experience of its adaptedness to relieve those terrors of the conscience, and those disorders of the soul of which you know something. Can you doubt any longer when thus you find this remedy attested, at once, by all you know of the disease for which it provides, from your own consciousness ; by all that you can understand of the nature of the remedy itself, as so marvellously adapted to the case ; and then by the universal testimonies of millions in heaven, and on earth, proclaiming, as the result of their experience, " This is a faithful saying and worthy of all acceptation, that Christ Jesus came into the world to save sinners ?" Nay, if you can refuse to believe and accept truth thus attested, ought not that fact satisfy you that the continued unbelief is evidence not of an understanding unconvinced, but of a heart " desperately wicked ?"

3. But perhaps there may be some of you who fully admit

the proof, and acknowledge the saying as faithful, and would gladly accept it, if you could only feel sure that Christ Jesus will accept such a sinner as you.   From long struggle with the soul disorders within : from a deep conviction of sinfulness, seeing that you have sinned so greatly, or against so much light, or in grieving the Holy Spirit ; or from discouragement about yourself, seeing how often you have resolved and vowed, and yet broken all solemn vows, this offer may indeed be gladly accepted by others, but is not to such as you.

I stand here in the Master's name, to say to you, that yours is the very case met, and you are specially invited to come first.   " Of whom I am chief," said the great Apostle, who had been the blasphemer and the persecutor.   And the argument is, the gospel that saved me will save anybody; the Christ Jesus that accepted me will accept anybody.   And such you will find to be the feeling of every sinner, saved by grace.   Knowing more of the depths of sin in his own heart than he can know of anybody else's heart, he cries " I am chief !"   And so far as his knowledge goes he judges rightly. Hence it is such a matter of amazement to him, that he should have been snatched as a brand from the burning.

Dora Greenwell, in the " Sunday Magazine,"—in the talk of the poor pitman to his wife—has expounded this principle with exquisite beauty and power.   Saith the poor reckless pitman :—

> I've got a word like a fire in my heart
>   That will not let me be—
> " *Jesus the Son of God, who loved,*
>   *And who gave himself for me.*"
>
> There's none on earth could frame such a tale.
>   For as strange as the tale may be—
> Jesus, my Saviour, that thou shouldest die
>   For love of a man like me !

Why only think now if it had been
    Peter, or blessed Paul,
Or John, who used to lean on his breast,
    One couldn't have wondered at all!

If He'd loved and He'd died for men like these,
    Who loved him so well—but you see
It was *me* that Jesus loved, wife,
    He gave himself for *me*.

It was for me that Jesus died,
    For me, and a world of men
Just as sinful and just as slow
    To give back his love again;

He did'nt wait till I came to Him,
    But he loved me at my worst;
He need'nt ever have died for me,
    If I could have loved him first.

And could'st thou love such a man as me,
    My Saviour! then I'll take
More heed to this wandering soul of mine,
    If it's only for thy sake!

Yes, it is the glory of the gospel, that it is "able to save to the uttermost;" that it is a gospel to save sinners,—the chief of sinners; and that its trophies, every one of them are living testimonies to encourage especially the soul who cries "I am chief!" "You" saith Paul "are the very sinner to come first. I, the persecutor and blasphemer have been accepted that I might be a standing assurance to the despairing!" Yea, and so Paul's Master before him had commanded it to be preached. The very commission which gives the Church her divinely appointed ministry, runs—"Preach the gospel to every creature,—*beginning at Jerusalem.*" The divine order of the work shall be the worst sinners first. Therefore before going into all the world, go first to the poor sinners hardened under the blaze of light and grieving the Holy Spirit. Go tell those who imprecated the awful curse

"His blood be upon us and our children," that the blood if they will, shall be upon them first, as the blood of sprinkling to bless, instead of an immortal curse. Go, tell the poor, compromising, cowardly Pilate that the blood with which he bought his peace with the mob, shall, if he will, buy his peace with God first of all, and wash off from his official hands that blood-stain that no water can ever wash off. Go, tell the poor heartless jesters, who jeered at my agonies, saying, " If thou be the Son of God come down from the cross,"—that I have not only come down, but, also, ascended to my throne, and if they will, my first act of royal clemency shall be their pardon. Go, tell the reckless gamblers who played for my seamless robe so eagerly, that they first, if they will, may put on the robes of my righteousness ! Go, tell the rough soldier who thrust his spear so brutally into my side, that he may first be washed in the blood, and first drink of the water of life !

Yes ! on the very front of this gospel saying, verifying it as God's saying, and distinguishing it from all human gospels, is this order of its offer. All human gospels seek first the least depraved—the finer natures, the morally elevated ; whereas this gospel ordains "begin at Jerusalem ;" take the chief of sinners first, to show that none need despair. What more do you want, in the way of proof, that " it is a faithful saying and worthy of all acceptation ?"

DISCOURSE XVII.

THE APOSTOLIC GROUND OF CHRISTIAN COMFORT AND COURAGE.

ROMANS viii. 28-31.—And we know that all things work together for good to them that love God, to them who are the called, according to his purpose.   For whom he did foreknow, he also did predestinate to be conformed to the image of his Son, that he might be the first born among many brethren.   Moreover whom he did predestinate, them he also called ; and whom he called, them he also justified ; and whom he justified, them he also glorified.   What shall we then say to these things ? If God be for us, who can be against us ?

THE Apostle resumes here, in the twenty-eighth verse, the subject of the afflictions which the children of God are called upon to endure in this life.   And as then he had assigned as one reason why they should not be allowed to crush the heart, that these "sufferings of this present time, are not worthy to be compared with the glory which shall be revealed in us ;" so now he assigns, as a second reason, that these sufferings are the means of good, blessings in disguise.

That apparent ills are often the means of good, is a fact which even men of the world may find out by experience. The disease brought on by sensuality has often restored a man to himself: the loss by some daring speculation in business has sobered his rashness, and trained him to self-reliance; the overthrow of his schemes of ambition has been a salutary discipline to make him a wiser man.   But more eminently, and more certainly, is this the case with the true Christian.   The crushing of his earthly hopes gives him a stronger set heavenward.

The humiliation of some fall into sin chastens his spirit. Even when death enters within the circle of his affections, and causes the deep wailings of nature to echo in all the chambers of the soul, he finds by experience that the affliction has been a means of spiritual good. Just as the trees that grow on the exposed summits and in the open fields are found to strike their roots far deeper down, and take firmer hold of the rocks beneath, than the trees that grow in the shelter of the forest : so the plant of divine grace in the soul is found to strike deeper root, and take faster hold of the rock of salvation, by the very blasts of the tempests of life which would seem to overwhelm it. The calamity, to the eye of sense tremendous, works out a far more exceeding and eternal weight of glory.

But troubles in this life are not apt to come alone : and, ofttimes, one calamity seems to follow another as though God, in his anger, were striking blow after blow. Here is the place at which true fortitude displays itself. Almost any man can nerve himself for the single great shock, especially if he sees the direction in which the blow is coming. But when called upon, while staggering under one, to measure his strength with another, and then another; or to stand sur-rounded by "a sea of troubles," boisterous and raging—then none but the greatest souls are found equal to the task. Hence the Apostle declares, not only that one calamity may result in good, but "*all things work together* for good." When the troubles come from this quarter and that ; when troubles from without come upon troubles within ; when news of evil from abroad comes in upon the heart already breaking with trouble at home ; when the storm rages fiercely,—the winds meeting from every quarter to lash the sea into fury,— then must God's children feel there is one at the helm, that will pilot them through ; one who has promised—"in six troubles I will be with thee, and in seven will not forsake thee." That though "many are the afflictions of the righteous, yet the Lord delivereth him out of them all." And though faith cries out—"deep calleth unto deep at the noise of thy waterspouts: all thy waves and thy billows are gone over me ;" still its cry also is " in the night thy song shall be with me." For—" out of the depths have I cried unto thee," and "in thee do I put my trust." Yea, " though he slay me yet will I trust in him." This is every Christian's practical doctrine of Providence.

It is surely strange, on any ordinary principles of human reasoning, that a doctrine so full of comfort, in a world so full of trouble, should have to fight its way against the most determined opposition of every class of worldly-minded men. Yet the opposition to this doctrine is manifold.

First, that of the natural heart; which, in its dislike to conceive of God as near to us, in even the ordinary affairs of human life, takes refuge in a natural sadduceeism, believing neither in angel or spirit as having any concern, at least with every-day life things, however God may concern himself about the Sunday services of his creatures. This is the practical philosophy of the multitudes who trouble themselves little about the grounds and reason of that which suits their natural inclination. Only in the time of alarm and deep affliction do they think of God as working all things.

Secondly, the opposition of that transcendental atheism, which with all its theoretic dreamings of God as the universe, or the universe as God, really leaves the world without a personal God to care for it at all. The very conception of an infinite personal and moral Being that moves and acts within the sphere of humanity, sympathizing with its sorrows, would dash in pieces their transcendental structures as inevitably, as the acceptance of the first truths of inductive science must dash in pieces the cycles and epicycles, and crystal orbs, of their visionary predecessors of antiquity. Hence this " science, falsely so called," not only cannot accept, but treats with passionate scorn the truth, that God works all things together for good, to any class of his human creatures.

So again, in the third place, this truth is assailed by a theological scepticism, which, while it professes to accept with reverence the revealed doctrine of God, yet cannot reconcile with its theories of how the universe is governed, and especially how man could be free under a government, which proceeds under a plan and purpose to accomplish certain ends:—and therefore cannot accept this doctrine of God's constant interposition in man's affairs. Jeremiah saw the working of the scheme of providence beautifully symbolized by the potter at his wheel, moving with his foot on the treadle his whirling stone, and with his hand fashioning into shape the clay as it whirled; and when the vessel was marred in his hand, lumping again and throwing back the clay, refined by the very marring process, to be moulded anew, into a better vessel. Both the philosophers and the theological sceptics accept Jeremiah's symbol so far as concerns the wheel. But the philosophers will have it that the wheel is moved, not by any intelligent power, but driven by some infinite blind impulse, as of steam power, water power, or magnetic power; and works out the fashion of the vessel to honour or to dishonour under the eternal laws of centrifugal motion! The theological sceptics, however, accept not only the potter's wheel, and the clay upon it, but also the wheel as driven by the intelligent motive power of the foot on the *treadle*, and the clay fashioned by an intelligent hand as it whirls; yet they cannot accept the theory, that the hand is working, according to a purpose and pattern, in the mind of the potter, and that the very marring of the clay in his hand is made the means of refining and preparing it, to be thrown back in lump and moulded anew according to his pattern.

There is a fourth form of this opposition, from what I may call the sentimental scepticism, more dangerous than any because it probably reaches more minds, and, by its plausible air of reverence and concern for the dignity of God, leads even the piously disposed astray. This sentimentalism is shocked at the inspired conception of Jeremiah and of Paul; and especially at the application of it in the teachings of Jesus, that God's care extends to the very humblest of his creatures, individually: that he marks the sparrow's fall, and numbers the very hairs of their heads; that God clothes, feeds, and protects them.

The sentimental sceptics by no means deny a providence, operating by general laws, having a care over general results, and even interposing on great occasions. But they regard it as the veriest fanaticism to hold, that each individual with his little sorrows and troubles fixes the attention of the great Ruler of the universe.

Now this whole conception of the sentimentalists, with all its show of special reverence for the dignity of Providence; of sensitive shrinking from the vulgar conceptions of the masses; and of compassionate concern for the feeble-minded enthusiasts, who talk of Providence, " working all things together for good to them that love him"—will be found, on analysis, to evince, in the first place, bad taste—in the second place, worse theology—and, in the third place, still worse logic.

Bad in taste is this notion that it is incongruous to the dignity of "the lofty One who inhabiteth eternity," to conceive of him as concerned with the little common-places of human life. For it is but the application, in religion, of that silly conceit of vulgar parasites, that it is preposterous to expect great people even to know or care for the little troubles of the obscure and lowly. Whereas all intelligent men conceive of it, as one of the marks of real dignity and greatness, that it stoops, without any condescending airs to sympathize with the lowly. Did any man of good sense and true taste, who ever noticed the case of Grace Darling, imagine that the imperial Queen of Britain compromised the dignity of her exalted station in stooping to caress, and do honour to, the fisherman's heroic daughter for her daring rescue of the storm-wrecked men ?

It is among the very sublimest of all the conceptions of God in the scriptures, when Jesus argues, "are not five sparrows sold for two farthings ; yet not one of them is forgotten before God?" " Fear not, therefore, ye are of more value than many sparrows." For how immensely does it add to our conceptions of the grandeur of God, that the Infinite Mind, which takes in at a glance the illimitable universe, notes distinctly, at the same time, every particle of it!

I have said it is worse theology. For however reverent seeming and pious this sentimentalism, with its language in the purest dialect of Canaan, yet for all practical purposes of religion, it really banishes God from the universe. Of what avail, to creatures such as we, to call upon us to love and adore a Being without sympathy for our little sorrows, sitting yonder at the centre of the universe abstracted in contemplating the outworking of the laws he has ordained for it, and watching their results ? Can the soul of man be drawn toward such a Being ? For all the practical purposes of worship this god is not a whit better than the gods of ancient mythology. Nay one could more readily bow down to their Jupiter, Apollo, or Mercury, than to this abstraction, or rather personification of the eternal laws of nature. For even the ancient heathen exhibited their gods in a human form, to suggest the thought of some sort of relation between us and them, that may draw out the feelings of our hearts in prayer to them.

The logic of this conception of God is still worse than the taste or the theology. It is in every aspect of it illogical. First, as a scientific statement of God's relation to the universe. If man is too little to be worthy of God's concern about his affairs, then what of the myriads of creatures *below* man in the scale ? As Dr. Chalmers well puts the case, somewhere, the same science which puts into our hands the telescope, through which we discern that innumerable worlds and systems of worlds are co-tenants of infinity with our world; until our scepticism, as it gazes cries out, "What is man that thou, the Ruler of these myriads of worlds—shouldest be mindful of him?"—puts into our other hand the microscope, through which we gaze down upon a universe of sentient creatures, far below the reach even of unaided human vision, until we cry out in response to our doubts, "Why not man, if the divine care so obviously extends to all those myriad races below him?" All knowledge of nature, from that of the hyssop upon the wall to the cedar of Lebanon, and to the knowledge of suns and systems, attests that throughout all its range, no marks have ever been found of any carelessness, in the smallest of the works of the divine hand, more than in the mightiest of them all. The structure and movements of the ant that creeps upon the wall, the antennæ of the gnat that floats in the evening sunbeam, not less than the movements of the planets in their courses, attest the presence and care of God.

And every man can attest from his own history that it is equally bad logic, as applied to individual experience, to say that God controls the great results of life, but not its minute incidents. For every man knows how the grand result often so turns upon some event of life intrinsically the most insignificant, as upon a pivot, that if God control not the little things, he cannot control the great things. The coming to a place a little too late; the accidental meeting of a friend in the street; the little disappointment that prevented the execution of some cherished purpose, has proved to be the event upon which the whole subsequent life and character turned. And had not God been working in "all things," he could not have brought out the grand result which followed from them.

Y

Every student of history knows that this is the very worst logic, as a statement of the law of universal history under God's providence. Let these theorists tell us what they could consider an event and a result great enough to be worthy the interposition of God's providence. Shall it be the discovery of the telescope, that revolutionized the thought of the world concerning the universe, of which we form a part; and caused the "heavens to tell the glory of God," as they never told it to former ages? Well, the event that led to this discovery, we are told, was the idleness of a spectacle-maker's boy engaged in grinding the glasses, who instead of attending to his work, was amusing himself with looking through two of the bits of glass, and to his surprise noticed that, looked at through two glasses held at a certain distance apart, the distant church steeple seemed to come close to him! Of course the telescope was within reach of any inventive genius then. If then God controls the discovery that revolutionizes the thought of the world, he must control the thoughts and acts of the spectacle-maker's lazy boy!

Or was it an event great enough to be worthy the interposition of God's providence, when one-third of the civilized world were led off into apostasy after the false prophet? Well, history tells us that there was an hour in the prophet's life, before he had deceived the nations, when the avengers of blood were in such hot pursuit that there seemed no human probability that Mohammed, in sight just before them, and exhausted with the race, would live another hour. But at a turn in the way, seeing a cave near the path, he, in despair, rushed in to hide himself. The pursuers coming up in a few moments, and noticing the cave also, were about to examine before they went on, but they observed a sparrow fly from her nest in the mouth of the cave, and a spider's web in the arch unbroken; and concluding that it would be a waste of time to search, since, if Mohammed had gone in, the sparrow would have been frightened off before, and the spider's web broken, they dashed on, and Mohammed escaped. See you not that if God would control this vast apostasy of Mohammed, he must also watch the sparrow as she builds her nest, and the spider as she weaves her web? Nay the lesson of all history repeats the maxim of Aristotle, "What the pilot is to the ship, such is God to the universe." There is no ground in any sphere of human knowledge for these clamours against the Apostle's view of God's relation to us, and his statement, "All things work together for good."

But not "for good" to all, but to a peculiar class—" to them that love God." And now perhaps some child of God who has followed our argument with deep interest so far, is ready to exclaim, "this is indeed a comfortable doctrine, but alas it avails little to me, since the afflictions work together for good only to such as feel and know that they love God. If I could but know with certainty that I love him, then the consolation would be indeed 'a song in the night' of my affliction. But—'do I love the Lord or no?' is the very question of questions with me. I hope I love him. I try to love him. I sometimes thought I did love him. Yet, at the very time when most I need the consolations of this doctrine, then am I least certain of my right to apply it. The tears of sorrow so dim the eye of faith, that I cannot see as before. The wails of sorrow in the heart seem to silence its utterances of loving trust. And in the darkness of my spirit, the record of many a forgotten sin comes out, as though memory had written it with phosphorescent ink that made no trace while the sun shone brightly. But now, when the darkness comes, the glaring record comes out to arouse the condemning conscience ; as when Reuben in his sorrow remembered the long forgotten sin, and cried, ' we are really guilty concerning our brother.' And while all these causes combine to make me doubt, I am in no state of mind to look down into the depths of my heart, and, by some skilful anatomy of the passions of it, or by careful applications of tests, as by some spiritual chemistry, ascertain the presence or the absence of any love of God there. How then shall I know whether the comfort is mine, and that all these afflictions are working together for good to me?"

I answer, not by any such search in the depths of your heart, nor by any anatomy of the affections, nor by any such spiritual chemistry. Observe, the Apostle seems to anticipate such a difficulty from the use of the general phrase, " to them that love God!" and therefore appends, as in apposition therewith, the explanatory clause—" to them who are the called." So that instead of directing you to look down into the depths of your heart, he directs you to look out of yourself altogether, and away from yourself. To listen not for the voice from within, but listen to the call that comes from without, saying " Look unto me and be ye saved, all ye ends of the earth." You test your spiritual state by simply referring to the calls of the gospel to sinners, and its offers to sinners, and then observing how your heart responds to that call. If gladly, willingly,—then " Whosoever will " are the terms ; and the doubt-generating sins are provided for. " Though your sins be as scarlet, they shall be as white as snow." And if you gladly hear that call, thereby you know you love him and the consolation is yours.

The scriptural philosophy of Christian experience is very beautiful. If you would either excite, or test the presence of any emotion in the heart, you must bring before the understanding the truth, which tends to excite and call forth that emotion. You can never by mere act of your own will call these emotions into play. Just as when you would have me love your friend, and when out of regard to you, I wish to do it ; yet I cannot at your bidding love whom you love. But you tell me of his many noble qualities, and recite the story of his generous and noble deeds, and while I listen to these truths, my heart warms in unison with yours toward your friend. So while the gospel religion is a religion of the heart, and lays all stress on the affections, it never assumes that sinners, by a mere volition, can make themselves love Christ, and the Spirit and the Father. But it tells you the wonderful story of Christ's generous acts, and of the Spirit's kind movings, and of the Father's yearning compassion, that, as you listen, the affections of love shall be awakened in the heart.

And it is just this principle of awaking and nurturing the Christian affections, through the truth of the gospel, that distinguishes the genuine religious experience from the current counterfeits of it by fanaticism on the one hand, and mere sentimentalism on the other. The fanatic has his moods of religious feeling. But it is a self-excited frenzy of the imagination ; or he dreams a dream ; or he sees a vision ; or he hears a voice from the unseen—these are the exciting causes ; not the simple truths of the gospel call. So the poetic sentimentalist has often his moods of religious feeling ; and no doubt is sincerely persuaded that the impulses of his spirit, under an excited imagination, are the true impulses of love to God. As I remember hearing a celebrated dramatic actor describe, how the music of the great organ at Haarlem as he was alone in the cathedral, made him so pious that he fell upon the floor, and prayed that God would let him die at once, while in a frame fit to die, and go to heaven. This sort of religious feeling substitutes music of the organ, "dim religious light," impressive ceremony, and the beauty of painting and statuary, for the truths of the gospel call, as a means of exciting the affections to love God. It conceives of these gospel doctrines as simply something to make a creed of, to swear by rather than something to live in the daily heart experiences of men.

It is a farther assurance to those thus called, and loving God, that God is working all things together for good to them, in that this call itself, is " *according to* his *purpose*," or pre-arranged plan, under the movings of the love wherewith he loved them before the foundation of the world." For in Paul's conception of it, the eternal purpose, plan and decree of God is not so much *a* doctrine among many others of the Gospel system as a point of view from which to contemplate all the doctrines. All that God hath done : all he is doing ; his entire work of creation and providence, are simply the development of the counsels of eternity. And, as he proceeds to show, the golden chain whose links run through all time, binds all time and the eternity that follows back to the eternity before time was.

" *For* whom he did foreknow." You will observe how this " For" connects all that follows, as explanatory of and ancillary to this phrase "called according to his purpose," in the twenty-eighth verse. Is it not very noteworthy that the theologians who do fierce battle against the doctrine of predestination should ever choose this twenty-ninth verse " whom he did foreknow them he did predestinate," as their battle ground; though this is merely ancillary and an explanatory appendage to, " called according to his purpose " in the twenty-eighth verse ? Surely one would think that, if a battle must be fought here, it should be on the chief passage, and not on the mere incidental appendage to it! That it is otherwise, should of itself excite the suspicion, that the difficulty with this great doctrine, arises not so much out of what the scripture saith, as out of what scientific theology and metaphysics saith.

" *Whom he did foreknow them he did predestinate to be con-formed to the image of his Son.*" How did he foreknow them—in what sense ? Some would tell us, " whom he did foreknow as holy,"—that is, " conformed to Christ's image—

them he did predestinate." But whatever else the place may mean, it cannot mean this. For instead of predestinating them *on account of* their foreseen conformity to Christ's image, that is precisely the thing they are predestinated *to.* That is the result of the predestination, not the cause leading to it. And just here, I imagine, lies the whole trouble which men make with the doctrine. They will insist on understanding it as meaning that God predestinated them, passing over this life, to heaven after death, whereas Paul says he predestinated them to be holy and conformed to the image of Christ. You will ask me, " But does not the Confession of Faith say, he 'predestinated some to everlasting life !'" So it does: and the objection to that statement as differing from Paul's here, arises simply from overlooking the fact that the Confession, after its manner, here uses the exact language of the scriptures for expressing this conformity, to the image of Christ as Paul hath it. You will observe that Jesus Christ says, "he that believeth *hath* (not *shall* have) everlasting life." That everlasting life begins here on earth when the sinner is born again ; and to that new birth he is predestinated, and as Paul here says whom he did predestinate them he also *called.* For remember all this account of predestination is appended to explain more fully that term "called," in the twenty-eighth verse. So the Confession, in speaking of the estate to which men are predestinated, and into which they enter here on earth, but uses the precise words of Jesus Christ. I have had occasion heretofore to show you how this conception of the heaven, or everlasting life, as beginning here on earth and carrying over death with it the sinless elements of the humanity on earth, is the peculiar distinction of Christ's doctrine of immortality.

But you will ask in what sense then did he *foreknow* them? I answer, in the sense of the word " know," when the Judge

shall say " Depart from me I never *knew* you"—though in the
ordinary sense he knows all men.   Or in the sense in which
Jehovah said, " Ye only have I *known* of all the nations ;"
though he, in the ordinary sense, *knew* all nations.   As in one
of these cases he means to say, " I never chose," or " preferred," you as mine, and in the other, "I have preferred," or
"chosen" you, only of all nations, so here the Apostle means,
obviously, to say whom he " *fore-preferred*," or " fore-chose,"
them he did predestinate, to become holy and Christ-like.
And as this predestination is to the result of a *call* obeyed,
therefore whom he predestinates, them he also *calls* by
his word and Spirit.   So that, in reality, the whole question in dispute between what is known as Calvinism, in
our day, and its antagonists, is the question, "who maketh
thee to differ ?"—a question on which, however rationalism
that believes not in any conversion by the Spirit of God
may mock, yet all true Christians must substantially agree,
discordant as may be their metaphysics of predestination.
How answer you this question :

> " Why was I made to hear thy voice
> And enter while there's room,
> While thousands make a wretched choice,
> And rather starve than come ?"

If you answer it as the same hymn,—

> " 'Twas *the same grace* that spread the feast,
> That sweetly forced me in,
> Else I had still refused to taste,
> And perished in my sin :"—

Then we have no need to quarel over that bugbear of modern
cavillers known as Calvinism.   Hence, true Christians of all
names are found singing and praying very much alike, however wide apart in their speculations.

The evangelical Armenian sings just as the rest of us ·

"Grace first contrived the way, to save rebellious man ;
And all the steps that grace display, which drew the wondrous plan.
Grace led my roving feet to tread the heavenly road.
And new supplies each hour I meet, while travelling on to God.
Grace all the work shall crown, through everlasting days,
It lays in heaven the topmost stone, and well deserves the praise !"

And yet when, or where, did Calvin ever distil a *bluer* Calvinism than that ?

Whom God " fore-chose," them he predestinated to be conformed to Christ, and in order to the accomplishment of that purpose, he " *calls* " them. Observe now we have the full account of " the called according to his purpose," in the twenty-eighth verse. And now the Apostle proceeds to show, how that image of Christ, in them, is brought about. " Whom he calls, them he also justifies." These sins that so darken their souls, and that burden conscience, are taken away by the blood of the Lamb having atoned for, and thereby " blotted them out." And the obedience of the " Lord our righteousness" becomes the sinner's obedience, so soon as, hearing the call, he accepts it, and by faith, is in " Christ Jesus," and represented both in his act of obedience and of atonement. And meantime the Holy Spirit, who has made the call effectual, and imparted the new life to the dead soul, whereby it puts forth this living act of faith, carries on his work of conforming it more and more to the image of Christ, until, with death, the body of sin drops off and the spirit becomes like Jesus and sees him as he is,—Thus " Whom he justifies he also glorifies."

Now we can see the power and beauty of the Apostle's logic —sorrows and affliction cannot do other than good to them that are called under such a purpose of grace. For since God hath such an end in view for them, all things that occur, however afflictive now, must work together to that great end

—the glory which shall follow. And we are prepared to accept his triumphant conclusion, " If God be for us who can be against us ?"

I have space only to add, in conclusion, a few brief suggestions touching the exact adaptation of this view of the grand system of gospel theology, from the stand-point of God's eternal purpose and plan, to all the wants of the human soul.

First, this is the only view of the gospel system of theology that can satisfy the logical requirements of man's intelligent faculties, which cannot receive, as from God, any system of truth inconsistent and self-contradictory. It may be easy to reason very astutely, about some one or other doctrine of the gospel system, and hew and shape it into conformity with some mere human theory; greatly to the puzzling of simple-minded believers. But the true test is whether the point, so hewn and shaped; will cohere with all the other points of the beautiful system. Just as the skilful workman from the great city, where the division of labour gives wonderful aptness in the several parts of it, may astonish the rude workman of the forest, by the almost divine skill with which he can carve a mantel, or a pillar, or a cornice ; while yet he is unable to construct, like the forester, a log cabin and keep its corners all square and its walls perpendicular. This *survey* of the great field of revelation is the only one that will *close*, without some of the arts and tricks of the incompetent or careless surveyor, who cannot make his *plat close*— his last line coming out at his starting point—without omitting a side, or enlarging or diminishing some line or some angle.

But, in the second place, what is still more important, is, that this is the only view of the gospel which can sustain the human soul, in danger and affliction, and inspire it to great and heroic acts.

For, unsupported by this consciousness that God is near him, and has a destiny for him to work out, in the "all things" of his life, man's spirit is feeble. He cannot be self-reliant, except as reliant on a power above his power. Hence the Cæsars, the Alexanders, the Napoleons of the world's history, have ever had some sort of blind instinctive impression of that great truth which the faith of the Pauls, the Luthers, the Calvins, the Knoxes, so clearly apprehended. Whatever else they may have done for the human spirit, Arminianism and Rationalism never yet constructed a true moral hero. All the world's spoken epics, all the world's acted heroisms, all the world's suffered martyrdoms, have had their roots struck deep in this conviction of Paul's, that "all things work together," to the purposes of God.

In the third place, and practically still more important than meeting either the logical, or the heroic necessities of human nature, this view of the gospel system is the only view which can meet the wants of the soul of man, in the hour of darkness and deep affliction. Hence, when in view of the controversies among Christians, the wish has sometimes been expressed for some compromise ground upon which all God's people could unite, I have ever felt that, whatever else might be yielded, if I am to minister in Christ's name, there are two great truths which I must cling to with the grasp of despair. One, the truth of justification by faith: so that as the poor dark-minded sinner comes inquring, "What must I do to be saved?" I may confidently point him to the Lamb of God, and say, "believe"—"only believe, and thou shalt be saved." The other, this truth concerning God's eternal purpose according to which he worketh all things: so that I may comfort his suffering children. How am I dumb under the wailings and complaints of the broken-hearted without this! How can I face this David, as he comes wringing his hands, and crying in his agony, "Oh Absalom! my son! my son!

would God I had died for thee "? What can I say to this poor "Rachel weeping for her children and refusing to be comforted because they are not " ? How shall I claim that my Master hath sent me with a gospel, " to comfort them that mourn and to bind up the broken-hearted," unless I may say to them—" This affliction cometh not by chance—it comes as the outworking of his adorable purpose," who " worketh all things together for good to them that love him ?"

And not less essential is this truth to sustain the church in the days of darkness and rebuke, than to comfort the individual soul. For it is in accordance with his great purpose, that days of affliction and rebuke shall come upon his Church also. And all history shows that however, in her days of sunshine and prosperity, the learned sons of the Church may amuse themselves with splitting metaphysical hairs and filling learned tomes, with their difficulties about the divine purpose, yet when the " storms of sorrow fall," then the universal heart of the Church must fall back upon this doctrine. When in the days of persecution, the smitten shepherd must gather his scattered flock to feed on lonely moor, or in wild glen, or under over-hanging cliff by the sea side, his thoughts irresistibly turn to this consolation —" For I reckon that the sufferings of this present are not to be compared with the glory which shall be revealed in us."

When the Church, his bride, cries in her anguish—" The Lord hath forgotten me !" her comfort is in the same glorious assurance. " Behold I have graven thee on the palms of my hands" so that in stretching forth the hand to work I am reminded of thee : and have care to " work all things together for thy good." When malignant infidelity shouts, " Christianity is a failure !" and the mocker from Seir calleth out to her prophet watchman, standing amid the midnight darkness of her desolations—" Watchman, what of the night ? Watchman, what of the night ?" Where now the promises of the " sure covenant with David ?" Staying his soul upon this great truth of God's eternal purpose of love, the prophet can answer back with heroic faith—" The morning cometh," ye ministers of hell ! " the morning cometh"—" and also the night" to you. And when in the times of spiritual decay and apostasy from the truth, worldly wisdom and prudence tempts the witnesses for " the truth as it is in Jesus" with the plea—forbear, withhold the offensive truth, and stir not up the storm that must overwhelm the Church : faith, resting on this same assurance of his purpose that " the gates of hell shall not prevail," can calmly say, " Let the storm come, it will scatter the sear leaves and dash down the withered branches ; but the God-planted tree shall only strike deeper root, and take firmer hold upon the great Rock of Salvation !"

And, in the fourth place, however much vilified as a doctrine, that cuts the nerves of Christian zeal and exertion, for the salvation of men, this is really the doctrine from whose encouragements all Christian zeal must derive its inspirations. For feeling that he is " a co-worker with Christ," the great shepherd seeking lost souls, whose purpose of love must be accomplished, that " he see of the travail of his soul and be satisfied," the Christian then can go forward, undismayed by all obstacles and discouragements. Observe how Paul, immediately after this triumphant demonstration, filled with burning zeal declares, " I could wish myself accursed for my brethren. My heart's desire and prayer to God for Israel is that they might be saved."

I may add in conclusion that this is the view of the gospel, which furnishes the strongest ground of appeal to sinners, crying, " now is the accepted time ! Behold now is the day of salvation." If your salvation were a thing within reach of your own unaided power, then we might feel less concern at seeing you going on to the grave in impenitence. For at any moment you could exert your power and secure salvation.

But seeing you helpless and able to "work out your own salvation," only because it "is God that worketh in you to will and to do of his own good pleasure,"—we are alarmed to see you so heedless of this *call* through obedience to which alone you can obtain the needful help. O spend not your energies, in trying to penetrate the dark cloud, that hovers around the lofty summit of this theology, and shrouds from mental view the secret purposes of God. Behold the golden link of the pendent chain that gleams here along the level of time—this *call* of the gospel. Seize hold of that, here and now, that you may be drawn up—justified—to be eternally glorified!

DISCOURSE XVIII.

II Tim. i.--10.—But is now made manifest by the appearing of our Saviour Jesus Christ, who hath abolished death, and hath brought life and immortality to light through the gospel.

I Cor. xv.-22, 53, 54.—For as in Adam all die, even so in Christ shall all be made alive.

For this corruptible must put on incorruption, and this mortal must on immortality. So when this corruptible shall have put on incorruption, and this mortal shall have put on immortality, then shall be brought to pass the saying that is written, Death is swallowed up in victory.

I take the second passage cited as exegetic of the first. As the one declares that Jesus Christ revealed the doctrine of immortality, and abolished death—reduced it to *zero* in the formula expressive of the soul's existence—so the other declares the mode in which this immortality is both secured and revealed. That it is by the connection of the race with Christ in his resurrection, as with Adam in his death ; and, consequently, it is not merely the soul that is immortal ; but, the power of death over the body being abolished, " the *mortal shall* put on immortality."

" *Brought life and immortality to light through the gospel.*" At the very enunciation of this proposition, in its broad sense, rises a many-voiced clamour, not only from the gospel-rejecting schools of philosophy, but from within the confines of the Church itself. " Was not immortality brought to light before Jesus came ?" asks the gospel according to the classics. " May not the doctrine of immortality be demonstrated independent of the revelation of Jesus Christ ?" asks the gospel according to College.

I propose to examine briefly : *First*, the grounds on which this argument for immortality, outside the gospel, is made to rest by the ancient and the modern schools. *Second*, In contrast with this, the grounds on which the gospel rests the argument. And, *Third*, the gospel teaching concerning the nature of the life and immortality.

I.—The notion floats, very vaguely indeed, but very generally, in the minds of our classically trained young men, that Socrates and Plato demonstrated, and Cicero, after them, expounded so fully the doctrine of the immortality of the soul, that little was left to be done by the gospel of Jesus on that subject. Therefore it seems to them to border on the extravagance of enthusiasm that the Apostle should thus claim that Jesus brought immortality *to light*, as though men had not heard and taught the doctrine of immortality before. But admitting, for the sake of argument, that Socrates and Plato had reasoned out, ever so conclusively, the doctrine of the endless existence of the soul, it cannot be claimed by their most enthusiastic admirers that they established a "life and immortality" so clearly as to "abolish death,"—that great unnatural fact—by setting before men hopes so glorious as to make the matter of the death of the body practically insignificant in their view. And, in the next place, the claim set up for Socrates, Plato and Cicero in this matter is much higher than the facts actually warrant. Any one, not content with admiring these philosophers on the basis of mere second-hand knowledge, must know this. Looking at the facts, rather than the poetry of the matter, it will be found that there is no ground for that excess of admiration which prefers Socrates to Jesus, Plato to John, and Cicero to Paul. For neither of these philosophers ever claimed to have proved a practical immortality, which one should greatly care for. Looking into the logic of the matter, it will be found that what they did undertake to prove, they rested upon such grounds as no intelligent man would be willing to rest his argument upon in any case of practical importance.

In the celebrated discussion of this question in Plato's *Phaedo*, Socrates in prison is represented as resting the argument, in chief, on the three points. First, the universal conviction of mankind that, after death, the soul exists in Hades; which argument he weakens rather than strengthens by his suggestion of the dogma of universal dualism, that contraries beget contraries—as darkness light, so death life, &c. Second, the dogma that all knowledge is reminiscence, and the ideas suggested by objects of sense are merely recalled as having existed in the soul before; and therefore as the soul existed before the body, so it, probably, shall exist after it. Third, that the soul being uncompounded, cannot be dissolved as the body is, and therefore must continue to exist. Now, aside from the many beautiful suggestions in the details of the argument, it is very manifest, that, beyond the fact of the general impression among mankind of their immortality, there cannot possibly be framed an argument on such a platform that could convince anybody, in any degree, beyond the conviction already felt from the instinctive impressions of his nature. And, indeed, as a practical proof Socrates himself did not seem to rely upon it; since we find him saying to his judges, " To die is one of two things : either the soul is annihilated, or it passes into some other state. If death is a sleep in which the sleeper has no dream, then death would be a wonderful gain. But if death is a removal to another state, and *what is said be true*, that all the dead are there, what greater blessing," &c. Divesting this classic gospel of its romance, thus, it will be perceived that even if the Apostle in this saying, " brought life and immortality to light," had Socrates, Plato and Cicero distinctly in mind, he had no call to vary the statement in the least.

It may be important, however, by way of dispelling the too

common delusion on this subject, to show further, not only that reason unenlightened by revelation did not, but in the nature of the case could not, demonstrate an immortality which could afford practical comfort to the spirit of man ; a " life" as well as an immortality.

If even it were granted that the certainty of a future existence had been established by philosophy, with a clearness greatly in advance of the native impressions of the common mind, that would establish neither a blissful immortality to be hoped for by all, nor a retribution whose discriminating award should secure it to a part. Leaving out of view, for the present, every other element than that claimed to have been proved—the existence of the soul after death, such existence of a human soul, as now constituted, must be nothing else than an immortal hell.

Every one knows the oppressiveness of time itself to the human spirit, when, in utter vacuity of thought, the progress of time, at every moment, is distinctly noted. Who that has been compelled in utter listlessness to watch the movement of the hand of the clock dial for a few hours, is not ready to define pleasure as that which causes time to pass unnoted ? If the world's tyrants could control the move· ments of the mind as they can those of the body, herein would they have found a method of torture beyond all the horrors of rack, and fire and faggot. They need only doom their victims to sit for years, and mentally note each second as it passes. Conceive, then, of such a soul on the threshold of the immortal existence which Plato has demonstrated for it— mere naked existence—contemplating the eternal prospect ! In the body it could " kill time," but how shall it kill eternity ? Devise, if you can, some measure of the progress of eternity analogous to our measurement of time, in order to impress more definitely and distinctly this point upon your mind. To measure time we begin with the movement of the

pendulum by the earth's attraction ; next by the movement of
the earth on its axis ; next by the movement of the earth
in its orbit.   Enlarging now these familiar measures, we may
conceive, according to our astronomers, of another cycle,
measured by the movement of our sun with his system around
some other sun in the remote depths of space, compared with
which all the circuits that earth has made since time began
until time shall end, are but as a point of time measured by
hundredths of a second.   And yet when this soul shall have
noted each moment of all this cycle, it is, as compared with
what is to come, but a single *tick* of the pendulum, to be
sixty times repeated, till a minute of eternity is measured !
Conceive, again, of this remote sun with all his systems
revolving in an orbit of almost infinite sweep around some
remoter central sun, in the depths of immensity, whose
circuit shall represent the minutes, and these minutes to be
watched—every moment of finite time in them—to the
sixtieth repetition of the circuit through immensity ; and at
last the clock of eternity strikes one : but this only to begin
again the movement and repeat interminably the same suc-
cession of cycles in the new hour again to be noted by this
soul still existing.   But the effort to grasp the notion, even
by feeblest approximation, is vain.   See you not that if
nothing but existence is demonstrated, Plato has demonstrated only an eternal burden to the soul.

But, next, add to this element of existence, in the inheritance of the soul, the co-existence of conscience with it as
another element, and you have only multiplied the horrors an
hundredfold.   For it cannot be claimed that any soul ever
having lived here goes into that state of existence pure, and
with a conscience absolutely clear ; and the existence there
must be consciously under the eye of a pure God.   True,
this soul has existed under the eye of a pure God here, for
" in Him we live and move and have our being."   But other

objects of consciousness veiled the sight of God ; and an atmosphere of mercy and grace here softens and reflects the glorious brightness. Well does the Apostle say, however, "Our God is a consuming fire," when conceived of by an impure soul, apart from his mercy and grace as manifested in the present state. Just as our sun is the glory and joy of creation, while shining through an atmosphere which softens the light from above and reflects it in a thousand forms of beauty : but the atmosphere removed from the earth, this sun would become but a glaring fire-spot in a single point of the heavens, and all the universe else as a pall of pitchy blackness. So we must conceive of an impure soul removed from the spiritual atmosphere of the present state of long suffering and grace, which reflects the milder radiance of God. The sinful inheritors of that endless existence must see God only as the " consuming fire," in all the intolerable brightness of the sun in heaven without an atmosphere, in the midst of a universe become the blackness of darkness for ever !

And as we now proceed to add to these two elements of eternal existence and the co-existence of a moral nature in an impure soul, the other element of the passions inherent in the soul itself, we but add infinitely at each step to the horrors of that estate, not of "life and immortality" but of death and immortality.

Nor can reason, unaided by revelation demonstrate, from the existence of a general conviction in mankind of a retribution as well as an existence in the future, any such theory of retribution as may relieve the foregoing difficulties. For, admitting that the existence in a future state is certain, and that men generally have an impression that the future state is retributive, with reference to character here ; still, the two cannot be logically connected, on the theory of the immortality of the soul merely. Thus, you argue, " I feel that I am not wholly material, nor to perish with my material part, and am conscious of some sort of capacity for immortal existence." Very well. You argue further, " I am conscious moreover of certain moral impressions that suggest the thought of rewards to virtue in that future existence which have not been bestowed here, and of penalties for vice, which have failed to be visited here. Very well. But now here interposes a difficulty. You are so constituted also as to feel that the awards of virtue and vice should be rendered to the same being who did the virtuous and the vicious acts. But death coming in dissolves this compound being who committed the acts, by stripping the mortal from the immortal, and sends the immortal part a purely spiritual, and therefore a different order of being, to stand at the bar and receive the award. So that the being that receives the reward is not even the same order of being that did the virtuous act : nor is the being on whom is visited the penalty of vice the same order of being as he who did the sin. Without some other fact to constitute a *nexus* between the idea of a future state and the idea of retribution, no skill of philosophy can bridge this chasm in the logic. And the discovery of such a chasm must naturally lead to the suspicion that the previous conceptions have been mistakes, mere dreams of the fancy.

As a matter of fact, moreover, the utmost extent of the argument of the classic philosophy is to prove that the soul *may* exist, because it has a capacity for endless existence. But this is very far from proving that it shall exist. Socrates argued that the soul is uncompounded, and, therefore, dissolves not as the body, and may continue to exist. But while the soul is an uncompounded existence, it is yet a *dependent* existence, and therefore, if God please, may cease to exist. God need only stop the out-goings of life from himself, and in a moment he would be alone in the universe. It is therefore possible that the human spirit should be

quenchable. And when we take into the account that it is
an impure spirit, and Godless, the possibility, apart from the
revelation of Jesus, becomes even a probability. For, seeing
how the impure, reckless and depraved must be excluded
from the purer society here, and remembering that the consequences of contagion there, in the presence of God, where
the slightest taint of impurity must sluice the fountain of life
and hoist the flood-gates of horror and pollution, does not the
probability seem to be all on the side of the suggestion that
God should quench such spirits as a protection to his moral
universe?

The assumption, therefore, that the classic philosophy
either did establish or could establish the doctrine of immortality upon any satisfactory basis, is purely a delusion. It
neither demonstrated the certainty of a future existence
against the contrary probabilities, so as to add in any degree
to the strength of the popular convictions; nor did anything
to satisfy the popular curiosity concerning the retributive
character of the future state; nor, even if it had done both,
could it possibly have demonstrated a blissful immortality,
but only an immortal hell.

It is, perhaps, a matter of still more practical importance
to examine into the claim of what I have called the gospel
according to college, to be able to establish so clearly the
doctrine of immortality, as to render the teachings of Jesus
on that subject unnecessary. Perhaps, in regard to no other
article of the Christian faith, does there prevail, among the
more intelligent class of the people, so vague and obscure
notions, as in regard to the nature of the Christian teachings on
the subject of immortality, and their relation to the teachings
of natural religion on the same subject. This arises, in large
part, from the confused and inadequate notions of the doctrine
picked up in the schools—all well enough in themselves
perhaps—which are unconsciously substituted for the teach

ings of Christ and his Apostles concerning immortality. The question having been discussed by the thinkers of all ages, and a favourite subject of thought and speech among the people, as well as among the learned, these reasonings of the leaders of human thought, gathered out of the books of the schools, become the groundwork of the popular faith instead of the Gospel. And most dangerous is the delusion, which prevails extensively, that the Gospel did not so much originally reveal to men the doctrine of a future estate, as improve upon the discoveries of natural reason; and that the improvement consisted chiefly in a more effective mode of presenting the doctrine to the masses, and, perhaps, adding a little to the force of the argument of the learned professor in the lecture room. The prevalence of this notion in the popular mind, opens the way for that singularly treacherous infidelity of our age, which instead of waging the open warfare of the infidelity of the last century, steals into the Church itself, in learned looking toga, solemn looking gown and bands, Episcopal lawn and sleeves, or sanctimonious white cravat, to undermine, by its various arts, the foundations of the popular faith. First, it proposes merely to relieve the gospel of some of the difficulties which a narrow-minded era of interpretation has put upon it; next, to fashion its interpretation to meet the demand from the "advanced thought" above, or from the Jacobinical philanthropism of popular opinion below; and, next, to find a higher, more spiritual, and less external gospel, outside the gospel of Jesus altogether, founded upon the nature of man. The masses, even of Christian people, under the illusion that on many topics of religion, especially this of the future state, natural religion has a sort of concurrent jurisdiction with the gospel of Jesus, are captivated with the idea of a more philosophical religion which shall catch all the learned and great men "with guile;" and discover not the cheat, save as some poor earnest soul, sorrow-stricken, and with guilty conscience, attempts to find a Saviour in the New Evangel; but comes back wailing, " *They have taken away my Lord*, and I know not where they have laid him."

Now a very simple analysis and classification of the facts and arguments, on this subject, which lie within the compass of reason and natural religion, must satisfy any intelligent man that, whatever else there may be in them, there is nothing upon which he can rest a practical faith in immortality; and that he needs, just as much as though the philosophers had never reasoned, the revelation from Jesus of life and immortality.

Beyond all doubt it is true that mankind, as a mass, have vindicated for themselves the claim to some sort of existence beyond the life that now is. The learned and the unlearned alike, in all ages, have agreed on the main question, however they may have differed in the detail, and in the clearness of their utterance on the subject. As widely as modern travel has investigated human opinion under every clime; as far as recorded history and tradition carry us; and even so far as we have been able to interpret the mysterious records of the earliest civilizations of the earth, on the Euphrates and the Nile, we find traces of the conviction that, somehow, and in some form, the human soul exists beyond the present earthly state. The mysterious oracles of the priests, directing the popular religious convictions; the strains of the poets that give utterance to the popular conceptions; the grave words of the greatest and best of the leaders and heroes of the people; and the profoundest speculations of the philosophers seem here all to unite in their testimony.

And, so far as it goes, this testimony is concurrent with that of the " Holy men of old, who spake as they were moved by the Holy Ghost." To a certain extent Confucius and Zoroaster are here at one with Moses ; Pythagoras at one with Solomon ; Hesiod and Homer, with David and Isaiah ; Socrates, with Jesus ; Plato, with John ; Cicero, with Paul. And so in all succeeding ages. The creed of the barbarous Goth and Visigoth, touching the fact of a future existence, was at one with that of his victim the semi-christianized, effeminate Italian ; the creed of the Moslem with that of the antagonist Spaniard ; the creed of the Buddhist with that of his conqueror, the Briton.

But when we proceed now to enquire for the origin of this singularly universal conviction, it will be found that, contrary to the current vague notions of the subject, it cannot be traced either to any suggestions of external nature, or to the arguments of the learned thinkers of the world. It is not from external nature, for all her analogies, instead of hinting an everlasting life, suggest decay, dissolution and death. All life, from the lowest form of vegetable, up to the highest forms of animal life, is seen to be quenched, and its physical organisms are dissolved, returning to the inanimate dust. Nor does the highest intellectual and moral life avail to lift its possessor above the doom of the meanest reptile that creeps upon the earth. It is not, therefore, in accordance with the analogies of external nature, but rather in spite of them, that humanity is possessed of this ineradicable convic. tion that its inner life shall not die.

Nor is this general conviction the result of faith in the reasonings and conclusions of the few profound minds that lead the thought of the people. For when these leaders have had occasion to reason of the matter, it has not been in the way of original suggestion or of positive argument, but rather in the way of critical and polemic argument—based upon the general convictions of mankind—against the exceptional, eccentric, sceptical minds who have pretended to dissent from the general belief.

Nor can this general conviction have originated among people unenlightened by revelation, in any tradition derived from the recorded revelation of God. For it will be found that the inspired writers, no more than the philosophers of heathenism and natural religion, undertook to demonstrate, as a new truth, the doctrine of immortality to the masses. Like the philosophers, they everywhere assume the prevalence of such a conviction in the human soul. And it is one of the very purposes of this revelation from Heaven to expound for men this paradox of his nature, how he, a mortal, should have these instincts and impulses of an immortal nature within him.

This is, probably, the true statement of the case, philosophically considered,—that the tendencies to such a belief in an immortal existence grow out of the very structure of the soul itself; or from some original instincts imbedded in its very constitution. Just as the geologists tell us of the traces of the forms of organized life—ferns—trees—reptiles—animals, which must have existed anterior to the rock itself, and have been imbedded in it in the process of its formation. So there are found in the depths of man's spiritual nature, these intuitions, as traces of another life, in another era than the present, which at once suggest to the soul these mysterious hints of another phase of existence than this; and would seem logically to suggest to the theologian, as the material phenomena suggest to the geologist, the idea of some great convulsion which has wrecked an anterior phase of life.

In addition to such intuitions and impressions derived from the original law of his nature, the logical processes of the human mind tend to develop and strengthen these impressions, in spite of the analogies of external nature which suggest the contrary. For man soon learns to differentiate himself, the thinking personal being, from the mere physical nature with which he is connected. And once he learns to make the inference, " I think, therefore I am not the dead matter nor the mere physical existence," he finds it no difficult logical leap to the other inference, " As I think and therefore I am, aside from the material nature, so I may continue to think when the material organism is dissolved, and therefore I shall continue to be." For nothing is more natural than that man, conceiving of himself as a self-conscious being, thinking, feeling, and willing apart from the unconscious matter, should conceive also of the notion that his existence is that of a perpetually self-conscious being whose life dissolves not with the physical organism which it animates.

Now on the back of this comes the fact of a mysterious moral nature in man, perpetually referring his feelings, words and acts to a God above him ; thereby leading to the suggestion of some power from without, moving upon him as subject to it, and causing him to anticipate not merely a perpetual existence, but an existence retributive in its nature in reference to the present. But how these two conceptions of existence and retribution are to be connected, so as to make the retribution upon the purely spiritual creature a just recompense of reward for sin done by the compound existence of a different order of being, reason alone has no means of determining.

Such in general are the sources of argument and the reasonings to which a true philosophy would trace this general conviction of an endless existence. And on such grounds as these true philosophy must reject not only the coarse materialism of the atheist, but also the wild dreams of the pantheist concerning the absorption of the soul in the great soul of the universe ; as a mere disguised, poetic form of the atheism which holds the annihilation of the soul. Manifestly, the claim of our modern pantheists to have both believed and proved the soul to be deathless is a miserable sham. For what else than practical annihilation is it when the self-conscious, thinking, willing, individual being is dissolved as a personality and merged into the soul of the universe ? On the pantheistic principle it might just as readily be proved that the body is quite as immortal as the soul. For the body does not die in the sense of annihilation ; it is dissolved merely, and merged in the matter of the universe, out of which it was fashioned at first. And if it is not the death of the spirit when it ceases to be an individual spirit and merges into the one great soul of the universe, why is it any more a death of the individual body when it dissolves and merges in the universe of matter ?

But while, on grounds of reason and natural religion, the atheist and pantheist may indeed be effectually silenced, yet we must remember that it is one thing to show what is not the truth, and altogether another thing to declare and establish practical truths on which men may confidently rest any important interest. For any such purpose this college gospel is as utterly useless as the classic gospel before considered. Nor is the professor in the lecture room, in any true sense, or in any degree, a co-ordinate teacher of immortality with the minister of Jesus Christ.

II. You are now ready to ask—" What then has the gospel done for the doctrine of immortality,—if it have neither originally demonstrated it, nor yet confirmed and enlarged the teaching of philosophy concerning it ? Much every way. Nay, I will say, *all*, every way ; but, chief of all, in enunciating, and practically demonstrating, this truth, that not merely the spirit of man shall live beyond the present life, but that the " *mortal* must put on immortality,'' also. For you will perceive that, in the Apostle's argument extending through this fifteenth chapter of Corinthians, and of which these words form the triumphant conclusion, we have a full and elaborate exposition of all these mysterious and otherwise paradoxical intuitions of humanity.

The substance of the Apostle's exposition is this : That though the creature man,—a compound being, the junction

of angel and animal in the same being—was constructed
upon a platform of endless existence for the compound
nature ; yet, since the original nature was constituted, a
huge moral convulsion has transpired wrecking the original
order of life. " In Adam all die ;" for as the head of this
new order of being he represented the whole order.   But,
on the other hand, this death has not been fully accepted as
the final condition of the creature ; for, immediately upon the
wreck, a mediator Christ interposed, and hath undertaken to
restore out of the race a body of people for himself ; and, to
that end, connected himself with it, as a second head to redeem.   " As," therefore, " in Adam all die, so in Christ all
are made alive."   As by the relation to the first head,
Adam, every creature that is born, is born to die, under the
sentence of the curse ; so, by virtue of the relation to the
second head, Christ, every creature that dies, must die to rise
again.   And rise again, not a different order of being—pure
spirit—but rise the same compound order of being physical
and spiritual as originally made.   Hence the separation of
the physical from the spiritual at death, is but a mere
incident of the creature's existence : a mere temporary suspension of the bodily functions to the spirit, analogous somewhat to the suspension of the intellectual and spiritual
functions to the physical nature during infancy.   The sum
total of the eternal existence shall be according to the original type, both physical and spiritual, a compound nature ;
the death is a mere incident, and its period reduces to *zero*,
—a not assignable quantity in the formula expressive of the
whole existence.   It is practically " abolished," therefore, in
the gospel theory.

  " In Christ all are made alive."   The gospel theory, as
stated by the Apostle in this argument, is that, besides the
peculiar special relation in which Christ stands to that part of
the race which is actually redeemed and restored by him, he

stands also in a very important relation to the whole humanity whose nature he assumed. In dying and rising again he stood, in an important sense, as representative of the race, while, in a special sense, he stood as the representative of his redeemed people. As every one born of Adam is born to die, because concerned in the disobedience of Adam, the representative head; so, also, because concerned in the obedience of Christ the representative head of humanity, every one that dies, must die to rise again. There is no need of any cautious limitations of such universals as this—" So in Christ all are made alive," or of the Apostle's other saying, that Christ, "by the grace of God tasted death for every man,"—in order to make them harmonize with such other declarations as, in accordance with obvious facts, represent Christ as dying for his elect people ; and that only a part of the race are actually redeemed. For besides the link that connects Christ specially with his people to secure their salvation, there is also a link which connects him with the race at large, so as to secure such movement of the Holy Spirit upon the fallen nature generally as to keep alive the religious consciousness, and prevent the race from sinking into a mere brutish and devilish animalism under its subjection to Satan ; and so as to secure also the resurrection of all who die, to be reconstituted the compound nature in which man was originally created. In a most important sense, therefore, the saying is true to the widest and most absolute extent,—that "Jesus tasted death for every man ;" and that " in Christ all are made alive." His resurrection was the resurrection of our nature, in so far that it becomes a law of the nature that it cannot remain under the power of death. It is not by an essential law of the nature, in the sense of natural religionism, that we are immortal and cannot cease to exist ; but because, by virtue of our relation to Christ, we are constituted immortal both as to soul and body. And if there never had been one sinner who would accept his mediation; if the earth never had contained any but rejectors of Christ, scoffers and infidels; still, by virtue of the work of Jesus Christ, the resurrection of all would have been secured, though the salvation of none had been secured. The despisers of his grace, because they share the nature with him, shall rise with him, and have an imperishable existence though it be rising to shame and everlasting contempt. As the untold myriads of the race were represented in the act of his rising from the dead, therefore the earth must give up its dead, and the sea the dead that are in it, and they shall join him risen to be judged and ruled by him. Thus the Apostolic argument finds the basis of an immortality, not as in the inherent nature of the soul itself, which is a dependent existence, and therefore if God please may terminate, but in the connection of the race with a Redeemer who has secured the immortality not only of the soul but of the whole compound nature—physical as well as spiritual.

You will perceive at a glance how such a theory of immortality furnishes the clue to all those puzzles which the classical and the college gospels find too hard for them.

We can understand now why these original intuitions of immortality are found imbedded in the nature of man as the geologist finds the traces of a primeval life in the rocks. The nature as originally constructed has been convulsed, upheaved, —" In Adam all died." And as the physical life now upon the earth's surface is nourished from the grave of an anterior life whose traces are still found, so this inspired science tells us that the spiritual life which now exists is nourished as it were, from the grave of an anterior spiritual life which this moral convulsion heaved into chaos.

This gospel theory expounds also the meaning of those impressions, ineradicable from his nature, of a future existence, as though an intrinsic necessity of such a nature, while at the same time reason must argue that, as a dependent existence, the life is quenchable, and, as a sinful soul, the probabilities are that God will quench out its life as a safeguard to the purity of his universe. When man has carried himself thus by his native impressions to the verge of eternity, and there is met with the sceptical doubts of reason, and stands shivering in turn at the prospect, not knowing whether he shall be permitted to spring forward, as his impulses would lead him, in the flight through immensity, or whether, on account of his sin, and as a just doom, he shall be blotted out of existence; just then this gospel of life and immortality comes to announce to him, from the Father of Spirits, that, by covenant with the Mediator representing humanity, the irrevocable decree of God is that the spark kindled by the breath of life breathed into him shall never go out nor wax dim. Therefore these intuitions of immortality and the hopes founded upon them are just, notwithstanding the doubts of reason to the contrary.

So, again, with the difficulty in connecting and reconciling the intuitions of future existence and the co-existing impressions of the moral nature concerning a retribution, while, according to reason, the retribution would seem to be visited, contrary to the natural sense of justice, upon another being purely spiritual for the sins done by a being of different order, a compound being with both soul and body. This gospel doctrine again confirms the correctness of both the intuitive impressions against the doubts of reason; and harmonises all by revealing that it is the mortal which puts on immortality, and therefore the same being—the compound being that did the sin here—shall receive the retribution there.

This gospel is needed therefore, if for nothing else, to expound to humanity the paradoxes of its nature which philosophy could not expound. And herein you have but another illustration of the fact that a revelation from heaven was needed, not only to explain the mystery of God, but also the mysteries of which man finds his nature so full. That the bible must be the most human of books as well as a divine book ; and furnish an articulate utterance for these strange, confused instincts of the spiritual nature. Not without reason, therefore, does Jesus make this the grand practical evidence of the divinity of his gospel, that it comes as bread of life exactly suited to feed their hunger, and as a water of life to quench the thirst of the soul.

But, that it thus expounds the cause and nature of these impressions of a future state, is very far from being all or even the chief of what the gospel does for the doctrine of immortality. All this is but the preliminary preparation, and laying the foundation for teaching the true theory and functions of immortality. The key to the whole gospel theory lies just in this proposition enunciated by the Apostle,—" this *mortal* must put on immortality." The prominent features of this gospel theory founded upon this fact, are set forth in these propositions :

First, that the immortality of our nature rests not so much upon the intrinsic nature of the soul itself, as upon the office work of Jesus Christ, the Mediator, for the race and the Redeemer of his elect ;

Second, that this immortality, as to its nature, consists in the restoration of the humanity to its original type at creation, a compound nature by reason of the junction of the physical and the spiritual in the same being.

Third, that the mode of this existence is exhibited to us as an actual fact by the mode of the existence of Jesus after his resurrection—he being the " first fruits of them that slept."

Fourth, that therefore the redemption by Christ includes the restoration of the physical nature of all that die—a " spiritual body" springing from the natural body as its germinal seed--as well as the restoration of the spiritual nature of those that are saved, by perfecting the growth of the " everlasting life" implanted in the soul here.

Fifth, that therefore the humanity, just as it is here on earth, only wholly purified or wholly depraved, shall inhabit eternity. The mixed state, existing here under the reign of grace, shall cease ; and the depravity gathered to itself constitutes the everlasting death ; while the purified shall be gathered to itself and constitute the " *life* and immortality."

Compare now, for a moment, these solid and sublime truths with the philosophic shadows and poetic dreams of the classic and college gospels ; their dreamy cloud palaces shifting over head, with this actual Jerusalem city of God come down out of heaven ; their feeble efforts to become the articulate voice of the unconscious prophecies of humanity in its longings, with this great utterance of great substantive historic fact ; their attempts to gather up the shadowy notions that floated down the stream of generations, with this actual incarnation of them all ! And thus will you be able to conceive something of the cool effrontery of this philosophic gospel which proposes to us to set aside the gospel of life and immortality, and let it devise for us a more scientific and better reasoned gospel. That would have us remove from the solid foundation of Jesus and the Apostles, that they may build our faith upon the foundation of baseless Platonic and Socratic dreams! That would put back the stone to the door of the sepulchre which, for four thousand years, humanity had been pushing at in vain till Jesus came ; put it back now, just to see how philosophy could roll it away if it were there !

No ! No ! brethren, you cannot afford that experiment ! It hath cost too much to make the first experiment in the blood and agonies of him who, as our representative, burst the bars of death that we might shout " O Death, where is thy sting ?" Even if, as the philosophy assures us, the thing could be done in a way to relieve the world of some of its superstitions and

fancies, and relieve the gospel from the sneers of the philosophic wits, still the new gospel of the " wise and prudent"
might be a hidden gospel to the babes.   As practical men we
say, " let well enough alone."

> " Better to bear those ills we have
> Than fly to others that we know not of."

III.   But the fullness and completeness of the gospel will
appear, in still more remarkable contrast, if we proceed to
the details of its teaching, and the manner of its teaching,
concerning the " LIFE and immortality," as a continuance of
the life which now is.   These details relate to the life,
considered simply as a life ; and the blessedness of that life,
both as a negation of all evil and the fullness of all positive
good.

First, the manner of the gospel, in its teaching, is to seek
a foundation on which to rear the structure in that fundamental
law of our nature which leads us to attach importance to *life ;*
to have a regard for the living thing which we cannot attach
to dead matter, except as imagination clothes it in the
attributes of life.   We feel a nearness of relation to the living
plant above the unorganized matter around it; to the insect
that creeps upon the plant, above that we feel for the plant
itself ; for the animal of higher order more than for the insect ;
for the intelligent human creature, more than for the animal ;
for the high intellectual human life, more than for the lower
and unintellectual ; and for the moral life, again, more reverence than for the merely intellectual.   Now the gospel, taking
fast hold of this law of our minds, when it would convey to
us some notion of its transcendant blessing, declares it to be
a life above all these,—a spiritual, and everlasting life.   " He
that believeth hath everlasting life."   " I am that bread of
life."   " A well of water springing up unto everlasting life.'
—These forms of speech are, more than any other, the favourite gospel expressions for the redemption which it offers.

Accordingly in the gospel representations of the estate of the immortality of the redeemed, its purpose is to show that in this immortality provision is made for all the forms of this life, whether the *sentient*, the *intellectual*, the *emotional*, the *moral*, or the *spiritual* life.

For the sentient, or lowest form of life, not only is provision made in the restoration of an immortal body in junction with the immortal soul, but in a "new heaven and new earth" prepared for it. And as in the life here this connection of the spirit with matter is the source of much of its pleasurable enjoyment, so in the "life and immortality" that form of enjoyment shall not cease. Such I take to be the meaning of the intimation of a new earth wherein dwelleth righteousness; of the city with its walls of jasper; of the crystal stream springing, as a river of light, from under the throne; of the green fields, shaded by glorious trees that bear the luscious fruits; where the Lamb leads them to drink of the river of his pleasures. What other significance have all such pictures, than that the sinless joys of which the senses are the inlets shall be ministered unto? That for the glorious bodies a new world shall exist over which the light of that estate of immortality shall be thrown, and kindle it into beauty and glory? Conceive, then, what visions of glory shall burst upon the crystal eye restored to the capacity it had in a sinless world! What new enchantments of melody to the ear attuned anew! What witchery of speech to the loosed tongue! In short, what sensations of exquisite delight from that restoration when the mortal shall have put on the immortality in the rest that remaineth for the people of God!

But this is the lowest form of life. Higher than all this must be the joys of the intellectual life and immortality. Here, as saith the Apostle, "we know in part and we prophesy in part. But when that which is perfect is come, then that which is in part shall be done away. For now we see

through a glass darkly; but then face to face." Here
the intellectual vision can see things only by their shadows;
as through a translucent glass, beyond which the shadows
are ever flitting. But there we shall be admitted within
the veil to a direct view of God, and knowledge shall
be intuitive. And the change must of itself vastly enlarge
the reach of human powers of intelligence. "We shall
know as we are known," says the Apostle. Now our appre-
hensions are confused by false notions mingling with the true;
then we shall know, as God knows, the true from the false.
Here our ideas, even when true, are often mere obscure
glimmerings of the truth; but there, those clouds will be dis-
pelled from the mental perceptions which the coming in of sin
has thrown over the mortal. Here we cannot grasp complex
ideas by reason of the obscurity of our perceptions and the
feebleness of our powers; there, relieved of all such trammel,
the power of combination shall be immeasurably increased.
Here the knowledge of the mortal is limited to such of the
two classes of being, matter and spirit, as exist in our universe;
there, being in direct communication with other orders of
being, the range of our knowledge shall be indefinitely
extended.

And the intellectual nature itself must vastly increase its
powers, under the new circumstances, restored to the original
greatness it had when first man was made in the image of
God. Conceive of the memory, as it passes on eternally,
gathering ever new stores into its treasury, and losing none
out through forgetfulness, until its contents shall be vaster
than all the libraries of the world. Of the powers of association, multiplying suggestions and trains of thought incal-
culably. Of the imagination, also, gathering all the while its
images and fanning into a glow its fires, as it passes through
the various orders of intelligence, and fashions its wonderful
creations. Of the reason, gaining even new cognitions for its

premises, and working out, unembarrassed by untruths, its conclusions. Of the executive energy of the will, and the reflex influence on the intellect of emotions always holy!

As we pass upward to the still higher emotional life whose laws we are less able to analyze, we but the more feel the force of the Apostle's declaration, " eye hath not seen nor ear heard, neither hath it entered into the mind of man to conceive" of the glory of the life and immortality. But if we have reasoned correctly from the scripture intimations announcing the restoration of the sentient and intellectual life, we perceive that, with such a platform of existence, sentient and intellectual, the emotional nature of humanity must then be projected upon such a scale that we have no analogies whereby to illustrate it. The ordinary play and ripple of the emotions of the heart, in this restored humanity, must, in the nature of the case, transcend all epic and all tragic grandeur of the mortal state.

Still less able are we to form adequate conceptions from analogies and approximations of the highest of all forms of life—the spiritual life in that estate of life and immortality. For we see it here only in its feeble manifestations, in perpetual struggles for continued existence in the soul, against the passions and depravity that naturally have had sway therein. Yet we may readily conceive, by contrast, what such a life must be when delivered from this bondage. How the soul, purified and restored to the full and free play of that spiritual life, sustained and cherished now, instead of resisted in its action, by all the powers of the other forms of life, must attain immediately to inconceivable heights of this life. " The pure in heart shall see God," is the expressive phrase of the gospel—" see him as he is." The war in the members over, all the spiritual energies, unembarrassed and untrammelled, are directed to the one object of near approach to, and closer communion with, God. " It is not lawful for man to utter," saith the Apostle, the things that belong to that life. "An exceeding and eternal weight of glory" is the accumulation of terms whereby he would enlarge our ideas of it. But our conceptions of the nature of that estate, in all forms of life, are materially assisted by various descriptions of the blessedness of that life in addition to what is taught of the nature of it. For,

Secondly, the gospel, by most expressive negations, furnishes us with many elements from which we may deduce something of its nature. It is described as a *rest*—cessation from toil and struggle. And this, in conformity with the gospel view of the mortal life as a condition of sin and ruin, and consequently of sorrow and spiritual languor and weariness. The fundamental conception of "the life and immortality" is of an estate from which all that is sinful is separated, and nothing allowed to enter that can disturb the quiet of the soul. The chaff hath all been winnowed out, the wheat garnered to itself. And there being nothing sinful, either within or without, there is no more struggle nor fighting the good fight of faith. So also the gospel declares, negatively, there shall be no more curse. Therefore, an eternal deliverance from all reproaches of conscience, and from the dread of God's displeasure. "They hunger no more nor thirst any more." All the longings and yearnings, and uneasiness of the mortal state shall cease ; "neither shall the sun light upon them, nor any heat." "There shall be no more death," nor "sorrow and crying," for "God shall wipe away all tears from their eyes." All these are expressive of the nature of that state as a deliverance from every conceivable form of uneasiness and disquiet of spirit.

And to the same effect are all those negations, by figurative description, which give rein to the imagination, and invite a contemplation through symbols of that estate. "There shall be no night there ;" "they need no candle, nor light of the sun." The mortal machine needs no longer to be wound up by these alternations between action and repose. There shall be nothing to interrupt incessant activity in the service of God. The mortal has become like Him whose attribute it is that "he never slumbers nor sleeps," and like the living creatures before His throne who *cease not day and night* singing "Holy, holy, holy, Lord God Almighty, which was and is, and is to come." And, just as it is a perfection of the God-head, and of these lofty-created intelligences, that they sleep not, so the mortal, in that estate of immortality, shall spring forward to take its place among the highest creatures to serve and enjoy God without a pause. There shall be no night either in any of its figurative senses of darkness and ignorance, of affliction and sorrow of heart, of treachery and secret crimes. To the mortal in a world of sin, how keen must seem this insight into the human nature, and that which is attractive to it, in thus negatively describing this immortality as no sickness with its languor, no sorrow of countenance, no death, no stormy passions with its wreck and havoc, no cares of life to agitate, no reverses to fill the spirit with gloom, no jealousy to trouble friendship, no treachery to watch, no evil to struggle against! Verily, this must be a divine skill that describes an immortality so precisely to meet the desires of humanity.

Thirdly. Far from resting in mere negations, however, the gospel descriptions represent a positive bliss also, displacing the idea thus negatived. If they need no light of the sun, it is because the "Lord God giveth them light." If they need no temple, it is because the "Lord God is the temple thereof." All the knowledge which could have been communicated to the mortal by means and ordinances will then seem insignificant as the light of the candle compared with the sun. The universe will be to the immortals one infinite manifestation of God. His righteousness and truth, and holiness and loving-kindness—all his attributes—will blaze and glow through immeasurable space. And the faculties and capacities of the immortal shall be equal to the task of comprehending God. No longer gathering conceptions from dim shadows and mysterious types, but, having entered into the very presence-chamber of Infinite Majesty, the mind shall have directly the power of the eye, and gather in truth as his eye takes in the scenes of nature.

I might show you also how this positive bliss is involved in the description of it as an " inheritance," as " glory and honour," as " reward," as a " kingdom;" all with reference to different aspects of the mortal state, and in contrast with it. Time fails, however, for further illustrations of the method of the gospel teaching concerning the life and immortality. For it is specially important to fix your attention, before closing, on the practical bearing of this whole argument upon the daily life of a mortal that is thus to put on immortality.

1. From the forgoing views of this whole subject, you will no longer be at a loss to comprehend why the Apostle, in his argument in the fifteenth chapter of Corinthians, makes the resurrection of Jesus the great key-stone fact of revelation, without which " our preaching is vain, and your faith is vain." Nor why, elsewhere in the gospel, this doctrine of the resurrection is made fundamental, and why the Apostles describe the substance of their message as " preaching Jesus and the resurrection." Not only is the doctrine of the resurrection logically, in idea, anterior to the doctrine of justification by faith, because the raising of Jesus from the dead is the assurance to us that God accepted the offering of his obedience and death as full satisfaction for our sins, so that " He might be just, and yet the justifier of him that believeth in Jesus ;" but the resurrection, and the carrying the humanity with him to the right hand of God, is the fundamental fact on which any real faith in our immortality must rest, in which

we find the key to the mysterious instincts of which we are conscious, and upon which any doctrine of immortality, adequate to the comfort of our souls in view of death, can be constructed.

2. You will readily perceive also, from this view of the gospel doctrine, that any and every attempt to subvert the great truth of the resurrection as an historic fact—no matter under what pious disguise, or from what intention—is nothing else than simple infidelity, and leading us back to mere heathenism. For, as the Apostle declares, "If Christ be not risen, then is our preaching vain, and your faith also is vain. Yea and we are found false witnesses of God, and those which are fallen asleep in Christ are perished." Assuming the correctness of our view generally, then nothing can be more inexorable than this logic, as any man that can appreciate a logical demonstration must see. So far, therefore, from rendering any aid to gospel truth by these classic gospels, or college gospels, which claim to establish immortality for man without any resurrection, there is danger that, however well intended, they remove the very foundations of the popular faith, and lead men to trust "another gospel, which is not another," as the Apostle saith when describing the teaching of "some that would pervert the gospel of Christ." Set it down in your minds, when tempted by your pride to hear and accept these learned and scientific gospels of immortality, that the most they can do for you is to confirm the testimony which your own inner nature has already affirmed of the probability of a future existence, and on that basis reason out for you an immortal hell, not a life and immortality. I hardly need remind you, even after what has been said, that the whole of that class of biblical expositors, who employ their ingenuity in so reading the inspired word as to make the story of the risen Jesus not fact, but a beautiful allegorical or philosophical fiction, whatever may

be their motive—whether sincere or insincere, conscious or unconscious—are simply perpetrating a sham upon you, in pretending that such interpretations may consist with any real faith in Christianity. Bear in mind that the grand anti-Christian movement of our day is not open and bold attack, but a flank movement to get into possession of the citadel of faith which has for near two thousand years proved impregnable to the gates of hell. Discovering that humanity must have a gospel to satisfy its longings, and that, therefore, the assaults of open atheism and deism were unsuccessful from disregard of the necessities of humanity, the assault by the infidelity of our age is chiefly by strategy—to substitute " another gospel, which is not another," but really no gospel at all. And the favourite strategy of all is to impose upon the people a gospel of Jesus, *with the part of Jesus omitted.*

There is of course no need of reminding well-grounded, sober-minded Christian men, of the treachery : but it may be important to remind our ardent young men of literary tastes and pursuits, that if the general ground of the preceding exposition be correct, then that seemingly Christian style of thought that is now pervading a large portion of our literature in every department ; which affects to be too spiritually intellectual to accept " the external " religion of the fathers, and their common sense readings of the scripture history—is but disguised infidelity, whether conscious or unconscious. And while it may seem to be Christianity, and to construct an attractive form of the gospel for the benefit of literary men, yet in the day that sorrow and trouble of conscience shall drive you in search of a gospel to rest your souls upon, this will surely prove " the baseless fabric of a vision." " Other foundation can no man lay save that is laid in Christ Jesus ;" however brilliant the genius, and profound the reasoning powers, of him that attempts it. And any foundation that pretends to be in Christ Jesus while ignoring his death as-

an expiation for sin, and his resurrection as the basis of our
life and immortality, is but a cheat and a delusion of the
human spirit.

3. But there are other lessons for the practical life in
this Apostolic view of " life and immortality." You will perceive that in this view the question of immortality is neither
any curious speculative problem, nor any beautiful poetic
dream to captivate the imagination : nor any mere sentiment
to play upon the affections of the heart.   It is a question of
stern realities that lie just ahead of us all : and in a few days
with some—a few months with others—a few years with the
youngest will be the one question in which all the transient
issues and excitements that now absorb us will be swallowed
up.   It is therefore no mere subject of debate to which you
listen as hearers having no concern, or only a very remote
concern.   It is a question of life and death—life and immortality, or death and immortality—to every one of you.

4. And it adds to its pressing importance that this is no
question of the future with which the present has little to do ;
and which therefore may be left to be settled when the future
shall become present to us.   If merely a question of the endless existence of the soul, in another and different order of
existence, it might be so.   But as it is the present mortal
that is to put on immortality, every man and woman, old and
young, is actually determining each hour what shall be the
character of the immortality.   The life that now is—this very
every-day, unromantic life—wearing away, hour after hour,
is the germinal seed of that immortal life.   And " what a
man soweth that shall he also reap.   He that soweth to his
flesh shall of the flesh reap corruption ; but he that soweth
to the spirit shall of the spirit reap life everlasting."   So
that every day the character of the immortality is in process
of development.   And every day, according as you are
sowing to the flesh, or by God's grace, sowing to the spirit,

is determining, just in that far, whether the mortality shall
put on an immortality of joy, or an immortality of sorrow.

5. It is altogether a delusion that it is left to men's choice
whether they shall stand in any relation to Christ or not, and
whether they shall be judged by his gospel or not. For, as
we have seen, even the Christ-rejecting sinners of the race,
just as much as the sinners who accept his salvation, are
already in such relation to Christ that his resurrection
secures their resurrection from the dead ; and therefore also
a retribution, in their present nature—rising to life and immortality or rising to shame and everlasting contempt. And
however men may say " we will not have this man to reign
over us," there is really no choice in the matter, save the
question whether he shall reign in their heart's affections, as
the Lamb in the midst of the throne leading them in life
and immortality, or as the Lamb in the midst of the throne,
whose wrath will cause them to cry, in vain, " Rocks fall on
us, and hills cover us from the face of him that sitteth on the
throne." The relation of Jesus to us, as head of the race,
is a matter settled in the counsels of eternity. His relation
to us as a pardoning and restoring Saviour is the question
which each must determine for himself.

6. You will observe that the very terms in which the
immortality is set forth, various as they are, all exclude
alike those hopes of a blissful immortality founded on the
illusions and dreams on which men at ease in sin are resting
their hopes. Not only is the immortality to spring from the
" mortal " here as its germinal seed, but all the terms used
as figures to express the nature of the life and immortality
imply that the mortal has settled its character. It is a *rest*.
Therefore it can be the award only to those weary of the
struggle with sin ; and with toils in the master's service. It
is an *inheritance*. Therefore only for the family of Jesus
Christ provided for in " the last will and testament " of his-

blood ; constituting them heirs of God and joint heirs with Jesus Christ.   It is a *reward*.   Therefore conferred upon those who have laboured faithfully to receive it.   It is *glory and honour*   Therefore properly conferred only upon those who have conquered and won the victory : not to the cowardly, and half-hearted, and double-minded who stood aloof from the conflict.   It is a *kingdom*, and therefore composed only of such as have been naturalized in the mortal : since otherwise they must remain everlasting aliens.

Not a term, not a figure of speech, not an argument or exposition setting forth the " life and immortality," but thus points to the mortal and proclaims to you—" Behold now is the day of salvation !"

DISCOURSE XIX.

THE GOSPEL ALARUM.   ITS IMPORT.

EPHESIANS v. 11.—Wherefore he saith, Awake thou that sleepest and arise from the dead, and Christ shall give thee light.

SEEMS it a strange and abrupt transition, brethren, that in the midst of these plain and homely admonitions concerning the duties belonging to the ordinary, every day level of the Christian life, here suddenly shoots up this alarum cry "Awake thou that sleepest," as shoots up mount Tabor from the plain of Esdraelon?

It is because of that tendency of the great Apostle's mind, ever absorbed with the two grand generalizations which constitute the essence of the gospel—man's estate of sin and death, and Christ crucified his all-sufficient Saviour—to see every other truth in the light of these two and in its relations to these two. Hence to him the Christian, primarily, is one who hath been awaked from the death of trespasses and sins by the grace of God; and all his dangers and temptations have their root in his tendency, from the drowsiness that is upon him, to fall back into the stupor of the death sleep again. Hence to the Apostle's view the end and aim of all counsels and admonitions is to counteract this tendency, and in effect to ply him continually with the alarum which first roused him from the death sleep.

The explanation of this abruptness is, therefore, analogous to that which the critics give us of the abrupt, irregular grandeur of genius such as Homer's, Pindar's, or Shakespeare's. That great truths lie hidden in their minds which other men do not see, and therefore the workings, under these truths, of the vast forces within is as the movement of those primeval volcanic fires of the geologists which, in their ordinary ripple and play, have heaved up, here a vast chain of mountains to span a continent : here the fantastic irregular heaps ; and here the solitary peak shooting upward to the sky as if having sought to cool its molten head in the regions of eternal snow !

Without further comment on its connection and relation, I propose to illustrate the fundamental truths expressed in this gospel alarum. First, Concerning the death-sleep, as the natural condition of men ; Second, Of the awakening from it ; Third, The encouraging promise annexed of aid to the awakened ; Fourth, The urgent hastefulness of the gospel call.

I. " Thou that sleepest and art dead." Such is uniformly the picture which inspiration paints of the native condition of man spiritually. And, without a proper apprehension of this truth, all the gospel truths become confused, obscure, or meaningless. Born into a world that has wandered from the spiritual orbit into which it was projected by the hand of its Maker, the change of orbit has produced a change of climate ; the intense chills of the spiritual winter have stupe-fied all the moral powers of man ; and no plants of holiness can endure it but such exotics as the great Lord of the garden shall, with unceasing care and attention, shelter from the chill blasts, and by the warm breathings of his love, expand the blossom and ripen the fruit.

This is declared not merely dogmatically in all the state-ments concerning the nature and character of man, in the scripture, but is assumed and implied in every invitation of the gospel mercy. This is a gospel for saving sinners, for calling not the righteous but sinners, for saving that which was lost; for quickening them that are dead in trespasses and in sins.

The very call of the gospel of love comes as a cry of compassionate alarm. As pastor Vinet beautifully illustrates this very call of the text. It is as the cry of some monk of St Bernard on the Alps scouting with his faithful dog, and finding, perchance, a traveller through the Alpine snows stretched out to sleep upon the white sheet of frost, and already beginning to be bound in the arms of that invincible slumber which precedes freezing, from which no voice but God's can ever wake him; he shakes the sleeper, and shouts the alarum in his dull ear, "awake that I may guide thee to shelter." Just such is the cry of Jesus Christ, in his gospel, to the slumbering sinners of earth already in the death stupor. "Awake thou sleeper—arise from the dead—I will give thee light." O, sinner, if it seem to you a very rough shaking up and a harsh call, when sometimes he lays his hand in affliction and trouble upon thee, still remember it is the roughness of love yearning for thy salvation. As I remember to have read in some of the journals, the story of that hardy sea-captain wrecked, mid-winter, upon our bleak northern coasts, under chill blasts that had sent all living things to shelter. Far down the beach he saw a light, and knew if he could keep up life and motion within his icy garments, long enough to reach it there was still a chance for life. His own stout frame could have endured, as the gnarled oak, all the blasts of the tempest, but with either hand he led a boy the very idols of his soul—eight and ten years of age. Their tender frames were soon chilled as a flower in the frost; and that heavy drowsiness began to fall upon them which is ever the precursor of death by freezing. At every step or two, as he urged them over the frozen sands, they would plead "Father, could'nt you let us stop and rest, and sleep, just a minute—then we'll go bravely on!" But, knowing it was a race with death to reach the sign of shelter, the poor father must, at length, with rude shakings, and even blows urge them on, while his heart bled at every blow and his heartstrings were breaking.

Just such is the rudeness of this Saviour Jesus, as, through his Providence as well as his word, he would arouse thee from this death stupor, saying in kindness and compassion— "Awake" now, "it is high time to awake out of sleep." The death stupor is upon thee, and if thou fall back after this awaking no voice of mercy may come to awake thee again."

It is difficult indeed to make the propriety of this figure apparent to the men of this world. For it seems to them, as they look upon the restless activity that surrounds them, that any other term than "asleep," should be the figure to describe it. "This world around us asleep?" they ask— these panting millions, pressing, dashing, trampling each other in the dusty highways of fortune, fame or pleasure? Asleep!—this restless raging ocean of life, over which the storm king rides in his fury. Humanity asleep, that neither night, nor sickness, nor satiety can check in its tumultuous course? Your figure of the Alpine traveller can surely apply to none save these stolid unthinking animals in human form ; or these sluggish drones whom neither pleasure nor danger can excite ; with whom the physical life is the all of them, and who, fastening themselves to some stable support as the oyster, care for nothing but their physical wants, and trouble themselves only to open and shut the mouth in receiving and retaining the needful sustenance of life!

The scriptures however make no distinction in this regard ; nor do they classify these sleepers into the active and the tranquil. But they do teach that this spiritual slumber may consist with great physical and intellectual activity. They are not only sleepers but somnambulists. They walk and still sleep; they speak, though still they sleep; with open eyes they sleep; but in the view of the gospel they have eyes and see not—ears have they but they hear not. They see what is not, and do not see what is ; things far off seem near to them; things near seem far off. While they walk, as wakeful men, their steps are not directed by the reality of things.

" This life's a dream, an empty show," with all its passions and agitations. These activities are but dreams ; visions created by the fancy, no longer restrained by realities, and running wild of the judgment. They live in a phantom world, in which they give to the phantoms the forms of reality, but on awaking to their true life, all these must dissipate. It is not a sleep therefore which suspends the physical and intellectual activities. But if it is to sleep when men have no longer power to distinguish shadows from realities ; if it is to sleep, when men's thoughts are all absorbed with gaining an end which does not exist ; and if it is to sleep when men are utterly unconscious of all the realities that surround them, while their anxieties and fears are directed to fancies that flit before them—then certainly the gospel utters no paradox in describing as sleepers, men who are applying all the energies of an immortal nature to perishable things ; and attributing to finite things a value and importance that can belong only to things infinite.

There is neither piety nor good sense in the sentimental tirades of discontented spirits against the vanity and worth-lessness of the world and of the life of men in it. The life in this world has its value, and the world in its own sphere has its value, but not as the reality and the great object of an immortal soul's existence. To that soul, framed for another life and for God as its great object, the world is the shadow of a great reality. As the physical universe is a shadow of God who made it and proves his existence, so all that belongs to life in this universe is a shadow of the infinite realities that exist in the life spiritual. What is this love of fame, and of the applause of other beings, but the shadow of that true

desire of the soul for the plaudit " well done good and faithful
servant," from God and holy beings? What is this desire to
live in the remembrance of men when we are dead, but
another form of the soul's natural desire for immortal
existence, and horror of ceasing to exist? What is this
greed of gain but the shadow of that passion of the soul to
have in store, for the future, treasures in heaven, where moth
and rust corrupt not? Nay, what is this incessant desire of
pleasures and the excitements of joy but the shadow of the
soul's inarticulate longing for " his presence where is fulness
of joy, and at his right hand where are pleasures for ever
more." To man, as an immortal being, there can possibly be
no reality save God and his relation to God.

The gospel, in this respect, but interprets for men those
suspicions and guesses which the sleepers have sometimes
made in their disturbed dreams. For this sleep of theirs is
the restless sleep of disease—sometimes almost coming to
waking. And, as it is in restless imperfect sleep that we
dream most, and the dreams are most like our waking
thoughts, so many of these dreamers, in different ages, have
seemed to come to a sort of half consciousness, and to the
suspicion of the true harmony of their nature with something
more real than this dreamy state.

II. Now there can be but one of two awakenings from this
death sleep; either the natural waking when death shall
come and dissolve the fancies and sham objects of sense from
the view of the soul; or the spiritual awakening under this
gospel alarum. For, obviously, if the nature of the sleep has
been truly described, then the awakening from it must be at
the death which dissolves the physical nature. If it seem a
paradox to say that one awakes from sleep in the sleep of
death; and that one arises from the dead at death; the
paradox is only apparent and verbal. When the scriptures
speak of death as a sleep, it is only by figure, to describe that

which is apparent and in accordance with human forms of speech and thought. Death is the true awakening of the soul from these dreams which have been described. If not, then it must be the beginning of a dreamless sleep, which it is unnatural and revolting to us to think of. Man himself, in his dreams, instinctively looks forward to death as some sort of awakening of his spiritual nature.

And what, think you, shall be the awakening of those who have all life long been pursuing phantoms; when suddenly God, the true end of the soul's existence, bursts upon its view after the long night of sensual revel and debauch? When "the Lord of the servant shall come as a thief in the night and find him asleep at his post." No finite mind can conceive it nor human tongue describe it. If you could ask yon traveller, who, in his sleep-walking, has stumbled over the precipice of a thousand feet, what kind of waking that was to find himself mid-air rushing down to destruction. If you could ask that father, awakened to find himself and children enveloped beyond all hope of deliverance in a sheet of glowing flame, what sort of waking that is! If either could find words to express the soul emotions of such a moment, then might you find words to express by feeble approximation the awakening of the sleeper at death.

The inspired writers find all language breaking down under the weight of the thoughts they would convey of the terrors of that waking. They seem to labour to convey some idea of it through analogies and approximations. They bid you try to conceive of the most terrific things in the sphere of the external world, and then intimate, "worse than all that." Nothing can be conceived more terrible than of a mountain at whose base one is walking, suddenly turning over to overwhelm us, or its huge land slide to rush down upon us. Yet saith the inspired vision, they pray to the mountains "fall on us," and to the hills "cover us from the face of him that sitteth on the throne." The most terrific of conceptions now, will then be regarded, in comparison, as favours to be prayed for. Perhaps the most exquisite of all human grief is the separation, to see their faces no more, from our kindred according to the flesh; yet in that awakening, souls shall esteem it the second best thing to be prayed for; that heaven will send and keep away the five brethren from the place of torment!

O think, sleeper! Even though you cannot think—as a waking spiritual man—yet *dream* of a soul, made in God's own image, with God for its great end, think of such an one waking from its night of debauch—all its dreams fled! All its connection with physical nature cut off, and it cast suddenly, a naked, shivering spirit as a wreck upon the shore of eternity. Its sources of pleasure all cut off in the destruction of their channel, the physical senses. Its passions, for want of anything to feed upon without, all turning in, with vulture greediness, to prey upon the soul itself! The scoffers have assured you that the gospel hell is no revelation from God, but only a dream of the poets. But the dullest fancy needs no aid of poets to conceive of the horrors of such a soul-waking as that. In comparison with the sober deductions of reason concerning the necessary results of such a waking, all the visions of poets are but the feeblest approximations. What, in comparison, is Dante's conception of the seven circles of hell increasing in intensity of torment downward to the centre? Or the lowest of Milton's " still lower deeps?" Or Shakespeare's picture of souls doomed:

> To bathe in fiery floods or to reside
> In thrilling regions of thick-ribbed ice,
> To be imprisoned in the viewless winds,
> And blown, with restless violence, about
> The pendent world?

Nay the solemnly, sober figures of Jesus in the gospel of

" the roaring of the lake that burneth," of the " crackle of
the fire that is not quenched," of the gnawing of " the worm
that dieth not," of " the weeping and wailing and gnashing
of teeth," seem no strong figures for the expression of such
a doom !

We may catch some faint glimmer of what the full soul-
waking must be from the partial wakings that are sometime
seen to occur this side of death ; the awakings under the
rough shaking of heart-breaking sorrow and disappointment
to utter despair ; sometimes producing frantic ragings, sometimes a cold, stony calmness still more terrible as the evidence
of hopeless remorse.   What agony of heart comes on then !
What utter wreck of the spirit !   The cells of the mad-house
give us the external of it, but Jesus Christ, the physician of
the heart broken, alone can tell the depths of that internal
horror !

I remember reading in our journals some years ago the
story of a poor creature, who half drunk or wholly drunk, lay
down in a skiff on the Canada shore above the great cataract ; and, by the additional weight in it, the skiff was loosed
from its moorings and floated out into the quiet but strong
current.   Loud were the shouts from either side when his
condition was discovered, " Awake thou sleeper," yet he
dreamed on, and floated on smoothly, but every moment
more and more swiftly ; till, approaching the mighty cataract,
the voice of its thunders seemed at last to wake him, and he
was observed to rise just in time to see that he was lost
beyond hope.   If you can imagine now the soul emotions of
that poor sleeper, as shooting over the fatal verge he hung
suspended mid-air for an instant over the boiling chasm below,
then may you conceive something of the emotions of a spirit,
that dreaming floats down the current of time, when suddenly
it wakes by the plunge into eternity !

I have read—perhaps in a discourse of the pastor Vinet

already referred to—the affecting story of a somnambulist, a young and joyous girl, who, in her sleep-walking, issued through the sky-light of the chamber to the roof of one of those lofty buildings so common in the old cities of Europe ; and there, sound asleep, walked and danced in sight of an excited crowd of passers-by arrested by the perilous movements. Dreaming she seemed to be, of some approaching *fête*, and, now was arranging her toilet, standing on the very verge ; now walking back ; now approaching and seeming to look down upon the crowd far below, as calmly as if from a balcony. None dared utter a word to wake the sleeper : all rather held their breath in horror. Till at length, as she stood once more on the verge, the flash of a light from an opposite window falling upon her eyes suddenly waked her. A shriek rent the still air an instant, and she fell to be dashed to pieces. The waking revealed the terrors of her position ; and the terror impelled her forward to death.

A faint type this of the soul suddenly waked to this despair by a light from some Providence of God falling upon the eye of the gay dreamer, and making him conscious of his true position.

It must be so. For remember, the true relation of the soul to God and things infinite can in no wise be changed by this dreamy sleep which makes it unconscious of the relation. True, very often we find men so thoroughly brutish in their nature that it is difficult to conceive of such creatures bearing any other relation to God and the universe than the brutes that perish. We sometimes say of this godless and debased Judas, that can conceive of nothing higher in the way of motive than the thirty pieces of silver,—" he has no soul ;" he " has no conscience." But he hath a soul and a conscience for all that. Buried far down in the depths of his nature, under all this moral filth and mire that covers up the spiritual nature in him, this Judas hath a conscience. And in due time, it may be before the full waking of death, that conscience will come struggling, and gurgling up from the depths and shriek in awful threnes of despair—" I have sinned—I have sinned—I have betrayed the innocent blood"!

And if such are the terrors of the partial wakings, even with the dim and confused notions of the relation of the immortal nature to God, and under the feeble workings of conscience, even in its best estate, this side death, what must be the horrors of that waking as all the dread realities of the unseen shall burst upon the soul, and of the arousing of conscience to sleep no more for ever?

But blessed be God! we are not shut up, without alternative, to this natural waking of the soul at death. For the gospel of Jesus Christ provides for an effectual waking by supernatural power this side of death, and for creating within us a waking life which, imperfect as it may be while yet existing in the body of sin and death, shall pass on over death to become a perfect and everlasting life. For not only hath a provision been made for taking away the sin that brings this death stupor on the soul, but, with that atonement for sin, a power also, even the work of the Holy Spirit, which makes this gospel a power of God unto salvation. This heavenly agent, who alone can make his voice heard by these sleepers, taking the things of Christ shews them unto them. Jesus, as represented by Him, comes now just-as really and truly as when he came in the flesh. Scouting over the Alpine sin-deserts and finding these wanderers stretched out on the sheet of frost, and dreaming as death is treacherously binding them fast in his invincible slumber, he sounds the alarum, shouting in their dull ear—" Awake thou sleeper"! "Arise from the dead"! for death is upon thee!

III. And now is made apparent the distinguishing glory of the gospel alarum. It not only arouses the sleeper to his impending danger—which is a cheap enough act of humanity that even the instincts of nature would prompt—but makes the tender of effective aid to utter helplessness—"*I will give thee light.*" Finding the poor wanderer bewildered and in darkness as he shakes off the stupor, instead of leaving him there to perish, this kind friend saith, " Come, I will light thee through the darkness and will guide thee to safe shelter. I will lead the blind in a way that they know not."

It is just here that all the ethical gospels, and moral power gospels, and rationalistic gospels, of human device in their origin, or counterfeits of the true gospel, completely break down. Whatever dispute there may be whether their voice hath ever had power to awake a soul truly, there can be no dispute as to their powerlessness to aid the perishing soul once it is truly awake. Your arguments of the beauty and propriety of virtue and the unwisdom of a life of sin ; your rules for the guidance of life by a vigorous discipline ; your arguments of the rectitude of God's moral government in punishing sin—all your ethics and disciplines and natural theologies are well enough in their place. And the moralities, which good government requires to be observed in order to attain the favour of God, may be all proper enough, but of what avail to a poor soul with the drowsiness of this death stupor upon it ?

Your gospels that, ignoring the depravity of fallen man and the death stupor that is upon him, play physician to them that are whole and not to them that are sick, may teach clearly enough in what way an unfallen nature may secure God's favour ; but are of little use for directing awakened sinners. The preachers of the old-fashioned moral gospels were good enough guide-boards at the *cross-roads* to point out the road to heaven, to those that have the power of spiritual locomotion. But of what use a guide board to a poor cripple lying at its foot powerless to move ! The preachers of the transcendental ethics who have succeeded them have only added to the difficulty by writing the inscriptions on the guide-board in a language that none but the initiated can ever read. Much after the fashion of a waggish guide-board that I remember in the valley of Virginia, which excited first the wonder, and then the mirth of childhood by its inscription— "*To Bunker Hill two miles. N.B. If you can't read, ask at the tavern.*" Of what possible use to the great masses of the people, whose thought and speech are limited to the every-day vernacular, these exquisite essays in ethics and æsthetics from men who pretend to speak in the name of Jesus?

"*I will give thee light*" is the offer of Jesus. It is one of the various forms of expressing the offer of grace and salvation of which there is such a variety in the gospel. For the forms of the offer are varied to suit the different phases of that state of soul when a consciousness of its sad condition is awakened in it; each one implying all the others. Here it takes the form of the offer of light with reference to the dark-ness of a soul awakened out of its night slumber by the sounding of the gospel alarum. That is one of the most vivid and impressive of all the gospel descriptions of the work of the Holy Spirit, in the renewal of a soul, which makes it analo-gous to the work of the spirit at creation, moving upon the chaos, and bringing all to order, as God said "Let light be; and light was." Saith the Apostle, "God who caused light to shine out of darkness hath shined into our hearts, to give the light of the glory of God in the face of Jesus Christ." Nor can we better conceive of the nature of the spirit's work in those cases of light suddenly breaking in upon the awakened soul, than by recalling the impression upon ourselves of the magnificent description, of God's work in the Oratorio of "Creation." Recall how with full orchestra the huge dis-cords describe, first the chaos, "without form and void and darkness upon the face of the deep," until the very soul is all

unnerved and in utter disorder.   Then how the single sweet
voice carols forth " God said let there be"—returning and
repeating as if afraid to pronounce the word of command—
till the whole force engaged, as if catching the inspiration
chimes in, shouting in thunders of sweetest harmony " Light"
" Light" " Let there be light"—till light seems to gleam
from every tone of the hundred-voiced choir ; light from every
note of the pealing organ ; light from loud trumpet and silver-
toned bugle and soft-breathing flute ; and the very atmosphere becomes a sea of effulgent glory.

Thus it is when, the voice of Christ heard and his offer of
light accepted, the soul at once is filled " with joy unspeakable
and full of glory."

But the experience of his promise fulfilled is not always
this sudden breaking in of light as when God first called
light out of darkness.   The analogy would rather be that
causing the light to shine out of darkness by the operation of
the laws which he had ordained for his great work when
finished ; as we may conceive it to have dawned that first
sabbath morning in the beautiful regions where he afterward
" planted the garden eastward in Eden."   First the faint
streaks of light in the east detaching the horizon from the
dark line of the mountains.   Then the mountain tops tinged
with light.   Next " the sun coming forth out of his chamber,
rejoicing as a strong man to run a race"—then the shadows
dropping down the mountain sides, and the light penetrating
the deep gorges.   Till now light seems to engender light and
all nature lies basking in the smile of its Maker as he pronounces all very good.   This is the gradual coming into the
soul of that " peace of God that passeth understanding."
And it is not less surely the supernatural work of the Spirit
on the soul, than when the light breaks suddenly in upon the
darkness.   For just so Jesus illustrates to us his methods in
his miracles of restoring the blind man.   In one case, he

simply speaks the word of power and the eyes are opened, and, in a moment, the glorious light of heaven rushes in. In another case, he uses external means, and at first the blind man sees, indistinctly, " men as trees walking." But both cases are equally acts of his divine power.

IV. One word as to the hasteful and urgent manner of this call. In this alarum, coming as the fire cry in the night —" Awake thou that sleepest," you have the true type of all gospel invitation. This is seen in the various forms of express call. " Escape for thy life, Look not behind thee, Tarry not in all the plain ! Escape to the mountains lest thou be consumed." " To day if ye will hear his voice, harden not your hearts." " Now is the accepted time." " Behold now is the day of salvation." But, besides all this, you will find that every invitation given ; every tender of his salvation ; every statement of its terms ; implies that it is now to be accepted. Not in all the word of God is there an invitation to come to-morrow : nor a statement of the terms that guarantees you those terms to-morrow.

Listen then to this call, and, if its appeals reach the dull ear of the soul, spring up at once and shake off the slumber. Say not a " a little more sleep, a little more slumber, a little more folding of the hands to sleep " ! Remember that the sleeper who is roused, and then falls back, only sleeps more soundly than before ! Say not wait, wait, while time waits not, and the current that carries thee onward to the abyss waits not, but becomes every moment fleeter ! Stay not to quarrel and debate about the terms, or the manner of the arousing. Stay not, pleading your powerlessness to move till God moves thee. Dream not of miracles, where God hath appointed means ! Lie not still waiting for God to compel thee to move, for he will have a willing service. Expose not thyself to all the soul temptations of the world, the flesh and. the Devil, expecting God to make thee world-proof, flesh-proof, Devil-proof: Take not the viper to your bosom and expect God to charm it that it sting not: Tamper not with the poison cup, and look to God to neutralize the deadly draught: " Awake thou sleeper " and bestir thyself. It is Christ calling and pointing thee to shelter and refuge; with the light in his hand to lead thee thither. Turn not back to thine idle dreams, lest thou be left to that dreadful waking where there shall be none to aid thee forever!

SECTION VI

DISCOURSE XX.

THE GOSPEL ADAPTED TO THE CONSCIOUS WANTS OF THE HUMAN SOUL—ITS ARGUMENTS, TERMS AND AGENCIES.

Revelation xxii. 16-18.—I am the root and the offspring of David and the bright and morning star. And the Spirit and the bride say, come. And let him that heareth say, come. And let him that is athirst come. And whosoever will, let him take the water of life freely. For I testify unto every man that heareth the words of the prophecy of this book, If any man shall add unto these things, God shall add unto him the plagues that are written in this book.

This remarkable gospel of invitation " The Spirit and the Bride say come," has a very peculiar significancy, my brethren, alike from *whence* it is, from *where* it is, and from *what* it is. As to the *whence*, it is a message of Jesus, back to the sinners of earth, for whom " he endured the cross, despising the shame," and comes from the throne of all power to which, sixty years before, he had ascended, carrying the humanity with him ; and after his finished sacrifice, and completed scheme of redemption, as developed in the new covenant of his blood, had been already proclaimed by his inspired Apostles to the utmost limits of the known world. But though now on his throne there is no abatement of his interest in that wonderful scheme of redemption, which he had been gradually developing, through the revelations " of sundry times and divers manners," under successive covenants for four thousand years. Referring to the last of these covenants, organizing the typical kingdom under David, he proclaims himself " the root and the offspring of David," now enthroned in the heavens as the "bright morning star" for whose rising faith had longed through all the darkness of prophecy. And, in full view of the scheme completed by the offering of the sacrifice once for all; of the outpouring of his Spirit; of the complete opening of the new and last era of redemption; of the dispensation of the Spirit; of the historic faith, now substituting facts *actual* for the types and symbols of prophecy; and of the Church of one nation, under the old covenant with Abraham, become the Church of all nations under the new covenant, he utters this last gospel as the climax of all the gospels which God had revealed through the prophets—through his Incarnate Son—and through the Apostles.

This then is the gospel according to Jesus ascended, delivered after his complete scheme of salvation had for sixty years been in the full tide of successful experiment. It is therefore peculiarly to our dispensation. It is the peculiar type of that Gospel which, without symbol or altar, or limit of nation, is to be preached till his second coming.

So also it is significant, from *where* it is, in the series of recorded revelations. It is the last paragraph, of the last chapter, of the last book, of God's revealed word. For you will observe that, immediately upon its utterance and record, that great seal—written all over, with curses against him, who shall by a single word add to, or subtract from the revelation here finished—closes up finally the communications from heaven. That it is such a general closing up of the whole volume of inspiration, and not merely applicable to this last

book, is manifest from the fact that while all previous revelations at the sundry times closed with a call for other
revelations to follow them, this closes with no call for more to
follow. Moses called for " a prophet like unto him," whom
they should hear. David and the prophets all call for more
glorious revelations to follow. Malachi closes up the Old
Testament with a call for the coming of the " Messenger of
the covenant" to develop the old covenants still more clearly.
Jesus, when ascending, called for the coming of the Holy
Ghost to lead his Apostles into all truth, and commissioned
them to speak still further in his name. Now the last survi-
ving of these Apostles, having traced on the prophetic chart
the history of this last dispensation down to Christ's second
coming to judgment, without any notice of any more revelations to come through all this era, closes up the communications from heaven by calling for no more but placing upon the
record this tremendous seal. All Mohammed Korans, all
Saints' legends of visions, and revelations, and miracles—all
Swedenborg dreams and communications with heaven—all
Mormon appendices, all stupid revelations, rapped or written
by silly spirits, are hereby anticipated, excluded, denounced
and threatened with all the curses written in God's book.
But before that great seal shall finally close communication,
Jesus has one more last word to say. In every conceivable
form of assurance and invitation, he had called sinners through
all the divers manner of his revelations before—yet still
yearning to see the travail of his soul, his love seems to stay
the hand that is putting on the seal, that it may first insert
one more invitation and assurance, lest some poor dark-minded
sinner should still despond and despair. And so there was
crowded in this last gospel, under the very seal itself that
closes communication.

And when we consider *what* it is, we must confess it to be
infinitely worthy of the source whence it comes, and the place

where it stands as the climax of all the gospel revelations.
"Stay," the ascended Jesus seems to say : " Put not on the
cursing seal, till there first be put in one more gospel assurance and invitation. And make it wide as human thought
can possibly conceive of it : plain as human language can
possibly utter it : and cordial as the heart of God alone can
give it. Assure them from me, David's creator, and yet, as
the offspring of David, their brother, partaker of flesh and
blood : assure them from me, the Day-star of all their longings,
now, beyond all dispute risen, and enthroned in the heaven—
that the fountain of life is now thrown wide open, and its
streams are gushing forth in all their infinite fulness, with
every barrier of approach to it absolutely taken away. Tell
them that not only have they *leave to come*, but every loving
voice in heaven and earth, pleads and urges them to come.
That my Spirit whispers to the depths of their spirits, saying,
" Come." That my bride, the Church, in all her divinely
appointed ordinances cries " Come" ! " Come." Nay more,
lest it be in highways and hedges where there should be no
Church ordinances to reach any one, every sinner that heareth
my voice himself, is authorized to say to any other sinner,
" Come." Nay more, lest there should be no such sinner to
invite him—tell any soul that feels the thirst not to stand on
ceremony, but, self-invited, " Come." Nay more still—lest
now some poor sin-darkened soul should stumble at the word
" athirst," and doubt if his thirst is real or great enough—
strike out even that, and say absolutely—" *whosoever will,
let him take* of the water of life freely." I will be the
Saviour of any that will have me for a Saviour. Only let
him cry in his despair, " O Lamb of God I come—just as I
am."

Brethren, I may well shrink from the task of developing
this gospel according to Jesus ascended, when I find all
human conceptions and human language breaking down in

the attempt to utter the infinite fulness and freeness of a
Saviour's love. Yet I may assist you in forming some conception of the great truths embodied in these beautiful
approximations and figures, by answering for you these
questions—

1. What ideas are involved in this figure of "the
water of life?"

2. What ideas in the correlative figure "thirst?"

3. What causes develop the consciousness of this thirst
in the soul?

4. On what terms may the soul conscious of it have the
thirst quenched?

5. By what agencies is the soul athirst brought to the
waters of life?

I. As suggesting at once the answer to the first inquiry, it
is needful only to remind you that, in all the eras of revelation
and under all the covenants, the familiar symbol for the
redemption provided by Christ is this of the living waters to
quench the spiritual thirst: Under the old covenant with
Abraham, the salvation guaranteed in it was symbolized to the
Church in the desert by the stream that gushed from the
smitten Rock in Horeb, and followed them in all their wanderings. For, saith the Apostle, "They drank of that spiritual
Rock that followed them: and that Rock was Christ."
Under the covenant with David the Church was taught to
sing in her liturgy, " As the hart panteth after the water
brooks, so panteth my soul after thee, O God." Isaiah
three centuries later, after presenting in prophetic visions the
scenes of the cross and the exaltation that should follow,
predicts this very gospel of Jesus ascended, saying—" Ho
every one that thirsteth, come ye to the waters, even he that
hath no money." Seven hundred years later, on the great
day of the feast, as the priest dipped up water with the
golden pitcher, and poured it upon the altar, while the vast

multitudes marched around in procession, singing from Isaiah—
" With joy shall we draw water from the wells of salvation"
—Jesus stood and cried saying, " If any man thirst, let him
come to me and drink." Thus it will be seen that this is
confirmatory of all the old gospels, and that in all cases this
symbol of the water for the spiritual thirst has reference to
the work of Christ in his incarnation, death, and resurrection.
It is a poetic synonym for " Christ crucified," the one great
idea of the whole revelation. For, above all books, the bible
is a book of one idea: and hence this tendency to those
magnificent generalizations that sum up and concentrate its
essence in a single sentence or phrase ; as, " when I see the
blood I will pass over"—" we preach Christ crucified." And
readily enough may the gospel be thus summed up, since it is
this death of Jesus as an atoning sacrifice which gives its
significance to every paragraph of the bible as the living word
of God. Just as, in the physical structure, the heart is the
seat of its life, and the blood driven from the heart to the
extremities, is all that makes them living flesh, rather than so
much dead clay : so the cross of Jesus Christ is the heart of
the revealed word of God, and the blood driven from the
cross into every sentence and word of it is that which gives
them their life, as the word of God instinct with living truth.

Nothing therefore can be more absurd than the very
fashionable form of Deism, which pretends, while accepting
the character of Jesus as perfect, to separate what it calls
the beautiful *morality* of Jesus from the gospel theology of
atonement, so offensive to the wisdom of this world. It is but
a gospel of Jesus with the part of Jesus omitted. For it is
the theology of Jesus, the atoning sacrifice, which imparts all
its vitality to the morality of Jesus as a law to the conscience.
Deism may indeed carve out of the gospel a beautiful ethical
system ; but when the work is done, it stands forth only as
the marble smitten by the chisel of genius into the beautiful

form of the living being, cold and lifeless as beautiful! Unitarianism may carve out of the oracles of God an elegant structure of natural religion ; but when the work is done, it stands forth a merely beautifully carved earthen vessel to contain the living waters; but, with no atoning sacrifice of Christ, there is no water of life for the thirsty soul therein.

"The water of life," therefore, which this gospel of Jesus ascended proclaims, as now accessible to all, means that provision for the everlasting life secured in the obedience and atoning sacrifice of Christ for sinners. It is here as elsewhere a generalizing formula, expressive of that scheme of grace, which, contemplating man as fallen from the lofty estate of holiness, conscious of guilt, and spiritually impotent, provides for taking away the guilt, clothing the sinner in a righteousness wrought out for him, and renewing and restoring his nature by divine power.

II. Accordingly, the wants of the soul for which the gospel provides are expressed by the term which forms the second subject of our inquiry, the correlative figure " *Athirst* "— " let him that is athirst come." It is peculiar to the gospel, in all its forms of revelation, that it assumes the existence, more or less conscious, in the human soul, of wants for which it makes provision ; of disease for which it provides a remedy ; of a guilty conscience for which it provides peace ; of spiritual hunger for which it gives the bread of life ; of a thirst in the soul for which it is the water of life. And on whatever other evidences of its divine origin the learned and philosophical may rest their faith in it as divine, the great practical evidence on which the gospel itself rests its claim to be divine, is that it meets the conscious wants of the human soul—an argument which the ignorant and the learned can alike comprehend. The greater part of those truths which constitute natural religion—as the existence of God, the immortality of the soul—are assumed by the gospel to be already known

and felt to be true by every man ; and therefore are assumed
as the basis of its offers, rather than made the subjects of
demonstration by proof and reasoning. Assuming that every
man in earnest must feel that there is a God, the judge and
the rewarder of every man according to his works; that the
soul shall continue to exist, and that there must follow a
retribution for the sins of the present life ; that the moral
nature of man is diseased and its powers enfeebled—the
gospel proposes to expound the attributes of God, and his
relations to the sinner ; to unfold the causes of the soul's disease, and the terrors of conscience ; and to point out the
infallible remedy both for the guilt, and the helplessness of
man.   In other words to provide a water of life for the soul,
of which " he that drinketh shall never thirst, but it shall be
in him a well of water springing up unto everlasting life."

Nor should we limit this thirst of the soul, in our conceptions of it, to that special state of conviction by the Holy
Spirit which makes men willing in the effectual call to salvation ; though indeed, that is the only " thirst " which ever
truly leads man to the water of life.   In a very important
sense this thirst may be said to belong to humanity at large,
and evinces itself in impulses of the natural man under the
ordinary movements of the Spirit. As there is a sense in
which the interposition of Jesus, the Saviour, affects the
whole race, and a sense in which, as the consequence of his
interposition, the Holy Ghost moves upon humanity at large
preventing the utter extinction of its spiritual faculties, and
thereby its utter degradation to a brutal devilishness as the
result of its subjugation by Satan and the fall :   So there is a
general sense, in which all men " thirst," for some such
" water of life," as the gospel provides.   Dr. Trench, in his
Hulsean Lectures on " Christ, the desire of all nations," has
illustrated with great force and learning, how humanity, in
all ages anterior to the incarnation, evinced this longing for

some such provision as the gospel makes for its moral and spiritual necessities, in the incarnation, death, and ascension of Jesus. How all its mythologies, all its sacrificial ritual, all its æsthetic culture, all its philosophic speculations, were but so many unconscious prophecies and longings of humanity for a divine-human prophet, priest and king. And I need only remind you how the objects of heathen worship were ever either gods made men, or men made gods ; thereby signifying their conception that the relief of humanity must come from some junction of the divine with the human nature. How their Hercules and Orpheus stories, and many stories of their class hint at their conception that their deliverer must somehow vanquish death and the grave, the great enemy of the race. How their sacrificial altars, even flowing with blood to expiate sin, and appease the wrath of offended divinity, evinced their conception of the substituting for the forfeited life of the offender, the " life which is in the blood " of the victim. How their most beautiful conceptions of the genius of sculpture were the results of efforts to set forth divine beings in the form of humanity. How the loftiest conceptions of their philosophy were in the efforts to devise some power which should elevate and restore from their feebleness the moral and spiritual powers which they recognized in human nature. What are all these but so many utterances of that inward *thirst* of the general spirit of humanity for something analogous to that which the gospel provides ?

Indeed we might at once illustrate and demonstrate the co-relation between the gospel doctrines and the necessities of human nature from the modern speculative philosophy no less than the ancient, as related to the revealed theology. For so intimate will be found the logical relation, that false systems of theology uniformly lead to false theories of the philosophy of human nature ; and false philosophies of human nature lead, more or less immediately, to false systems of theology

The modern neologists have seized upon this general correspondence between the gospel and the longings of humanity in all ages, as evinced in its mythologies and sacrificial rituals, as a point of assault upon the gospel's claim to have had a higher than human origin. With elaborate learning they have gathered and analyzed the poetic myths of the religions of all countries and ages, to show us how these conceptions of a divine-human deliverer, of an atonement for sin, of a victory over death, and of a renewal and restoration of human nature, have ever flitted as shadows before the imagination, or have been dreamed as beautiful dreams by the poetic souls of the world in all ages. Therefore, say they, the gospel of Christ is only a step in advance, a condensation of the shadows into more definite shape. Now we admit the premise of fact, but reason to precisely the opposite conclusion that instead of being a shadow, because the soul thirst of the world had created shadows before, this must be the reality and the substance which cast the shadows. For the shadow cannot exist without the substance to cause it. And as, when looking down into the smooth waters of the lake ⁻⁻ see, far below, the trees, and green meadow, and flocks feeding upon it, we infer, without looking up for the proof, that though all we see is shadow, yet the shadow is there because the reality is above ; so when we contemplate these shadows reflected to the vision of the human soul, during all time, we infer that some reality, somewhere causes the shadows to exist ; and when now we find, in this revelation of Jesus, the counterpart of all these shadowy conceptions, as great facts, substantially existing, we naturally conclude that the existence of such facts has caused the shadows.

A story of our early colonial times in America illustrates our argument. It is the story of the pilgrim colonists still dependent on the mother country for their food, reduced, by the long delay of the supply vessel, to the very verge of starvation. Day after day, we are told, they stood on the beach straining their eyes in vain; and night after night, prayed in agony for its coming. Till one evening, as they gazed, behold, far out at sea, they discovered the image of a vessel, just such as they expected, painted far off on the eastern sky, though no ship was within their horizon. They received it as a token from heaven in answer to their prayer, sent that their faith might not fail; and in a day or two, the long wished-for vessel, just such in appearance as the image on the sky, came, bringing them relief. The simple-minded colonists devoutly believed that, supernaturally, God had given them a sign to cheer their desponding faith. But as discoveries in the science of optics advanced, the philosophers found an explanation of the image of the ship on the sky, in the laws of refraction, by which, in certain conditions of atmosphere, images of real objects by the refraction of the sun's rays may be cast in the air, and thereby become visible, even when the object itself is below the horizon. And now the pilgrim story became a subject of dispute—some still holding that the vision of the ship was a supernatural answer to their prayers; others that it was a creation of their imagination under the terrible excitement of famine; others that it was but the operation of ordinary natural law. But a few summers since, the question received a solution that left little room for debate. The crowd of visitors on the beach at a celebrated sea-bathing resort, looking out to sea, beheld on the sky an image so distinct that they recognised it as the steamer " Asia," from Europe, not yet due by two days. And by means of the telegraph, the whole continent was informed of the phenomena, so that the people everywhere might note for themselves whether the coming of that particular vessel would verify the prophetic shadow. And sure enough, at the expected time, the " Asia " came. From the real object, far below the horizon, the sun had painted the beautiful image on the sky. Now, in like manner, we argue it was neither a supernatural revelation from their gods, nor a mere delusion of excited imagination which caused this vision of the deliverer of humanity in the souls most conscious of the soul-thirst among the heathen. It was the shadow projected on the soul's horizon by the real object yet far below its horizon of vision. It was the gospel "Asia" coming in, freighted with the bread of life and the water of life for famishing spirits.

The gospel of Jesus Christ claims indeed to be the " great mystery of godliness, God manifest in the flesh," and to be foolishness to the wisdom of this world. Yet it by no means claims to be out of analogy with all that men had ever thought or felt before. On the contrary, it glories in bringing out to the clear light of day the mysterious truth which the spiritual nature of man suggested to him dark hints of the existence of. It represents all creation as groaning and travailing in pain till now; and Jesus Christ as the stiller of creation's groans, himself at once the Eternal Son of God, and the leader of humanity in its final march to victory, and the realization of its unspeakable desires. The vision of the world's dream has in him its waking reality. The shadows and shifting cloud palaces that floated on the world's spiritual sky became, through Jesus Christ, the real city of God. Jerusalem come down out of heaven, and standing stable on earth. The ladder of the world's night visions, reaching from earth to heaven, with superhuman beings, gods many and demigods many ascending and descending upon it, is realized in the coming forth of Jesus from the bosom of the Father to declare him, and through him the ascending and descending of " ministering spirits, sent forth to minister to them which are heirs of salvation."

Hence the ineffable folly and effrontery of these trans-cendental sophists who, affecting to regard all historical and external religion as a clog upon the lofty devotional flights of its spiritual insight, say to us, " Destroy this temple, and in three days we will raise it up," a far more gorgeous spiritual temple for the worship of the soul, in which shall be celebrated the rites of the absolute and universal religion. What is their proposition in effect but to ask us to turn away from the fountain of living water, and, with the heathen, struggle to quench the thirst of the famishing soul at the shadowy rivers and lakes which have ever been projected to the view of thirsty men upon the spiritual horizon of humanity, from the reality of lying far out of sight.

I have extended these illustrations rather for the sake of impressing a great general truth too much overlooked, than because I take the primary or chief reference of this " thirst " in the gospel of Jesus, ascended to be the general want, felt by humanity at large, of something analogous to the provisions of the gospel. And because, also, with this general truth in mind, we can the more readily appreciate the force and beauty of the figure " athirst " as applied to that state of the individual soul to which special reference is had in the saying " Let him that is athirst come."

III. This leads to our third proposed inquiry, into the causes which develop this consciousness of thirst in the individual soul to which reference is here specially made. These are natural and supernatural.

A first natural cause tending to such a result is the consciousness, in every intelligent spirit; of instincts that fail to be met by corresponding provisions in the nature of the life that now is ; and of powers of action and tendencies to action which have no theatre wide enough in the present life, for their proper development. Every man who reflects at all on his inner nature discovers in himself a singular paradox—the powers of a giant fettered within the limits of a cradle ; passions that find no corresponding objects in life, upon which to expend their energies, ideals of heroic life that he can never actualize. Hence the restlessness of the human spirit, never content with the attained but ever gazing forward and eagerly grasping at the unattained. Hence the peculiar tendency of man, above all other animals, to excessive indulgence of the merely sensual appetites. It is simply the attempt to feed the hungry soul, " on the husks that the swine do eat ;" to satisfy that spirit with "bread alone," which was made to feed upon "every word that proceedeth out of the mouth of God." And even among the few who rise above these grosser conceptions, and grasp after fame, as men of wealth, of learning, or of high position—there is in the end always the same disappointment.

After a life spent in pressing along the crowded and dusty avenues to wealth, honour and fame, the poor cheated spirit must sit down and review life with discontent and disappointment. The whole of it—even at the best estate—is now seen to be but the repetition, over and over again, of the delusion of childhood, when he ran eagerly in chase of the end of the beautiful rainbow that stood in the meadow, to find the pot of gold, which the faith of the nursery always held to be buried there. Or, in case the passions have been specially called into play, in the pursuits of life, then the review of it is rather analogous to that of the poor famishing emigrant, rushing, all day long, over the hot sands and under the burning sun of the Sierra Nevada desert, in desperate chase after the cool streams and refreshing shades which the treacherous miasma has created on the horizon before him ; only to find himself at last deluded, and nothing left him but to lie down on the burning sands and die. Hence to the more reflective of men there must ever be some sort of consciousness of this " thirst" instinctively in the soul.

On the back of this negative comes in, oft times, the positive cause of deep sorrow, affliction, and disappointment to excite this thirst—for such is the ordinary lot of human life. And it is ever the tendency of sorrow that darkens the soul to awaken instinctive impressions of guilt, and of wrong done, that has caused God to send the affliction. There comes also the suspicion of the treacherousness of these promises of satisfaction which the world has been holding out, and of the risk that at any moment *all* may be swept away and the spirit beggared, and for the time the thirst burns in the soul.

On the back of these again come those impulses of the natural conscience, which, though ordinarily it may sleep, is often aroused by the fall into some unusual sin, or the coming in of some unusual sorrow. It alarms the fears, by suggesting retribution in store, and an angry God who sees the sin with special displeasure.

But over and above these natural causes come the movings of the Holy Spirit whose office it is to convince of sin. And especially, in the case of those who are brought within the reach of that word, which is the sword of the Spirit,—do the great truths of the gospel sometimes take fast hold of the conscience. Even in these cases, it may prove to be those ordinary movements of the spirit of God, whereby the natural conscience is excited to action, and the spiritual nature within kept from being utterly crushed. But in other cases the mere, " sorrow of the world that worketh death," becomes the true, " godly sorrow that leadeth to repentance." Then begins a longing for deliverance from sin, which cries out— " as the hart panteth for the water brooks, so panteth my soul after thee, oh God ; my soul longeth, yea thirsteth for God."

Now, while this gospel according to Jesus ascended, extends to all these cases, yet it has specially in view this last case of the earnest soul, under the movings of the Spirit, thus " thirsting" for that which will relieve its thirst.

IV. And on what terms now may such have relief ? On. no other than simply to take it, " freely !" " Freely" is the.

answer of the gospel of Jesus ascended. As I have shown you before—even after putting the offer in terms so wide as to say, " let him that is athirst come"—the compassionate Saviour, as the last words that shall ring from heaven in the sinner's ears through all our dispensation, proclaims still more absolutely, " *whosoever will,* let him take the water of life freely." No matter who he be, no matter how great his guilt, no matter how depraved his nature, no matter how dark and damning the stain of sin upon his soul! Brethren, I have shown you in a former discourse, how all the expressions of the terms of salvation in the gospel of Jesus incarnate and of his Apostles, whether literal or figurative, when reduced to their last analysis amount to this, that whosoever will may come. And now we have in the last gospel of all—the gospel of Jesus ascended—and the last of that gospel, the direct confirmation of that argument. The climax of all the gospels preached from Abel to Abraham, and from Abraham to David, and from David to Jesus Incarnate, and from Jesus Incarnate to the last of his Apostles—the climax of all, the key'to all, and the final development of all is this—" whosoever WILL, let him take of the waters of life FREELY. Surely this is enough—nor can human thought conceive er human language utter any offer freer than that! But the compassion of Christ for lost sinners is not exhausted with the throwing open the fountain of life and saying, " whosoever will let him take freely.". Had it been left thus, no sinner would have been saved. He hath devised a system of agencies to " draw all men unto him," as he is thus " lifted up," and the fountain of life opened.

V. What are these agencies? They are, again, both natural and supernatural. In the first place, availing himself of the power of human sympathy, he constitutes every sinner " that heareth," and thereby quenches his own thirst, a missionary to tell others also to come. The very act whereby he is created anew, awakens in him the desire, " O that all would believe." So that surrounding every sinner wherever this gospel has been preached, there are those who can testify by experience to its efficiency, as a means of quenching the " thirst." Is there not reason to fear, brethren, that this agency of personal effort is not employed as extensively as, under the terms of this gospel, it would seem to be authorized and enjoined? Is there not too much timidity, on the part of many who have truly heard, about permitting the natural impulses of the new life to have defer course in uttering the invitation—" Come ?"

In the next place, the results of this scheme of salvation are organized by Christ into a great body, whose chief function it is, to extend the invitation. The Church of God, the bride of the Lamb, saith " Come." This is the sum and substance of all her ordinances.

The one grand mission of the Church on earth, is to hold forth this water of life in the view of perishing sinners, and cry " Come." And, organized as this peculiar body is of " the families that call on the name of the Lord," many of you find your life so woven into the web of other lives about you, that every holy tie which binds you to earth, is a cord about you to draw you to the fountain of life. Not only the voice of the venerated pastor of your youth, in the word, sacraments and prayer, a voice of authoritative invitation, but the voice of personal affection—of Sabbath teacher, friend, father, mother, wife, sister, brother, child, are all to you voices of special and perpetual invitation.

And if fretted by the importunity of the voices from the bride on earth you seek to retire within yourself—then, in your deepest solitude, comes the voice of the bride, as the redeemed Church in heaven. For a thousand holy memories and associations so connect you with the departed of the Church in heaven, that voices of personal invitation whisper thence to your spirit also. It may be the whisper of the venerated father, now at rest from his toils, gently chiding you, as he used kindly to chide your folly, saying, ' Why forsake the fountain of living waters for broken cisterns that can hold no water?'' Perhaps it is the soft mother's voice that so fascinated the ear of your childhood with her cradle song of Jesus, that now seems to awake with the familiar strain:

> "Delay not! Delay not! O loved one, draw near;
> The waters of life are still flowing for thee;"

Thou doating father—perhaps it is the voice of the cherub boy whose Sabbath school choral once so charmed thee, now singing to soothe and comfort thee:

> "Jesus the Saviour in mercy said 'come!
> Joyfully, Joyfully haste to thy home!'
> Death with his arrow indeed laid me low.
> But, safely with Jesus, I feel not the blow.
> Jesus hath broken the bars of the tomb,
> Joyfully, Joyfully, I have got home."

Thou sad sister—perhaps it is the noble brother whose sun went down ere yet it was noon, and who, wrapping himself in the robe of his manly beauty, lay down to sleep in Jesus—that now beckons thee to come and "take of the water of life," that thou mayest walk with him on the banks of the river of life. Or thou brother—it may be that sister, who parted with thee at the river of death, waving back so cheerfully her farewells, that is now waving the invitations from the river of life!

Thou weeping Rachel—it may be the little one for whom thou art refusing to be comforted, that from that glorious kingdom of Heaven stretches its eager hands, with the immortal smile upon its countenance calling to thee "Come! mother, come! Come, learn the love of Jesus who took me from your arms to his own; come up here where they never die any more, and never cry any more. Come! just taste this

water of life, for they who taste it never thirst any more!"
Yes, the bride saith come! on earth and in heaven alike!
Yet, alas! such is the power of sin in the soul—even in the
thirsty soul—that all these eloquent voices of invitation are
unavailing in themselves! But the same love which opened
the fountain of life hath provided an agency of persuasive
power enough to " make them willing in the day of his power."
For, in addition to these natural agencies, " THE SPIRIT SAITH
COME."

Brethren, having no space now left for any adequate development of the great gospel doctrine of the work of the Holy
Spirit, in persuading and enabling sinners to embrace Jesus
Christ, offered here as the water of life so freely, I may with
a single explanatory remark, appeal simply to your own
experience, for the testimony to the reality of this, as of the
natural agencies moving sinners to accept the offer. The
teaching of the gospel is that, while the work of the Holy
Spirit is supernatural, in opening the blind eyes and renewing
the will, and persuading the soul to willingness, he yet, ordinarily, operates through the natural avenues of approach to the
soul. " Behold," saith he, " I stand at the door and
knock." He makes use of the usual method of gaining
admittance, operating in and through the agencies already
described. Hath he not, therefore, often said to you
" Come?" In those deep and solemn impressions which the
truth hath made ofttimes—in that impulse, that led you to
resolve to accept the offer—in those solemn providences,
which so much impressed you—in those movings of conscience, charging you with sin—in those uneasy longings
for something better, and that dissatisfaction with yourself—
It was the Spirit saying " Come." O heed the voice and
grieve Him not away!

APPENDIX.

NOTE A TO DISCOURSE III.

THE SCRIPTURE ARGUMENT FOR THE SABBATH.

The recent mournful defection in the Church of Scotland, to thoroughly rationalistic views of the obligation of the Mosaic law in general, and its law of the Sabbath in particular, having occurred since the discourse on the Gospel Covenant and worship of the lost Eden was written; and having awakened a fresh interest in the discussion of the Sabbath question, the Author presumes that it may not be unacceptable to his readers, if he shall append to this paragraph touching the Eden Sabbath, at least a reference to some views in this volume which seem singularly to have anticipated the new ground upon which Dr. Macleod proposes to void the authority of the Fourth Commandment in the Christian Church, viz., the fact that the Sinai revelation was in the nature of a Covenant transaction with Israel, and therefore passed away with the Mosaic dispensation save in so far as its precepts were of universal moral obligation anterior to and independent of the revelation at Sinai.

In Discourse VI., on the Sinai Covenant, will be found the general principles on which he thinks the argument against the Anti-Mosaic Rationalism should be founded. To wit, that the whole Anti-Mosaic theory arises from an entire failure to perceive the nature of the Sinai revelations as a Covenant with the Church of that age, *as representative of the Church in all ages*—as both Moses and the Martyr Stephen assert—prescribing a rule of life to convince of sin, and a ritual to teach how sin is taken away. That nothing enacted by Jehovah Jesus, through Moses, has been repealed any more than what Jesus enacted through Paul; however some concrete forms of the law in its application may fall away, and become obsolete by the progress of ages, and the fuller revelations of redemption. That the reason, therefore, for the comparative silence of the New Testament on the subject of the Sabbath, to which Dr. Candlish refers with so much effect in a recent lecture, is the same as the reason for the silence on the subject of the organization of the Church, and the membership of the children in the Church; namely: That the Church was regarded as already organized, and the children in it under the Covenant with Abraham; and the Sabbath as already established in the Covenant with the Church, at Sinai, as all other precepts of the holy life. Therefore, it devolves on those who deny the Sabbath, to take the labouring oar, and show where it is repealed in the New Testament.

It will be perceived, moreover, that not only the general principles suggested in Discourse VI., but the argument of his whole series of discourses illustrates how the fact of the identity of the visible Church in all ages—and together with the fact of the representative character of Israel at Sinai, who, as Stephen says, "received the lively oracles *to give unto us*" of the Christian dispensation, furnishes the key to the interpretation of the whole scripture as a history of redemption; and therefore Dr. Macleod's device for avoiding the force of the argument from the Fourth Commandment, drives him to the assertion of a principle on which it is impossible to interpret the scriptures in the sense of the symbols of his Church, or indeed in any other than the rationalistic sense.

In the unfortunate controversy among the Protestants of the Reformation, respecting the sacredness and perpetual obligation of the Sabbath, as a Divine ordinance—which controversy may be traced, perhaps, to the almost Antinomian zeal of Luther and Calvin, against even the semblance of Judaical legalism, as well as their just hostility to mere ecclesiastical ordinance, as of authority over the conscience—the British, and after them the American Churches, have generally held the stricter views of the sacredness of the Sabbath, against the laxer views of the Continental Churches.

Yet at the same time, both in Britain and America, a perpetual conflict has been necessary to maintain this stricter view against the combined influence of semi-Popish Churchism, of the type of Laud and the " Book of Sports," immigrant Continental Protestantism, Popery and open Infidelity—all of which unite with the secularism of the masses to overthrow the Christian Sabbath, or at least to pervert it into a mere holiday instead of a day wholly consecrated to the public and private worship of God.

In this struggle too, there is reason to fear that in their zeal to gain the popular verdict, and meet the popular prejudices, as in the Sabbath Mail controversies, and other efforts to gain legislative sanction and protection for the Sabbath—its advocates have based the argument a little too exclusively on grounds of *expediency;* and have sometimes even attempted to enforce their views by doubtful illustrations, to the effect that Providence directly interferes in the ordinary events of life, to reward the obedient and punish the Sabbath-breaker, and thereby appealing to interest, rather than conscience, to demonstrate that Sabbath observance is on the whole *a good speculation.*

No doubt also the true doctrine of the Sabbath, as an article of Christian faith, has been obscured somewhat to the public view, by the zeal for legislative enactment of the Sabbath on grounds that imply some sort of authority in the civil legislature to enact religious laws with pains and penalties. Even in America, where, theoretically, the sphere of the state is wholly political, the leaven of the original Puritan conceptions of the State relative to religion, has led to plying legislatures with theological arguments for the Sabbath. The Sabbath, as an article of Christian doctrine, and as one of the covenant engagements of the Church with her adorable Head, "the Lord of the Sabbath," is one thing; the Sabbath as a public necessity, and enacted by the will of a people permeated with Christian ideas, through their servant the legislature, is quite a different thing. The consequence, here as in all other cases, is that the "confounding things which God hath sundered leadeth to decay of true religion."

It will add another to the instances of good coming out of evil if this new phase of the Sabbath controversy shall lead to a thorough exposition of the theory of the relation of the " Church in the wilderness " to the Christian Church and the obligations of the Sinai Covenant upon the Church of all ages.

NOTE TO DISCOURSE IV.

OF THE PLACE OF THE CHURCH IN THE REVEALED SCHEME OF REDEMPTION; AND THE DOCTRINE OF THE CHURCH AS FUNDAMENTAL IN THE GOSPEL THEOLOGY.

It has occurred to the author that perhaps students, and others accustomed to the closer methods of thinking, into whose hands this volume may fall, would be pleased to have, in a form more elaborate than is suited to popular discourses, a brief statement of his theory of the place of the Church in the scheme of Redemption;—the more especially, as they will discover that the theory of Biblical interpretation, and the method of preaching, exhibited in these discourses, gives prominence to the churchly idea, in our holy religion.

Aside, however, from this special reason for such a statement, it is the profound conviction of the author that among all the sources of our controversies in the Reformed churches, and of the Rationalistic perversions of the gospel, none has been more fruitful than the failure of Protestants to perceive clearly and grasp firmly the great doctrine of the Church as a fundamental truth of the gospel revelation.

It was the observation, perhaps of Kleiforth, whose own views on the subject of the Church diverge very widely from the scriptures, that of the four great branches of sacred science—Theology, the science of God, Anthropology, the science of man as related to God, Soteriology, the science of salvation, and Ecclesiology, the science of the Church—the three first have had their full development in the history of the Church but *the fourth remains to be developed.* That the controversies touching the nature of the Godhead which closed under the labours of Athanasius fully developed Theology; the labours of Augustine against the Pelagians fully developed Anthropology; the labours of Luther and Calvin against Rome, to establish salvation by grace, fully developed Soteriology; thus leaving Ecclesiology still to receive its development in the Protestant Churches. Unfortunately this development has been slow; not because the Reformers did not catch glimpses of this great doctrine also, but because their exposed condition compelled them to take shelter under civil governments which would not permit the full and free development of a doctrine which seemed directly to affect their absolute control over their subjects. The jealousies and divisions growing out of this connection of the churches with civil governments; the popular prejudice against church authority arising out of the terrible abuses of it by the Church of Rome, and the gradual growth of the error that the gospel doctrines may be held and propagated without the gospel Church, have hitherto prevented any progress in this development.

The fundamental error of many of the Protestant theories of the Church lies in overlooking the fact that the doctrine of the Church is a fundamental truth of the gospel, and is entitled to the same sort of consideration as other articles of theology. Nay more, that not only is this doctrine intimately connected with the other articles of Protestant theology, but it enters as an element into all those doctrines, and to a large extent moulds and shapes the scientific statement of them. It will be the purpose of the remarks now submitted, gathered from a previously published tract on this subject now out of print, to illustrate this view of the question.

There is in the minds of many persons, and even students of theology, a prejudice against such reasonings, as too transcendental, and out of the sphere of practical Christian knowledge. But students, at least, should know that by celestial observations alone can safe and practical terrestrial charts be constructed. And while the mariner may, indeed, learn to find his way over the ocean by his chart, as men learn a trade, yet, in order to any true and intelligent guidance by the chart, scientific observations to determine the relations of the Earth to the bodies in the heavens becomes a prime necessity. So it is absolutely necessary in order to any true ecclesiology, to study the relations of this idea of the Church, to those other great ideas which entered into the plan of redemption framed in the councils of eternity.

No student of scripture needs to be told that the Apostles give no ground for this notion of separating practical religious thought from the profounder views of God's method of Redemption. That—in exhibiting the practical truths of the doctrines of grace—they ever look backward to eternity and forward to eternity from the stand of the revelation given through them. As after the method of those immense triangulations of the modern trigonometrical surveys, which, from some known base line measured upon the plain, take observations, forward and backward, of the prominent mountain-tops at immense distances, from which, again, other observations are extended, till the measuring-line of their science is laid, encompassing half the globe, and determining with marvellous accuracy, even to a single inch, the distance :—so these inspired Apostles, assuming as the ground-work of their argument that which they now see and hear under the outpouring of the Spirit, from this direct their vision back to the prominent facts in the past dispensations of God, and onward to the prominent heights of the prophetic views of the dispensations yet to come ; and from these in turn they determine new points of the argument. With a logic at once sublime in its reach and infinite in its comprehension, they determine the measure, the proportions, and the relations of that transcendent problem of man's salvation, which has its primary elements in the depths of eternity past, and its conclusion in the depths of eternity to come.

So in every department of revealed knowledge, they alone shall succeed in obtaining adequate conceptions of the significancy of the several parts thereof, and the highest practical knowledge of the whole, who, under the guidance of the Holy Spirit, shall have studied the "pattern in the heavens," as it existed in the mind of the Infinite Author of salvation.

Since the Reformation, four chief theories, and these inclusive of all other theories of revealed theology, have had currency in Christendom,— the Papal, the Zuinglian, the Lutheran, and the Calvinistic. Of these the first named is the original error against which the last three may be regarded as successive forms of just protest. All three of these protests are true in their general idea intrinsically, and successful in developing the chief truths of the gospel, but with widely different degrees of clearness and completeness, and with still more widely-different degrees of success in preserving pure and incorrupt the doctrines of grace. Recurring again to the analogy just employed, these four theories may not unaptly be compared, as to their relative value, with the four different theories of the visible universe which have in different ages had currency in the world. The Papal theory of theology, like the ancient mythological theory of the universe, scarce pretended to have any foundation other than in mere human fancies and its general prevalence among men. And just as the Ptolemaic, the Copernican, and the still more modern theory of the *Mécanique Céleste*, are successive protests against the mere prejudices and dreams of men; yea, just as by each of them the fundamental facts of the *Cosmos* had in some sort their explanation, but with different degrees of consistency, clearness and beauty, so with the three Protestant theories of theology. The Zuinglian, taking as the central principle of its structure the truth that the word of God alone can be any authoritative rule to the conscience, developed from that point a true, in opposition to a counterfeit gospel; yet a gospel too easily perverted by reason of its tendency to exalt the rational man of earth into a centre of the spiritual system, or at least, from its narrowness of view, to obscure the higher truths of the scheme of Redemption. The Lutheran theory, taking as its central principle the justification of the sinner by grace alone, through faith, after the fashion of Copernicus, exhibited Jesus Christ, the Sun of Righteousness, as the real centre, to whom the rational man of earth, with all that concerns him, is attracted, and around whom he revolves. Calvin, whilst perceiving that the central truths of both Zuingle and Luther were indeed great truths, yet, with the still wider vision of La Place and the moderns, beheld not only the rational man revolving around the mediatorial Sun of Righteousness as his true centre, but also that man and his Central Sun revolved again around a still profounder centre, even the Eternal Purpose of God, fixed in the counsels of eternity before the world began. Such, generally, is the relative position to the others of that remarkable theory of theology which, however men have cavilled at, they must be constrained to admit both its singular accordance with the very language, and its logical development and elucidation of all the great facts of revelation.

Of this system of theology the eternal purpose of God is, ideally, the great central truth. All that has transpired under the reign of grace and under the administration of Providence, since the world began, is conceived of as simply the gradual manifestation in time of the purpose formed from eternity.* The revelation which God has made of himself in his word is but the record of the execution of his Eternal Decree, and the publication to the world in time of the proceedings had in the counsels of eternity. The revelation of Himself, experimentally, to the souls of his people is but the manifestation of the love wherewith he loved them before the world began. Every syllable of truth revealed in the scriptures is conceived of as having its significance and its importance determined by its relation to the purpose previously existing in the Divine Mind; so that the doctrine of the Decree and Predestination of God is not so much a doctrine of Calvinism—one distinct truth in a system of truth—as a mode of conceiving and setting forth all the doctrines which make up revealed theology.

Now, pursuing the hint already suggested touching the connection

---

* Eph. i. 4-12, iii. 9-11; Rom. viii. 28-33; John xvii. 2-5.

between the system of theology and the idea of the Church, and taking this theory of Calvin as correct, a sure and reliable central point will be found for the doctrine of the Church, likewise, in the eternal purpose of God. For the fundamental idea of the Church, as a separate and distinct portion of the human race, is found in the peculiar *mode* of that purpose itself. It is set forth as a distinguishing feature of the purpose of redemption, that it is to save not merely myriads of men as *individual men*, but myriads of sinners, as composing a Mediatorial body, of which the Mediator shall be the head ;[*] a Mediatorial Kingdom, whose government shall be upon His shoulder[†] forever ; a Church, the Lamb's Bride, of which He shall be the Husband ;[‡] a bride whose beautiful portrait was graven upon the palms of his hands, and whose walls were continually before him,[§] when in the counsels of eternity he undertook her redemption.

The mission of Messiah, undertaken in the covenant of eternity, was not merely that of a teaching Prophet and an atoning Priest, but of a ruling King as well. His work was not to enunciate simply a doctrine concerning God and man's relations to God, as some Socrates, for the founding of a school ; nor even merely to atone for sinners as a ministering priest at the altar : it was, as the result of all, and the reward of all, to found a *community*, to organize a *government*, and administer therein as a perpetual *king*.

It will be perceived, therefore, that the primary and fundamental conception of the Church of God has its germinal source far back in the purpose of God, and that the Church naturally and necessarily grows out of the very form and mode of the scheme of redemption for sinners, as it lay in the Infinite Mind. As the purpose was to redeem not only elect sinners, but a *body* of elect sinners,—an organic body with all its parts related to each other, and the Mediator himself the head thereof,—it is manifest that in that purpose is involved ideally the Church as an elect portion of the race under the Headship of the Messiah, and distinct from another and reprobate portion of the human family.

The elementary conception of the Church, therefore, and that conception of it which must be presupposed and enter into every definition of the Church, is of that elect body of men which was contemplated in the covenant of redemption, as constituting the mediatorial kingdom of Christ, and for the sake of which body he undertook the work of salvation. Other elements, as we shall see, must necessarily enter into the definition as this *ideal* of the purpose of God becomes *actual* in the external manifestation of the purpose in time ; but this element must obviously be found involved in any and every form which the notion of the Church, as actual and external, can take. In this view of the case is found the reason for the fact that a Calvinistic theology cannot long retain its integrity and

---

[*] Col. i. 18-20.   [†] Isa. ix. 6, 7.   [‡] Eph. v. 20.   [§] Isa. xlix. 16.

purity save in connection with a Calvinistic ecclesiology, and for the more general fact, already referred to, of the intimate connection between a wrong theology and wrong views of the Church.

As the general ideal purpose of God becomes actual and revealed in time, so every part of the purpose has its corresponding actual external manifestation. The Mediator of the ideal eternal covenant becomes the Jehovah, in various forms manifesting himself to men; the Angel of the covenant, not only the ideal covenant of redemption, but of the actual covenant of grace, in its successive renewals and various forms; the King of Zion; the Word, speaking "at sundry times and in divers manners to the fathers," and in the last time becoming incarnate to finish the atonement for sin; the ascended Son of Man, that hath the seven Spirits of God, to send forth the Holy Spirit, in his place, to carry on the work of redemption on earth till he shall return a second time in glory.

So in like manner the ideal *eklektoi* of the covenant of redemption become the actual *kletoi* (called ones) of the manifested purpose in time. Inasmuch as they are called by an external *klesis* of the word, they are gathered in successive generations to constitute the external *ekklesia* on earth. In as far as they are called also by the internal *klesis* of the Spirit, they are gathered to constitute the invisible *ekklesia*, the full and complete actual of the eternal ideal. For whilst, indeed, the effectual call of the Spirit can alone fulfil the promise of the eternal covenant to Messiah, yet, as that call is externally through the word and the visible ordinances, the very process of calling and preparing the elect of God creates the visible Church in the very image of the invisible. And it is in this visible body that the Mediator carries on his administration, works by his Spirit, gives laws and ordinances for the present, and exceeding great and precious promises of that which is to come; and through this body carries on his purposes of mercy toward a world lying in wickedness.

This statement concerning the actual and visible Church as the development of the ideal elect body of the covenant of redemption is by no means exclusive of all other aspects of the Church in the gospel scheme. The visible Church is an important, if not a necessary, means of revealing to men the whole counsel of God; and, for aught we know, such is the constitution of the human mind that by no other method could have been communicated to human intelligence that peculiar feature of the purpose of God which contemplates the redeemed not as individuals merely, but as the mediatorial body of the Redeemer. In another view, the Church is an indispensable means of accomplishing the great purpose of his love to his chosen people, as an institute for the calling, training, and edifying the elect. What is intended in the foregoing view is to exhibit the external Church in time as, primarily in the logical order of thought, the development of the ideal body of the covenant of redemption. Contemplated as a part of the process of manifesting to men the purpose of God to gather an elect people, the Church is a means through which God makes known his counsel. Contemplated as to its immediate end, the Church is a divinely appointed institute, by which and through which to accomplish his purpose in his calling and edification of his elect. But both these views, however important and essential, are, logically speaking, secondary and incidental to the idea of the Church—a Church on earth, as the development of his Church ideal—" the pattern in the heavens."

It is a marked peculiarity of the Abrahamic covenant that it brings into view the Church visible, not simply as the external manifestation and development of the ideal mediatorial body of the Redeemer in the eternal covenant, but at the same time, also, as an actual institute for the calling and training of the elect people of God. From this time forward, through the entire revelation, the visible Church is exhibited as a body externally called to the privilege of receiving the oracles of God, and of being specially under the charge of Jehovah as his peculiar nation, the special beneficiary of his promises, and enjoying the special agency of his Holy Spirit. It is no longer limited in extent of numbers to the true κλητοί,—the called internally by the Spirit according to the eternal purpose,—but also to the called [κλητοί] who are externally called by the word only. Now, as several times intimated in these discourses, and assumed as the ground, of their arguments and expositions, every revelation ever communicated, every ordinance appointed, every promise and covenant made of God, has been, not to and with men as men, or as constituting nations, but to and with the Church, as such,—a body organized or contemplated as the elements of an organization. In the widest sense, to the ancient Church were committed the oracles of God. The successive revelations come not from God as Creator to men as creatures, but from Messiah as Prophet and King over his Church to his own peculiar people. The revelations of Sinai are expressly declared to have been made to the covenant-people; and when Moses wrote the words of the Lord in the book, they were formally ratified as the covenant between God and the Church. After Moses, all additional records of inspiration are given to the Church as the depository of the Oracles of God. Here, as in all other points, Rome does not invent pure falsehood, but only counterfeits the truth. The Church is in truth *anterior* to the Scriptures, the receiver of the Scripture, the guardian of the Scripture. Rome adroitly perverts all this to mean that the Church is *superior* to Scripture, the maker of Scripture, the infallible interpreter of Scripture. Less monstrous indeed, but not less deceptive, is the Rationalistic assumption that the idea of the Church is something extraneous to the Scripture,—having no other relation than that of an expedient or even a necessity superinduced upon the Scripture, simply by the outworking of a system of revelation made to the world of men at large, and when received by any portion thereof, attracting them together to constitute a School of Religious Philosophy.

From the foregoing views of the relation of the idea of the Church, first to the plan of Redemption in the Purpose of God, and secondly to the record of the manifestation of the Purpose of God in time, we derive these general observations concerning the idea and nature of the Church.

1. The primary and germinal idea of the Church of God is of that elect body of men which was contemplated in the covenant of Redemption as constituting a mediatorial body, of which Messiah is the Head, and for the sake of which he undertook the work of Redemption.

2. It being an essential feature of the Plan of Redemption that the purpose of God have its manifestation through successive ages of time, and its accomplishment through external instrumentalities, even the call (κλῆσις) of the word, providing the instrumentality through which shall be made the call (κλῆσις) of the Spirit,—together with the other external ordinances for the edifying and training of an elect people in external convenant-relation to the Mediator,—the very outworking of the purpose of God in time brings into existence an actual external (εκκλησία),—a called out and separated body of men, corresponding to the ideal of God's Purpose.

3. In accordance with this relation between the ideal and the actual, the Purpose of God is revealed by means of convenants, as between the Mediator and a separated portion of the race; and in particular one covenant, as a charter, specially and formally organizing into a community the portion of the race to which the Mediator shall specially reveal himself and give the oracles and ordinances through which he will execute his mission to the race at large, over which he shall exercise spiritual authority as its Founder, Lawgiver, and Head; and in which he will set officers to teach and rule, and by the Holy Spirit as his agent carry on the work of recreating his people.

4. This body visible on earth is perpetual and identical through all ages. It may vary in its degrees of purity, down to utter apostasy; it may have its seat exclusively in one nation and run in the line of natural descent, or it may have its seat alike in all nations and treat as one blood all kindreds of men; it may be now conspicuous before the world, or now humble and comparatively hidden; it may vary as to the degree of Divine knowledge current in it, having now only a partial and now a fully-completed revelation as its rule, and of course, therefore, may vary as to the form of its ordinances and instrumentalities for teaching Divine truth :—but, withal, it is essentially the same body of people, organized for the same purposes, administered in by the same Head and Ruler, and, under him, ministered to by the same sort of ministering servants, having the same sort of duties to discharge, for the attainment of the same great ends. And in this fact, doubtless, is the true solution of the comparative silence of scripture

history touching Church government. There being no organic changes from the first institution of this government, there is no call for any special reference to that subject in the history. The events which constitute the true life and glory of a nation—the natural and healthy development of its organic laws—are not those which find a place in history, but rather the events which destroy and disorganize. Hence the saying of men, "Blessed the nation whose annals are tiresome." But the Divine history records no tiresome annals merely to fill out in rhetorical proportion the history of a given space of time. In this history *Silence* takes the place of the tiresome annals of other history. Hence the silence concerning the external constitution of the kingdom whose history it records is simply expressive of the continued sameness of external government through all its progressive development.

5. The idea of the Church being thus a complex idea, the proper definition of the Church must not only enumerate the essential elementary ideas that enter into the complex whole, but also make such an enumeration as shall arrange in logical order these several elements according to their relative position and prominence each to the other. From the foregoing views, the definition of the Church—as simply a fact of revealed theology—should describe it as that body of men, taken as a whole or any part thereof, which, according to God's eternal purpose to call out and organize a part of mankind into a kingdom, is called successively in time by his word and Spirit to a confession of Christ, an engagement to his covenant, and subjection to the laws of his kingdom. This general description, however, while comprehending all the elementary ideas, must have certain modifications, according as one or another aspect of the Church is prominent in the mind. But these modifications can only change the relative prominence of the several elements one to the other, neither adding any element, nor taking any away. Thus, in defining the Church as actual and visible, the constituent elements of the Church are persons not only as individuals, but also as representing families, according to the general principles of all the covenants of God. So in defining the Church in greater or less extent by corresponding modifications, according as the mind has prominent before it the whole or the part, the definition of it embraces, according to scripture usage, any variety of extent. As it is gravitation—involving the same general idea—whether as embodied in the phenomenon of the apple falling from the tree in the sight of the philosopher, or in that of the earth retained in its orbit; so, by reason of its connection with the great ideal, it is the Church of God, whether it be the Society in the house of Priscilla, the Church of the Saints at Philippi, the Church of many congregations and languages at Jerusalem or Antioch, the Church at large which suffered persecution, the General Assembly and Church of the First-born whose names are written in heaven, or the ideal Church of the Pur-

pose of Redemption,—which Christ loved before the world began, and for
which he gave himself in the Eternal Covenant.

Such accordingly is the definition of the Church, as a point of Calvinistic
doctrine, in the Westminster Confession. The entire article forms one
definition, containing, in their logical order, the three elementary ideas
which enter into the complex whole, in three distinct paragraphs: first,
the Church ideal, or invisible; second, this ideal as manifest and actual in
the Church visible; third, this visible body as an organic body, receiving
visible officers, laws, and ordinances from her great Head.

Any definition of the Church, therefore, is doctrinally defective, which
ignores either of these elements, the internal call ($\kappa\lambda\tilde{\eta}\sigma\iota\varsigma$) of the Spirit, the
external *klesis* of the word, or the organic nature of the *ekklesia*. As with
the peculiar ordinances of the Church,—Baptism and the Lord's Supper,—
the three elements of the internal grace, the external act, and the Divine
appointment thereof are all essential to the true definition,—and that is
ever a dangerous description which ignores either of the three; so with the
definition of the Church itself, and for precisely like reasons. And hence,
as a matter of fact, defective conceptions of the Church and of the sacraments
go ever hand in hand. When the Church is conceived of only as external
and organized, to the exclusion of the internal element of its structure,
then the sacraments become merely external rites, and the administrator
the authoritative dispenser of grace through them. When, on the other
hand, the Church is conceived of as wholly an internal thing as to its
essential nature, then the tendency is ever to conceive of the sacraments,
in their external character, as simply appropriate and suggestive cere-
monies, representing internal acts of the soul merely, rather than as the
means of grace to the soul; and the administrator of the sacraments, not
so much God's authorized minister, as one chosen by the company to
preside merely in the performance of a solemn ceremony. So of any
other defective view of the Church. The entire system of the gospel has
in truth all its parts so related, that error in regard to any one part must
in some form affect every other part. Considering that the gospel hath
sprung from an infinitely perfect Mind, it cannot be otherwise.

The importance of the foregoing views, in order to the practical exposition of the scripture, either devotional or practical, in the Church, will be
manifest. In fact, one of the chief causes of the confused and conflicting
interpretations of many portions of the word of God arises from the previous want of a decision of the question whether there be a Church at all.
With the advantage of this vagueness as to the general subject concerning
which the appeal is made to scripture, it is obviously impossible to settle,
from the mere words of the scriptures themselves, the true significancy of
their teachings on the subject. Hence errorists, though pretending to
appeal to the scriptures, may give illimitable range to the imagination,

and, being free to give any one of all possible meanings to the words of the sacred record, thereby deprive them of any real significance. If, however, it has been established previously that a visible Church, in some form or other, is an absolute necessity of the plan of redemption as revealed in the scriptures, demanded by the nature of the plan itself; presupposed by the very mode of revealing the plan ; essential as a means of communicating one of its fundamental facts to the world, and not less essential as a means of accomplishing the divine purpose; required as a key to the interpretation of the Sacred History, the prophetic expositions of the doctrine of Messiah, and the apostolic teachings concerning his kingly office ; then there are limits fixed within which the language of prophets, evangelists and apostles, concerning the Church and its ordinances, is to have its interpretation, and which fix the meaning thereof with remarkable accuracy.

Having obtained this general conception of the Church, we assume this as a positive standard, and turn now on the other hand to consider the relation to this idea of the Church of the more important and obvious of the abstract principles which underlie the structure of this peculiar body, the Church visible—the great government not reckoned among the nations. These may be considered as relating to four general points—the source of the Spiritual power—the delegation and vesting of the power—the mode of exercising it—and the distinctions and limits of this ecclesiastical power, and that secular power which also God has ordained to the civil magistrate.

1. The source of all Church power is primarily Jesus Christ, the Mediator. As this is manifest from all that has gone before touching the nature and idea of the Church, so also it is manifest from the most explicit declarations of every scripture relating to the subject. Anterior to his coming in the flesh, as Jehovah he administered through prophets, priests, and extraordinary ministers. The preamble to the apostolic commission asserts this power as the foundation of their authority. " *All* power is *given* me, [as Mediator:] go ye, therefore," &c. And, accordingly, all power in the Church is exercised by him and in his name. His apostles teach in the name of Jesus.* In the name of the Lord Jesus the offender is cut off.† His promise to the courts of the Church is to be present when two or three are gathered together *in his name*.‡ And, in like manner, all the prophetical views of his relation to the Church declare in effect the government shall be upon his shoulder.§ Nay, as actually containing in himself, by way of eminency, all the offices of the Church, he is styled the Apostle,‖ the Shepherd,¶ the Chief Shepherd and Bishop,** the Head of the Church.††

---

* Acts iv. 17, 18. † I Cor. v. 4. ‡ Matt. xviii. 20.
§ Isa. ix. 6, 7, 8; Luke i. 32, 33. ‖ Heb. iii. 1.
¶ John x. 11. ** 1 Peter ii. 25.
†† Col. i. 18, and Eph. i. 22.

2. As to the delegation and vesting of this power, it is expressly taught that he hath made such delegation, vesting the power in men. Throughout the Old Testament, such is represented to be the method in which he carried on the administration of his kingdom. Men ruled and administered the ordinances and spake in Jehovah's name. In that civil theocracy, in which he ruled as local king,—set up to be a type and historical prophesy of his fully developed spiritual commonwealth, the New Testament Church—men commissioned by him ruled as judges and kings over the nation, though Jehovah was King. So in the delegation of power under the last dispensation, distinguished as the ministration of the Spirit, to the Apostles he said, " As my Father sent me, even so I send you."

But in neither case, whether under the Old or New Testament dispensation, was this power vested in the prophets, kings, or apostles personally, but as representative men. Not in the office-bearers of the Church, either, as distinct from and irrespective of the people; nor yet in the people contemplated as an aggregation of individuals. In all cases the power is vested in the Church as an organic body, composed of both rulers and ruled. For as God hath *set* the members of the body, so hath he *" set* in the Church, first, apostles, secondly, prophets," &c. In every inspired allusion to the power of rule in the Church, the power is represented as vested in an organic body, as the human body with its several members and their functions.* And as it has been shown before that the idea of the Church from the very first, even in the purpose of redemption, was of an organic body, the reason for this peculiar view of the scripture, as to the vesting of the power is very manifest.

The power vests in the body as such; the administration of the power is in office-bearing members of the body whom the Great Head selects, calls, qualifies, and commissions to rule ministerially in his name. The Holy Ghost makes them overseers. But yet the vocation to the exercise of the office is in the people, who must try the spirits, and judge whether they be men full of faith and of the Holy Ghost. As in the ancient civil theocracy in which Jehovah reigned as local king invisibly, through a visible king as his minister, chosen and commissioned by himself;—though Jehovah's own prophet has formally anointed David king, that call and commission from God did yet not actually constitute David king until, after long years of trouble and darkness, Judah first, and then all Israel, called him to the throne. So in this spiritual kingdom of Christ, though the appointment to office, the qualification and commission, are from him, the true invisible Head of the kingdom, yet the vocation to the actual exercise of the office so conferred is in the people. In this sense of vocation alone, and not in the sense of power delegated by the people to their office-bearers, are they, in

---

* Rom. xii.; 1 Cor. xii.: Eph. iv. 4.

any case, the representatives of the people. If, as has been shown, the idea of the Church, as one great body, is essential in the system of redemption, and if in the body as such are vested the powers of external government, and that in the form of office-bearers provided by the Great Head and given to the Church, to be called to the actual exercise of these functions only by the people, then they are ministers of the Church of God, and hold relations to the whole Church of God which preclude the idea of their being exclusively the representatives of any given part of the people. Hence the parallel between the Church as a spiritual commonwealth and the civil republic is wholly fanciful, or implies a theory of the idea and nature of the Church fundamentally different from that presented in the former part of this discussion.

3. As to the mode in which the power of government shall be exercised, there is this remarkable peculiarity in the view set forth in the Scripture history of every era of the Church,—viz.: that whilst the office-bearers have severally certain functions to discharge, as of teaching, administering sacraments, and oversight, yet all power of jurisdiction is to be exercised only through tribunals. The fundamental and only office of jurisdiction, alike in the Church under all dispensations, is the office of elders, *Presbuteroi*. The title *Episcopos*, occurring not over half a dozen times in the New Testament, seems used only in speaking to or of Gentiles unfamiliar with the ancient ecclesiastical language of the Church, and hence επισκοπος is really nothing more than a Grecian equivalent for the Jewish ecclesiastical term *Presbuteroi*. From the first to the last of the dispensations of God recorded in Scripture, as before shown, the uniform exponent of a government in the Church is the office of the elders, *Presbuteroi;* and if a name of distinction for the Church visible, considered as a form of spiritual government, is to be applied to it, "*Presbyterian*" has been the proper title from the days of Israel in Egypt to the present. Of course we mean this in no offensive denominational sense, but simply as the statement of a philological fact of the scriptures.

Now, taking this title to be expressive of government in the Church, the fact that, uniformly, throughout the Scripture, a plurality of these office-bearers is always indicated, whether referring to their existence in a particular community or Church, or to the exercise of jurisdiction therein, is, in itself, little short of demonstration that their power is exercised only jointly and in tribunals. It is ever the *elders* of a city or Church in any locality, never the *elder;* it is ever the elders who sit in council, who act in the name of the people, who consult together of the things pertaining to the Church. There is not a case that the author is aware of, in all the scriptures in which an ordinary office-bearer ever exercised jurisdiction alone. He acts always as one constituting a member of a tribunal.

And whilst this power is thus limited in the mode of its exercise, it also is limited as to its end, which is wholly spiritual. In full accordance with the idea of a kingdom not of this world, and of the power of men in it as wholly ministerial, is the end for which it is exercised. It is spiritual: it is to gain our brother. It is that the spirit of him against whom this power is exercised may be saved in the day of the Lord Jesus. It is for the edification of his people, and for the Lord's business for the peace and harmony of the Church, for the extension of the Church, and for Jehovah's glory.

4. Touching the distinction between the power ecclesiastical and the civil power,—which latter is ordained by God also,—the points of contrast are so numerous and so fundamental that nothing but the confusion of mind arising from the oppression of Cæsar, and Antichrist backed by the power of Cæsar could ever have caused the obscurity and inconsistency of the Church's testimony in modern times. For they have nothing in common except that both powers are of divine authority, both concern the race of mankind, and both were instituted for the glory of God as a final end. In respect to all else—their origin, nature and immediate end, and in their mode of exercising the power,—they differ fundamentally. Thus, they differ :—

(1.) In that the civil power derives its authority from God as the Author of nature, whilst the power ecclesiastical comes alone from Jesus as Mediator.

(2.) In that the rule for the guidance of the civil power in its exercise is the light of nature and reason, the law which the Author of nature reveals through reason to man; but the rule for the guidance of ecclesiastical power in its exercise is that light which, as Prophet of the Church, Jesus Christ has revealed in his word. It is a government under statute laws already enacted by the King.

(3.) They differ in that the scope and aim of the civil power are limited properly to things seen and temporal; the scope and aim of ecclesiastical power are things unseen and spiritual. *Religious* is a term not predicable of the acts of the State; *political* is a term not predicable of the acts of the Church. The things pertaining to the kingdom of Christ are things concerning which Cæsar can have rightfully no cognizance, except indirectly and incidentally as these things palpably affect the temporal and civil concerns of men; and even then Cæsar cannot be too jealously watched by the Church. The things pertaining to the kingdom of Cæsar are matters of which the Church of Christ, as an organic government, can have no cognizance, except incidentally and remotely as affecting the spiritual interests of men; and even then the Church cannot watch herself too jealously.

(4.) They differ in that the significant symbol of the civil power is the sword; its government is a government of force, a terror to evil-doers; but the significant symbol of Church power is the keys, its government only ministerial, the functions of its officers to open and close and have a care of a house already complete as to its structure externally, and internally organized and provided.

(5.) They differ in that civil power may be exercised as a *several* power by one judge, magistrate, or governor; but all ecclesiastical power pertaining to government is a joint power only, and to be exercised by tribunals. The Head of the government has not seen fit to confer spiritual power of jurisdiction in any form upon a single man, nor authorized the exercise of the functions of rule in the spiritual commonwealth as a several power.

It is unnecessary to digress here into a discussion of the *rationale* of these fundamental distinctions. It would not be difficult to show, however, that they are neither accidental nor arbitrary, but spring out of those fundamental truths concerning the nature of the Church itself, and of its relations to the gospel, which have already been pointed out. These distinctions, therefore, are of a nature to forbid all idea of any concurrent jurisdiction, and to render certain the corruption and final apostasy of any part of the Church which shall persist in the attempt to exist as a governmental power concurrent with the State,—it matters not whether as superior, inferior, or equal. They are the two great powers that be, and are ordained of God to serve two distinct ends in the great scheme devised for man as fallen. The one is set up, in the mercy and forbearance of the Author of nature toward the apostate race at large, to hold in check the outworking of that devilish nature consequent upon the apostasy, and to furnish a platform, as it were, on which to carry on another and more amazing scheme of mercy toward a part of mankind. The other is designed to constitute of the families of earth that call upon his name, and into the hearts of which his grace has *put* enmity toward Satan and his seed, a nation of priests, a peculiar nation, not reckoned among the nations, of whom Jehovah is the God and they are his people. That not only the utter disregard of this distinction in the formal union of the Church and State—either merging the Church in the State or the State in the Church —is destructive of the Church, but that, also, any degree of confusion in respect of this distinction is proportionably dangerous and corrupting, the history of the Reformed Churches generally, and in particular of the Church of Scotland, is a most striking illustration. Nay, the entire history of the Church, from its first organization, testifies that his people must render to Cæsar the things that are Cæsar's as distinct from rendering to God the things that are God's, or the Church suffers.

But, it may be proper to add here to prevent misapprehension of the author's views, that the Scriptures, in their teachings concerning spiritual government, go beyond the enumeration of certain abstract truths merely. They set forth with equal clearness the specific forms in which these truths are embodied in the scheme of government appointed for the Church, both in reference to the officers and the courts thereof. As to the offices to be executed in a community whose real ruler is invisible,—Jesus Christ,— whether considered either as acting personally or through the movements of the Holy Ghost the functions are necessarily ministerial only, and are therefore readily determined by the nature and design of the kingdom itself. If, as we have seen, this kingdom is in its nature the outward development and a mode of revealing a purpose to gather an elect body out of the race, and, considered as to its design, is an institute for the calling, gathering, and preparatory training of the elect out of the successive ages of time, then these official functions have reference to developing the purpose and accomplishing this design, and therefore must relate to three things exclusively,—viz.: the call of the elect into communion and keeping up their communion with Christ the Head,—that is the ministry of the ordinances; the preserving the order and harmony of the body,—that is, government and discipline; and the provision for and care of the revenues of the community.

In perfect consistency, therefore, with these views of the nature and design of the Church, and the corresponding functions needful for the ministry of "doctrine, discipline, and distribution," the scriptures exhibit, as the three classes, of divinely appointed officers, first, ministers who both rule and administer the ordinances,—a double office necessarily growing out of the essential connection between the word and the spiritual government founded upon it; second, ministers of rule only, and in spirituals only,—an office arising out of the nature and joint power of the government as, in idea, distinct from the several powers of administering ordinances, both of which unite in the first-named office; third, the minister of temporal things pertaining to the community for the keeping prominent that ordinance of the fellowship through which is expressed the relation of one to another, and of one part to another part of this body, even as the other ordinances and government are expressive of the relation of one and all to the Great Head.

It affects not the substantial correctness of this view of the permanent offices in the Church as growing out of the very nature and design of the Church, and therefore necessarily in substance the same in all ages of the Church, that under the several dispensations recorded in scripture God raised up extraordinary officers at divers times and of divers sorts, as judges, prophets, apostles, &c. Nor does it any more affect this argument and threefold classification of the officers that, under different dispensations, any one of the three offices should have been discharged by two or more persons in the different aspects of it, as when both priest and prophet of the Old Testament discharged in effect the functions of the preacher of the word of the New Testament. For if the offices arise out of the nature and design of the Church, the fundamental element of a proper classification is the function itself, rather than the functionary. During the era of immediate inspiration, such changes of mere form were made by the same great authority which first instituted the office; and, indeed, during the progress of the Church under a progressive and incomplete revelation, such changes must occur, in the nature of the case, with the changes of the forms of the ordinances, according as successive new revelations presented Messiah, the great object of worship, in new aspects. It is only after the revelation is complete and the immediate inspiration withdrawn from the Church that the forms of the ordinances, government, and offices of the Church must thenceforth remain stationary, and just at the point in which the last and highest development of the revelation left them. The limits of this note forbid, and the general familiarity with this branch of the subject renders unnecessary, any argument in detail to show that the last and complete development of the Church under the apostles exhibit, as the three ordinary and permanent officers thereof, elders who rule,* the fundamental office of the Church, as a government, from the first to the last; elders who both rule and labour in word and doctrine;† deacons‡ who represent the fellowship of the members of the Church in each other's gifts, and who have care of its revenues and the necessities of the poor.

As to the courts of the Church, the essential relation of these to the foregoing general views of the idea and nature of the Church is manifest, and, indeed, has already been pointed out in what has been said touching the governmental power in the Church as exercised always jointly and by *tribunals*. But the other principle needs here to be brought into view which also has already been referred to in a preceding part of this discussion as a fundamental peculiarity in the definition of the Church. This is the fact that the oneness of the Church is so absolute by reason of the connection of the visible with the invisible, as the actual development of the ideal, that the definition of the Church is substantially the definition, at the same time, either of the whole or any part thereof. From this it follows, in coming to regard the Church as a governmental power, that the power of the whole is over the power of every part thereof, and also the power of the whole in every part thereof. Hence, therefore, the same power is in every tribunal that is in any tribunal, whilst the power of the greater part is over the power of the smaller part. As it is, the Church of God, whether considered as the body meeting in a single house, or the body in Jerusalem, or Ephesus, or Antioch, composed of bodies meeting in different houses and worshipping in different languages, or whether considered as the whole body of the Churches of Judea, Samaria, and Galilee; so tribunals, in a corresponding extent of jurisdiction, must of necessity exist in order to the discharge of the functions which we have seen are an absolute con-

---

* Rom. xii 8; 1 Tim. v. 17; Heb. xiii. 17. † Heb. xiii. 7, 8; 1 Tim. v. 17. ‡ Acts vi. 4, 7; 1 Tim. iii. 8.

dition of the existence of the Church as one visible body, all the parts thereof in active communion with the Head. And here also is involved the consequence that in all ages of the Church the tribunals thereof, as to their functions, must be essentially the same, notwithstanding, as in the case of the officers of the Church, the progressive revelation under the administration of men immediately inspired may and must produce changes in the form of discharging these functions, until the completed revelation and the withdrawal of inspiration shall at last leave them permanent in form as well as in substance.

Now the Scriptures exhibit, accordingly, this actual uniformity of government, by a series of tribunals representing the different extents of the meaning of the word Church, as existing under every dispensation. Elders and ministers of the word form their constituent elements,—and that in tribunals having jurisdiction of various degrees of extent, from a single community of worshippers up to that over the whole visible body. Such was the structure of the ecclesiastical tribunals, as distinct from the civil, under the first general organization of Moses; such it appears in all the subsequent history, whenever occasion calls for a reference to it. Such we find it, beyond all controversy, at the opening of the New Testament, as appears from the numerous allusions to the synagogue with its elders and chief ruler, and to the sanhedrim of chief priests, priests, and elders; and such, with scarce a single important modification, do we find the government of the Church under the apostles; and so left as the perpetual order of government for the Church.

Thus, with remarkable consistency, the Scriptures are found exhibiting the same great idea of the Church, as pervading all the details of office and government embodied in the actual forms which the Church assumed through all the ages of inspiration.

As concerning the form finally developed at the close of inspiration, and which, therefore, is to remain the perpetual form of government for the Church under the dispensation of the Spirit till the second coming of Christ, it would not be consistent with the design of a volume not intended to be distinctively denominational to enter upon the discussion of that question. The purpose of this note is to set forth the fundamental importance of the doctrine of the Church as part of the gospel doctrine, not to discuss the merits of the distinctive forms of the author's own Church.

The importance of this idea of the Church, and its direct bearing upon the question of worship in the Church, will be pointed out in a brief note to Discourse X.

If this note may seem to any to be very extended, or in any way aside from the general subject of the volume, it is needful only to remind such that the principles here set forth furnish the clue to a large part of the biblical interpretation upon which the discourses are founded.

THE NATURE OF THE SEVERAL ORDINANCES OF PUBLIC WORSHIP AND THEIR RELATION TO THE IDEA OF THE CHURCH.

THE fundamental conception of all true external worship and ordinances of worship is, on the one hand, to be the channel of communication for the voice of God to the soul, and, on the other, of the soul of the worshipper answering back to God.

Concerning the ordinances of public worship, what they are in kind, and in what manner to be performed, there can be little question among those who agree in holding the scriptures to be the only rule of faith and worship. Reading, expounding, and preaching the word; blessing the people; prayer, singing praise, and the act of fellowship in the collection; these, together with the sacraments, (which as complex ordinances are best left to a separate consideration,) and discipline, which cannot here be considered, are the ordinances of scriptural authority in the public worship of God. Here, then, are plainly appointed the two sorts of acts of worship which express the communion between the Great Head of the kingdom and the citizens thereof. The minister of the worship stands, in the reading, expounding, and preaching the word, and in the benediction and pronouncing sentence of discipline, to speak for God to men; and in the prayer to speak for men to God. And in addition to the prayer, by which the people, in one form, make response to the voice of God through the representative voice of the minister; in the ordinance of singing praise provision is made for each worshipper to make response for himself; and therefore the choice of this form of utterance in harmonious sounds, that the voice of response from the great congregation, each for himself, may, as an external act of worship, be without harshness and confusion. The bearing of this view of singing praise in public worship upon the question whether it, like the prayer, shall be done representatively by a few, or by the whole congregation, is very obvious.

Once the nature of the ordinances of worship is properly apprehended, and their relation to the idea of the Church, it at once separates them in idea from every other kind of acts analogous to or resembling them. The reading of the word in the public worship is a solemn official ministration for Christ, and the utterance of his voice to the people. Hence the custom so earnestly urged as an expediency by many who hold high views of the dignity and sacredness of the ministry, of reading the scriptures at public worship in alternate portions by minister and people, originates in a manifest misconception of the nature of that ordinance of reading the word, and tends to obscure in the minds of the people its true relation to the worship as belonging to the class of acts in which the minister speaks for God to men. The expounding of the word is no mere display of critical learning or skill, but the solemn unfolding of the mind of the Spirit in the word. The preaching of the word can no longer be mistaken for skilful teaching, or elegant speech, or profound reasoning, or labouring to convert men; all these may be involved in it as incidents; but the preaching of the word is essentially the uttering the message of Christ to men, and applying it to the soul; it is the taking that word which Christ, as the Prophet of the Church, hath uttered, and, through the usual forms of operating by speech upon the human soul, and by the aid of the Holy Ghost, making it still the voice of Christ to men now, as really as it was to those to whom it was first uttered. In this aspect of his work, and assuming him to be both teacher and pastor, the preacher of the new is the true successor of the prophet of the old dispensation. In the one case, the revelation not yet being completed, the prophet gathered from direct communication with God his message to be delivered, and then permanently recorded it as God's voice; in the other case, the revelation being now complete, the preacher has that, as the permanent oracle, from which, led by the Spirit, he is to gather the message of God, and, by every proper means of reaching the human soul, lodge it there, as the message of God. So the benediction upon the people is the word of God to men. It is not of the class with the prayer and praise which it resembles in form, but belongs to the other class of acts in which the minister speaks for God to men, and perhaps is most nearly analogous to the authoritative sentence of discipline which it is his office also to pronounce. The act of fellowship in the collection for pious uses is more complex as an act of worship, but is properly reckoned also among the responsive acts of the people, whereby they give expression to the communion that exists between all the members and all the parts of the one great body, through the communion of each and all with Christ the Head. Thus every ordinance of the Church in detail is perceived to have its significancy, its reason, and its distinction from every thing else that is not an ordinance of worship, on account of its relation to the same fundamental idea of the Church external and actual, as at once the development of the great ideal, and as the instrument for the final and perfect accomplishment of the great ideal of the purpose of redemption.

Still more direct is the relation of the idea of the sacraments to the idea of the Church visible as an organized spiritual community. For the two sacraments of the Church, alike under the Old and New Testaments, are but the signs and seals of the two special covenants in the great series of covenant-revelations, by one of which the Church visible was constituted, and by the other, the full and complete redemption of the Church so constituted was guaranteed. The sacramental seal of the charter covenant of the Church, circumcision, as all other ordinances of the Old Testament, expressed faith as from a prophetic stand-point, and a desire for regeneration as the cutting off of the filth of the flesh; baptism expresses faith from a historic stand-point, and contemplates prominently the outpouring of the Holy Spirit as the power which alone can effect the regeneration. Thus, however apparently unlike the symbol, the thing signified in both is the same,—viz., the Holy Ghost, as the regenerator and sanctifier of the elect ones of the eternal covenant.

These observations bring into view a peculiarity of all these seals of the covenant, alike in the Old and the New Testaments,—viz.: that the seal is itself of such kind and form as to signify visibly the great idea contained in the instrument to which it is attached. Thus, as just observed, the circumcision or baptism symbolizes the renunciation of the sin character-istic naturally of the seed of the serpent, and that regeneration of the nature by divine power which puts the enmity between the seeds; thus it becomes significant of a translation into the body of the elect seed to become the Lord's people. The passover, or the Lord's Supper, is at once commemorative of the deliverance of the elect body from death, and, at the same time, the spiritual life as nourished only by communion with their King and Deliverer. So that in each case the seal becomes a sign also, and therefore the sacraments, as external acts of worship, become seals and signs of internal grace, and involve, in one and the same act, both parts of the communion which constitute worship,—the word of God to the soul, and the response of the soul to that word,—both words made visible to the senses, and at the same time used as the instrumentality of the Holy Spirit to confer the blessings symbolized.

As circumcision or baptism, therefore, is the seal of the covenant which first constituted the visible Church, so, in the very nature of the case, it becomes the sacrament which continually perpetuates the visible Church. It is the entering into solemn contract to be Jehovah's people, as he contracts to be the God of all such in the original instrument. As that original instrument expressly provides that the family principle, which had obtained in all the previous as in all subsequent covenants, shall still be recognized as fundamental under this covenant charter of the new visible community, so that principle must continue to be recognized under all dis-pensations and changes of the form of the seal. As the original social organization out of which the Church grew was the family, so the consti-tuent elements of the visible Church, from the first, were *families*. Its members are not individual believers merely, but their seed also with them. And, as we have already shown that this community, in essential idea and in fact, remains the same under all changes of dispensation, so it is still constituted of the same elements as at first.

And as the one sacrament is thus made the instrument of a perpetual process of creating the visible Church itself, so the other sacrament is a per-petual attestation of the great promise to redeem his elect covenant people, and on their part of their simple reliance on that promise for salvation, and

their renewal of the engagement to be his people, ruled and guided by him
as their King and Head. As, then, in the ministration of the word, the
minister commissioned of Christ speaks for Christ to men, so in the sacraments he stands as Christ's authorized attorney, to exhibit his covenant and
receive from men their seal to it. The sacraments thus become special
means of grace, exhibiting, as they do, the whole promise of the gospel in
substance in the form of a solemn bond closed and sealed. His people, by
reason of sin and manifold temptations, ever prone to doubt, unbelief, and
confusion of ideas as to the terms on which they may receive salvation, are
herein reassured in the strongest form,—even the bond of Jehovah; and
they are at the same time reminded that the simple terms of this covenant
alone are the terms of salvation, and there are no open questions touching
them, nor need they ever concern themselves as to anything behind the
covenant.

It is scarcely needful to add the inference from the foregoing view that
where there is no Church there can be no sacraments, and, conversely, no
sacraments, no Church, in the sense of a visible organized body.

NOTE D. TO DISCOURSE X

RELATION OF THE TEMPORAL AND SPIRITUAL POWERS HISTO-
RICALLY CONSIDERED. THE SCOTO-AMERICAN THEORY.

No logical Christian mind can avoid the suspicion that the first principles of the true doctrine touching the relation of the temporal and
spiritual powers must have very generally fallen out of the consciousness
of Christendom, as he contemplates the singular fact that, after 1800 years
of experiment, the whole question seems as unsettled as ever; and that
all parts of Christendom alike are still divided and agitated by antagonist
theories on the subject. In Papal countries, everywhere, he finds the old
contest going on as keenly as ever, between the various theories of Ultra-
montanism which make the State a creature and subject of the Church,
and of Cis-Montanism which make the Church the creature and subject
of the State. He finds the continental Protestantism aroused to new vigor
in the 19th century, in the conflicts between the various forms of the old
Zuinglian, semi-Erastian theories, which ignore the separate and independent existence of the Church, and the new theories of the school of Hegel,
that the Church is but an incidental and temporary aid to the state in
developing its moral ideal of a religious commonwealth or theocracy—
that, as Strauss hath it, " *The Church is but the crutch of the State;*" the
theories of the school of Stahl and Kleiforth, that the Church (not the
congregation, but the incorporated officers and orders of the Church) con-

stitutes a government above the state; or of Schleirmacher, contending for the co-existence of Church and state. In Great Britain, independent of various semi-Erastian denominations of Dissenters, he finds the Anglican Church agitated by earnest conflict between the theories of the Lords in council and the lawyers, that the Church is merely a head servant of the Crown, incompetent to dismiss even her infidel servants from the priesthood, except at the bidding of the Crown; the Broad Church theories of Arnold, ignoring the separate existence of the Church, and, with Hegel, contemplating the Church as a temporary means employed by the state in the process of developing its ideal of a Christian state; and the theories of the school of Palmer, claiming the independence of the Church, and, at the same time, support from the revenues of the state. In Scotland, he finds the descendants of the Covenanters divided between the theories of both state support and submission to state dictation by the Church; of support from the state without submission to state dictation, and of neither support from nor dictation by the state to the Church. And even the yearnings after ecclesiastical union between the evangelical bodies whom the secularism of state support and dictation has driven out of the state Church at various eras, are seriously impeded in giving effect to these Christian truths by grave dissensions on the theoretic question whether the Church may not sell her birth-right for the state's "mess of pottage!"

But, what is more remarkable still, he finds the American Churches, whose boast it has been for near one hundred years that here at last the Church's independent existence has been recognized by the civil power, apparently eager to assume the secular yoke again as if tired of their liberty, to engage in the service of Cæsar, and shout with the mob, "We have no king but Cæsar!" And, in consequence of this tendency, they are agitated by conflicts similar to those of the Churches under the state yoke, between the theories—First, of what may be called the Virginia, or Scoto-American school, denying any connection or co-ordinate jurisdiction in spirituals or temporals between the state and the Church; the theories of the New England school claiming the Church as one of the agencies fostered by the state for secular purposes and to develop the Christian state; and the theories of what may be called the Gallio school of entire indifference to the whole question of the relation of Church and state which so agitates all Christendom.

Meantime, he finds without the enclosures of the Covenant in all Christendom, two great classes of thinkers among the politicians and jurists. One class disposed to patronize the Church as an important agency for controlling the civil masses of the people and strengthening the civil Government; another class who look upon the Church and all claims on her part to authority and control with extreme jealousy, as a spiritual despotism which is ever making war upon liberty of thought and liberty of conscience. According to these thorough-going secularists, the Church has for centuries past been the great enemy of popular liberty and free governments; and the martyr-spirit of the politicians alone has sheltered the people from the cruelties of the priesthood. The woolfish sheep have been constantly worrying the lamb-like dogs; the priests, by some super-human subtilty, have befooled and subjugated the lawyers!

That such a suspicion of some general error underlying all these theories is well founded, will appear if, after the favourite method of the critical philosophy of the 19th century, we proceed historically to review the various phases of this conception of a relation between the secular and the spiritual powers from the earliest forms of its existence up to what, in our judgment, is the true and scriptural view of it, namely, that presented in the views of the fathers of the Scottish Reformation, on the ecclesiastical side; and in the views of the fathers of the American Republic, on the civil side; and which therefore we denominate the *Scoto-American* theory.

It will, we think, appear from such historical review—First, that the conception of a use of religion for state purposes is Pagan in its origin, and, therefore, impossible, in any form of it, to be actualized under Christianity. Second, that the union of the Church with the state, whether as subject to, superior to, or co-ordinate with, the state is due in all cases to the usurpations of the civil, rather than the ecclesiastical power. Third that the troubles and agitations on the whole subject cannot be removed save by a full recognition, both by Church and state, of the doctrine of Jesus, "My Kingdom is not of this world."

Nothing can be plainer from history than that the idea of some direct and necessary connection of the civil power with religion came not first from the Christian civilizations. In all pagan nations, in all ages, the secular and the spiritual powers have been blended as inseparable parts of the same governmental machinery. In the Egyptian, the Greek and the Roman civilizations alike the head of the state was at the same time the head of a college of priests, and the civil government depended for its sanctions upon the mysterious power of religion. In all alike religion assumed directly the place of law to the citizen, or stood a "power behind the throne higher than the throne." The wars which ravaged the ancient world were wars of religion; each battle determined the relative power of local gods. The key to the Old Testament history is found in the fact that the wars between the chosen people and surrounding nations were wars of religion. That, in the Pagan conception, each battle decided a theological question, and the relative power of Baal, Ashteroth, Isis, Apis, or Osiris, as compared with the Jehovah of Israel. Of this you will find a striking illustration in the history of the defeat of Benhadad and his royal colleagues with his Syrians in the 21st chapter of I. Kings; who, when the "committee on the conduct of the war" inquired the cause of the repulse from the hills of Judah, was gravely told, "Their gods are the gods of the hills—therefore, they were stronger than we. But let us fight them in the plain and surely we shall be stronger than they."

Much as has been said of the mingling of civil and ecclesiastical in the Mosaic constitution, it is a fact that in that constitution only of all the ancient governmental constitutions was the distinction beween the civil and the ecclesiastical powers carefully distinguished, as Gillespie, of the Westminster Assembly, has abundantly shown.

The idea of a blending of the two powers, secular and spiritual, is purely a Paganism in its origin. Only in the Jewish nation, of all the nations of antiquity, is to be found any exception to the general practice.

In all the inspired expositions of the mission of Jesus Christ, whether in the Old or the New Testament, two ideas are fundamental. The first, that his design is not merely to teach a doctrine, and make an atonement, but also to found a community and establish a *government*. The other idea is that the power of administration in this government, of which he is King, is something distinct from that civil power under which human society is organized for protection of the life, liberty, and property of man. That there are duties to Cæsar altogether distinct from the duties due to him as spiritual King. That "His kingdom is not of this world." Accordingly after the full setting up of this kingdom, with the Pentecostal organization, his Apostles went forth, not only proclaiming a doctrine but organizing a community ; and establishing a governmental power over it not only distinct from, but in defiance of the civil governments of the world. The same men who are dragged continually before civil tribunals, and immured in dungeons, yet go on discharging all the functions of officers of a government; from their very prisons sending forth their rescripts and expositions of the Christian law ; and are obeyed as implicitly, by the new community, as if clothed with all the authority of Cæsar. With no other resources of power than its own inherent energy as a spiritual government, it spread its conquests and survived all efforts for its extermination ; and before three hundred years elapsed it had become a more truly universal kingdom than any of the Cæsars ever ruled.

But at the opening of the 4th century, just when, through the genius of Cyprian, the notion of the ministry as the incorporate Church, and of the central episcopate in the Church as a visible bond of unity for the Christian community had obtained general currency, the Roman Emperor himself suddenly became a convert from Paganism to Christianity. His previous heathen notions of the relation of religion to the state as an element of governmental power combined with the state policy of that particular time, and with the novel ideas of Cyprian concerning the Church to suggest the *establishment of Christianity in place of Paganism*. Constantine had no conception, as a statesman educated in the heathen school, of the possibility of governing the state without the aid of religion ; while Constantine as a Christian convert could not longer make use of Paganism. What more natural, therefore, than that the Christian religion and its Priests should be called upon to discharge for the state the functions which Paganism had heretofore discharged as part of the government machinery! The common form of stating the origin of that tremendous ecclesiastical despotism which ruled the world for the subsequent thousand years is to describe it as a gradual encroachment of the ecclesiastical upon the civil power. Whereas facts show it was by a single step, and that a step taken by the civil, not the ecclesiastical power. The intelligent inquirer on this subject need only study carefully the enactments of *jus ecclesiasticum* in the last sixteen books of the Theodosian, (A.D. 429,) and the first books of the Justinian code, a hundred years later, to perceive that the process by which the Christian Church became established was not through the triumph of the ecclesiastics over the lawyers, and the scheming of the Church against the state. The order and dates of the "constitutions" or edicts of the emperor trace clearly the process. First, the prohibition of persecution of the Christians. Next, the permission, to the Church, of the *jus acquirendi*, or power of holding estates through the Bishops. Next the provision for the support of the ministry by the state. Next the grant of a large portion of the spoils taken in war to the Church, after the old heathen fashion. Next giving the administration of the Church to the Bishops. Next, immunities to the clergy, as a privileged class. Next the transfer of all matters relating to marriages and wills to the ecclesiastical court. Then the successive gifts of territories to the Church, and finally, under Otho, in 1201, the formal establishment of the Popedom as a temporal power in the states of the Church.

Of course the State made no such extensive grants of favors without a consideration. The Church must enlist in the service of the State, by way of compensating its pious kindness. To secure this service the State soon begins to claim to nominate Bishops, and to exercise a veto upon ecclesiastical legislation. Then to decide questions of doctrine and liturgy. Thus, as, according to Cyprian's ecclesiastical theory, the unity of sacerdotal power in the See of Rome gives the Church all the elements for a central power of control; so, according to Constantine's political theory, religion being an essential element of power to the state, it is therefore a plain consequence that through the Church, that is the clergy, we may rule the world. Once thus inaugurated by emperors from Constantine to Clovis, it is not surprising that, as the civilism of Constantine and Justinian becomes broken up into feeble polities, the Church still holding fast to her organic unity, should cease to feel dependence on the State; till soon the Church rises higher than the State, and the Pope is above Cæsar. What though the State now begins to raise remonstrance and resistance? Starting upon Constantine's theory, as a premise admitted, recognizing as the sum of all law the Theodosian and Justinian codes,—and receiving, as undoubted, the Pagan axiom that the state must have a religion—how were the lawyers and publicists to resist the logic and the towering genius of Gregory VII, when he reasoned out and enacted the conclusion of the Church as supreme and independent, and the state as dependent upon the Church? That the mediæval publicists should hold the Pope to be the head of all states—to dethrone princes as his vassals and absolve subjects—is by no means so absurd a conclusion, if the semi-Pagan premise of Constantine and Clovis be true. Nay, we may go further, and say that if the premise of modern publicists, as Vattel, Grotius and Puffendorf, be true, that the state, as such, must have a religion, it is not easy for modern lawyers, more efficiently than the middle-age lawyers, to resist the conclusions of Dr. Brownson, who has recently revived these doctrines of the mediæval Popes, that the spiritual is supreme and over the temporal. For all the maxims of these Popes are a direct logical deduction from the original Constantine constitution, and from the Pagan notion of religion as a part of the state government.

Resisted, as it often was, this order of things continued for 1000 years, to the Protestant Reformation. Let us now notice briefly how the Church-State doctrine was affected by this great revolution. The Protestant Reformation brought about a return, in faith and order, to the model of the primitive Church. It was, moreover, a successful effort of the civil government to shake off spiritual despotism. But it must be confessed that it was a failure, on the part of the Church, to shake off *temporal* despotism.

The Reformation of the 16th century developed indeed such views of the doctrine and order of the Church, as would, if permitted to work out their logical results, have led to a restoration of the spiritual independence of Christ's kingdom. Luther's first ideas of the nature of the Church were in revolt against the Cyprianic theory, and his definition of the Church as "the congregation of faithful men, in which the word is purely preached and the sacraments rightly administered," is an overthrow at once of the Cyprianic notion of the clergy as constituting the Church; and it logical'y works out a separation of the Church from the State. It is plain on comparing the earlier with the later ideas of Luther that he was driven, by pressure from without, step by step to recognize the civil magistrate in a Christian land as somehow a part of the Church. So in the constitution of the Reformed Churches, so called, who embodied the first ideal of Luther. But Zuingle, while admitting the right of representation in the people, conceived that mayors and counsellors might be assumed to represent the people, in the Church organization, and appoint for them their Church officers. Calvin's ideal Church necessarily flowed from his theology; and, far more assiduously than either Luther or Zuingle, he laboured to establish the Church as a perfect spiritual government. But while holding with Luther's first ideal that the Church and State are two distinct powers, he held also with Zuingle that the State may suppress heresy by force. While claiming that the Church is a complete autonomy under her divinely appointed rulers, yet like Zuingle he supposes that the "little council" of state may be assumed to represent the people and by advice of the clergy appoint her ruling elders. Bearing in mind that Calvin, being educated a lawyer, was imbued with the ideas of the Justinian code, then still in the ascendant as the source of all law ; it is not so surprising that Calvin, the lawyer, should have failed in organizing a government according to the ideal of his gospel theology. In so far as Calvin failed it was as a lawyer, and in spite of his theology.

As the Anglican Reformation differed from the Lutheran, in that the king rather than the people took the initiative in throwing off the Papal yoke, we therefore may, naturally enough, expect to find the Anglican theory, from the very start, more Erastian, that is, tending to merge the Church in the state than the Lutheran. Besides Cranmer, who more than any other ecclesiastic, gave shape to the Anglican system, was thoroughly an Erastian in principle, even to the extent of denying the necessity of any other authority for ordination than the king's commission. Hooker, to whose brilliant genius the exposition and defence of the Anglican system owes more than any other man, devotes the eighth book of his great work to the special denial and refutation of the proposition that the power of ecclesiastical dominion may not be given to the civil ruler or prince. His argument assumes the broadest ground of the ancient Paganism in making the Church and the State but two forms of the one and the same thing. "Just as," says Hooker, "though a triangle, contemplated one way, hath two of its lines called sides and the other base, and, contemplated another way, may have this base one of the sides, and a side the base thereof; so the Church and State is one society, being called a commonwealth, as it liveth under secular law, and a church, as it liveth under spiritual law." All the various theories of the modern English parties assume in substance this idea. Dr. Arnold's theory is but a slight modification of Hooker's. Such writers as Palmer, while revolting at the slavery of the Church under such an idea, and at the coarse logical results that rationalistic liberalism derives from the original system, are driven to curious logical expedients to shield the system, and at the same time to assert the independence of the Church.

The Scottish of all the National Churches of the reformation came nearest to realizing the true Protestant ideal of an independent Church To whatever cause we may choose to ascribe this—whether because of less exposure to the temporal power of the Papacy or to the necessity felt for resisting the Erastianism of the English reformation, or to their clearer ideas of the gospel, it is unquestionably true that in Scotland more clearly and consistently than in any of the reformed churches, was developed from the first, not only an ideal, but an actual doctrine of the relation of the Church to the State, as an independent governmental power, which is consistent with the true Protestant theology. Indeed, so far were the Scotch fathers in advance in their views that their zeal for " Christ's crown and covenant," which motto embodies the essence of the whole truth on this subject of the Church's relation to the State, has strangely been made the target for the gibes and jeers of the English-speaking world ever since. And those who have gibed and jeered have done s) chiefly from their want of ability to comprehend the thoughts of the profounder thinkers than themselves, even after those thoughts have been worked out for them. The preliminary chapter of the Second Book of Discipline—the great symbol of the Scotch Church prior to the Westminster form of Government—is beyond comparison the profoundest philosophical disquisition on the principles which underlie constitutional law existing in any language. Its great first truth, that the power ecclesiastical is from Jesus Christ the Mediator, and is distinct in its own nature from the civil power given by God to the magistrate, is the great germinal principle of all freedom in Church or State. For the space of a century this noble army of the martyrs attested the truth of the freedom of Christ's spiritual kingdom, in spite of fire, and fagot, and thumb-screws, and iron boot. It was only after the seductions and arts of the civil power cheated the Scottish Church out of what violence could not wrench from her martyr grasp, that, in the act of settlement under Queen Anne, her testimony for this great truth was silenced, and she was left to degenerate in the eighteenth century nigh to spiritual death. For just in proportion as the Church has been purest in doctrine and most fervent in holy zeal—and most spiritual in feeling, has this conception of the two distinct powers been developed in the consciousness of the Church. It is only at such an era that Erskine of Dun could declare boldly to the Regent Mar—" There is a spiritual jurisdiction and power which God has given unto his kirk and to them that bear office therein. And there is a temporal power and jurisdiction given of God to kings and civil magistrates. Both the powers are of God, and most agreeing to the fortifying of one another if they be rightly used." It is only at such an era that Andrew Mellville dare say to the tyrant James, " There be two kings and two kingdoms here in Scotland. There is King James, the head of the commonwealth; and there is Christ Jesus, the King of the Church, whose subject James Sixth is, and of whose kingdom he is not a king, nor a lord, but a member."

The sum of the whole matter as gathered from the reformation history is, that while the true theory of the relation of the Church as independent of the State was conceived of generally, and in the Scotch Church fought for during a century, yet there was a general failure to actualize the theory for three reasons—1st. That the reformation was not only a spiritual but a political revolution. The chief aim of the civil governments was to emancipate themselves from the Papal yoke, under the ecclesiastical constitutions of Constantine and Justinian. 2nd. Whatever ideas the Churches might have, being compelled to take shelter under the civil power against the legions at the command of the Pope, they were not permitted to develop them. 3rd. In any attempt to develop actually the Church, as an independent spiritual government—a "kingdom not of this world"—the jealousy of the civil powers, on whom the Church was dependent for protection, suppressed the effort. 4th. The current notion among the civilians of that era was that of the Theodosian and Justinian code—the whitewashed Pagan theory—of the right of the state to employ religion as one of its governing powers.

It may now be added in passing, that, for two hundred and fifty years after the reformation it was again the generally received doctrine—not of the *ecclesiastics* but of the civilians—that the state must control religion. This was the doctrine even of the most sceptical and liberalistic of them all. Hobbes claimed the right of the sovereign to dictate religious opinions; and it is doubtful if any thing more ridiculous to an enlightened Christian man can be found in the times of the school-men, than Vattel's Chapter on religion—though he is still a great luminary in our schools of law. In Chap. 12th, Book 1st, on "Piety and Religion," Vattel thus presents the whole theory of modern liberalism.

" § 125. To the practice of piety all mankind are indispensably obliged, and those who unite in civil society are under still greater obligation to practice it. *A nation then ought to be pious.*

" § 127. Religion consists in doctrines concerning the Deity, and the things of another life, and in the worship appointed to the honour of the Supreme Being. So far as it is seated in the heart it is an affair of conscience; so far as it is *external* and publicly *established, it is an affair of state.*

" § 129. The establishment of religion by law, and its public exercise, are matters of state, and are necessarily under the ¹urisdiction of the political authorities.

" § 130. If there be as yet no religion established by public authority, the nation ought to know and use the utmost care in order to establish the best. That which shall have the approbation of the majority shall be received and publicly be established by law, by which means it will become the religion of the state.

" It solely belongs to the society the state to determine the propriety of those changes (in religion); and no private individual has a right to attempt them on his own authority nor consequently to preach to the people a new doctrine. Let him offer his sentiments to the conductors of the nation, and submit to the order he receives from them.

" § 139. The prodigious influence of religion on the peace and welfare of societies incontrovertibly proves that the conductor of a nation ought to have inspection of what relates to it, and authority over the ministers who teach it."

Here let us remember is the highest result of liberalism in religion amid the opening glories of the 19th century, and from a profound civilian! We are sometimes asked how is it, if Gillespie, and the London Ministers in the Westminster Assembly era, held the theory of the entire separation of politics from religion, they yet should have assented to so many acts of the Church inconsistent with that theory? The answer is very easy when it is borne in mind how arrogant were the claims not merely of the Stuarts, but of the civilians and publicists as late even as the era of Vattel. It will be seen that this eminent publicist propounds just as solemnly and *ex cathedra* the fundamental maxims of the semi-pagan Justinian theory of Church and State as though no Reformation had ever occurred, and no progress in the world's history for 1500 years. What pagan Pontiff or Papal bull ever uttered heathenism worse than Vattel's. If such notions still passed current among civilians, down to the very era of the American Revolution, is it wonderful that the Scotch Reformers should have been compelled to accept from the civilians and politicians, a partial actualization of their theory, and fail to establish a free Church? Nay, if such are the notions with which students of law are imbued, from the high sources of legal wisdom, is it wonderful that even in the American States we should find such hazy and confused notions among American lawyers of the relation of the state to religion? Is it wonderful that, even in face of the American Constitution, semi-pious, and occasionally pious politicians and cabinets, losing the confidence of the people should rush eagerly for aid to the Church, in their political sicknesses? and that republican monarchs should assume authority to appoint, and the Republican mob to enforce the observance of sacred days, and dictate liturgies to the ministers of the Church?

Thus the Scottish doctrines of the independence of the spiritual commonwealth, though not crushed out under the heel of civil usurpation over the Church, at once, as on the continent, yet were restrained, confused, and corrupted by the overpowering influence of the civilians and publicists for two hundred years. The Scottish fathers "came unto their own, but their own received them not." It was reserved for another age to witness the unfolding of their great principles, once the pressure of the civil power should be shaken off. It is one of the beautiful laws, in the economy of nature for the propagation of certain plants, that the seeds are endowed by nature with gossamer wings, which, unfolding in the ripening process of autumn, enable them to mount upon the winter blasts and travel to distant islands and continents, to fall there and germinate, to the great surprise of the inhabitants of the far-off land. It is a beautiful emblem of the processes in the spiritual economy of Christ's kingdom, whereby truths sown in tears that seem fruitless and apparently forgotten shall, as if endowed with wings, float upon the winds of human passion and strife, and find a resting place and a germinating soil in far-off climes, and then produce the harvest in joy. Let us notice now briefly how the law had its exemplification in the case of the great distinctive truths of the Scottish Reformation.

As colonies of Great Britain, the general principles of the Anglican

State system obtained in America until the period of the Revolution. In New England the Puritans had actualized their ideal, not of a church, but of a community of churches. They had sought relief against the despotism of Church and State at the opposite extreme of State and Church, not making the Church a part of the State, but the State a part of the Church. The relation of religion to the civil power in the practical working of the system soon became thoroughly Erastian. At the era of the formation of state constitutions, the old fallacy was embodied in the organic law of Massachusetts, that "as morality is essential to liberty and good government, and religion essential to morality, therefore the state should provide for the temporal support and propagation of religion." The premise is true enough, but the true inference is—therefore the state should keep its sooty fingers off religion—for, as all history had shown, the fostering of the state means, rather, to kill out all spiritual religion. Even as late as 1830, perhaps, a levy continued to be made in Massachusetts for the support of religion. The result of the modification of Church, and, Statcism, which compelled a man to pay for religion, and yet allowed him to choose to what form of religion and denomination his tax should go, was practically this—that, as usual, the majority of men having little taste for earnest spiritual religion, were disposed, if they must *pay* for religion anyhow, to pay towards the salary of that minister, who *would trouble them with the least of it.* Thus a bounty was offered practically for sham religion—for "the form of godliness that denied the power." And probably to this more than any other source may be traced the growth of the innumerable *isms* in religion for which New England is so famous.

The evil effects of the fallacy of the New England logic on the subject extended far beyond the masses. Drilled into the minds of their educated men in their youth, these fallacies hide themselves in the minds of the most illustrious, not only of their theologians, but also of their jurists and publicists, and seem to render them incapable of perceiving that great truth of the gospel which the Scottish fathers saw so clearly ; that there are two powers, and two commonwealths ordained of God ;—one in the hand of the civil magistrate for the protection solely of men's temporal interests ; the other in the hand of the Church for the protection of men's eternal interests.

Even men so illustrious as Justice Story and Mr. Webster,—in face of the very principle of the constitution, of which they were the great expounders, allow themselves to promulge—and think they do God and their country service, by propounding—principles on the subject of the functions of civil government, as thoroughly heathenish, if not so broadly stated, as those of Justinian or Vattel. Says Judge Story—(on the Const., p. 260) :

"The right of a society or government to interfere in matters of religion will hardly be contested by any persons who believe that piety, religion and morality are intimately connected with the well-being of the state, and indispensable to the administration of civil justice."•••

" It is impossible for those who believe in the truth of Christianity, as a divine revelation, to doubt that it is the especial duty of government to foster and encourage it among all the citizens and subjects."

Now the author of these discourses humbly trusts that he "believes in the truth of Christianity in a higher and stricter sense even than Judge Story did; and believes also in the importance of " piety, religion and morality," &c.; yet he equally disbelieves what Judge Story declares impossible of disbelief to such ; namely, that it is any special duty of the civil government to foster religion ; or that it has any right to interfere in matters of religion.   And if, by making this confession, he writes himself an infidel in the judgment of the body of Christians—so called—with which Judge Story is supposed to have sympathized, he has the consolation of feeling, that, as will be shown presently, that he stands with Waddel, and Graham, and Stanhope Smith, of the Old Hanover Presbytery, who, if infidels, were men very zealous for piety and religion.   He holds, as they held, that the state has nothing to do with religion, except to let it alone, that it may be kept pure and spiritual, and thereby promote a pure morality of a somewhat higher type than events show the New England theory has been able to produce for the benefit of the state.

So also, Mr. Webster, in his oft-cited speech on the Girard will case—for whom, indeed, the apology may be offered that he is playing the advocate and not the judge :—

" We have in the charter of Pennsylvania that the preservation of Christianity is one of the leading ends of all government.   This is declared in the charter of the state.   Then the laws of Pennsylvania, the statutes against blasphemy, the violation of the Lord's day, and others to the same effect, proceed upon this great broad principle, *that the preservation of Christianity is one of the main ends of all government.*"

It is needless to say, in response to this declaration, that, if true, it is difficult to see for what end Jesus Christ set up a distinct spiritual government; or how the Apostles could declare the Church of the Living God " to be the pillar and ground of the truth."   If this is true, then, obviously, the conception of Hegel and Strauss, that the Church is simply " a crutch of the state," for the purpose of preserving Christianity, is the true one! And, therefore, the charter of Pennsylvania is directly in the face of Christ's order, of the state for temporals and the Church for spirituals.

In the middle, and especially in the southern colonies, as Virginia, the English state-system was formally established—and so thoroughly fixed in the popular mind, that its ministers were encouraged to demand a continued establishment, even after the independence of the colonies.   This brought on that remarkable conflict which led to the celebrated " Act for establishing Religious Freedom," which is probably the first recognition, by any civil power, in all history of the doctrine of the Scotch Reformers on the civil side of it, and therefore to the full and final development of the Scoto-American theory.

That the famous Act to establish religious freedom was the legitimate result of the Scottish Reformation, and the actual shooting forth of the seed wafted over the ocean from the minds of the Scottish fathers—a single glance at the history of that Act will suffice to show.

At the era of the Declaration of Independence, the dissenters—Presbyterians and Baptists—not only outnumbered the Established Church, but greatly exceeded it in zeal for independence. These dissenters, in the struggle for civil liberty, naturally enough demanded religious liberty and equality also. As the result of their first movement, we find in the Bill of Rights, prefixed to the Constitution of the State, passed in, 1776, this significant declaration. Religion or the duty we owe to the Creator, and the manner of discharging it, can be directed only by reason and conviction, not by *force* or *violence* ; And therefore all men are equally entitled to the free exercise of religion according to the dictates of conscience. This declaration, however, was merely abstract, and did not stay the effort of the Old Establishment to seek to be continued, at least so far as to be incorporated and supported in common with others, and to retain its glebes. That we have not ascribed too much influence to the teachings of the Scotch fathers in directing Jefferson and Madison to the great conclusion reached after nine years' struggle in the Virginia Legislature, appears from the fact that the civilians were guided in the matter largely by a series of memorials from the Old Hanover Presbytery, drawn by such men as Waddel, whom Wirt has immortalized as the "blind preacher," by Scotch William Graham and Stanhope Smith. And it needs only the citation of a few passages from their memorials for religious liberty, to the Legislature of Virginia, to show that they were thoroughly imbued with the spirit of the Scotch fathers ; and that in the wilderness, under the encroachments and persecutions of the Colonial State Church, they had been led a step in advance of the Scotch fathers. From the first memorial of Hanover Presbytery to the Legislature of Virginia, we select the following :—

" We embrace the declaration of rights (Mr. Jefferson's bill already quoted) as the *Magna Charta* of our commonwealth. Certain it is that every argument for *civil liberty* gains additional weight when applied to liberty in the concerns of religion. Neither can it be made to appear that the gospel needs any such civil aid. We rather conceive that when our blessed Saviour declares his Kingdom is not of this world, he renounces all dependence upon state power. And we are persuaded that if mankind were left in the quiet possession of their unalienable rights and privileges, Christianity, as in the days of the Apostles, would continue to flourish in the greatest purity by its own native excellence and under the all-disposing Providence of God. We would humbly represent that the ONLY PROPER OBJECTS OF CIVIL GOVERNMENT ARE THE HAPPINESS AND PROTECTION

So again, in a memorial of Hanover Presbytery in 1775, against a general assessment: "As every good Christian believes *that Christ has ordained a complete system of laws for the government of his kingdom*, so we are persuaded that by his Providence, he will support it to the final consummation. In the fixed belief that the kingdom of Christ and the concerns of religion are beyond the limits of civil control, we should act an inconsistent and dishonest part were we to receive any emoluments from human establishments for the support of the gospel. If the Legislature has any rightful authority over the ministers of the gospel, *and it is their duty to levy a maintenance for them, as such, then they are invested with a power, and it is incumbent upon them to declare who shall preach, what they shall preach, and to whom they shall preach.*" So again in a fourth memorial in August in 1785, against the incorporation of the English Church:

"As Christians also, the subjects of Jesus Christ, *we are wholly opposed to the exercise of spiritual powers by civil rulers.* We conceive ourselves obliged to remonstrate against that part of the Incorporating Act which authorizes and directs the regulation of spiritual concerns. *This is such an invasion of divine prerogative*, that it is highly objectionable on that account, as well as on account of the danger to which it exposes our religious liberties. *Jesus Christ hath given sufficient authority to his Church for every lawful purpose; and it is forsaking his authority and direction, for that of feeble men, to expect or to grant the sanction of civil law to authorize the regulation of any Christian society.*"

It will be seen at once that here is the revival of the ancient Scotch testimony to the completeness and independence of Christ's spiritual government; and differs only in going one step in advance to the first practical inference from that doctrine, which inference their peculiar circumstances prevented the Scottish fathers from making. In consequence of these persistent testimonies, when the Act of Incorporation was put upon its passage, Mr. Madison took a sudden turn upon the friends of an establishment, by moving to substitute for their bill, a bill which, seven years before, Mr. Jefferson had prepared as a part of the revised statutes of Virginia, under the title of "An Act to establish Religious Freedom," since so celebrated, and whose principle was intended doubtless to be embodied in the article of the Federal Constitution forbidding any establishment of religion or interference with it.

To perceive the connection between this bill and the memorials of the Presbytery it needs only that we cite a sample of Mr. Jefferson's bill. It declares among other things:—"that the attempt to coerce the mind by civil penalties is a departure from the plan of the Author of our holy religion. That the impious presumption of legislators and rulers, both civil and ecclesiastical, in this regard, hath established and maintained false religions over the greater part of the world in all time. That to compel a man to furnish contributions of money for the propagation of opinions which he disbelieves, is sinful and tyrannical. That *to suffer the civil magistrate to intrude his powers into the field of opinion, is a dangerous fallacy which at once destroys all religious liberty.*" "That it is time enough for the rightful purposes of civil government for its officers to interfere *when principles break out into overt acts against peace and good order.*" Such was this great disavowal—the first in all history so far as known to the author—of all claim to extend its power over the Church and religion by the civil government; and the formal adoption, on the civil side, of the great truths enunciated by the Scotch fathers on the ecclesiastical side.

These principles, as we have seen, were not fully accepted in all parts of the United States. In New England, not only by reason of the continued influence of the ancient Erastian theory—but also from peculiar prejudice against Mr. Jefferson, as a sceptic in religion, these principles were regarded with suspicion. The prejudices against Mr. Jefferson, as a sceptic, in other portions of the country, combined with the prevalence of many prejudices imported into the American Churches with a ministry reared under the established systems of England and Scotland, made many Christian men slow to receive them. All alike seemed to forget that even if Mr. Jefferson were a sceptic, God often has made use of unbelieving men, as Cyrus a heathen, and caused them to be the greatest benefactors of his Church. Perhaps had Mr. Jefferson not been, as they charged, an *infidel*, the current religious prejudices of his time would have prevented him, as they did the great Patrick Henry, from perceiving the force of the statements and reasoning of the Hanover Presbytery memorials. But, in spite of all this, these principles were so obviously in conformity with the political doctrines of the constitution of the young States; and the influence of Mr. Jefferson and Mr. Madison so powerful, that they gradually became at least theoretically the American doctrine of Church and State. The subsequent success of the experiment in the Church added also continually to the strength of the argument.

Much has been said and sung of the results of the American Revolution to the civil liberties of mankind. But the day will probably come when these results shall be held as nothing to its results for the Church of God in relieving her from bondage to the civil power. Of all the acts and sayings of Mr. Jefferson, illustrative of his far-sightedness, this is perhaps the most remarkable, that in selecting from among the great acts of his life one significant act to be recorded on his tomb-stone—he should have selected this, "Thomas Jefferson, author of the act for establishing religious freedom." This note having already been extended far beyond the limits intended, the author must refer the reader, for a succinct statement of the truths concerning the relation of the secular and spiritual powers, which distinguish the true gospel from the Pagan theory whose history has here been traced, to the note on Discourse IV. in this Appendix.

www.ingramcontent.com/pod-product-compliance
Lightning Source LLC
Chambersburg PA
CBHW032018110726
47901CB00004B/1127